Confessions of a White Educator

Stories in Search of Justice & Diversity

Lisa Delpit
Ron E. Miles

Kendall Hunt
publishing company

Lyrics from "Ella's Song," composed by Bernice Johnson Reagon, from her film score created for Joanne Grant's film *Fundi: The Story of Ella Baker*. Used with composer's permission.

Cover image © 2012 Shutterstock, Inc.

Kendall Hunt
publishing company

www.kendallhunt.com
Send all inquiries to:
4050 Westmark Drive
Dubuque, IA 52004-1840

Copyright © 2012 by Joan T. Wynne, Lisa Delpit, Ron E. Miles

ISBN 978-1-4652-0893-4

Printed in the United States of America
10 9 8 7 6 5 4 3 2

Joan Wynne:

This book is dedicated to my Mother, Catharine Wynne, whose intellect, wit, and bravery always inspired me.

To my four wildly wonderful sisters, Patty, Margaret, Michael, and Debby who have nurtured and sustained me personally as well as professionally, with special support for all of my writing adventures.

To my daughter, Catharine, who has been the sunshine of my life, who continues to read and critique my "stuff," who while she was teaching children with special needs, taught me how to see students' spirits not their "disabilities," and who, from her first breath, has dazzled me with her genius and laughter.

And to my husband, Fran Skwira, an indefatigable emotional and financial supporter of my professional life inside and outside of classrooms, a critical reader of everything I write, and the teacher of unconditional love.

Lisa Delpit:

To all of my students, of every age, gender, creed and color - you have informed my work and enriched my life.

Ron E. Miles:

To my late mother, Kathleen, my loving wife, Shondelle and our two delightful treasures, Jasai and Senaya.

CONTENTS

ACKNOWLEDGMENTS

To my astounding African American mentors who are all named in this book;

To three wonderful women, Marla Swartz, Stefani DeMoss, and Renae Horstman, for their editorial advice and gracious nudging to finish this book on schedule.

To my friends, Carol and Woody Bartlett, Lisa Delpit, Wendy and Bob Probst, Bev and Vic Riccardi, Louise and David Smith, whose nonjudgmental spirits in earlier decades helped keep me glued together, which demonstrates an amazing endurance for the absurd.

To all the students in high schools, colleges, and universities who have nurtured, trusted, taught me, and patiently suffered my failures, especially those of you who took the time to contribute to this book.

To my young colleagues/friends, Maria Lovett, Hilary Landorf, Carlos Gonzalez Morales, Louie Rodriguez, and Alex Salinas, who taught me new worlds of adventurous pedagogy.

To Janet Moses, who keeps my political-self informed, alive, and "in-check."

To my great family of brothers-in-law and creative nieces and nephews and son-in-law who tolerate all of my political rants and who always support my professional work.

To Mamoo, who teaches us every day that age is just a number and life can always be lived with zest and humor.

To my daughters, Lindsey and Barbre, who taught me that love has no bounds and that courage comes when you call it.

To all of you, I offer deep gratitude for helping me in a variety of ways to tell the stories that I needed to tell and to share a space for others to do the same.

INTRODUCTION

Joan T. Wynne

I am saying as you must say, too, that in order to see where we are going, we not only must remember where we have been, but we must understand where we have been.—Ella Baker[1]

"Why are you, a southern white woman, teaching here at an all-black, male college?" This question or some version of it was asked by a random student almost every semester for the twelve years that I taught at Morehouse College in Atlanta, Georgia. Now, although I reside in a different state, I'm still trying to answer that question for myself.

What led me there and what kept me there for twelve years? I'm not sure, but I do have some hunches. Sometimes, a big event or a lived experience can help shape a life, or, at least, choices in life. I think that growing up in a segregated south was one of those defining experiences for me and possibly a reason for my ultimate need to immerse myself into another culture. Because my parents philosophically stood against racism and segregation, as a family we lived in contradiction to the society we were born into. No one in my neighborhood nor in my catholic school or university seemed to share the same world view as my family. So, although my white skin advantaged and protected me, I became accustomed to feeling intellectually and politically alienated. And because of that, I've come to believe that in the South at that time, only in the black community could I have possibly found a large number of like-minded people. Hence, my sojourn at Morehouse.

Certainly over time I have found white people who shared similar philosophies about the evil of racism but, frankly, not many. Those people simply have not galloped into my orb in abundance. And whether I'm in the North, the South, the East or the West, many white associates and friends seem to congregate typically among themselves. They say they welcome diversity, yet the systemic nature of racism begets the ease of their living in all-white neighborhoods, hosting all-white events, and, thus, remaining socially segregated from people of color—which is all fine, I'm sure. I understand the human tendency to move within familiar circles, whether one is black, brown, or white, but because of the forced segregation of my developing years in the South, white-only circles still make me uncomfortable. Actually, any all-white gathering feels like the confederacy to me.

Escaping those "white-only" circles through immersion in the African American culture and the lessons learned from that experience helped shape many of the narratives found in this book. To share those lessons with teachers, I believe, can create a space to invite others to engage in a search of justice and diversity. An imperative for such an exploration became even clearer when I awoke this morning to another headline in the *Miami Herald* [2] that yet one more unarmed black male teenager had been shot and killed in a Florida neighborhood, and this time by an "overzealous" neighborhood watch captain—so my outrage is getting the best of me this morning. I want to shout from my orange tile rooftop, "White people, let's wake up—to our complicity, our denial, our failure to not just rid ourselves of the institutional racism in schools but to the pandemic killing of black youth in every large city in this nation." At these times, I feel like the "good" German who refused to acknowledge the smell of human flesh burning in massive ovens. When black males in this country are only 7% of the nation's population, yet they are 50 to 80% of the populations in urban U.S. jails and prisons,[3] I have a difficult time believing that there's no analogy here to the German's ghettoizing of the Jews before the attempted final extermination. And I keep hearing the words of Ella Baker, immortalized in the song composed by Bernice Johsnon Reagon, "We who believe in freedom cannot rest, until the killing of black men, black mothers' sons is as important as the killing of white men, white mothers' sons."[4]

Many of the political and educational epiphanies in my life have resulted from the wisdom of people of African descent, especially when I became silent and listened. I listened not because I was smart enough to know that silence was the right thing. Rather, I shut up because their intellect dazzled me. And now I find a deep listening to the African American community by white educators is desperately needed. Often, in my head, I'm murmuring: "Can we white folks, please, just sit down and be quiet?"

Some of my friends and family suggest that I am overzealous in my struggle to unlearn racism and to raise that awareness in the larger society. Two personal experiences made me think, however, that my focus on ridding racism from our nation's practices was maybe not any more obsessive than others who have managed a recurring theme in their lives. The first was that of meeting a man who had served in the army in World War II who referred to his war experiences in most conversations. Although his experience in war was over at the age of 21, when 60, he still regularly referenced the war. After noticing that phenomenon, I began to believe that maybe segregation had been a comparable experience for me, one that kept me preoccupied with unraveling racist thinking that even today continues to surround me.

The second one happened while reading an autobiography by Benjamin E. Mays.[5] In the book, Mays said that racism was a theme in his life, all of his life. I believe because of living in a segregated South, I, too, became engrossed in his theme. And this journey to learn how to eradicate the disease from my own psyche and from others' has led me to believe that if we unravel racism, we might unravel all of the "isms." African Americans' voices, both present and past, led this liberation battle in the South. They have been leading it, as Bob Moses said, since the first African stepped off the first slave ship in chains.[6] Because of their experiences, my voice is unnecessary in the cultures of people of color. So, I've focused most often on communing with my white brothers and sisters, who are either in or out of the struggle for a world beyond racism. We carry the pathology and continue to spread it; therefore, we need to talk to each other so we can find the cure. If we fool ourselves into thinking that the disease no longer exists or that it's about "them" not "us," then racism raises its ugly head again and again, crippling the whole nation.

Edward T. Hall,[7] a researcher of cultures, said that we can never fully understand our own culture until we step outside of it and immerse ourselves in another's. I first became immersed in the African American community when teaching in an all-black high school during the first year of school integration in Atlanta. That year the system integrated the faculty at some schools, but not the students. From that year and many others in the African American culture, I've learned and continue to learn some serious lessons.

Unraveling those lessons has become an attempt to crystallize the inchoate thoughts rambling around in my brain for decades as I moved from being perplexed in my youth by racism to anger toward it; to recognition of my own complicity in it; and to my ultimate discovery that, because American history, literature, film, art, music, religion are drenched in racism, probably the best any of us who are white can be is recovering racists. From reading Toni Morrison, I also became aware that even the language I think, speak, read, write and hide in "can powerfully evoke and enforce hidden signs of racial superiority, cultural hegemony, and dismissive 'othering' of people . . ."[8] Therefore, the act of writing this introduction is fraught with navigating those "hidden signs," a kind of schizophrenic conundrum of finding-while-fighting my place in the national scheme of white supremacy—snarled in the web of veiled utterances that protect it. How do I disentangle my tongue twisted for decades in making sounds sustained for hundreds of years in the dismissive dominant discourse? This is one of the thorny issues considered in this book.

Similar convolutions, also explored in the book, arose during a public forum I attended in Atlanta where "Quality education as a constitutional right" was examined. To begin a conversation about the origin of that movement, the young facilitators arranged us in small groups and passed each group a photo of a young, 5-year-old black boy ferociously holding onto an American flag while a white policeman attempted to snatch it from his hand. Groups were asked to discuss feelings that the picture evoked. The memories and politics the photo elicited emerged as well as stories of past and present issues of justice and equity. The majority of the audience, especially the people of color, seemed pleased with the discussion. The white audience gave a more mixed review. One white man abruptly walked from the room. Several white people later explained to me that the photo caused divisiveness, that it spoke of the past not of the present, that such photos no longer had a place in discussions within an "integrated" audience, and that such photos had no relationship to quality education as a constitutional right. Some of the white audience seemed to be suggesting that white people are only interested in conversations that speak to "Can't we all just get along," and that photographs, like the one described, have no relevance to today's realities. These folks seem to lack the understanding of what Ella Baker, William Faulkner, and others like them knew only too well, that "The past is never dead. It's not even past."[9] We only need read *Slavery by Another Name*,[10] a Pulitzer Prize winning and wrenching, documented tale of the eighty-two years of criminal industrial practices perpetrated to re-enslave African Americans in the deep South, to understand that the past is more present than last night's nightmares.

The Atlanta photo discussion, although only one episode, typifies my experiences over many decades. The pain of the past seems difficult for many in the mainstream to connect to the pain of the present. When asked to engage in linking the present to the past, too many seem either to palpitate in fear or in a stance of "How dare you dredge up the past?"—as though the past were completely severed from the present. Or, for those of us who see ourselves as white progressives, then it sometimes becomes "How dare you think that I harbor racist notions—I'm one of those 'good' white people." After years of wrangling with this phenomenon, I still cannot figure out why white people get so angry when African Americans tell their stories. Where does that white anger come from? Can anyone truly understand the nation's present realities without connecting the dots from its past? Author and Atlanta Bureau Chief of the *Wall Street Journal* Douglas Blackmon explains those dots when he insists that "As painful as it may be to plow the past, among the ephemera left behind by generations crushed in the wheels of American white supremacy are telling explanations for the fissures that still thread our society." And only such plowing, he insists, can "reconcile the paradoxes of current American life."[11]

Coming to grips with my "white" reactions to history's painful present evolved primarily from my engagement in the black culture. Without that, I, too, might still be stuck in anger or fear, for I've been just as deluded as any other white woman/man. I've been lucky, though, that from the first day I stepped into that all-black high school to teach, African Americans have taken me under their wings. One of my most significant transformations, however, came through meeting Lisa Delpit. I found her vision, writing, wit, and humility so compelling that I left Atlanta, where I was born and had lived for fifty years, to work with her in Miami. And, as I sat mulling over the reactions in that Atlanta forum to the photo of that daring young child in a tug of war for the American flag, a particular passage from a Delpit book,[12] kept firing at the synapses in my brain:

As a result of careful listening to alternative points of view, I have myself come to a viable synthesis of perspectives. But both sides do need to be able to listen, and I contend that it is those with the most power, those in the majority, who must take the greater responsibility for initiating the process.

To do so takes a very special kind of listening, listening that requires not only open eyes and ears, but open hearts and minds. We do not really see through our eyes or hear through our ears, but through our beliefs. To put our beliefs on hold is to cease to exist as ourselves for a moment— and that is not easy. It is painful as well, because it means turning yourself inside out, giving up your own sense of who you are, and being willing to see yourself in the unflattering light of another's angry gaze. It is not easy, but it is the only way to learn what it might feel like to be someone else and the only way to start the dialogue.

That piece of wisdom continually surprises and challenges me—keeps me twitching to practice it. It speaks to my imagination as well as to my common sense. It speaks to everyone who sits in a seat of power, whether it be the white male with females and "othered" men; middle and upper caste people with those living in poverty; teachers with students; etc. But, especially, Delpit's wisdom speaks to white people who "want to run as fast as we can from conversations about racism."[13] Her practice of deeply listening to "the other" is one that holds lots of promise for us to begin to understand the repercussions of the power and privilege that we and our ancestors have held for over 500 years in the United States and the impact of it all on the present policy decisions. If we practiced it well, this deep listening might lead toward a much needed national truth and reconciliation.[14]

Newly discovered national truth became a topic of conversation at a recent family dinner, when a niece who is working on a graduate degree at one of the former citadels of the southern confederacy explained some of the biggest lessons she learned in her graduate classes. Her number one lesson, she said, was a revelation of the power and privilege that she gained from simply being white. Because of reading Peggy McIntosh's article about white privilege,[15] my niece opened a discussion in the room that until reading Delpit's, "The Silenced Dialogue," [16] I, too, had not understood. My niece's story of sudden recognition of centuries of white privilege is another reason that I want to write this book. We may not alter the attitudes and behavior of those who for generations have held tightly to erroneous notions of earned privilege, whether consciously or unconsciously. But offering the young another way of looking at the past and present inequities that prevail in the nation and world has all the possibilities for shifting the dialogue about what a real democracy might look like.

Yet my niece's epiphany is not the only such awakening that has been shared with me. Since moving to Miami, I have heard similar revelations from "white Hispanic" pre-service and in-service teachers when exposed to issues of power and privilege. Many have confided within the classroom space that until they read the works of African Americans, they were unconscious of their own racist attitudes toward other people of color. Many of my Cuban students related tales of parents or grandparents warning them not "to bring black boys home." Some of these and other students tell their stories in this book.

Their stories and other surprises awaited me on coming to Miami. One surprise was the separation of white and black Hispanic identities. In Atlanta and other large cities, I had never heard people of Latino descent classify themselves as white or as Hispanic. Yet here, many Cubans and South Americans were quick to tell me that they were white. After one of the first faculty meetings, a Cuban colleague explained this phenomenon to me. So I learned quickly that using the phrase "people of color" when referring to "Hispanics" in Miami was problematic. And from my Caribbean students, I learned that many people from the islands held fierce, unconscious racist notions about African Americans. In a recent search committee meeting, one of the professors from South America criticized a candidate for referencing our "Hispanic" student population as students of color. The professor commented that her South American grandmother would have been horrified if anyone had called her a person of color.

But, also in Miami, I learned from my "white Hispanic" students the great sacrifices that they and/or their parents had made to flee to this country from rigidly repressive governments; therefore, their learning the history of excluded people's bloody battles for freedom in our nation evoked a lot of pain—painful because my students had imagined that they had arrived in a place where if people work hard enough, everyone's dreams come true. So in those contexts, I struggle to do what Delpit requests, to suspend judgment, and with compassion, deeply listen to their angst—while we together probe our national dilemma of hegemonic institutions and policies.

Still my ignorance of the intensity of the racist nuances of the city has plagued me. Although Delpit and I came here together, in many public spaces when we were not together, we were treated differently because of our different skin color. Although we shared the same community club in our predominantly Latino neighborhood, she and her daughter were ostracized, while I was always welcomed. In one of the few cafes in our neighborhood, owned by Venezuelans, I was warmly greeted whenever I brought visiting relatives or friends. Yet after the café vanished in the night, I learned that Delpit and her daughter, the few times they went, were ignored until everyone else had ordered. Such examples abound, allowing me to live in yet another community where I can obliviously swim in my unearned privilege.

So this book is not about euphemistic talk of celebrating diversity. No, it is not—because I believe we need to first name the demon that is in our midst, otherwise, we won't know what it is we're trying to chase away. If we can't name the problem, we cannot solve it. If we cannot recognize our bloody past, then we will continue to replicate it. But if we stake our schools on the courage and creativity to name racism/ sexism/homophobia/classism/elitism, and all the "isms," smoke them out, confront them, and stop teaching them, then we will have something to celebrate. Then we can talk about diversity and the claim by scientists of its necessity for survival on the planet. Then we can talk about how without diversity physicists suggest the universe might implode. But we cannot get to the positive declarations of celebrating difference until we name and reckon with the negative policies at play in our nation. And we must talk about them in the context of how they are institutionalized instead of examining them as individual pathologies. For what is killing the nation is their presence in all of our institutions. Most of us, regardless of our culture, don't really care if individuals like us or not, but we do profoundly care if our institutions cheat us out of our constitutional rights for equity and justice. Ask any white man who thinks he lost a job or a seat at an

Ivy League school because of "affirmative action." He immediately attacks the policies of the institution and often sues for his sense of justice.

Recently, law professor, James Forman Jr. wrote, "Today, too many Americans refuse to acknowledge the continuing impact of race and prejudice on public policy."[17] His statement demands attention, and it reminded me of a conversation that seemed to illustrate his point, a conversation in Boston with a young white lawyer whom I was walking alongside. He asked me why African Americans must continuously talk about their history in this country. Why couldn't they just "move on" into the present? Often asked, this question seems to indicate a desire for selective national amnesia. Yet not until returning to my hotel, did I recognize the irony of his question within the context of "place." We had spent the afternoon walking on the "Freedom Trail" toward Paul Revere's home, a tour that boasts the stories of "the protests of Samuel Adams and James Otis, the Boston Massacre and the Boston Tea Party and the liberation of Boston in 1776 by General Washington."[18] Taking a walk down memory lane, reflecting on the history of white rebellions in the United States felt completely legitimate to this white man. But, to him, African Americans talking about their liberation struggles in the nation are seen as somehow divorced from American history, an unnecessary digging into the past. No matter whose past we're exploring, though, I wish I had remembered to share with my young friend James Baldwin's astute perception that "American history is longer, larger, more various, more beautiful, and more terrible than anything anyone has ever said about it."[19] Ignoring its breadth, depth, complexities, and relevance to present policy decisions, it seems to me, may keep us all chained in Plato's cave, analyzing shadows.

I also wish I had shared, at that moment, the advice of Arundhati Roy, novelist and activist, to her friend who lives in NYC. Roy advised her "To never get used to the unspeakable violence and the vulgar disparity of life around you. . . . To respect strength, never power. Above all, to watch. To try and understand. To never look away. And never, never, to forget."[20] But I didn't remember those words either.

Nonetheless, some facts about life in this country are just undeniable. White people, with few exceptions, own the banks and the bombs, the Congress, the Supreme Court, the museums, the zoos, the hospitals, the media, most of the schools and universities, and the corporations (who seem to own everything). Approximately 84%[21] of teachers in public schools are white and mostly female. With all of this power and access to public education, why have we failed to effectively educate black and brown children, especially those forced to live in poverty, including the white poor? Why have we allowed people who look like us to make tons of money from a school-to-prison pipeline? Why have we failed to teach white children about their civic responsibility to become agents of social justice and equity? Why have we failed to effectively educate every child in the United States? Even though some are offered academic rigor, few in public schools are taught the real convulsive history of the nation's continuing struggle for democracy. We lie, we omit, we distort the diverse cultural sagas that could teach us powerful lessons on how to "establish justice" for all citizens. And if we imagined ourselves in those stories and understand them as the great American mosaic of freedom struggles, then we, too, might be proud to be part of that collective national heritage.

Evidently, though, the mere phrase "social justice" is scary to many. In 2011, an ad-hoc committee of state educators, revising the Florida Principal Leadership Standards, asked me to join them on a call to discuss my research about equity issues. The committee was conflicted, I was told, about including the phrase "social justice" in one of the ten standards for principals. The standard under question was *Professional and Personal Ethical Behaviors: Effective school leaders demonstrate personal behaviors consistent with community values and morals, are resilient and promote integrity, fairness, equity and social justice.*[22] During that call, a district superintendent argued that many of his constituents did not understand what that phrase "social justice" entailed. They, he insisted, had strong aversions to the phrase, afraid that it might unleash ideologues to distort curriculum and school leadership responsibilities. In a response to his concern, I mentioned that the Preamble to the U. S. Constitution specifically declared that "We the People...in order to form a more perfect union" must "establish justice." Because of that nationally revered document, his constituency, I argued, surely could be persuaded that principals in a democratic society should be expected to "establish justice" in schools and communities. Apparently, his argument to exclude the phrase "social justice" eventually won. The final version now states: *Professional and Ethical Behaviors. Effective school leaders demonstrate personal and professional behaviors consistent with quality practices in education and as a community leader.*[23] So much for bringing the Constitution into school reform!

Wrestling with social injustice has dogged my steps during my long teaching career. And for all of these years, white people have dominated educational institutions. Yet the problems of sorry education for students of color are still the same as then. Black children are still left at the bottom to suffer instructional delivery systems of outrageous inferiority. If we white folks are so smart, why is this still happening? And why are whites taught disdain for the rich histories of other cultures who also helped shape this country? Hoarding power seems to demand a huge intellectual vacuum for the privileged.

Clearly a multitude of diverse ethnicities sculpted this nation's existence, but because I grew up in a "black and white" world of the segregated South, my most intimate knowledge is that story, and the only one I can tell from a lived experience; yet I fully recognize that the other cultural battles—First Peoples', Chicanos', Latinos', Chinese, Japanese and other liberation narratives—are equally powerful and essential to the American story. In telling my tale, however, I hope to make it clear that I'm not blaming white teachers for all of the ills of bad public schools—most teachers are as maligned as the students who don't learn in their classrooms. I am insisting, however, that we white females, with our sheer numbers as teachers in public schools, need to come to grips with our unconscious complicity in a morally and academically bankrupt system. But if we do nothing else, we can at least stop blaming the victims and their parents for the sorry education our schools deliver. In addition, I think it's time to ask ourselves, "When are we going to sit down, hush, and listen to the multitude of African American scholars, educators, parents, students who do know what education their communities need and deserve?" I say this while understanding fully that, like many women who are devalued in a hegemonic system and, thus, have internalized oppressive notions about themselves, some educators of color have internalized faulty beliefs about poor black and brown children and about why schools fail. Therefore, I am not suggesting that I will hitch my wagon to the star of the people of color who sound no better than my people. I am saying, however, that as a white woman I must join, only as an ally not as a leader, the forces of non-whites who do advocate for education as liberation. I don't believe any of us white people, no matter how enlightened, can trust that our power and privilege won't distort our good intentions for America's liberation from an apartheid society and schools.

With all of this, I'm not proposing that white educators don't know some good stuff, nor am I implying that we are completely useless. Nor do I believe that white teachers cannot teach black and brown children. After all, a number of the pieces in this book are authored not only by people of color but also by some of my "white Hispanic" students and by me, a white woman, telling research stories that evolved as I worked alongside African Americans. But, none of my stories come from my wisdom, only that which unfolded while being mentored by Delpit, Asa Hilliard, Robert Dixon, Bob Moses, Theresa Perry, Charles Payne, and others.[24] So I am advocating that we listen deeply and well to "the othered" and use their strategies, their advice, their research, their expertise if we intend to work with their children. Actually, it seems pretty stupid to continue to listen to the same ole folks from the same ole white culture who created and sustain this broken system we're operating in now.

Brilliance and courage often seem to burst forth from the margins of a dominant culture—at least the likes of Jesus, Gandhi, MLKing Jr., Ella Baker, Cesar Chavez, etc. did. Therefore, I suggest we start listening for those kinds of voices to bubble up and avoid being drowned in our own noise. Nikki Giovanni, when asked to keynote at a NASA conference, wrote the poem "Quilting the Black-eyed Pea (We're Going to Mars)."[25] In the poem, after reminding us of the terrors of the Middle Passage[26] and the courage of those survivors of the unknown, she says, *"When we go to Mars.........it's the same thing . . . . it's Middle Passage . . . . NASA needs to call Black America. They need to ask us: How did you calm your fears . . . .How were you able to decide you were human even when everything said you were not . . . How did you find the comfort in the face of the improbable to make the world you came to your world . . . How was your soul able to look back and wonder."** So those are some of the people I hope we choose to hear when we want to create a new world of education that depends on flights of the imagination, courage, and wonder.

Years ago, Hilliard taught me that it is not the *knowledge* our nation lacks on how to teach all of its children, it's the *will* to teach all of its children. And this book shares research that documents Hilliard's premise. Yet regardless of whether we can agree with Hilliard, we can probably all agree that white people—who dominate the seats of power in this country—have failed to deliver to this nation coherent and just policies that create a world-class educational system worthy of a democracy. The recently published statistics about the achievement of educational systems around the globe validate this premise.[27]

Over the last fifteen or so years, I have been playing with another premise. It has morphed into something like this: We white educators must stop grabbing foundation, federal, state, local funds for our pet projects that concern research or practice in educating students of color. If we were really honest, really knew and respected the work of African American, Latino, and other "othered" educators, then we might give our award money to their research, their projects, their systems of thought; or at the very least, only apply for those funds if the principal investigator is a scholar/teacher of color with a proven track record. When it comes to educating black and brown students, we well-meaning, white, liberal, progressive educators need to get out of the way of the many equally progressive and brilliant educators of color so they can lead the charge toward quality education for their children. We can be their allies, but not their leaders; we can be their support system, but not their competitors. For, in their battle to demand quality education for their children, they enhance the education for all of the nation's children.

Certainly I am aware that, as Howard Zinn[28] consummately documented, audacious white people have led, joined, and died in struggles for justice and equity in this country for centuries. Their rebellious stories, also ignored in most history books when I was young, are necessary to be known and honored. And my research about inequities in communities and schools has been influenced as well by the work of white activists/educators like Joe Feagin, Herb Kohl, Jonathan Kozol, Jeannie Oakes, Tim Wise, the editors of *Rethinking Schools*, etc. Educator Charlie Billiard taught me about the value of diverse dialects and Bob Probst about the rights of student readers. So, no, my angst is not with white people per se, but with the policies of white supremacy that undergird our every institution. Nonetheless, it's time to step back and let black and brown people lead this new struggle for quality education as a constitutional right because it is

*From *Quilting the Black-Eyed Pea* by Nikki Giovanni. Copyright © 2002. Reprinted by permission of the author.

primarily their children who are being cheated of that right. We must participate in the struggle with them, at every step, but we shouldn't be seizing the funds for us to lead it. Rather, I believe that we white educators should be uniting as a force to insist that the Kellogg, the Ford, the Spencer, and all of the other foundations fund not our projects, but revolutions like the Algebra Project (AP), with a thirty-year success record in teaching higher level mathematics to children at the bottom, or The Young People's Project (YPP), where youth develop youth into high school and college math literacy workers. The only impediment to their work going viral is money—money to pay students to be knowledge workers instead of burger flippers; money to guide teachers in rethinking the way they teach mathematics and language arts; money to fund public school/university summer institutes so students at the bottom can experience the academic rigor denied them during the school year. These are some of the components of their work that have been researched by NSF and proven effective in major cities in this country.

If we got out of the way and stopped holding our hands out for the educational dollars and insisted those dollars be used to fund these successful programs, poor children of color might receive the education they deserve, and they, in turn, would help lead the nation toward a real democracy. And, frankly, programs that rescue students at the "top" from bad schools do nothing to change the elitist paradigm that allows inferior schools to exist. Unlike those programs, Moses, AP, and YPP are demonstrating how marginalized students, ignored by schools so they can fill up prisons,[29] can be taught academically rigorous curriculum in public schools. These projects offer the children the content typically reserved for "the gifted" because, like Asa Hilliard and Shin'ichi Suzuki, they demonstrate that hard work, not IQ, creates genius; and they believe it is our job as teachers to excavate that brilliance so these students can contribute to their communities, not be "freed" from them. Moreover, AP and YPP illustrate how to raise the voices of the disenfranchised to make a demand for quality education in their communities. Moses and AP reveal how we can make schools both "public" and outstanding for every mother's child. Former UN Ambassador, Andrew Young, in a recent interview, said, "Dr. King used to say 'I admire the Good Samaritan, but I don't want to be one. I don't want to pick up people on the Jericho road after they've been beaten up and robbed. I want to change the Jericho road so that they don't get beaten up and robbed.' That's public policy."[30] And that's the kind of paradigm shift Moses seems to be after. Not rescuing children from bad schools, but changing public policy so that there are no bad schools where children need rescue.

Sonia Nieto recently in a keynote address at FIU College of Education said, "Our public school system is sick."[31] I believe her. And I think that as white people, our pathology is too thick, too deep, with too long a history for us to avoid tainting much of what we touch in schools for children of color. We swim in power and privilege every day so no matter how enlightened we become, we can never see the same world that a Delpit or a Moses or thousands of "othered" educators see. Nor can we really know what the parents of children of color know about their own children. If we are not deeply listening to those communities' voices and experiences, then we are surely lost.

Our white skin protects us and all of our children from ever being victims of "sick" racist institutional policies described by Nieto. Thus, I can feel disgust at the ghastly statistics of the criminalizing of young African American and Latino men who are marched out of schools for insignificant offenses and rushed along a path leading into prisons, but I also know the statistics[32] that tell me that this will not happen to my young nephews. I can intellectually recognize the injustice of a black Harvard professor being arrested for trying to get into his own home, but I can be pretty sure that as a white professor, that injustice will not happen to me. I can still writhe from the horrors of African Americans' plight in New Orleans after Katrina, yet I know my white skin would have allowed me to cross that infamous Danziger bridge into a safe haven instead of being gunned down. And, yes, in nightmarish images, I can intuit that if my black mentors had been unlucky enough to be stranded in New Orleans, they would have been left there by their government to die. But, we, my progressive white sisters and brothers, no matter how much we bloody ourselves fighting for justice and equity, we know that all of us would have been allowed to cross that bridge. And no matter how many "hoodies" our children wear, we know they will not be murdered because they looked "suspicious." So, my knowledge of the institutional racism that drowns black and brown poor children in a backwash of rotting educational policies can never equal the intimate knowledge that a Perry or a Payne or an African American parent and child bring to the battle to stop the sinking of our darker children into the maelstrom of "sick" schools.

Yet when hashing out these ideas in my head, I'm brought back again to Baldwin's wisdom: "I'm not interested in anybody's guilt. Guilt is a luxury that we can no longer afford. I know you didn't do it, and I didn't do it either, but I am responsible for it because I am a man and a citizen of this country and you are responsible for it, too, for the very same reason. Anyone who is trying to be conscious must begin to dismiss the vocabulary that we've used so long to cover it up, to lie about the way things are."[33]

Hopefully, we can commit to taking that responsibility Baldwin addresses; of reaching across social, cultural, religious, and ethnic boundaries; of building bridges; of spanning gaps. We've sometimes done so in the past. But are we, am I, ready for truth and reconciliation? Are we, am I, ready to give up the power and privilege that has become what Hilliard and others have called a pathology for those who savagely hold onto it? Can we, in releasing that grip, dramatically lessen our anger, anxieties, fears, shame? Can we recognize that if Richard Leakey was right when he claimed he dug up those first human bones in Egypt, then we are all of African descent—at least those of us who claim to be human.

Along with those reality checks, I am also tussling with the act of humility—a lesson a few lines from a Native American poem I've kept for decades reminds me, ". . . .Wherever you are is called Here, And you must treat it as a powerful stranger, Must ask permission to know it and be known . . . .Listen."[34] So am I humble and brave enough to sit and listen to "the other" while taking my hands off the pots of gold that foundations use to seduce us into thinking our research is holier than those "others"? Am I humble enough to take a "back seat" on the foundation bus to my black and brown progressive educators, who daily wrestle institutional Darth Vaders, to extract their children from the vise of poverty, prison, and extinction? Is funding our careers more important than funding the integrity of those educators' urgent battles to save their children, our nation's children? We simply need to stop hoarding the money.

In 1999, Jeannie Oakes, a bold, brave, progressive researcher, scholar, writer, and white activist participated as a discussant for an AERA panel[35] where I was describing research resulting from an Annenberg grant that Delpit directed. After sharing with the audience my surprise that Atlanta foundations would not support the work of an African American, MacArthur "genius" scholar like Delpit, yet gave barrels of money to white urban educators, Oakes spoke. She said that my remarks gave her pause to ponder as she reflected on the fact that foundations "threw money" at her projects. Oakes is now the Director of Education and Scholarship at the Ford Foundation. So, I guess, I'm now asking Jeannie Oakes the same questions I'm asking myself, "Are we ready to walk away from the money? Are we ready to heap those funds into the hands of the multitude of reputable black and brown educators and their communities who are determined to pull their children out of the well of damnable schools and prisons?"

When growing up, I heard my mother often say when talking about activism, "Put your money where your mouth is." Can we do that as progressive white educators? Can we walk away from the foundation trough and, thereby, make room for the funding of the public school programs targeting students of color that are led by black and brown mothers' sons and daughters?

And can you, who are pre-service and in-service teachers, as you study about instructional strategies and issues of diversity impacting children, parents, schools, the nation, regardless of your ethnicity, gender, caste, religion, culture, do what Delpit challenges us to do: *Put your beliefs on hold . . . give up your own sense of who you are, and be willing to see yourself in the unflattering light of another's angry gaze?* Can you read this book with that kind of openness to the unknown—to the struggles and triumphs of *"other people's children"?* And by doing that, can you, then, own all cultural liberation stories as our collective battle as humans to be free?

Can you consider Payne's research into the strategies of the organizing tradition of the Southern Freedom Movement as a study to guide your instruction of students?[36] Can you capture in your classrooms the lessons from the lives of those ordinary people—sharecroppers, maids, mechanics, children—who became s/heroes, who for one brief shining moment turned America upside down, creating the "great, inspiring moral event" of that century?[37] Can you let that saga unfold for students to learn how as ordinary people, we can lead ourselves out of the desert of dysfunctional belief systems and disempowered schools?

And as present or future teachers, can you explore, as Perry does, how to teach all of our students a counter-narrative to the one that society weaves about this same culture?[38] Can we teach, especially our privileged, that the nation's African Americans for hundreds of years risked their lives and limbs to learn to read and write, preach poetry, sing theology, dance philosophy, challenge epistemology? With such insights, can we recognize that those records can fortify us all to confront the demons who daunt us in our struggles to evolve as humans worthy of the bounty of this small planet, earth?

Or can you do as Dixon suggests, "Intuit from the long ago boasts of Greek mathematician, Archimedes, that if we give students 'a place to stand upon, they might move the world'"?[39]

And finally I ask, can we as teachers start a dialogue exploring the wisdom in Hilliard's words: "I have never encountered any children in any group who are not geniuses. There is no mystery on how to teach them. The first thing you do is treat them like human beings and the second thing you do is love them."[40]

ENDNOTES

1. Moses, R. & Cobb, C. (2001) *Radical Equations: Civil Rights from Mississippi to the Algebra Project.* Boston: Beacon Press, p.3

2. Robles, F., A shooting in the neighborhood, *The Miami Herald*, March 16, 2012 (Broward & Keys edition). After this introduction was written, another unarmed black male reported shot 11 times and killed by a security guard in Miami, Guard held in fatal shooting, *The Miami Herald*, June 9, 2012.

3. Jackson, P., Black America loses gamble in electing first black president, *The Black Star Project*, Chicago, 2/12/2010; Stevenson, Bryan 2012., We need to talk about an injustice, TED Talks, TED. com www.ted.com/talks/lang/en/bryan_stevenson_we_need_to_talk_about_an_injustice.html

4. Lyrics from "Ella's Song," composed by Bernice Johnson Reagon, from her film score created for Joanne Grant's film, *Fundi: The Story of Ella Baker* (Icarus Films, 1981). Used with composer's permission. Ella Baker, keynote address, Mississippi Freedom Democratic Party Conference, Jackson, MS. 8/6/64. Also found in Ransby, B. (2003). *Ella Baker & the Black Freedom Movement: A radical Democratic vision.* Chapel Hill: The University of North Carolina Press, p.335.

5. Mays, B. E. (1971). *Born to rebel: An autobiography.* New York: Scribner.

6. Moses, R. & Cobb, C. (2001). *Radical equations: Civil rights from Mississippi to the Algebra Project.* Boston: Beacon Press, p. 174.

7. Hall, E. T. (1976). *Beyond culture.* New York: Anchor Books

8. Morrison, T. (1990). *Playing in the dark: Whiteness and the literary imagination.* New York: Random House

9. Faulkner, W. (1951). *Requiem for a nun.* New York: Random House.

10. Blackmon, D. A. (2009). *Slavery by another name: The re-enslavement of Black Americans from the Civil War to World War II.* New York: Random House.

11. Blackmon, pp. 401–402.

12. Delpit, L. (1997). *Other people's children.* New York: The New Press

13. Feagin, J. (1997). *Reflections on education and race: Examining the intersections: Select addresses from the Public Education Network 1996 annual conference* (p 22). Public Education Network.

14. Stevenson, Bryan 2012. TED.com www.ted.com/talks/lang/en/bryan_stevenson_we_need_to_talk_about_an_injustice.html

15. McIntosh, P. (1988). "White Privilege and Male Privilege: A Personal Account of Coming to See Correspondences through Work in Women's Studies." Working Paper #189, Wellesley College Center for Research on Women, Wellesley, MA 02181.

16. Delpit, L., The silenced dialogue: Power and pedagogy in educating other people's children, *Harvard Educational Review*, 58:3, pp. 280 298. Copyright @1988 by the Pres. and Fellows of Harvard College.

17. Forman, J., Racial critiques of mass incarceration: Beyond the new Jim Crow, *Racial Critiques*, 2/26/2012 11:08 AM.

18. www.bostonbyfoot.org/tours/Heart_of_the_Freedom_Trail?gclid=CKLu_6j4664CFQFgTAodciH8Ig

19. Baldwin, J. *The Price of the Ticket: Collected Nonfiction, 1948-1985.* (1985) New York, N.Y.: St. Martin's Press.

20. Roy, A., Come September (9-29-2002), ZNET: A community of people committed to social change. Retrieved July 21, 2012 www.zcommunications.org/come-september-by-arundhati-roy

21. Feistritzer, C., *Profile of Teachers in the U.S. 2011* (2011) National Center for Education Information. Retrieved May 30, 2012: www.edweek.org/media/pot2011final-blog.pdf

22. 8-24-11 draft revisions FPLS, document sent to conference call participants for review for August 29, 2011 call.

23. Florida Department of State, Division of Library and Information Services, 6A-5.080, Florida Principal Leadership Standards 12/20/11, www.flrules.org/gateway/ruleno.asp?id=6A-5.080

24. All are African American scholars, researchers, writers, teachers.

25. Giovanni, N. (2002) *Quilting the black-eyed pea.* New York: HarperCollins, p 4. By permission of author.

26. Middle Passage refers to the brutal transport of Africans in ships across the Atlantic to serve as slaves. Some sources cite as many as 16-20 million being transported with possibly half never making it to Europe or the United States alive. www.pbs.org/wgbh/aia/part1/1p277.html; Palmer, C. (2002). *Captive passage: The transatlantic slave trade and the making of the Americas.* Newport News, VA: Smithsonian Institution Press.

27. Anderson, N., International test score data show U.S. firmly midpack, *The Washington Post*, 12-7-10. www.washingtonpost.com/wp-dyn/content/article/2010/12/07/AR2010120701178.html; Strauss, V., Darling-Hammond: the mess we are in, *The Washington Post Post Local*, 8-01-11.

www.washingtonpost.com/blogs/answer-sheet/post/darling-hammond-the-mess-we-are-in/2011/07/31/gIQAXWSIoI_blog.html

28. Zinn, H. (2005). *The people's history of the United States.* USCOM: Harper Perennial Modern Classics.

29. American Civil Liberties Union. School to prison pipeline. www.aclu.org/racial-justice/school-prison-pipeline; Special Issue: the School-to-Prison Pipeline. *Rethinking Schools*, Volume 26, No.2 Winter 2011/2012

30. Ross, K. The policy of Andrew Young: Atlanta icon lends his legacy to GSU. *GSU Magazine*, Summer 2012.

31. Nieto, S., Good teachers in difficult times: Challenging teacher bashing and promoting the health of our public schools, Keynote, College of Education, FIU, 1/12/2012.

32. Special Issue: The School-to-Prison Pipeline. *Rethinking Schools*, Volume 26, No.2 Winter 2011/2012; Alexander, M. (2010) *The new Jim Crow: Mass incarceration in the age of colorblindness.* New York, NY: The New Press

33. Baldwin, J. (1985). *The Price of the Ticket: Collected Nonfiction, 1948-1985.* New York, N.Y.: St. Martin's Press

34. Wagoner, D., Lost, *Collected Poems 1956-1976* © Indiana University Press.

35. Wynne, J., Racism, research, and reform, April 19-23, 1999, AERA panel for national conference, Montreal, Canada.

36. Payne, C. M. (1995). *I've got the light of freedom: The organizing tradition and the Mississippi freedom struggle.* Berkeley: University of California Press.

37. Rorty, R. (1995, September 24). *Color-blind in the marketplace.* Book Review. *New York Times.*

38. Perry, T. et.al. (2003). *Young, gifted, and black: Promoting high achievement among young African American students.* Boston: Beacon Press.

39. Dixon, R. (1997) Keynote Address, Morehouse College Science Institute, Atlanta, GA.

40. Hilliard, A. G. III. Alonzo A. Crim Center for Urban Educational Excellence, Georgia State University website. http://education.gsu.edu/cuee/index.htm accessed 4/12/2012.

SECTION 1

HONORING DIVERSITY BEGINS WITH UN-LEARNING RACISM

Image copyright mchaeljung, 2012. Used under license from Shutterstock. Inc.

Life's camera had caught the images of two six-year-old black children who, attempting to be the first to integrate a southern elementary school were walking down a street lined on either side with angry white adults . . . . the image of the thick, heavy chains that many of those men and women held, threateningly waving them, shouting taunts at those two young but courageous children. . . . With the picture of those chains, Life magazine had dramatically captured . . . the moral deprivation that racism inflicts on the racist, thereby, diminishing the whole community.

—Joan T. Wynne "The Elephant in the Classroom"

CHAPTER 1

HOW DOES AN ORPHANED CULTURE EDUCATE ITS CHILDREN?

Carlos Gonzalez Morales

"For a long time the Universe has been germinating in your spine."—Hafiz

I live and work in the South Florida bioregion. This area is framed by Lake Okeechobee in the north, Florida Bay at the southern end, the Gulf of Mexico to the west, and the Atlantic to the east.

This bioregion is quite young in terms of its current manifestation. Its shape and form are only about 12,000 years old. Humans have been around most of that time. The two major people who were the original inhabitants of the area were the Calusa and Tequesta.

South Florida's current social/cultural incarnation is about 100 years old. Modern Miami (named after the Calusa word for sweet water) develops when the Flagler Railroad moves to the area in search of warm breezes and agricultural and tourist dollars. The center of the city is physically built upon the sacred burial grounds of the Tequesta people, a nation that was killed off by European disease and persistent Spanish slave raids.

When Flagler built the first hotel on the mouth of the Miami River, photographs were taken and used as postcards of his men digging the site and dumping what seem to be rocks into Biscayne Bay. If one looks closely at these photographs, however, one can see that the content of the wheel barrows are human remains. Not all of the skeletons were disposed of this way; some were kept and given to special guests who would come and stay at the hotel. VIP status sometimes came with the privilege of a hand, foot, and/or skull (1997, p. 53).

Flagler's legacy is not just of disregard for the sacred essence of land, he also physically carved into the limestone and culture of South Florida a form of apartheid that still is evident 100 years later. If one looks at a map of Florida's east coast, from Jacksonville to Miami, one can see that all of the northwest sections of each of the major towns that Flagler developed are African-American.

Flagler segregated each of his communities, placing Blacks farthest away from tourists but close enough to provide a cheap labor force to run his businesses. If one visits Overtown, the historic African-American community in Miami, one can clearly see the economic logic of Flagler and his men. In the late 1950's another form of institutional racism was inscribed in South Florida. This happened when I-95 was brought south. There were several choices where to lay the freeway, but the one made went right through historic Overtown. Within a short period of time the community lost about 44,000 people and its middle-class base. Businesses closed, substandard housing became the norm, and the seeds for the riots of the 1980's were sown. The freeway came with shackles.

At the same time that Black Miamians were being expelled from their homes, Cuban migration became a reality that also changed the South Florida landscape. The area next to Overtown, Little Havana, became the hub of the Cuban exile community. What happened next is classic and a story that has taken place many other times in US history. Conflict between new immigrants and established poor minorities created a dynamic ripe for injustice, violence, and an even deeper memory loss.

At the same time that humans were injuring one another, South Florida became an engineering water theme park gone wrong. Lake Okeechobee was dammed so that farmers and, more significantly, sugar growers could produce a federally subsidized product at the expense of massive environmental destruction to the Everglades. In a matter of a couple of decades, the Everglades shrunk by 50%. Bird populations plummeted and water supplies have become threatened and mercury laden. What the engineers had not figured was that if one alters the water flow of the Everglades by creating an extensive canal system taking water out to the ocean, that the aquifers where the major population areas get their water supplies, do not get recharged. More significantly, because population increases demand even more water, these aquifers become susceptible to salt water encroachment, making the future questionable for those who call South Florida home.[1]

South Florida is an ecological landscape of deep loss. Tourists come and go without realizing the tragedy that is happening under their sun tanned bodies. More importantly and sadly, the current inhabitants of the area lack a clear understanding of the loss.

We are an orphaned culture, one where violence and greed have undermined the possibility of fully belonging, of becoming integrated not just to the diversity of the human family but also to the diversity of the natural ecosystems that support the very life of the area.

How does an orphaned culture educate its children? For me this is the central question regarding so called environmental education and education in general. The answer to this is clear in many if not most of our schools in South Florida: We do so with great internal violence, coercion, ugliness. We may have science curriculum that touches on the importance of conservation and biodiversity, but the schools are structured from their physical form to their pedagogies to see themselves as separate from the life systems around. They also perpetuate a dominator mindset that sees nothing wrong with consistent and ever increasing growth, development, and profit. The American dream so many of my own people come seeking is nothing but a parasitic vision which leaves areas like South Florida in ecological and social shambles.

True ecological education is rare in my region. I don't think I have really seen it. It does not exist because we have built our culture not on top of sand as a scripture would say, but on top of sacred remains. Maybe each school community in the nation does not have the same exact story; however, I have a sneaky hunch that the themes are similar and the bones have been scattered or given away as souvenirs. Industrial education is incompatible with true human needs. We were not meant to be treated as objects and subjected to the cruel indoctrination of a capitalist system turning out children who can test well but not live in harmony with themselves and life around them.

How to work with what we have is a great challenge. I think that whatever we can do right now to provide pockets of sanity in otherwise dysfunctional schools is important, not just for the children but for those of us who want to see a different kind of society. The key for me is to change the dream. I'm not sure how to do this working within our current system. I do know that this work is profound and calls for my own transformation as I seek to find ways to invite others in the process.

Thinking from a media perspective, reporting on true ecological literacy involves understanding and being touched by plants, animals, rocks, soil, water, air, and the very energy of the planet. I say this because there is no way to get the story right if we are doing so from a dominator bio-phobic paradigm of privilege and status hungering. For me what's true for teachers and school policy folk holds true for those who would write about such things.

END NOTES

http://philliswheatley.wordpress.com

1. Most of this information comes from conversations with Dr. Marvin Dunn, retired FIU professor and from the text: Dunn, M. (1997). *Black Miami: In the twentieth century.* Gainesville, FL: The University Press of Florida.

THE ELEPHANT IN THE CLASSROOM: RACISM IN SCHOOL REFORM

Joan T. Wynne

"Why is it that White women will not raise the issue of racism when engaged in serious conversation about issues that concern us as women?" That question spoken by Mattie Avery,[1] an African American woman, at a women's retreat in Boston has troubled me for several years. At the retreat a small group of women from around the country and two women from other countries had come together to learn strategies for creating and sustaining meaningful dialogue with each other and with other more diverse groups to whom we were connected.

We had spent a weekend bonding as a newly formed group, experiencing the strategies we were there to investigate, and discussing issues that affect us as women in a world that seems to become increasingly hostile to women and children. Ms. Avery's question emerged on the last day, which means that we, the other fifteen women all of whom were white, had been there for two days consciously or unconsciously refusing to raise the issue of racism. Stunned by her question, I puzzled over my part in this group's willingness to remain silent. What is it about racism that makes white people assume it concerns only people of color? Why is it that we seem unable to enter into honest discussion about it with each other, knowing that it plagues the planet? And what irony, that fifteen supposedly intelligent and sensitive women had come together to learn new ways of talking openly and honestly about serious issues yet had ignored an issue so fundamental to our personal and societal realities. As a veteran teacher, I could not help but wonder about the ramifications of those kinds of silences for all of our children in and out of school.

Because of those children, I've sat with Ms. Avery's question for a long time letting it simmer inside of me, wanting to let it go, to keep it from gnawing at me. Though I knew I had raised the issue of racism in all-white circles at other times in my past, I wondered what it was that kept me and the others oblivious to it this time. Avoiding the issue concerns me most because of its consequences on children. I am frankly scared for them because the political tenor of this country has turned again toward a paranoia of all groups of children and adults who are comprised of anything that is not mainstream white Euro-centric. The Internet, radio talk shows, and other media are full of vitriolic condemnations of diverse groups of people. In an issue of the *Harvard Educational Review*, Bartolome and Macedo echo this same fear:

The racism and high level of xenophobia we are witnessing in our society today are not caused by isolated acts by individuals such as Limbaugh . . . . Rather, these individuals are representatives of an orchestrated effort by segments of the dominant society to wage a war on the poor and on people who, by virtue of their race, ethnicity, language, and class are reduced at best to half-citizens, and at worst to a national enemy responsible for all the ills afflicting our society (Bartolome and Macedo, 1997).

Here we are in the 21ˢᵗ century, and their words still ring true and Limbaugh is still spewing hate. It seems too easy for those of us who think and feel differently about diversity to ignore the need of our voices in rebuttal. Hearing Toni Morrison in a television interview say, "When they send the trucks, I know who they are sending them for; they're sending them for me," I understood fully the danger of white people's failure to initiate the dialogue about racism, because I know Morrison is right. In fact, when I look at the statistics showing the disproportionate numbers of African American males in prisons; the disproportionate numbers of children of color living below the poverty level; the numbers of children of color doomed to failure in our public schools, I think we've already sent the trucks. Those trucks in Nazi Germany could have been stopped. One of the factors that allowed them to operate was the early silent global complicity about the persecution of Jewish people. Silence can be dangerous. We have a chance to stop those trucks. We've been silent long enough. As members of the dominant culture, we must say out loud that racism is crippling our nation, ravaging our children, and draining the country of its most precious resource, brilliant human minds.

But it is the silence of white women that particularly concerns and confounds me. It concerns me because in our nation the overwhelming majority of teachers in our schools are white women (Feistritzer, 2011) and the National Education Association (2011) indicated the proportion of women teachers continues to rise. Therefore, if we don't confront the issue for our children in schools, who will ever voice it in the larger context? When schools are failing to teach 85 percent of black and 84 percent of Hispanic/Latino students to read on grade level; and in math, they are failing to teach 85 percent of black and 79 percent of Hispanic/Latino students to achieve on grade level (CDF, 2010), how can we excuse ourselves from addressing the issue? Researchers from John Hopkins University designated 2000 American schools as "Drop-out" factories. Forty-six percent of the nation's black students and 39 percent of its Latino students unluckily attend those schools (CDF, 2010).

Our silence about these atrocious realities for the nation's children confounds me because we as women are considered by the larger society to be the nurturers, the protectors of children, the very life's blood of children. Yet here we sit, most of us, in comfort while over 16 million children live in poverty (Edleman, 2012). Millions of American children go to bed hungry every night because of an unjust system of economics and politics. And too many of us do nothing, assuming the problem is too big for us to tackle. But we can do something. We can educate our students and teachers about these ugly realities, then maybe millions of children won't always go to bed hungry.

Volumes have been written about the damage of educational inequities on children of color. The research is replete with our failure to teach these children because of our erroneous assumptions about their ability to learn. When serving economically disenfranchised African American children, school systems often assume that because these children are poor and because their culture is different from the mainstream, these students will be unable to achieve academically at the same levels as their white counterparts. Many times without being aware of their own biases, teachers and others, operate from a framework of low expectations of success for these children. Assuming that the capacity for learning is somehow hampered by the children's life circumstances, we as educators too often allow these children to get by with less, because less is all we believe they can do. Society in general supports these notions, thus, making it difficult for schools to shift their thinking.

Consistently some educational experts continue to bombard us with the belief that the learning potential of children of the urban poor is forever limited. An article by Richard Rothstein in *Education Week* once claimed that "academic performance of the [Los Angeles] district's students will always be and should always be considerably below national averages." He bases his argument on the supposed fact that "for 30 years, experts have acknowledged that the most important determinants of student achievement are family and community characteristics." I wonder if his experts are those with white skin. As I will share later, the research of many African American educational experts has found the absolute opposite to be true. He continues, however, insisting that "children from literate homes with secure economic environments will always, on average, have better academic outcomes than children without these advantages." Therefore, he later concludes that inner-city teachers "who guide their students to the 30th percentile on national achievement tests may bring as much 'value added' to the educational process as teachers in more comfortable communities where students coast to the 70th percentile" (Rothstein, 1997). His newest work published in 2004 furthers this theme by researching the effects of social and economic factors that impact education in America, certainly a valuable investigation; yet he still seems to misunderstand the power of great teaching for students at the bottom. One only needs to look at the 30 years of work of Bob Moses and the Algebra Project to see an impeccable counter to Rothstein's assumptions about quality education. Through his research assumptions, Rothstein, with all of the best intentions, releases any responsibility for teachers and schools in inner-city neighborhoods to demand excellence from their students because he believes that mediocrity is the best these students can give. Once again, we well-meaning white liberal, progressive thinkers get off track when we don't listen and learn from the African American experts who have been working magic in their schools for hundreds of years with socially, economically, unhealthy children in spite of the nation's total disenfranchisement of their people.

Years ago African American scholars and practitioners like Asa Hilliard and Barbara Sizemore (Hilliard, 1991, Sizemore, Brosard, and Harigan 1982) documented a multitude of effective schools where the majority of students who attend those schools come from single-parent, poor neighborhoods or housing projects yet achieve academic excellence and knock the tops off of national standardized tests. These high-achieving schools produce successful students, despite extreme poverty or dysfunctional home environments. Such schools exist in communities around the country, in Los Angeles, Pittsburgh, Detroit, Lansing, West Virginia, Texas, etc. Many of these schools operate on ridiculously low budgets and limited resources, yet common to all are a firm belief and demand by teachers that their children will excel. I find it interesting that few, if any, mainstream scholars ever investigate or cite these schools.

Another African American scholar, Vanessa Siddle Walker, documented the high achievement of black children in black segregated schools in the south, where most black people were forced into poverty, socially isolated, and denied access to adequate health care. Later teachers, scholars, and students in *Quality education as a constitutional right* (2010) documented a number of examples of raising the academic achievement of the children that Rothstein and others give little hope for unless society changes its bad economic, health, and social policies. All of us want those policies eradicated. But schools and teachers don't have to wait until that happens. The act of education can trump bad policy when good teachers stand strong. In the midst of chaos, brutal oppression, bloody recrimination, African American people throughout their long history in this country, especially in the south, found a way to educate their children. Yet too many studies from current research literature, ignore these histories and these scholars, and unfortunately, suggest limited possibilities for the children of the poor, especially those of color, illustrating the pervasive and insidious nature of the messages sent by, I assume, well-intentioned educational experts. To suppose that teachers walk into classrooms untouched by these biases is naïve. For many who teach, there seems to be a struggle to, first, believe that all children not only can learn but do learn and are always learning. Whether it be what we want them to learn or not, all children are innately curious and they are in the constant process of learning. And second, it seems to be a struggle for many teachers to believe that they can teach all children.

Yet to be a good teacher, both beliefs are imperative before we can expect to be effective in teaching any children. All children, regardless of their economic status, whether their mother is on drugs or their daddy is in jail will learn and do learn at prodigious rates. And as long as we believe we can teach them and demand that they achieve academic excellence, they will learn whatever it is we want to teach them (Hilliard, 1998). A number of research studies have documented that most children, regardless of economic backgrounds, come to school with the same capacity to learn and at the same performance levels, yet the longer most African American children of the poor are in school, the more they fall behind. (Levin, 1988) This fact seems an indictment of the inability of the school rather than the incapacity of the student.

As early as 1995, The Educational Policy Research Institute in West Virginia completed a two-year study of elementary schools in their state. The results of the study convinced the researchers that: "Effective student performance *is* possible despite extreme adverse conditions. In fact, this research identified high student achievement in effective elementary schools irrespective of the degree of poverty, high or low parent education, high or low parent income or high or low parent involvement" (Hughes, 1995). What makes us pay so little attention to studies such as these?

Hilliard in the 9th Annual Benjamin E. Mays Lecture insisted that "there really is no pedagogical problem to producing academic success among children no matter what their social class, cultural, or gender circumstances may be" (1997). Because I have taught and worked with teachers in urban schools all of my professional life, like Hilliard, I, too, believe that the fault of low achievement of many children in urban schools lies not with the children but with the educational systems that devour them.

THE RESEARCH RESULTS OF THE UACC

I and several colleagues in a co-reform effort, the Urban Atlanta Coalition Compact (UACC), engaged with six public schools to explore ways to create better places of learning for disenfranchised African American children. This project was initiated and driven by the research and vision of Lisa Delpit who passionately believes and has documented that poor African American children, like all other children, are brilliant and only wait for us to help that brilliance unfold (1995, 2012). Yet, in this collaborative reform effort, led by two African American women, we observed that insidious messages of racism played a significant role in the failure of the schools to meet these children's academic needs. However, as Ms. Avery had suggested at the Boston retreat, no one seems to want to name it. No one wants to say the word out loud. Consequently, I keep hearing her question ringing in my ear. Why won't white folks raise the issue? Why don't we want to confront it head on? Part of the answer probably lies in the fact that our "white privilege" consciously or unconsciously allows us to benefit from racism (McIntosh). But I continually wonder if there is more than privilege playing out in this game.

I seem compelled to explore the question for two reasons. First, my personal history is interwoven in the history of America's racism. I grew up in a segregated South. I rode buses where African Americans sat in the back. I drank from "white only" fountains, and frequented "white only" restaurants. My youth was spent in the midst of Jim Crow laws. My schooling was in all-white classrooms. The second is that, as a teacher, I've witnessed the consequences of racism on children's learning. So its impact on people's lives has been a theme, all of my life.

And I think I've been asking myself Ms. Avery's question since I was eight years old, when I was first visually assaulted by the perverse consequences of the Jim Crow laws. I had returned home one day from my segregated Catholic school and picked up a copy of *Life* magazine from the coffee table. *Life's* camera had caught the images of two six-year-old Black children who, attempting to be the first to integrate a southern elementary school were walking down a street lined on either side with angry White adults. In that same photo, National Guard soldiers stood as the only barriers between those two small children and the hostile bodies of hundreds of grown men and women. What stuns me even now as I bring it back from memory, is the image of the thick, heavy chains that many of those men and women held, threateningly waving them, shouting taunts at those two young but courageous children. Though later in my life, I have read books and seen movies that detailed more horrific depictions of racial hatred, that picture remains the most vivid: the anger, the chains, and the sheer numbers of adults intimidating two vulnerable and innocent children. What in the world could so twist adult human beings that they would want to strike out so menacingly at such small, defenseless beings? With the picture of those chains, *Life* magazine had dramatically captured for me, even as an eight-year-old, the moral deprivation that racism inflicts on the racist, thereby, diminishing the whole community. That consequence on the spiritual lives of the privileged seems today as ignored as the debilitating consequences of racism on the lives of its victims—a systemic reality that ultimately makes us all victims, even though some of us materially benefit from it.

But the children, both the privileged and the disenfranchised, are still my major concern. For both are stunted by racist rhetoric and practices—poor children of color because they are forced into failing schools, the privileged because if not taught about racism, they will never understand why their nation is failing as a real democracy, nor how to help put it back on track. Too often, while working with the UACC and with other projects, I sat at meetings and listened to well-meaning white educators discussing the low achievement of the urban child. These educators seem sincere in wanting to change that reality, yet they never raise the impact on classroom instruction and student achievement of racist assumptions about the capacity of poor children of color to learn. In *Educational Leadership*, Sandra Parks explained our challenge. She said, "Past and present conditions of racism contribute to reduced expectations, opportunities, and resources for students of color who live in poverty. The influences of racism result in policies and conditions that are debilitating for children and young adults, perpetuating rather than reducing the cycle of poverty"(Parks, p.18). I keep wondering when we as white educators will bring it to every table for discussion? That discussion drove part of our work in the UACC. We continued to ask ourselves and our partners to investigate the consequences of racist thinking on the academic performance of urban children. Our work demanded that we explore how, as a community of educators who are committed to empowering children to excel academically, we can together confront the issue of racism and class bias in a meaningful way so that our children's capacities for learning are enriched not stifled?"

In the rest of my discussion I have used the terms culture and ethnicity wherever possible when talking about the issue of "race" because I have been persuaded by the work of a number of African scholars that there is only one race, the human race, and that the "racial" differences among us are actually cultural and/or ethnic. From these studies, I have learned that the construct of different races was developed four hundred years ago to further divide people for the purposes of domination (Carruthers and Harris, 1997). Unfortunately, because the construct of race is so ingrained in the language, at times, using the term "race" can explain people's unconscious rationales for particular behavior.

Patricia Williams suggests that "racism is a gaze that insists upon the power to make others conform, to perform endlessly in the prison of prior expectation, circling repetitively back upon the expired utility of the entirely known"(Williams, 1997). Her definition seemed to manifest itself in some of the UACC schools. Some in our schools in interviews and program evaluations insisted that what mainstream researchers have discovered as pedagogical "truths" are universally suitable for all children, regardless of cultural heritage. White and sometimes black teachers also insisted that the children of the poor, especially children of color, have been so "impoverished" by their life circumstances, that we can expect very little from them in academics; that the best we should hope for is to offer "life skills" to get them ready for jobs.

But, as Williams' definition suggests, our educational success with disenfranchised black children is thwarted because we are "imprisoned" by our expectations of failure for these children. Some of our UACC teachers, as well as many other educators across the country, share a pervasive attitude that there is nothing of merit that these children bring to the classroom; that nothing of value happens in their communities; and that any change that happens must happen in the "disadvantaged" children and their homes, not in the classroom and the school. Because what teachers do and know is often unquestioned by them, they assume that the trouble lies in what the students don't know rather than in what the teachers don't know about the students. Therefore, again as Williams' definition suggests, there is a constant circling back to the uselessness of known mono-cultural strategies and curriculum. And I observed in UACC this insistence on the pedagogy of the dominant culture, an insistence to do more of what was not working for the urban poor.

I watched, astounded again and again, as these educators ignored the lessons learned by black scholars whose national and international reputations had been built on substantial research and practices examining how urban children of color learn. Exposed to these scholars' expertise, mainstream teachers and administrators, knowing their schools were failing African American children, still seemed not only to resist but to resent suggestions based on this proven research.

In addition, I almost became speechless when local foundations denied funding to such scholars while at the same time making major contributions to white organizations who had no record of success in urban schools. Wherever those decisions were made, I wish Ms. Avery had been there to raise her question. I wish somebody had asked these program directors why they insisted on giving money to unproven white educators to tamper with urban schools where black children are miserably educated while turning their backs on the work of famous black researchers with successful track records. How can I reasonably assume that racism, unconscious or not, plays no part in the decisions of these foundations?

Some of my African American colleagues have cautioned me to maintain a balanced view when I look at this thing called racism. They have encouraged me to avoid demonizing white people. I have made a sincere effort to think within those parameters. For I really do believe as Adam Michnik, a Polish freedom fighter once said, "There are no angels, no maggots." (Schell, 1986) Somewhere in our collective histories, there's probably blood on all of our hands. I believe, too, what Parks says that "learning to face racism and to talk about it transformatively with others requires compassion toward oneself and others" (1999). But when one of my white colleagues suggested I call racism something else when speaking about individuals trapped by it, I began to wonder that if I became too concerned about a balanced view, I might lose sight of the very thing I was trying to get a handle on. If we can't say racism out loud because the word may offend those whom it doesn't exactly fit, then how do we eradicate the disease that's bloodying all of our children? It becomes the "elephant in the classroom" that everybody pretends isn't there. And my experience has taught me that white people want to call racism everything but racism. We will explain it as personality clashes, misunderstandings, over-sensitivity, impropriety, and a hundred other euphemisms. We will call it anything but what it is to avoid recognizing our silent complicity in it. Refusing to call its name reminds me of the military calling missiles, which tear bodies, buildings, and whole cities to bloody shreds, "peace keepers." Our language often masks our hypocrisies. Thus, for my own need to keep myself from abandoning Ms. Avery's challenge, I must say the word out loud, racism.

As Beverly Tatum suggests, institutional racism and white privilege are so imbued in American culture, history, politics, and economics that they become like smog in Los Angeles; if you live and breathe in L.A., you are a smog breather. Living in a racist culture, we consciously or unconsciously breathe in racism. (Tatum, 1997, p. 6) Another understanding about racism that is important to grapple with is the impossibility of "reverse racism." Many of us White people whine about this mistaken notion whenever people of color seem to "prejudge" us. Yet if we understand racism as *a system of advantage based on race [ethnicity]; a form of oppression which is the systematic subjugation of a social group by another social group with access to social power; and that racism = power + prejudice*" (Wellman, 1977), then, I believe we should be able to understand that people of color can be prejudiced but not racist. There is only one culture in this country that has overwhelming power in all of our institutions, and it is not African American. "Every social indicator, from salary to life expectancy," as Tatum says, "reveals the advantages of being White. (1997, p. 8)

Because of the ingrained reality of racism in our culture, I also believe that the best we in the dominant culture can be is recovering racists (Feagin, 1997, p 22). But if we don't come out of denial, we will never be able to be in recovery. Calling ourselves and others racists is, of course, unproductive; however, recognizing our assumptions as they unfold is essential. As Probst suggests, if we don't question "culturally established norms," they "become so deeply ingrained in consciousness that they come to seem as substantial and immutable as physical reality itself."(Probst, 1984, p 67). We become "trapped" by our single cultural lens.

Tatum's and Probst's definitions consistently manifested themselves in the work of UACC. In the earliest discussions of funding for the project, issues of ethnicity arose. In a steering committee meeting when members were discussing the language used in the proposal for initial funding, one of the members, an African American educational consultant, suggested that we take the words "African American" out of the proposal when identifying the children we would target. He said that some foundations might reject the proposal because it specifically designated black children. A discussion of the efficacy of keeping that description in the proposal ensued amongst the fifteen committee members, a committee comprised of mixed ethnicities, genders, and professions. The committee's conversation ended when one of its members, an elementary school teacher, insisted that because African American children across this country were systematically poorly served in educational institutions, deliberately acknowledging a focus on these children demonstrated an honest attempt to address the problem. That the very naming of the ethnicity of these children could be seen as a problem suggests the power of the unconscious societal agreement to be silent about anything that evokes "race."

When funding finally became a reality for the UACC, we presented the project to three school systems who had been contacted concerning their interest in becoming involved. After the central administration of one system decided to invite their elementary schools to apply for the two available slots, I received a phone call from their associate superintendent. He revealed that their board was concerned about the piece of the proposal that designated the targeted population as African American. He asked for me to explain the project at their next board meeting. This system consists of a majority white and 40 percent African American student population. The district's test scores indicated that the performance of the majority of the African American students was far below that of the white students. Because of that, the central administration, was enthused about the possibility of the UACC changing this discrepancy. Some board members, however, did not want to support the initiative.

Consequently, I did attend and explained the main components of the project. Afterward, one board member, a white female, asked a number of questions about the project. Her major concern about UACC, she said, was the targeting of one segment of the district's student population. At one point she also asked just what we meant by the term, "children of color." I attempted to explain the necessity of targeting those children who are least well served by public schools because reform efforts have taught us that if we don't specifically target them, nothing changes for them.

The seven-member board (five white and two black) eventually approved the proposal with one dissenting vote, that of the white female. Her resistance to citing ethnicity seemed symptomatic of the complicity in this nation to deny the reality of racism. Even with the district's hard data of test scores revealing its failure to create schools where black children can excel, part of its ruling board still wanted to ignore that inequities played a major role in the system's incapacity to effectively teach all its students. But two of the district's elementary schools eventually applied for participation in the UACC.

After all three of the systems approved the project's proposal, the selection process began.[2] During that process, again issues of cultural differences manifested. The process included visits of two or three steering committee members to each of the schools, meeting with leadership teams, with random teachers in their classrooms, and with parents. Because we had no director of the project at that time, I visited all of the schools, talking to teachers, administrators, and parents as well as looking at school documents that addressed institutional vision, mission, goals, and records of student achievement. Two of the schools (Peters & Winchell Elementary[3]) that applied had white female principals and mostly white faculties. One of those schools had a majority white student population, and the other had an African American student population.

At Winchell when the African American parent representatives, invited by the principal that day, were interviewed, they complained about feeling alienated from the school; that African American children at Winchell were retained at higher rates than the other children; and of their frustrations that their children were treated differently at the school. (Wynne, 1997) Several mentioned that when they came to visit their children in the school, they felt unwelcome. After the hour's session with the parents, I asked the principal if I could meet with her whole faculty and share the perceptions and issues raised by these parents. My request was based on my need to ascertain the willingness of her staff to address the concerns of their African American parents and to make any necessary instructional or institutional changes. I walked away from that 1-1/2 hour meeting with serious doubts about the faculty's level of awareness of their own ethnic biases. They had spent that hour blaming the parents for being disconnected to the school and for their unwillingness or inability to help the children at home with their studies. In this discussion, the staff manifested a defensiveness about the school's failure to raise the achievement level of their African American students by consistently reminding me of the learning deficits of these children due to their "impoverished" backgrounds and lack of parent involvement, a defensiveness that forced their unconscious racist attitudes to bubble to the surface.

After the meeting, I mentioned to the selection committee my reservations about Winchell's selection. An in-depth dialogue ensued about the efficacy of accepting their application. After a full discussion, it was agreed that the committee would accept them as a partner in the reform effort for two reasons. The first was that the leadership at Winchell as well as the staff had vowed they were committed to school change that would more effectively raise the level of achievement for their black students. Their staff consistently in interviews acknowledged their need for help. The second reason was that our committee believed the school probably reflected the ethnic make-up of a large percentage of schools around the country; and, thus, if the partnership could effect positive change at Winchell, more African American students in the nation might benefit from the experiment.

Once the schools had been selected, the work began. Because the actual grant monies were slow in coming, we had to delay the director's hiring. Thus, I remained intimately involved with the initiation of the project. Our first meeting, a two-day over-night orientation retreat in early August, was designed to build relationship among the schools and universities and to communicate the UACC mission and goals. Fifteen constituents from each school, including parents, staff, and teachers were invited as well as university fellows and district administrators. Most schools sent at least twelve participants. During the retreat it became obvious that everyone there sincerely wanted to raise the academic achievement of the schools' African American students. Cultural differences, however, surfaced immediately as participants responded to the different retreat experiences. The mainstream faculty responded less favorably to experiences that incorporated music and relationship building, feeling those experiences took too much time away from discussion of goals and strategies. While the African Americans responded positively to goals and strategy sessions, they expressed a greater interest than their white counterparts in team-building activities. And three of the majority African American faculties repeated the team-building experiences for their faculties when they returned to school in the fall. These early responses reflected the difference in preferences manifested in the two cultures in the context of the larger society. Wade Nobles suggests that typically, central to the African worldview is the necessity for the sense of relatedness, the belief that "I am because we are," a philosophy that reveres community (Nobles, 1973). The Western worldview seems typified by Descartes' notion, "I think; therefore, I am," a philosophy that holds sacred individual rights. Often, these two conflicting views played themselves out in the discussions of the individual schools on how they could change to meet the academic needs of their African American students. White faculty often assumed that specific strategies, programs, or more outside tutors were the answer to the problem of low achievement, rarely examining the teacher's relationship to her students as a legitimate means of impacting the achievement levels of these children. In fact, in only one of my interviews with white faculty was the instructional benefit of a personal relationship with students ever specifically mentioned, and this teacher devoted her Friday evenings to spending time with students. Other instances emerged of white teachers creating classrooms where African American children could excel; however, too many teachers seemed unaware of their inability to connect with their students.

Though manifestations of racist assumptions unfolded during our first year, we were convinced that most of the teachers and staff, white and black, consciously wanted their black children to achieve. Their denial of racist suppositions about children speaks to, I think, the pervasiveness of those notions in the larger society, making it more difficult for these educators to recognize their own biases. Their failure to see through these assumptions might strengthen Tatum's explanation of the power of institutional racism.

Besides recognizing denial, what was also important to understand while participating was another outcome of our culture: "internalized oppression . . . believing the distorted messages about one's own group "(Tatum, p 6). During those first selection interviews, I began to notice that many of the African American teachers had absorbed the notions of the dominant culture against their own children. As often is true with oppressed peoples, the distortions of the oppressor become the beliefs of the oppressed. These teachers, too, could be heard blaming the children's low academic achievement on the plight of their parents, on the consequences of their poverty, and on the intellectual damage of these children due to their "disadvantaged" backgrounds. I had come up against this before when working with teachers in other public schools. Once an African American teacher, at a middle school serving children who lived in a housing project, informed me that her class of low-achieving science students could not go to the science laboratory because they could only handle "pencil and paper work." She insisted that they didn't have the social skills needed for laboratory work and, evidently, saw no responsibility to teach them those skills.

As I visited all of the schools, some of the insights from talking to their teachers led me to believe that most of the faculties lacked a sense of the potential genius of the children they taught. (Delpit, 1997, 2012). They consistently talked about the shortcomings of the children, the skills they lacked, their poor neighborhoods, the lack of support for schooling from their parents, the consequences of their poverty, the negative impact of their single-parent homes, etc. The sense of doom about the chances of these children to excel could have sunk a ship. In none of the interviews did I hear teachers or administrators mention the strengths of these students. Often during the interview process, after a litany of deficits was proclaimed, I interjected the question: "What are these students' strengths?" Too many times there was complete silence while teachers or administrators struggled to think of some. Their voices echoed society's message that the people in poverty, not the economic and political systems, are the cause of their own dilemma.

Because of most of the faculties' propensity to externalize the causes for the academic failure of these children, I wanted our first Town Meeting[4] of representatives from all the schools to focus on the "Ten Factors Essential to Success in Urban Classrooms"[5] that Delpit had developed. I thought her research discoveries, grounded in building instruction on the strengths of our urban children, their families, and their culture, could inform the individual and collective investigations for school reform. For I knew that her writing and research had worked magic on thousands of educators like me. Thus, I believed a discussion of her principles might help to dispel the schools' general acceptance that poor African American children, as Rothstein insists, could only achieve at minimal levels. After Delpit's talk, however, to my amazement, many of the white faculty and administrators present walked away thinking they had heard her say that only African American teachers could effectively teach African American children. Because I was there and I had heard no such reference or intimation made by Delpit, I asked several of those teachers for the specifics which had given them that impression. None of them could pinpoint any particular word or words. Several mentioned, however, that when Delpit cited examples of teachers who used the culture of the children as part of their classroom instruction, she was insinuating that only African Americans could know that culture; therefore, only they were most suitable to teach their children. The irony of the misconception of these teachers is that Delpit said at that very meeting that some African American teachers don't understand the culture of the urban poor and, thus, are ineffective. She also gave examples of excellent white teachers of African American children.

The repercussions of that same misconception arose again months later when I was teaching a master's methodology course for the university. One of the students who enrolled was a white teacher from one of the UACC schools. On a night when I was explaining the mission of the UACC, the teacher reiterated the same contention, that at the first Town meeting, Delpit had claimed only African Americans could effectively teach African American children. Once again I asked if the teacher remembered what Delpit had said that implied such a belief. The teacher then admitted that she actually had not attended the meeting, but that she had heard a conversation of teachers at her school who insisted that Delpit had voiced this assumption. Because I know Delpit's work well, I know that she sometimes uses the work of white teachers as examples of exemplary teaching. My professional experience in working with her convinces me that she harbors no such belief about the innate incapacity of white teachers to effectively teach African American children. I also know that she insisted on including in UACC white educators and professionals as steering committee members, as university fellows, as associate director of her Center for Excellence in Urban Education. The evidence of her amazing openness to the voices of others should have prevented anyone from assuming she held a bias against white educators. The consistent misconceptions, though, reminded me of how easily people's predispositions can distort information. Rokeach's research concerning ethnocentrism explained this phenomenon:

> Persons who are high in ethnic prejudice and/or authoritarianism, as compared with persons who are low, are more rigid in their problem-solving behavior, more concrete in their thinking, and more narrow in their grasp of a particular subject; they also have a greater tendency to premature closure in their perceptual processes and to distortions in memory, and a greater tendency to be intolerant of ambiguity. (Rokeach, 1960)

His research discoveries again and again became apparent in our work. Because of the unconscious ethnic and class prejudice of many teachers, parents, and administrators, research by African American scholars was distorted, ignored, or disbelieved. The propensity of some to stick to the "known" in their problem solving about raising the achievement of their African American students, without exploring the new ideas the Compact offered, suggested the trap of their unconscious ethnocentrism.

Shortly after the Town Meeting which was held in November of the first year, the white principal of Peters Elementary, a school with predominantly white faculty and mostly African American students, without consulting her faculty, chose to withdraw from the UACC. This principal, Ms. Feldman,[6] was the only principal who had not attended the Orientation Retreat. This may have been a factor in her lack of connection to the work of UACC. One of the major reasons she gave for withdrawing from the project was its divisive quality. She blamed the UACC for splitting her faculty along "racial lines." I have found in my years of work with schools as well as other organizations that when racism becomes obvious to the community at large, the culprit becomes whomever brought it to light, a diversity consultant, a diversity committee, student committees examining the issue, etc. So Ms. Feldman's mistaken source of blame for the divisiveness of her faculty came as no surprise, given that in our early interviews, members of her faculty complained about the division of the staff between white and black.

Later when I interviewed representatives of Peters Elementary about their exit[7] from the project, that division as well as unconscious racist beliefs about the children surfaced. One of the white staff, Ms. Smith,[8] when interviewed said, "It broke my heart when the principal made the unilateral decision for the school to end its partnership with the UACC. I, in the beginning did believe, and still do, that the project offered our best hope to change the achievement level of our kids." In her authentic attempt to be fair in her assessment of the reasons for the quick exit, the staff member explained it as a result of mutual misunderstandings and miscommunications between the university partners and the school's administrator and staff. She, however, mentioned at great length, the perception of the white faculty who attended the Town Meeting that Delpit had proclaimed the inability of white teachers to teach African American children.

The respondent insisted that the young white teachers had come away from that meeting with the impression that they were "inadequate" as teachers. The respondent also reported that the white faculty kept asking: "After African-centered pedagogy, then what?" She intimated that the African-centered activities, suggested by some of the black teachers as a way of being more responsive to the children's culture, seemed trivial to the white teachers as a means of teaching "basic skills."

When asked later in the interview if racism had played a role in the demise of the partnership, she insisted that while racism was a societal problem, she felt it had little impact on the problems in her school because "the young white teachers today don't share the prejudices and ignorance that white people of our generation did. They [young White teachers] live in integrated neighborhoods, have shared experiences like "cheerleading camps" with other cultures, are exposed to other cultures more than we were." Though her assumptions here may be accurate, they still do not take in the failure of those kinds of experiences to change institutional racism. No matter the increased exposure of whites to African Americans, societal racism is still alive, well, and wreaking havoc on children, even if unconsciously so by the mainstream masses.

Ms. Smith's biggest criticism of the project was its invitation to one of Peters' faculty to become a member of the UACC steering committee without first consulting the faculty. She insisted that the administrators of the Compact should have asked Peters' staff to choose a representative from their school, a concern which seemed completely legitimate and a decision that we had regretted immediately after it was made and immediately had rectified. Ms. Smith also insisted that none of the staff would have ever chosen the teacher that we had invited. Nevertheless, knowing that the person selected was African American, and noticing the inordinate amount of time Ms. Smith seemed to want to talk about this decision, I wondered if there were other unspoken issues underlying her comments.

For my initial exit interview, I had deliberately chosen Ms. Smith to interview because she had been with the project from the first orientation meeting, had early on verbalized an enthusiasm for the project, and had actively participated in the work the several months that the school was a partner. I sensed that she was well intentioned and that she sincerely wanted what was best for the children at her school. She seemed, however, unable to recognize the role racist notions about children played in the failure of the school to adequately teach its students, an inability that typified the responses of most White partners in all of the schools.

When I asked Ms. Smith what caused the academic failure of the low-achieving students at her school, she cited the lack of proper nutrition and health care, both prenatal and pre-school, parents' lack of education, poverty, lack of appropriate parental support, etc. There was never a mention of instructional inadequacy, only child and parental flaws. Again her responses were not unique. They typified the assumptions of many faculty members at all of the schools. And as she talked, I couldn't help but remember saying similar things about the families of my "disadvantaged" students almost thirty years ago as a first-year teacher when I taught in an African American high school located in a low-income neighborhood. Had it not been for a group of African American teachers who took me under their wing that first year and taught me how to teach, I might still be saying the exact same words as Ms. Smith. Her comments especially saddened me because I sensed that she wanted her students to achieve yet had no understanding of the insidious nature of the assumptions she held as truth, assumptions that kept her students from achieving. And sometimes I wonder how could she understand when there is such an overwhelming conspiracy by the media and others to keep silent about racism. It was another reminder for me of the necessity to address Ms. Avery's question, and to raise the issue of racism.

Another white teacher who was interviewed at Peters also said that she had walked away from the Town Meeting assuming that Delpit had indicated that only African Americans could adequately teach African American children. Interestingly though, after having heard Delpit's talk, she reported, she bought *Other People's Children* but was still convinced that Delpit believed white teachers could not effectively teach African American children. Like Ms. Smith, this teacher also seemed to love her students, yet, as Rokeach suggested, she filtered new information through her unconscious ethnic prejudices. Unlike many others, though, her interview suggested that she was open to the value of knowing about and using the culture of her children in their classroom.

However, one of the African American teachers whom I interviewed was as surprised as I when her white colleagues misread Delpit. In addition, she related that before the partnership, she believed, the faculty at Peters assumed instruction "couldn't be done any other way" than the way it was already being done. She believed that one of the best things about the partnership was that it got people talking about change. Before the partnership, she said, no one listened to parents, and no one "was used to someone watching what was going on" in classrooms. "All of a sudden," she continued, "When the director of UACC began visiting the schools, it put a different set of eyes on the school; people began to pay attention to what teachers were doing or not doing in their classrooms."

After a number of interviews, it became clear that many mainstream faculty at Peters did not want to confront any assumptions of racism. This, of course, was probably not the only reason for the withdrawal. The mutual miscommunications, misinformation, and misunderstandings as reported during several of the interviews suggest that other factors may have played a role. However, the cultural and ethnic tensions that existed among the faculty, which surfaced as they briefly participated in the school's self-assessment, seemed to be a significant factor in the ending of the partnership.

During the first year of UACC, in the three schools where a large mix of white and African American faculty worked, teachers and parents, most of whom were African American, confessed to the director and to university fellows, concerns about racist attitudes present in their schools. Yet in larger faculty meetings with us, these concerns were rarely raised. Another echo of Ms. Avery's words.

I witnessed such avoidance at a school's faculty meeting called specifically to deal with its first year's evaluation. One of the components of the UACC was the school's self-assessment of what worked well and what did not work well in raising the level of achievement of their African American students. Part of the assessment included "a university fellow" interviewing some administrators, faculty, students, parents, and staff about their interpretation of the school's strengths and weaknesses. The data were to be used in the school's design of an action plan for school change. At one of the schools, the fellow asked me to facilitate the meeting while she reported the findings of her interviews and asked the faculty to brainstorm three main themes for school change. Though the issue of racism was reported as a concern of some of those who had been interviewed, when the faculty decided in that meeting on its main themes for school change, it ignored racism as a possible issue to be explored.

A year later, however, this school, with the constant prodding of its university fellow, was investigating anti-racism workshops for interested faculty, parents, and staff. Though only a handful voiced interest, it was a beginning.

At the start of our second year of the project, we heard rumors that the school with the predominantly white faculty and students was considering withdrawing from the UACC. The principal, Ms. Jones,[9] shared this decision first with the principal of one of the neighboring UACC schools. When our director learned about it from the other principal, she attempted to contact Ms. Jones to suggest a meeting to discuss the school's decision. It took a number of weeks for the phone calls to be returned.

Eventually, though, a meeting was agreed upon. Late in the fall, the director, the university fellow, and I met with the principal to discuss her reasons for ending the partnership. During that meeting the principal related the concerns of her faculty. A major concern, she said, was the African-centered pedagogy recommended by some of the experts who participated in an Educational Expo sponsored by the UACC. The Expo was designed to bring together school staffs from around the country who had proven successful in raising the academic achievement of urban African American children. These experts were invited to present their "best practices" and educational philosophies to representatives from the UACC schools. The Winchell faculty, Ms. Jones said, believed that some of the African-centered strategies demonstrated at the Expo relied too heavily on memorization and rote drills. The faculty believed that strategies typically supported by UACC lacked opportunities for developing higher order thinking. They maintained this belief even though at the first Town Meeting, Delpit emphatically had said (and illustrated with examples) that "whatever methodology or instructional program is used, *demand critical thinking.*" Her ten factors had also been reprinted in the participants' orientation retreat notebooks. (See factor 2 in footnote [5])

Another concern of Winchell's faculty was the UACC's suggestion that the schools use the greatest amount of money from the grant for staff development. Her faculty, Ms. Jones said, felt that they wanted to be free to spend the majority of the budget on after-school tutors to teach the low-achievers to read as well as to use grant money to purchase more reading materials for the students. Their action plans for change seemed to focus on what others could do for these children, outside the normal school day, and on what more or better materials could do.

She also said that her faculty believed that for the amount of money received from the grant, there was too much time and energy demanded. The faculty, she reported, believed that their teaching strategies were sufficient to meet the needs of most of their children and that parental involvement was their major challenge, and, she insisted, they could and were already attempting to accomplish that on their own. Most of their assumptions contradicted the research on effective schools of students with low socioeconomic status. In an extensive study of "unusually effective schools" in Louisiana and California, it was found that:

The clearest differential between unusually effective [with low socioeconomic status (SES)] and less effective middle SES schools involved a tendency for teachers in the former group to push students harder academically and to take greater "responsibility" for students' achievement than did teachers in "typical" middle SES schools. (Levine and Lezotte 1990)

The insistence of the Winchell faculty to hold to their assumption that they were doing all they could do to help these children achieve, and that only better parental involvement, better materials, or outside tutors could make a difference was a fascinating dynamic. Not only did these assumptions contradict the findings of the research on effective schools, but also they compounded the low academic achievement of their African American students who lived in public housing.

Ms. Jones also mentioned that her faculty was interested in the whole language approach and insinuated that phonics programs were not acceptable to them. Some of the experts at the Expo as well as Delpit suggested that poor children of color, who are not exposed in their preschool years to literate activities, often need a stronger emphasis on phonics than their middle-class counterparts. Most of the current literature on language literacy and the urban poor support these conclusions. The misinterpretation of the Winchell faculty about African-centered pedagogy as well as their assumptions that phonics supporters were arguing against whole language suggested the propensity of us mainstream teachers to either resist the voices or misinterpret the messages of African American educators, with those educators who have been proven effective with the same students whom this faculty was failing. Although I have lived in the thick of racism all of my life, this particular behavior never ceases to confound me.

Later when the Winchell faculty was individually interviewed, they repeated many of the same beliefs reported by the principal, especially the budget concerns. A number of teachers mentioned the faculty's desire to spend the money received through UACC for more reading materials and more tutors or more computers, indicating again their denial about a need for teachers to change strategies, attitudes about learning potentials, or expectations of achievement. The fault for the low achievement was firmly placed in the laps of the children and the parents. When I asked each teacher what was the cause of the academic failure of their low-achieving African American students, the majority plainly said the lack of parental involvement in the school life of the child and the assumed dysfunctional home lives of children living in the projects. One teacher said "I can't imagine having some of the problems that these children face and coming to school and excelling." The same teacher said, "We've reached a level [with some of these children] where it's not going to go any further." To consciously write off the potential success of anyone who is ten years old or younger astounds me. Nevertheless, many of the teachers shared this same sense of hopelessness for their low-achieving students who lived in the projects.

I asked several teachers, "What would you say to a parent who came to you and said, 'Well, you have my child six to eight hours a day, why do you need my involvement to teach him to read?'" One of the teachers responded that "There's nobody that just six to eight hours a day is going to do it." Another, responding to the same question, said, "Six to eight hours a day is not enough time to do everything with the children. Children need to see that parents value education in their school." These assumptions seem to go unchallenged with most teachers. Even though there is a body of research that indicates that children can achieve academic excellence through instruction during school hours without the involvement of their parents, the pervasive idea is that parental involvement is a necessity for academic excellence. Not only from research studies but also from my own experience with children in housing projects, I have learned that this is absolutely false.

Interestingly, two of the teachers who were interviewed suggested that the faculty assumed that they didn't need to change their instruction:

I think the other thing is that teachers began to realize that they were going to have to be willing to look at other alternatives from what they had always done. There are just some teachers over here that aren't willing to do that. They have all the answers and there's just nothing you can teach them. Even if it was trying these with just that one little group. It's sort of like they want something that supposedly works for everybody and if it doesn't it's not their fault . . . . That's not every teacher over here but it's a large majority of the teachers.

This observation of the teacher supported Williams (1997) definition of racism, of "circling repetitively back upon the expired utility of the entirely known." Often mainstream teachers, as well as others, believe that what they know about instruction is all that anyone needs to know. Thus, if the methods they know don't work, they blame the child or the parent, instead of the instructional practices.

Both of the teachers, who voiced observations about the overall faculty's propensity to stick to instruction that they already knew, seemed to have a better sense of the culture of the African American children in the school than the rest of their faculty. The majority of the mainstream teachers that I interviewed at both Peters and Winchell had difficulty answering the question: "What have you learned about the culture of the African American students at your school?" One teacher, while stumbling over the question, "What are the strengths of your African American children?" blurted out, "Their strength is definitely, at least, they can dance." The other two teachers, however, talked about the power of the extended family of their African American students, the value of the students' involvement in churches, and their talents in "drawing and other cultural and performance arts."

While interviewing the teachers and the principal, I got a sense that the faculty worked hard, thought they were open to change, and sincerely wanted their children to succeed. Yet there was this pervasive feeling of doubt about the capacity of their low-achieving African American children to learn at any higher level. The realities of the home lives of these children seemed to convince these teachers that there was little that they as teachers could do to overcome those life circumstances which the teachers assumed kept the children from learning to read or compute. Their suggestions for school change of more tutors for the children and more involvement of the parents seemed to indicate a belief that teachers lack the power to increase the level of academic achievement for these children. The responsibility and the solutions for these particular children's achievement, the teachers seemed to imply, lay outside their classrooms. On the other hand, their interviews suggested that the teachers had every confidence that their instruction made a difference in the lives of their mainstream students.

Yet the studies in California and Louisiana of "unusually effective schools in low SES" neighborhoods found that "home-school cooperation was weak and parent involvement was 'limited' and that high expectations for students originated largely from the school rather than the 'home and school.'" Our mainstream myth about the children's incapacity to learn without appropriate support from parents is time and again dispelled. The research in the last several decades by numerous scholars like Delpit, Hilliard, Irvine, Ladson- Billings, Nobles, Sizemore, etc. has indicated that economically disenfranchised African American children, regardless of what's missing in their home lives, can and do achieve academic excellence if teachers expect and demand it of them. Why is it, then, that we in the mainstream keep resisting these documented messages? Is it because the messages come from people of color? The principal and the teachers at Winchell Elementary had all read Delpit's book, which emphasized the need to learn the culture of the children *from the children* and their parents and then bring it into the instruction of the classroom whenever possible. This, of course, is a strategy dependent on developing personal relationships with those students. Her book also stressed the need to include explicit instruction, like phonics, with children who needed it within the context of demanding critical and creative thinking. Again after having read her book as well as after hearing African American educators at the Expo prescribe the same, Winchell's teachers insisted that their method of teaching "critical thinking" and "whole language" was far more valuable. These same teachers had heard and applauded Hilliard when he had spoken to an assembly of all of the faculties in their system about the success of students in classrooms where teachers expected and demanded excellence of all African American children. Nevertheless, the teachers at Winchell, with no empirical data of their own to suggest that their strategies worked for their low-achieving African American children, still chose to ignore the research of these noted African American scholars. They continued what Williams saw as the behavior of racism, "circling repetitively back upon the expired utility of the entirely known." What reasons but racism are we left to consider?

I've heard university educators and others suggest that maybe the reasons for resistance rest in the fact that some teachers just don't want to change. But from listening to the teachers at these schools and observing them in their classrooms, I was convinced that they and the administrators worked hard at what they knew to do, and on a conscious level wanted to change if they thought it could make a difference. But there was the "rub." The teachers' unconscious racist assumptions about the children, the African American children of the poor, drove their expectations and their pedagogy, and their resistance to the voices of African American educators with proven records of success.

At all of the schools, even those who chose to end the partnerships, there were, of course, both White and African American faculty who took time to develop lessons that incorporated the culture of their students. They used creative strategies that built on the interests of the students. In one school a White teacher used movement to teach reading. In another school, a White male teacher used drama and role playing to teach abstract ideas and asked students to develop a dictionary of African American language. In another school where a white and African American teacher were team teaching, their connection to each student in the class manifested itself in a myriad of ways, including the language they used to address their students that signified a caring community of learners. And in one school, the white principal continuously searched for new ways to meet the needs of her African American students. She, from the beginning of the project, admitted with great concern, "We are not giving our black kids what they need to excel. We need to make serious changes in our school to make that happen." Some of the African American teachers regularly used the culture of the children to teach them new concepts. Two of those teachers at one school said, "We are helping other faculty members learn culturally responsive pedagogy by sharing our materials and strategies." Yet at all the schools, there was a pervasive battle to transcend societal racist notions about the ability of their poor African American students to succeed.

Through this work with the UACC, I have become even more aware of Ms. Avery's question. Yet I am still no closer to the answer. I have continuously watched as too many of us white people refuse to talk about or recognize racism. I've sat in meetings for hours where we talk about the inadequacies of the education of the urban child, yet we never discuss the role that racist politics, economics, and educational attitudes play in the mis-education of these children. The complexities of their "inadequate home lives" are often bemoaned and the incompetence of some of their teachers, but the consequences of racism in educating children seems never to be raised. As I continue to sit in these meetings, work with public schools, and remember my own silence in Boston, I am convinced that Joseph Feagin, a white professor is right when he says, "Most whites in this country are running as fast as they can from a candid, honest, open discussion of race and racism in the United States."(Feagin, p.18)

Nevertheless, until more of us of the dominant culture begin to break the silence about racism, my experience suggests that in many classrooms of white teachers and some African American teachers very little will happen to support the academic achievement of our children of the poor. And in most of those classrooms, it will not be because the teachers don't want these children to achieve. It will be because their unchallenged and unconscious racism thwarts these children at every turn. So I think the first step in allowing these children to excel is our willingness to listen to the children, the parents, and the communities we serve. We also need to begin to listen more attentively to African American researchers, scholars, and teachers who understand the culture of the children we teach and who know how to move these children toward excellence. We need to engage in the kind of listening suggested in Delpit's, *Other People's Children* of "giving up your own sense of who you are, and being willing to see yourself in the unflattering light of another's angry gaze" (Delpit, 1997). Though what Delpit suggests can apply to all of us when we occupy seats of power, her words are especially significant for white women who teach in the public schools. We must be willing to see ourselves in the "unflattering light" of the stories of our past, the histories of our abuses against people of color as well as the stories of our present privileges. Those realities, along with our positions of power in our own classrooms, demand that we continually examine our racist assumptions, be unafraid to raise the issue, and begin to create safe places where children can learn about it, talk to each other about it, and learn how to disengage from it. If we refuse to raise the issue, we, then, as Rokeach indicates, damage the development of our children as well, perpetuating the cycle of fear and hostility that cripples the country.

But before we open up the dialogue with our students, we need to talk about racism to each other as teachers. Because white teachers make up at least 84% of the teaching work force in America (Feistritzer, 2011) and because racism is damaging the children we teach, we have a responsibility to struggle with it amongst ourselves. We need to discover how to create for ourselves safe spaces for such serious dialogue. Confronting racism head on is uncomfortable and often wrings guilt, shame, anger, or despair from us. We need, therefore, to explore together how to sit with the discomfort long enough to move through these emotions toward a place of healing. But if we continue to wallow in denial about the impact of racism on our children, we can never rid ourselves or society of its abuses, much less begin to heal as a community of humans.

To suspend our beliefs about racism so that we can hear the experience of others, especially those of our children, seems imperative. We cannot continue to deny it, be defensive about it, see it as only the problem of people of color. It is our disease, white people's disease. And, thus, it is our responsibility to initiate the conversations. We cannot wait for people of color to raise it. I think, they're weary of the conversation. Black educational leaders like Alonzo Crim (Crim, 1991) and renowned scholars like Delpit and Hilliard don't really talk about racism because it seems to get them and their people nowhere. Instead they spend their energies teaching teachers and the rest of us how to respectfully serve children. And, I believe, they are right to resist the conversation with white people. In my experience, if black people name it, whites simply accuse them of being "too sensitive," of misreading their words or behavior. Some white folks seem to assume that if we don't use the word "nigger" then we must not be racist. We are crippled by a disease that we can't even call out loud, yet we are drenched in a bloody American history of hundreds of years of racism. Whatever our level of awareness, racism still exists within every institution we are associated. We cannot escape it. As Taylor Branch says in *Parting the Waters*, "Almost as color defines vision itself, race shapes the cultural eye: what we do and do not notice, the reach of empathy and the alignment of response." (Branch, 1988, p xi)

Many African American educators and parents are busy helping their children heal from the abuses of racism so these children can achieve in spite of it. We can't expect African Americans to heal us. They focus on cradling their communities, creating safe places for their children and families. Yet on some level we all know that if white people don't deal with racism, none of our children will be safe.

Starting the dialogue, raising the issue, is probably the next step after learning to listen to those who have been most damaged by it. And it's a big step since we all know our penchant in the dominant culture for running away from such dialogue. Yet until we address the issue, as Parks suggests, we cannot adequately solve the myriad of problems that emanate from it:

. . . teen violence, safe schools, gang behavior, drop-out and suspension rates, diversity and equity in personnel policies and school administration, poor achievement among students of color, inequity in school funding, and the needs of children living in poverty. Such school problems directly or indirectly reflect past or present racism and may not be meaningfully remedied until racism is addressed. (Parks, 1999, p.14)

But after addressing racism, then what? I think the "then what" becomes designing education for all children, white and children of color, as Paulo Freire defined it, as a liberation of the mind, because all children need to be liberated from an education that supports elitism. White children's minds are stunted as well by a system that supports "the pathological contamination of a large body of its clients" (Clark, 1989, p 33). Those contaminated clients are the children living in poverty, especially children of color, but also privileged children. In a system where the histories and cultures of Africans, Indigenous Americans, Asians, Latinos, etc., are minimized, trivialized, or completely ignored, everyone's children lose. They lose because all children then absorb a truncated view of world realities, a seriously limited sense of the cosmic whole. In a 21st century world where only 4-1/2 % percent of its population lives in the U.S., (UN, 2010) how will our privileged white children ever learn to operate in the world, if all they ever explore in school is Euro-centric cultural truths? How will they understand, much less communicate with those who represent 95% percent of the planet's population? Our ever-expanding global village will demand that they communicate in far more effective ways than most of the present adults in their lives do.

There really are no winners in an elitist system of education. For, ultimately, even at home, the elitist suffers. He is afraid to walk down some of his own streets in the cities he has helped build because he has engineered a permanent undereducated underclass who is angry, and out of that anger, is exploding in violence. That violence is perpetrated not only by some of the angry poor but also, as witnessed recently, by children in middle-class communities. It is practiced as well by the elite, whenever their "knee jerk" reaction to global resolution of conflict is building more tanks, bombs and missiles to terrorize other countries when the behavior of those countries does not serve "our national interest." If that's the best in "creative problem- solving" that the graduates from our present educational systems can muster, then our schools are cheating all our students. I believe that when education ignores racism, supporting notions of privilege and supremacy, all of our children's minds are trapped into a never-ending cycle of violence.

When I consider the kind of change that our educational system needs to make, I always think of Hilliard's challenge to school systems and university teacher preparation systems:

Revolution, not reform, is required to release the power of teaching. . . . Virtually, all teachers possess tremendous power which can also be released, given the proper exposure. We can't get to that point by tinkering with a broken system. We must change our intellectual structures, definitions and assumptions; then we can release teacher power (Hilliard, 1997).

In the UACC, Hilliard's words continuously echoed. It wasn't that these teachers were incompetent. They knew what they assumed was "correct pedagogy." It wasn't that they didn't want what was best for their students. It was that they were operating out of a system whose "intellectual structures, definitions and assumptions" are based on racist philosophies and epistemologies. Those notions prevented them from seeing black children and parents as real three-dimensional people (not statistics) with brilliant potential. Those philosophies stole the teachers' power. When talking to these teachers, I heard intimations of how powerless they felt to teach black children who live in poverty. The media, school systems, probably every institution had convinced them that they could do very little for these children's academic success because their poverty, lack of parental support, or emotional needs had crippled them. The teachers were so steeped in their own unconsciously elitist belief systems that they either could not hear or refused to listen to the messages of African American scholars and researchers, messages that could have given them back their sense of power. And by reclaiming the power to teach all children, the teachers, in turn, could empower all children to excel. And then, we'd have our revolution, one where everybody wins.

Maybe the why of Ms. Avery's question about racism is not as important as the question itself? Just asking the question might, at least, initiate a conversation that could lead us to a search for integrity, a wholeness that this country has only dreamed of. Nevertheless, the "why" of her question still plagues me. But one of the answers to her "why" may have been explained in a conversation I had with a friend when Maya Angelou was in town for the Black Arts Festival. I invited my "liberal" white friend to attend the event with me. After the powerful performance of Maya, I asked my friend how he enjoyed the evening. He said he thought she was quite exciting. I asked him what he liked best about her recitation, and he said it was her humor and her last poem of the night, "And then, I rise." We both raved about those moments in her presentation; and, then, sensing some unsaid dissatisfaction with the night, I asked him what he liked least. And he said, "Her racist comments at the beginning." Surprised at this response, not having heard any racist remarks myself, and believing, as Hilliard suggests, that an oppressed people cannot be racist, I asked what specifically did she say or intimate that smacked of racism. He said that it was her comment that blacks were in America before Columbus as well as her comments on the racist practices of white Americans. I pushed him further by saying that, to me, those comments didn't represent racism rather they represented historical fact. And, then, he said "Well, it all made me feel uncomfortable." Continuing to probe, wanting to get at his rationale, I asked him what he thought was the source of his discomfort. Was it really racism or something else? Finally, without any further questions by me, he said "shame." Shame was the source of his discomfort. Shame as a white man, he said, "for the hideous crimes against blacks and Native Americans." In that moment he crystallized for me what for years I have sensed might be at the core of our refusal as white people to address racism.

Maybe it is this shame that many white people don't want to face because we don't know how to get past it. Nothing in the culture teaches us how to experience it, then move through it toward reconciliation. Unlike many modern psychologists, however, I think there are times when shame is appropriate. When my Euro-centric culture has for four thousand years committed heinous crimes against other peoples of the world (Carruthers), feeling remorse is probably one of the most sane things I can do, that is, if I intend to avoid getting stuck there; and instead move toward redress. After all, nobody wants to be in a room filled with people stuck in shame.

Nevertheless, during the work with the UACC as I watched people shut down whenever the word "racism" came into the conversation, I thought about the "why" of Ms. Avery's question. My hunch is that unconscious shame could have been at the core of how 15 white women sat silent about racism in that room in Boston. Perhaps, somewhere in our collective unconscious is the memory of how our grandmothers or great grandmothers "forgot" to voice their objection to other women and children being enslaved, beaten, raped, murdered. Perhaps somewhere in our unconscious is the memory that our mothers or someone's mothers paid slave wages to the women of other cultures to clean our houses, take care of our children, cook our meals. That, maybe, somewhere in our psyches are the realizations that we, women, continue to pay "illegal immigrants" slave wages to work in our homes or their husbands in our gardens, then refuse to allow those women decent health care or their children the right to education. These memories and realizations, if surfaced, most likely would create shame. Why else would we keep them so deeply buried. If not, then why are we afraid to explore the consequences of institutional racism on children? How is it that white people come together over and over again to talk about serious issues and rarely, if ever, initiate a dialogue about racism?

If we believe, as do many mystics, poets, scientists, psychologists, and African cultures that we are all one in the universe and are inextricably bound to one another, then we in the dominant culture must own our part in the plight of the oppressed. We must stop blaming the victim of the oppression and look into our own past and present for the responsibility as well as the privileges resulting from racism. Then, maybe, we can move through the shame and into healthy resolution of the conflicts we have unconsciously masterminded. Like Martin Luther King, Jr. and Andrew Young and all the freedom fighters of the civil rights era, I believe that through confronting racism in our culture, we can begin to "redeem America's soul" (Young, 1996, p 2).

That redemption, I do understand, will not come from attempts to bludgeon others with the righteousness of any ideology. Righteousness is rarely effective and usually damaging. I also clearly understand that, whatever our culture, we have deep seated, learned prejudices that surface every now and then, uninvited maybe, but very much a part of us. And dealing with that reality is a life-long challenge. To be able to admit to those ugly realities, though, especially those of us who are in the dominant culture, is, I think, the first step toward the redemptive process, a process that makes all children winners.

REFERENCES

Bartolome, L. I. & D. P. Macedo (1997). "Dancing with Bigotry: The Poisoning of Racial and Ethnic Identities," *Harvard Educational Review*, Vol. 67, No. 2, Summer, p. 226.

Branch, Taylor (1988). *Parting The Waters: America in the King Years 1954-63* (p.xi) New York: Simon & Schuster,.

Carruthers, J. H. & Harris, L. C., editors (1997). *African World History Project: The Preliminary Challenge, Association for the Study of Classical African Civilizations.* Los Angeles, CA.

Clark, Don (1989). "High Expectations." *Effective Schools: Critical Issues in the Education of Black Children* (p. 33). Detroit: National Alliance of Black School Educators.

Crim A.A. (1991). "Educating All God's Children." *Reflections: Personal Essays by 33 Distinguished Educators.* Bloomington: Phi Delta Kappa Educational Foundation.

Delpit, Lisa (1995). *Other People's Children,* New York: The New Press.

Edelman, M. (2012). Children's Defense Fund. Retrieved May 30, 2012: http://www.childrensdefense.org/policy-priorities/ending-child-poverty/

Feagin, J. (1997). *Reflections on education and race: Examining the intersections: Select addresses from the Public Education Network 1996 annual conference.* (p 22) Public Education Network.

Feistritzer, C., *Profile of Teachers in the U.S. 2011* (2011) National Center for Education Information. Retrieved May 30, 2012: http://www.edweek.org/media/pot2011final-blog.pdf

Hilliard III, A.G.(1991). Do We Have The Will To Educate All Children? *Educational Leadership,* 49(1), 31-36.

_____(1997). "The Structure of Valid Staff Development." *Journal of Staff Development.* Spring, Vol.18, No.2.

_____(1998). "Characteristics of Effective Teachers." Conversation about his research.

_____(1997). "Tapping The Genius And Touching The Spirit: A Human Approach To The Rescue Of Our Children." The Ninth Annual Benjamin E. Mays Lecture, Atlanta, GA.

Hughes, Mary F. (1995). *Achieving Despite Adversity: A Study Of The Characteristics Of Effective And Less Effective Elementary Schools In West Virginia.* West Virginia Education Fund.

Levin, Henry M. (1988). "Accelerating Elementary Education for Disadvantaged Students." *School Success for Students at Risk* (p. 213). New York: Harcourt Brace Jovanovich, Inc.

Levine, D.U. & L. W. Lezotte (1990). *Unusually Effective Schools: A Review and Analysis of Research and Practice* (p. 66). Madison, WI: Board of Regents of University of Wisconsin System,

McIntosh, P. "White Privilege: Unpacking the Invisible Knapsack," Working Paper 189, *White Privilege and Male Privilege: A Personal Account of Coming To See Correspondences through Work in Women's Studies* (1988). Wellesley, MA: Wellesley Women's Center

National Teacher Day spotlights key issues facing profession. (2011) National Education Association Issues and Views. Retrieved 5-20-2012 http://www.nea.org/home/43744.htm

Nobles, Wade (1973). "Psychological Research And The Black Self Concept: A Critical Review." *Journal of Social Issues*, 29, 1.

Parks, Sandra (1999). "Reducing the Effects of Racism in Schools." *Educational Leadership*, Alexandria, VA: ASCD, Vol. 56, No. 7, p. 18.

Probst. R. E. (1984). *Adolescent Literature: Response and Analysis* (p.67). Columbus: Charles E. Merrill

Rokeach, M. (1960). *The Open and Closed Mind*. New York: Basic Books, Inc.

Rothstein. R. (1997). "RX For A New Superintendent: A Hand up to the Students Not a Back of the Hand to Teachers." *Education Week*, Vol. 17, Issue 42, July 09.

Rothstein, R. (2004). *Class and schools: Using social, economic, and educational reform to close the black-white achievement gap*. New York, NY: Teachers College Press.

Schell, Jonathan (1986). "Reflections," *The New Yorker*. New York: February 3.

Sizemore, B.A., Brosard, C. and Harigan, B. (1982) *An Abashing Anomaly: The High Achieving Predominately Black Elementary Schools*. Pittsburgh, PA: University of Pittsburgh Press

State of Americas children 2010 report. Children's Defense Fund. *http://www.childrensdefense.org/child-research-data-publications/data/state-of-americas-children-2010-report.html*

Tatum. B. D. (1997). *Why Are All the Black Kids Sitting Together in the Cafeteria? And Other Conversations About Race* (p.6). New York: Basic Books.

United Nations, Department of Economic and Social Affairs, Population Division (2011): World Population Prospects: The 2010 Revision. New York. Retrieved from: http://esa.un.org/unpd/wpp/Excel-Data/population.htm Also found on: http://en.wikipedia.org/wiki/World_population

Wellman, D. (1977). *Portraits of White Racism*. Cambridge: Cambridge University Press.

Williams, P. (1997) *Seeing a Color-blind Future: The Paradox of Race*. New York: The Noonday Press.

Wynne, J. (1997) Field notes.

Young, A. (1996). *An Easy Burden: The Civil Rights Movement and the Transformation of America*. New York: HarperCollins Publishers, Inc.

END NOTES

1. Pseudonym
2. Selection was based on signed commitments by the schools that included:
    1. Agreement of school administration to engage in collaborative decision-making with faculty and staff
    2. Agreement by teachers (80%) to staff development and to engagement in the planning and the implementation process to create an exceptional learning setting for low-income children of color
    3. Agreement to seek parental involvement and support for this effort
    4. Agreement to take on the role of a teaching/learning site as a source of assistance for other schools attempting to change.
    5. Utilization of community resources

3. Pseudonyms for both schools

4. A gathering of faculty, parent, administration representatives from all seven schools to cross-pollinate best practices and common challenges across districts

5. Lisa Delpit, "Ten Factors Essential to Success in Urban Classrooms":

    1. Do not teach less content to poor, urban children, but understand their brilliance and teach more!

    2. Whatever methodology or instructional program is used, demand critical thinking.

    3. Assure that all children gain access to "basic skills," the conventions and strategies that are essential to success in American education.

    4. Provide the emotional ego strength to challenge racist societal views of the competence and worthiness of the children and their families.

    5. Recognize and build on strengths.

    6. Use familiar metaphors and experiences from the children's world to connect what they already know to school knowledge.

    7. Create a sense of family and caring.

    8. Monitor and assess needs and then address them with a wealth of diverse strategies.

    9. Honor and respect the children's home culture(s).

    10. Foster a sense of children's connection to community—to something greater than themselves.

6. Pseudonym

7. EXIT QUESTIONS:

    1. What do you think causes the academic failure of the low achieving African American students in your school?

    2. What plans have you or the faculty made to raise the level of achievement of these children?

    3. What parts of the Urban Atlanta Coalition Compact worked well for your elementary school?

    4. What parts of the Compact did not work well for your school?

    5. What have you learned about the culture of the African American students at your school?

    6. What do you see as the strengths of your African American students?

    7. What do you want your African American students to know and to be able to do?

    8. What are some of the staff development needs of your faculty?

    9. What is the involvement of your African American parents at your school?

    10. What plans are being made for more inclusion of these parents in your academic programs?

    11. If you were given extra money to use to enhance your teaching capacity, how would you spend it?

    12. If you were given extra time to use to enhance your teaching capacity, how would you use it?

    13. What do you think is the most uniquely beneficial piece of the work of the UACC as it relates to school reform?

    14. What do you think that the UACC could do to be more effective?

    15. How significant a role do ethnic differences play in your school environment?

    16. To what parts of the UACC would you like to continue to be connected?

8. Pseudonym

9. Pseudonym

Section 1: Honoring Diversity Begins with Un-Learning Racism

Please take ten minutes and write in the space below the answers to the following questions:

1. What were two compelling ideas that you discovered while reading Carlos Gonzalez Morales' article? (If you need more space to answer any of these questions, please use the back of this page or other paper as well.)

   _____

   _____

2. Were there any ideas in "The Elephant in the Classroom" that were similar to the ideas discussed in the Gonzalez Morales' article? If so, write those similar ideas in this space.

   _____

   _____

   _____

3. Describe the difference between individual prejudice and institutionalized racism.

   _____

   _____

   _____

When you have finished writing, please consider the following activities:

- Choose a partner and share your ideas about the articles.

- Then you and your partner arrange yourselves in a group of two other partners.

- In your group of six students (more or less), together create a statement that you all can agree upon that answers Carlos Gonzalez Morales' question:
  "How does an orphaned culture educate its children?"

- Write that statement and ask a reporter from your small group to share your group's answer to the question.

   _____

   _____

Now please go to website www.tolerance.org/tdsi/cb_adapting_instruction Then, scroll down to Sonia Nieto's 2-minute video on the first page of the site: ". . . in order to know their students well, teachers need to be aware of their own dispositions about race, culture and class."

- Discuss with your partner how Nieto's ideas inform your belief system about teaching diverse students, especially her comments on institutionalized racism.

◆ Why do you think she uses the metaphor of "smog" to describe racism?

_____

_____

_____

_____

_____

_____

_____

_____

SECTION 2
SEARCHING FOR JUSTICE WELCOMES EVERYONE INTO THE DIALOGUE

Image copyright Konstantin Sutyagin, 2012. Used under license from Shutterstock. Inc.

When I was growing up . . . I knew black teachers in our community, who once schools were integrated, were rejected by the white schools. Those black teachers were no longer employed. A few black teachers fresh from college were hired, but veteran black teachers were not. These older teachers were part of our community, attended our churches and socialized with us. Their expertise was not valued by white educators.

—Wanda Blanchett

CHAPTER 2

WELCOME HOME (LIFE IN THIS PIGMENT)

Mike Baugh

When we sit in the classroom,
The teachers ignore us, the children laugh at us.
The schoolhouse marginalizes us.
The school system never wanted us.
They **teach** *us that we are out of place.*

When we are out in the world
Buying, perusing, dining,
laughing, gathering, praying,
walking, sleeping, dancing
They tell us that we are vermin, yes a plague attempting to destroy everything that is pure

When our eyes have made a pact with sorrow,
When words no longer come out of our mouths,
When our surroundings deteriorate, and we are forced into smaller and smaller communities,
They say that our suffering is not enough.

They tell us to leave, go, vanish, vacate, quit, desert, flit, retire, say "goodbye"
Die in silence, Die in pain, Die struggling to keep our heads above the clouds,
They explain to us that the world is their kingdom, their utopia, their love . . . not ours.

But, when we walk between their prison gates
Sit hopelessly behind metal bars
Clothe ourselves with orange, white, blue, or pink
Attach a number to our person, befriend misery,
    and finally walk ourselves into **our** *necropolis*
They smile, open their arms, close their fists
    and say "Welcome Home"

REFRAMING URBAN EDUCATION DISCOURSE: A CONVERSATION WITH AND FOR TEACHER EDUCATORS

Wanda J. Blanchett
Joan Wynne

This article represents a conversation between two urban educators—one African American and one White. Not only the influence of race, but also the influence of personal and cultural histories on urban classrooms and colleges, unfold during their conversation. Providing important insights into the nature and significance of the work of urban education, their dialogue also demonstrates the need for, and examples of, multiple divergent voices in the struggle for practical and theoretical thinking in urban education to give direction to meaningful improvements.

Joan: THE READER MIGHT WONDER how we came into this conversation. I remember only that one of your Ph.D. students contacted me by e-mail, requesting a satellite dialogue with your class and me.

Wanda: Yes, it began in a doctoral seminar three years ago. I required students to read two texts: *Power Plays, Power Works* by John Fisk (1993), and *The Urban Underclass Debate* by Michael Katz (1993). Students were also required to arrange a video-conference with an expert in urban education whose work is pertinent to today's realities. One student was interested in the work you and Lisa (Delpit, 1995) had been doing.

The session moved me because you did things with the students that very few people can do. All of the students in my class were White students. They had been exposed to the issue of racism's impact on education. Many of them had participated in a previous seminar I had taught. Thus, they came to the class with certain frames of reference and very well read. But, at the same time, they saw racism and discrimination as something that was in everyone else's knapsack, not theirs.

Joan: Exactly; all of us White people are, I'm afraid, eaten with that disease.

Wanda: Your candor about racism, how pervasive it is in every aspect of one's life, your personal story as a White southerner reached them in ways that I could not. One statement that you made that night really stuck with me and with them too. You said it's impossible for a White person, growing up in America, to not be a racist. For the first time ever they thought about themselves as racists. They had never made that connection.

Joan: A frightening statistic I recently read suggested that about 88% of the nation's teachers are White. So if White teachers don't grapple with our unconscious racist thinking and behaviors, we will continue to sustain racism in our classrooms and in our U.S. culture.

Wanda: I've thought a lot about growing up in Arkansas, in a rural poor part of the Delta. My parents were sharecroppers, an unusual ancestral category for a 40-year-old woman, but I was the youngest of a large family.

Growing up in the south, or wherever you grow up, helps shape you. Some of my childhood experiences significantly shaped my values as an adult. I grew up in the 60s when the south and Arkansas, in particular, were not kind places. We had seen a lot of political action and local activism for civil rights. This was on the heels of the famous Little Rock Central conflict in 1957. Black people then received little to no respect from White folks.

The Southern Negro Leaders Conference on Transportation and Nonviolent Integration currently known as the Southern Christian Leadership Conference (SCLC) was organizing itself in the south. I remember my father and brothers getting in the back of a pick-up truck, putting a cover over the truck to conceal themselves. If the Klan knew they were going to the NAACP meeting, the Klan would throw bottles through our windows, burn crosses in the yard. Anything could happen. The law was not there to protect us, only to maintain the status quo. My early memories were of just being terrified of White people. Usually when White people came around, it meant trouble. My other memories involve going to an integrated school: all of my siblings attended and most of them graduated from segregated schools.

It is helpful to educators to think how their personal stories impact their teaching. For example, you have been able to move on beyond your upbringing in Georgia. You talked extensively with my class about some of your experiences with African Americans, particularly in Georgia. You were able to operate for many years from an unconscious position of power and privilege, but you've grown toward awareness.

Joan: What may have made my shift easier than many Whites was that my parents were, or, at least thought that they were, liberal thinkers. They fought racism in the south all of their lives, yet I'm not sure that any of us, then, fully understood the consequences of our places of power and privilege. But my parents' modeling made a huge impact on my ability to make substantive changes later.

The biggest growth for me, though, resulted from being immersed in another's culture. That immersion happened while teaching in an African American high school. I became close to my students, close to the faculty who were all African Americans except for five of us who were transferred there to integrate the faculty. I learned the richness of that culture from the culture itself. Edward Hall (1989), in *Beyond Culture*, said that we only learn about our own culture by stepping outside that culture. That was certainly my experience.

I taught at another all Black institution, Morehouse College, for 14 years which is also all-male. In those places I began to see the limitations of my worldview and how my position of privilege had actually kept me ignorant, had kept me from dealing with my own racism. I was like one of your White students. I never thought that I was racist. I had fought racism the whole time I was growing up, never knowing how many of those assumptions were buried deep in my psyche. So when you talk about unlearning racism, I really believe it's a life-long process. Like Beverly Tatum says, you can't live in this culture without taking at least some of that racist thinking in. She uses the analogy of smog in L.A. If you live in L.A., you're going to be a smog-breather. And if you live in America with a 400-year history of racism, which is still unexamined today, then you are going to be, at the very best, a recovering racist. We rarely examine today's realities that have racist underpinnings. Without that public discussion, we must constantly unravel it in ourselves as we discuss it with others. But I believe that White people have to be willing to be vulnerable in that conversation.

Wanda: These students, many White folks, and unfortunately, some misguided folks of color, often think because some discriminatory policies, like segregation, have changed, that with the policies went the racism. They don't make the connection that there are residual effects from segregation, from slavery, from the history of racist policies and practices, and that often people's perception, ideas, reactions, and interactions don't change.

Joan: Students are rarely asked to examine public policy and the racism that undergirds it in every institution, especially education; they are seldom taught that racism has existed since Europeans invaded the country, that our nation's history, art, music, epistemology are steeped in it. In my teacher preparation experience, I was never taught to investigate those assumptions, nor was I taught culturally responsive strategies.

Students that I work with now in Miami (and it was true in Atlanta too), young teachers in our master's programs who have been teaching for 1 to 3 years, love the kids and want to help them learn. But too many teachers are clueless as to how to do it. They've rarely been taught to infuse their instruction with the students' cultural experiences. But the most significant barrier to quality teaching that I have observed is an obsession about parents and their children's purported dysfunctions. Teachers too often assume that if the kids aren't learning, then it's the kid's fault or the parent's fault. They rarely assume that the school is at fault or that teacher inadequacy—the lack of knowledge of content or pedagogy—is at fault.

Wanda: Yes. And there are a couple of common misperceptions I discovered through my work with graduate students. They don't see the connection between public policy, between laws that govern our society, and the ways we interact as social beings. Because of these misperceptions, I ask students to examine the Declaration of Independence, the Constitution, to think about who crafted those documents; how African American slaves were portrayed in the original document; and how they were treated in subsequent years. I also ask students to look at housing policy, at laws and social programs, and how those have been structured; what impact those programs and laws had on Whites' perceptions of Blacks. I ask them to examine these policies in light of White supremacy. Students typically have not thought about these things. Because of their place of privilege, they don't have to. They sometimes think they're better even if they are the ones who are the most dysfunctional.

Joan: What a great dialogue. And because of that ignorance of the country's history, White people don't understand what it is that people of color are "upset about." I think that's a huge failure of schools, especially teacher education programs. Our bloody history is an uncomfortable subject. We don't like to talk about it, and so we don't. Teachers go out there unarmed with historical facts that could lead them into a better understanding of the children they teach. I learned in an urban leadership masters program that many of the African American teachers did not know their cultural history because they had grown up in integrated schools where they were not taught the richness of their culture.

Wanda: No matter what class I teach, I teach some history. History is important to help correct teachers' faulty notions about other people and other cultures. Another strategy is developing teachers as reflective thinkers. Until you can get educators to do that introspective work, forget about everything else. If I'm teaching a methods class, I not only help students understand teaching strategies, I help them understand the historical context of the educational system they will work in; who they are and how that will impact everything they do in their classroom. I was taught that I just needed a set of skills to master that could be effective with any set of students within any teaching environment. I now know differently. So I instruct our students that to be effective, they need to understand themselves, the prejudices, the misperceptions, and all of the baggage that they bring with them to the classroom.

Joan: Yes, many teachers are convinced that poor kids can't learn at the same rate as their suburban counterparts. Most teachers want to teach well, but their attitudes about the capacity of all children to learn at high levels keep poor children out of the loop of quality education. Hilliard (2000) says U.S. educators have a "pathological preoccupation with capacity." Our failure to face that pathology in teacher education programs is a serious problem. We must grapple with teachers' attitudes about poor children of color.

Wanda: And we must expose our teacher candidates to culturally responsive pedagogy. I show our teachers the cultural connections between the home and community life of White students with the school's practices and curriculum. I try to guide my students in examining how it empowers White students to move forward and to think that they can and will excel in school. Then, we examine culturally responsive instruction and pedagogy of African Americans and other students of color. My students typically have never thought that the curriculum was developed for White students with a purpose in mind and that students who are not White are not affirmed by that curriculum. Teachers need to look at existing practice and analyze who benefits from it.

Because most teacher educators are White, and most do not understand the imperative of teaching as a cultural practice, they don't push their students to understand and use culturally responsive pedagogy. Many of these professors also still perceive preservice teachers of color as deficient, forcing these students to consistently prove themselves worthy to be at the university. When these are the professors who help develop educators, you know we're in trouble.

Joan: Yes, we're in trouble, and I don't think we even know it. We're asking the wrong questions in colleges of education. In most of the universities where I've served, we discuss our need to streamline our courses so we can be competitive, or we focus on more competitive recruitment processes or tenure processes. While necessary, these issues seem to dominate the conversation, and the large questions, the issues that strike at the heart of our mission—racial, economic, and class disparities—are typically superficially addressed.

By sticking only to the minutia of structural changes, by talking only about institutional survival, we cheat ourselves and our students. We don't deserve to survive as institutions if we are not courageous enough to engage in dialogue about the big issues of racism, poverty, war, and the impact of those diseases on the teachers and students that we teach and the children that they teach. Without those conversations, our intellectual discourse becomes that of T. S. Eliot's "The Hollow Men."

Wanda: In my office, I have a quote on my wall by Malcolm X, which says, "The colleges and universities in the American educational system are skillfully used to miseducate" (March—April 1965, p. 196 as cited in Breitman (1965)). Students come in and ask, "Why would you put something like that up?" And I say, "Because it's true."

Joan: Yes, I hear you, and I also understand people's fear that professors might try to ramrod their political beliefs down the throats of their students. However, I think that what you and I are saying is that we can and must legitimately hold discussions where students are able to discover that politics is in the mix of all of education, and that students have to unravel that for themselves and for the culture. We are not suggesting that anyone of us become ideologues.

Wanda: I want to go back to this question you raised, given the history in this country and our present reality, can America really be remade? What would it take for us as teacher-educators to help all teachers believe that they can educate all children and that they, teachers, can unlearn their racism?

Joan: I think those are incredibly important questions, and I don't know that I have any answers. Other than I think that we and our students must grapple with those questions. But I don't think colleges of education can do it in isolation. We separate ourselves from the communities that we serve; at our tables of discussion, only we are present talking to each other. We need to have community organizers, parents, public school teachers, and students—all of us—talking together about these issues because professors don't have all the answers. Bob Moses has taught me more than anyone else on the planet about community building. The way he models finding what it is the community knows, wants to learn, and wants to change is remarkable. Bob reminds us that there is a deliberate intent in this nation to maintain sharecropper education for the descendents of slaves; that we know how to educate our poor children in rural places or innercities; we simply have no intent to do so. Society needs that underclass. And in *Radical Equations* (Moses and Cobb, 2001), Moses says that we can advocate for the children and the parents, but change ultimately will come from those parents and students who sacrifice to demand the change. Like Ella Baker, Bob Moses believes in the intelligence and leadership abilities of low-income, grassroots people.

Wanda: As Moses and Noguera suggest, America lacks the will to educate all of its students. Yet, as teacher educators, we can't prepare teachers unless we retool ourselves. Too many of our professors have no real understanding of the communities that teachers are serving, nor are they inclined to question their misperceptions about those communities. Many people see teaching students of color and other marginalized groups in rural and/or urban communities as a challenge. I see it as a privilege. As professionals, we need to rethink our assumptions about students, parents, and the communities we serve.

If we are ever to eradicate racism, it has to be a dual process. First, all races must be given the opportunity in this culture to be who they are and be allowed to live fully without obstruction on the basis of color. If you are a racist who is trying to unlearn your racism, I can live with you. I can tolerate you. I can even help you, but I can't tolerate you if you are in complete denial.

We must help educators process race in a straight-forward way-to process the inequities that people experience solely on the basis of race.

Joan: So how do we, as teacher educators, create those conversations among ourselves? How does a College of Education take responsibility for creating a safe space for professors to first participate in those conversations themselves so that they can learn to facilitate those conversations with the teachers who come into their courses? We don't seem to know how to talk about racism with each other. And until White people climb out of denial, say *mea culpa*, admit the historic presence of institutional racism, and our responsibility for sustaining our power and privilege; I don't think there's much hope of any real healing in this country. Most White people I know think that racism is about Black and brown people. They don't think it has anything to do with their positions of power. They are unconscious of the automatic privilege given them solely because of their White skin. We need some serious coaching.

Wanda: I agree. As long as people are not forced to face it, then nothing will ever happen.

Joan: I think—because I have seen it in my classroom with White teachers—that once teachers are exposed to other ways of thinking about it, they often change. Some of my Hispanic teachers, who are new to the country or whose parents are new, didn't understand the country's issues around racism, and yet once here they begin absorbing the racist notions that resound in the country. Yet my White and Hispanic/Latino students, once they have read and discussed the work of Delpit (1995), Hilliard (1997, 1999, 2000), Moses (Moses and Cobb, 2001), etc., often say out loud in classes, "I never knew any of this." Some of them have confessed, "I was guilty of racism and didn't even know I was." They are the reason I believe that people can change and will change; if we continue to struggle to get the knowledge to them and help them confront the ugliness, they will shift. Otherwise, I'd go mow lawns for a living and give up this education game.

Wanda: I become more and more frustrated because we're running out of time to get it right for kids, and it's not just kids of color, though they are suffering the most. Their daily experiences in schools are not preparing them for the future. We need a sense of urgency about eradicating inequality, particularly in public education. Our children are literally dying as a result of not being properly educated. We're cutting them off at the knees before they're out of elementary school. A responsible society wouldn't do that. Schools of Education play a major role in developing educators who are charged with teaching kids who are increasingly diverse, and in public city schools, those children are Black and Brown.

Here, when we interview new faculty, we tell them overtly about our commitment to equity and diversity, and the role we expect them to play in helping us achieve that. We have five values in our School, and we tell candidates, "If you can't commit to these values, this isn't the place for you."

But I would go one step further and insist that adherence to these values be part of the promotion and tenure process. We should measure people by their performance in preparing teacher candidates to effectively deal with these issues. The reward structure of salaries and bonuses should be connected to those values; otherwise, you're not going to get consistency and diligence to these causes. We need to stop hiring deans that can't address these issues and fire those who tell the same old lies of "We can't find diverse candidates; they're not out there."

Joan: You're right. For instance, my sister told her corporate search team who were charged to find diverse candidates, "I not only want you to bring back a slate of candidates that has some people of color, I want you to bring a person of color that we will hire. Failure is not an option. And when I hire that person, if that person fails, I'm going to hold you accountable because it will mean that you did not give that person adequate support to succeed." That phrase "failure is not an option" really struck a chord with me. That's what Colleges of Education need to understand, that there are a multitude of people of color that have the credentials to teach at our universities, and we've got to find them—whatever it takes. Too few qualified diverse candidates is a myth. I know plenty who have Ph.D.s who are not invited into the university for phony reasons. At a university in a large city where I taught, an African-American female who was interviewed was eliminated because her focus was "too urban." We have to counter that nonsense.

Wanda: One final mission that we didn't talk about is that while we continue to work with White teachers to unlearn their racism so they can be effective with all kids, we need to continue to diversify the teaching force. We can't give up on that one. We need to bring more teachers of color not only into the university but also into the public school classrooms. Cannot all children benefit from teachers of diverse cultures?

CONCLUSION

After reflecting on our conversation together, we believe that all teacher-educators should examine the following assumptions:

1. "In a society stratified by race, class, and gender, schools are by no means politically neutral. Schools are major socializing mechanisms which help maintain existing hierarchical relationships of power and privilege" (Bowles & Gintes, 1976; Shujaa, 1993).

2. Colleges of Education can lead the nation's dialogue about confronting racism and poverty in urban schools and communities so that never again will black and brown children be left to die in the aftermath of disasters like Katrina.

3. The teachers of our children in all public schools need to know how to grapple with the hard issues of social justice.

   With these assumptions as a context, we believe the following questions should be asked of colleges of education (COE):

   ◆ How do COEs deliberately and consistently create safe spaces for faculty conversations around issues of social justice, power, and privilege? Where do they find the resources to commit to building an infrastructure that will support these difficult dialogues?

   ◆ How do we develop these professors' expertise in developing the competency of preservice and in-service teachers to recognize and engage in the discussion of social justice issues, especially racism, with their students, parents, and schools?

   ◆ How do COEs lead their professors toward a more effective examination of the impact of the nation's history, their personal histories and biases, and those of their students on the children in public schools?

   ◆ How do COEs create rewards within the tenure process for professors to become genuine advocates for unlearning racism and for demanding diversity in our educational thinking and practices?

   ◆ How do COEs demand equal representation of professors from diverse ethnicities on their faculties?

   ◆ How do we use the knowledge and experience of people like Bob Moses to engage the grassroots community in honest discussion about COEs as advocates for quality education as a civil right for all students in urban, rural, and suburban schools?

   Within that same context, COE professors might help their K-12 teachers navigate the following questions:

   ◆ How do my personal life experiences influence my educational philosophy and practices?

   ◆ What are some of the biases that I hold about other cultures, ethnicities, religions, etc.?

   ◆ How might those biases influence my attitudes about my students?

   ◆ What is institutional racism? How does that impact the students in my classroom?

   ◆ What are some of the "bloody facts" of the country's history that are not talked about in schools yet impact what happens in my classroom?

   ◆ How can I find out about the history, art, music, spiritual, and cultural mores of the students I teach?

   ◆ What does White privilege mean and how does it play a part in the power inequities in my school?

   ◆ Who is privileged in my school, in my classroom?

   ◆ Do I see the parents of my students as respectable collaborators in my students' educational lives?

   ◆ How am I complicit in the miseducation of my students?

   ◆ What am I doing to integrate the community into my classroom?

   ◆ What if the children in my classroom were deeply heard, what would they say?

REFERENCES

Bowles, S., & Gi ntes, H. (1976). *Schooling in capitalist America*. New York: Basic Books.

Breitman (1965). *Malcolm X speaks*. Grove, NY: Merit Publishers and Betty Shabazz.

Delpit, L. (1995). *Other people's children*. New York: New Press.

Eliot, T. S. *The Hollow Men Poetry X*, ed. Jough Dempsey. Retrieved June 13, 2007, from http://poetry .poetryx.com/poems/784

Fisk, J. (1993). *Power plays, power works*. London; New York: Verso.

Hall, E. (1989). *Beyond culture*. New York: Anchor Books edition/Double Day Dell Publishing Co.

Hilliard, A. G., III. (1997). The structure of valid staff development. *Journal of Staff Development, 18*, 28–34.

Hillard, A. G., III. (1999, February). *The spirit of the African child*. Unpublished speech at the Urban Atlanta Coalition Compact Town Meeting, Atlanta, GA.

Hilliard, A. G., III. (2000). *Awaken the geniuses of children: The nurture of nature*. Unpublished speech for Skylight 6th International Teaching for Intelligence Conference, (Cassette Recording No. 00227-1160). Elkridge, MD: Chesapeake Audio/Video Communications.

Katz, M. B. (1993). (Ed.). *The "underclass" debate: Views from history*. Princeton, NJ: Princeton University Press.

Moses, B. & Noguera, P. Unpublished panel discussion, Urban Expo, Center for Urban Education & Innovation Conference at Florida International University, Miami, November, 2003.

Moses, R. & Cobb, Jr., C. (2001). *Radical equations: Math literacy and civil rights*. Boston: Beacon Press.

Shujaa, M. J. (1993). Education and schooling: You can have one without the other. *Urban Education, 27*, 328–351.

Section 2: Searching for Justice Welcomes Everyone into the Dialogue

Please take five minutes and write in the space below the answers to any two of the numbered questions* from "Reframing Urban Education Discourse." Then write about how you see the Baugh poem relating to the issues discussed in the Blanchett/Wynne article.

---

*Questions for K-12 Teachers:

1. How do my personal life experiences influence my educational philosophy and practice?
2. What are some of the biases that I hold about other cultures, ethnicities, religions, etc.?
3. How might those biases influence my attitudes about my students?
4. What is institutional racism? How does that impact the students in my classroom?
5. What are some of the "bloody facts" of the country's history that are not talked about in schools yet impact what happens in my classroom?
6. How can I discover the history, art, music, spiritual, cultural mores of the students I teach?
7. What does white privilege mean and how does it play a part in the power inequities in my school?
8. Who is privileged in my school, in my classroom?
9. Do I see the parents of my students as respectable collaborators in my students' school lives?
10. How am I complicit in the mis-education of my students?
11. What am I doing to integrate the community into my classroom?
12. What if the children in my classroom were deeply heard, what would they say?

_____

_____

_____

_____

_____

_____

_____

_____

_____

_____

After writing those answers, please consider the following activities:

- Join at least four other classmates and discuss your answers.

- Once discussed, choose one or two ideas from your group's discussion and create a 3- to 5-minute skit that illustrates your ideas about confronting racism in or outside the classroom.

- After 15 minutes of designing the activity, present the group skits to the class.

- Then, as a class, critique the value of the use of skits in K-12 classrooms as a method of assisting students to learn abstract ideas via the performing arts.

Please view the 8-minute *YouTube* video about a story of two schools:
www.youtube.com/watch?v=MgvpRoAn-ro&feature=related
Discuss with your small group what actions teachers can take to make schools more equitable.

_____

_____

_____

_____

_____

_____

_____

SECTION 3
EXPLORING WHOLENESS CREATES POSSIBILITIES FOR ALL OUR STUDENTS TO SOAR

Image copyright mangostock, 2012. Used under license from Shutterstock. Inc.

I learned more than my students that first year. . . . that books, philosophies, rhetoric, dogma, pedagogy, lesson plans, mandates, teacher performance assessments, and my college degree meant squat if I didn't believe—if I didn't absolutely without reservation accept that every student I touched had the potential for learning, discovery, enlightenment, communication, interpretation and enjoyment from being a part of a whole—a part of something expected, a part of something like their peers, a part of their community, a part of society. That was one of the biggest truths I found. My students, our students, whoever they were, whatever they emotionally or physically did or did not bring with them, wanted to be a part of the whole— and whatever I needed to do to make that happen was my responsibility, my obligation.

—Catharine Graham "Inclusion into the circle of life"

CHAPTER 3

INCLUSION INTO THE CIRCLE OF LIFE

Catharine Yvonne Graham

'What do you do?'
'I teach high school.'
'Oh what do you teach?'
'I teach students in special education.'
'Oh, wow, you must be really patient.'

Many of my conversations used to start that way, right before the person walked away. In the late 80s and most of the 90s I taught students who had orthopedic impairments and students who had behavioral and/or learning challenges. I taught in a public high school that also housed the largest ESOL (English as a second or other language) program in our metro county. We were a poorer school and extremely diverse in population. We struggled on almost every level for: attention from the county, involvement from community and parents, money for our extracurricular activities, sports, uniforms, tournaments and even our physical facility. We did, however, excel at caring deeply for our student body & each other.

I came into the profession as a fledgling teacher prepared to teach elementary students with visual impairments. Due to an extreme need for teachers in another area, I ended up teaching high school students with various orthopedic impairments as well as behavioral & cognitive challenges. I am confident I learned more than my students that first year. I learned that books, philosophies, rhetoric, dogma, pedagogy, lesson plans, mandates, teacher performance assessments and my college degree meant squat if I didn't believe—if I didn't absolutely without reservation accept that every student I touched had the potential for learning, discovery, enlightenment, communication, interpretation and enjoyment from being a part—a part of something expected, a part of something like their peers, a part of their community, a part of society. That was one of the biggest truths I found. My students, our students, whoever they were, whatever they emotionally or physically did or did not bring with them, wanted to be a part of the whole—and whatever I needed to do to make that happen was my responsibility, my obligation.

OUR STUDENTS' STORIES

TIM

One of my students, Tim B., was a young man with an indomitable spirit and an IQ in the gifted range who had cerebral palsy. Physically Tim was significantly affected by the cerebral palsy. He had limited motor control and significant spasticity. He used a power wheelchair for mobility. Due to his spasticity, orthopedic restraints were used to position him in his chair in a way that kept him stationary and gave him greater control of his body. He operated the chair on his own with a foot switch. He had more fine motor control of his right foot than any other area of his body so that is what he used to accelerate and guide the chair. Due to his physical demands, his speech was so affected that he was quite difficult to understand. He drooled. Yet, if people chose to pay attention to only his body, they would miss out because Tim was incredibly smart and incredibly social. He was mainstreamed for all classes except study hall, which he took in my room.

During the school day and at school sponsored functions, Tim was involved, engaged and happy. The other teachers and students accepted him, included him and learned to be patient with Tim's differences. Tim and I did have discussions, though, at times when he was feeling left out of non school related activities. His mode of transportation, when not a specially designed school bus, was an expensive van designed with a wheelchair lift, so he couldn't just hitch a ride to after-school events or activities. All had to be planned well in advance. Obviously this inhibited his social activities. But in school, Tim made every effort to become fully integrated into the student body.

ANTHONY

Another student, Anthony, had muscular dystrophy. He, too, used a power wheelchair for mobility. Like Tim, Anthony had daunting physical hurdles. He had little control over any of his body with the exception of his fingers, feet and mouth—exceptions which underpin a story we'll get to in a moment. Anthony 'drove' his chair with a joy stick mounted to the armrest at exactly the spot his left hand rested. He was a pro at propelling that machine. He could and would whip that chair around like any experienced Indy driver. Because he did not have the strength to hold his head up on his own, he had a padded head rest on his chair that supported both the back and the sides of his head. He could when motivated hold his head up without the support for brief moments and tip it slightly from side to side. Anthony supposedly tested at "average" intelligence, had a wicked sense of humor, a flair for the dramatics and a mastery of sarcasm.

My first year teaching was Anthony's junior year. I found out that people had assumed that he was not going to make it through the summer after his sophomore year, due to the progression of his disease and a bout with pneumonia. But he did make it and bounced back with a vengeance. Upon his return for his junior year, one of my fellow teachers, who was extremely fond of him, played into their typical banter with each other by acknowledging his hard summer with the comment, "Well Anthony, I thought you told me at the end of last year you wouldn't be back? I'm glad you decided you would give me another chance."

Anthony replied, "Hey Miss B, you know only the good die young."

Anthony's humor was not limited to wry comments, however. The principal at our school had some idiosyncrasies about the physical aspect of the school. One in particular was that all blinds should be raised 8 inches from the bottom of the window thus creating uniformed curb appeal. *I know. I'm shaking my head as I remember it.* Anyway we got to be pretty rigorous about it to avoid useless, I mean, needless feedback. The students, of course, picked up on this, and it became occasional classroom fodder. One day after Anthony had received some bad news, was especially feeling the effects of his disease and was just generally in a rotten mood, cajoled one of his fellow students to let him into Miss B's classroom while she was at lunch. By using his wheelchair to bump the cord of the window blinds so they would swing back and forth, he got it swinging enough to grab it with his mouth. He held the cord with his teeth, used the joy stick to move the chair in reverse and ripped the blinds all the way to the top of the window.

Eventually Miss B figured out the culprit's identity. She did give him detention, although, she spent it with him, uncovered the reasons for the misbehavior, listened intently and then laughed uproariously with him. She praised him for his ingenuity but told him if he ever did it again, his body would never be found. He promised to resist the next temptation, and they made up.

BJ

BJ's temptations were different. He always aimed to please. He was a student who came to me because his father was taking custody of him. Leaving the group residence he had attended for years, BJ was changing not only homes, but also parents, educational facilities and his day-to-day circle of people. He had cerebral palsy and was labeled as "below average" intelligence and sat in a manual wheelchair. BJ was kind, soft spoken and desperately wanted to be liked and to please those around him. He had not been pushed physically or cognitively but had obviously received quality instruction and coaching in regards to social skills. His manners were outstanding.

Consequently, BJ did fairly well assimilating. He got along swimmingly with his peers in his special education classes and because of his friendly disposition, he became known by the rest of the student body and faculty too. As I said he could operate his wheelchair on his own but was not strong enough to negotiate the opening of the school's main & hallway doors like many of the other students who used manual chairs. Because of this his independence was inhibited, and often he needed someone to accompany him in order to access certain classes and activities. Building the coordination and strength to open and get through these doors became a big goal of mine and BJ's. I wanted him to have greater independence around the campus for his self esteem. In addition, I was running out of folks to accompany him to class. It would be a win / win for both of us! Wildly enough and without expecting it, my biggest obstacle to this was not BJ or his ability. It was my assistant principal.

My AP was a wonderful, caring, strict, seasoned educator who had been at my school for almost longer than any other faculty member. He had a visible physical impairment due to an illness from his youth. He never missed a day of school but some days his pain was obvious in his gait and his mood. It was very difficult for him to watch BJ struggle while pushing the heavy doors with his chair, especially while I stood by and watched. Only after catching my AP for the 4th time assisting BJ with this task, did I school this administrator, insisting he stop being a helper. The AP was not pleased with me, and I'm not sure he ever agreed with me, but he did stop, at least when I was around. BJ sustained some minor injuries during the first few months of his efforts. Those entrance doors were heavy. His knuckles got pinched and bruised but his efforts were valiant. He mastered it and became quite independent on campus. He was so proud that he could get around without me or others' assistance.

RINA

Like BJ, Rina, too, enjoyed the feeling of independence. She was a student with muscular dystrophy and used a power chair with a joystick for mobility. She was bright, articulate, funny and shy. She was on the student council and was in honor's classes. She came to me once a day for study hall. I gave her any assistance she needed in getting books, helping with dictation of assignments and taking care of her bathroom needs. Rina was so well mainstreamed that I was just there to monitor her Individual Education Plan (IEP), be an advocate on the campus if she ever needed one and take care of her school day physical needs. Although most days she ate lunch with friends, occasionally she would eat with my class if she wanted to visit with me and catch up. She was quite social at school. Because she was on the student council, she, of course, was invited to the student council national convention in Florida. Her parents desperately tried to support her independence, extracurricular activities and overall development into a young, responsible adult. Yet for her parents, a weekend trip to the student council convention on a greyhound bus, staying away from home in a hotel with 500 high schoolers from all over the country was a lip biter. But Rina was adamant. She absolutely wanted to go, but she did not want either of her parents to go. She did not want to go separately from the other students—for the 10 hour bus ride with all of the other kids was half the experience.

So I rode 10 hours to the student council national convention. We loaded Rina's power wheelchair under the bus with the luggage. I carried her up the stairs to her seat and used pads and pillows to position her as close to the way her wheelchair supported her as possible. Rina did enjoy much of the bus ride, but by the 7th hour she was so uncomfortable from the lack of proper support in her seat that the last hours of the ride, both ways, were painful. In spite of the bus trip, though, Rina enjoyed the weekend's events. She made every meeting, meal and night time activity. I tried to stay scarce except for our agreed upon meetings for bathroom breaks and scheduled check-ins about upcoming experiences where my assistance might be needed.

Wow, that kid wanted to be a part of every piece of that convention in a big way. And she was. Rina worked hard at it. She worked hard at making it seem effortless, natural and normal. I tried to follow her lead as best I could. I saw firsthand the extremes to which individuals, teenagers, would go to be a part of their community. Once again, my student taught me richly textured lessons about the importance of being accepted into the whole.

So while "inclusion" (2007) may be just a theory or a lexicon of educational jargon to many, to me it shouts out the many stories of my students' sometimes excruciating but often joyous struggles to belong. Inclusion won't allow us to make others invisible. It won't settle for excuses in lieu of human connection. It sings to us of courage and wit, of anger and defeat, of small victories and burgeoning human power. But most of all, it begs the best in each of us to come out and play together—in the circle of life.

REFERENCE

Turnbull, A. et al (2007). *Exceptional lives: Special education in today's schools*. London: Merrill Publishing.

CRITICAL GLOBAL MATH LITERACY

Bob Peterson

"I didn't know fractions could make such a powerful point about the world," one of my fifth graders reflected after finishing her math assignment. The assignment was an out-growth of the class watching an anti-consumerism Adbusters commercial (see "Videos With a Global Conscience," p. 368). In the 30-second video spot, an "American Excess" pig emerges out of a map of North America, burps, and announces: "A tiny 5% of the people of the world consumes one-third of its resources and produces almost one-half of the non-organic waste. Those people are us."

The assignment had been to change the percentages to fractions, to draw a graph contrasting the data, and to write about the significance of the information. The mini-project took only one class period and was integrated into our study of percent, fractions, and decimals. It allowed me to observe students' understanding of one aspect of percent and fractions, as well as their graphing and thinking skills. It also allowed students to begin to see the power of math and express their concerns about world problems. During one such lesson we had a lengthy debate about responsibility that wealthy countries have towards the earth's environment and people. After the discussion one of my students wrote, "When I think about the poverty I feel sad. I think the problem is 'countryism' as we are supposed to be at the same level. It's like sexism when men and women aren't at the same level."

Mathematics, like language, is both a discipline unto itself and a tool to understand and interact with the world and other academic disciplines. Just as written and oral language help a student understand one's surroundings, so too can written and oral mathematics.

Most of my students learn that mathematics is a powerful and useful tool because I flood my classroom with examples of how math is central to many "hot topics" that kids like to discuss and study. I regularly clip news articles and file them for future use—articles such as "25% of the Mammals Species Now Extinct," "Women Government Leaders Under-represented," "10 Million Land Mines Threaten Afghanistan." Through lessons that integrate math and social studies and science, students see how math is central to understanding issues of social and ecological justice (and injustice) in our world.

For example, after my students participated in the International Beach Sweep (sponsored by The Ocean Conservancy) one September we tallied up all the types of debris that we had found on the shores of Lake Michigan. Of all the items found, 51% were cigarette butts. As students made graphs of their data we spoke of both individual and corporate responsibility towards the earth. We practiced understanding big numbers and place value by looking at the profits that tobacco companies made in one year and the number of deaths caused by tobacco each year in the United States (more than 400,000) and around the world (6,000,000). Using data that the tobacco industry spent over $65 million dollars lobbying Congress in 1998, students calculated the average amount of money spent per U.S. Representative. We examined why Congress has failed to put limits on the U.S. tobacco industry as it expands its global reach—two-thirds of U.S. tobacco company sales and nearly half of their profits come from overseas.

The Adbusters video has other "un-ads" alerting students to the influence of advertising and consumerism on the earth. Every day, students are targeted by corporate advertising to consume. When they see anti-consumerism ads, students stop and take stock. I explain that studies show that kids are three times as sensitive to tobacco advertising than adults and are more likely to be influenced to smoke by cigarette marketing than by peer pressure. We use statistics from UNICEF to show how small amounts of money can buy life-saving medicines and then contrast the cost of those items with advertisement-related tobacco costs. We figure out how much medicine could be bought with the money spent by just one individual who smokes a pack a day and by the tobacco industry that annually spends $8.4 billion dollars on advertising and promotion in the United States.

Throughout the year, students examine different social and ecological problems using math. I encourage students to bring in math-related items they see in the news. I regularly search the Internet for background statistics on topics like global warming, deforestation, water depletion, land mines, tobacco, and child labor to bring my math lessons alive. For math "class," I pose problems that have social significance that help students practice whatever particular skill we are focusing on. All together, by the time students leave my fifth grade classroom their skill and understanding of math is improved, and their understanding of the world is sharpened.

ROOM 214: NURTURING AN EVOLVING CLASSROOM CULTURE

Princess Briggs
Give light and people will find the way.
—Ella Baker, 1944

"How long you gon' be here?"
"Excuse me?"
"How . . . long . . . is . . . you . . . gon' . . . be . . . here?"
"What do you mean? Here where? Here in this classroom?"
(Heavy long sigh) *"Here wit' us! How long you gon' be our teacher?"*
"Sweetie, I don't plan on going anywhere. I'm your teacher. You're my students. This is our class. I'm here."
"Oh." (Rolls eyes. Turns and walks away.)

The above exchange took place between one of my students and me about a month into my first year as a special education teacher. Although it has now been more than a decade and a half, I remember this conversation vividly. This student, who I will refer to as Tiffany, shielded her feelings and did not show much emotion. She manifested an *"I-don't-take-crap-from-anybody"* attitude in her body language and facial expressions. Tiffany, like many of my students that first year, found it difficult to develop a relationship with me as her teacher. The other students were also guarded and untrusting of my attempts to reach out to them. They were unsure of my motives, and more importantly, unsure of my commitment to them.

Before I was hired, my students had been without a permanent teacher for months. From the beginning of that school year, they experienced a revolving door of teachers and substitutes. Not only were my students deprived of their right to a certified and qualified teacher, they were also left without books and instructional materials. They had been provided with only a filing cabinet full of newspapers and a few torn, outdated workbooks. The situation was dismal. These students, I felt, would never recoup what they had lost. Having been deprived of an adequate instructional atmosphere and having missed one hour a day, every day for the first five months of school, it seemed that little could replace this incredible loss of developmental time.

Unfortunately, many other classrooms in this county suffer these deficits, either lacking a permanent classroom teacher or with a teacher who is under-qualified. The demographics of the students sitting in those classrooms are no different from the demographics of my students (Aud, Fox, and KewalRamani, 2010). Specifically, most of the students who attended the school where my teaching career began were African American, and they resided in the public housing projects located within one or two miles of the school.

The school was located in a poor community where many children witnessed criminal activity while playing mere steps away from their front door or down the street at the neighborhood park. As is typical of many urban families, my students grew up in households run by one parent, usually the mother or grandmother (Children's Defense Fund, 2011). All of the students in my class had a familiarity with incarceration, either having a parent, sibling or close relative in jail, or having seen or heard about neighborhood kids being cuffed and taken down to "juvey." This community and the children who grew up here were deprived of what most of America would consider "The American Dream."

The children in this community lived with limited financial, social, and familial resources. Adding to their already burdened young lives, the students in my special education classroom, in particular, faced academic challenges and learning difficulties. Their academic level was no less than two years below their actual grade level, with most of them being four years behind in reading and about two years behind in math. Their writing skills also lagged significantly behind those of their same-age peers without similar learning or cognitive challenges.

So when Tiffany asked, *"How long you gon' be here?"* she was interested in more than just the length of my stay at the school. She was questioning my commitment to her. She needed to know if she could trust me with her fragile core despite its rough exterior. She needed to know if I respected her enough to allow her the time and space to grow educationally, emotionally, and socially. She needed to know if she could depend on me to provide a safe haven to run back to when her world became overwhelming.

Like Tiffany, many students in my class needed the security of a stable school environment to counterbalance the instability they faced outside of the school walls. Some of these children faced seemingly insurmountable circumstances including poverty, malnutrition, homelessness, neglect, and physical, sexual, and mental abuse. Any attempt I made at reaching them would have to be intentional, consistent, and enduring. I would need to make them and their realities a central focus of my teaching and of my interactions with them. This method of teaching, in which the teacher responds to the students' cultures and personal lives, has been coined *culturally responsive teaching* (CRT) (Darling-Hammond et al.).

Learning culturally responsive teaching practices have been crucial in my development as a teacher. I have learned that those practices are not a "step-by-step, how-to" guide to teaching. Rather, as researcher Linda Darling-Hammond suggests, they "… develop over time as teachers learn from their students' experiences and develop ways to incorporate diverse perspectives" (pg. 109). My students that first year taught me whole new worlds of cultural understandings and pedagogy. One of the most important components of CRT helped me that first year before I had learned to name the theory, a theory which includes four major components: *Respect for students and belief in their potential as learners* (Smith et al., 2007); *Cultural congruity between home and school;* (McCarthey, 2000); Active teaching and authentic assessment; and *Caring environment and personal connections.*

This last aspect of the theory, "caring and connection," is the focus of this paper. As a novice teacher, I had to capitalize on my strength of forming bonds and personal connections with young people. My students and I made connections with one another, which helped shape an environment of mutual respect and trust. Although all four areas of the Culturally Responsive Teaching concept are meaningful, the focal point of this article illustrates how a supportive and caring environment over time was cultivated from my students' interactions with me and my sensitivity to their needs.

BUILDING TRUSTING RELATIONSHIPS

Although I was only one of the six teachers my students would see on a daily basis, my presence was needed to balance their world, to sustain them. Because they had lived the reality of teacher after teacher coming and leaving, from the moment I became their teacher, the possibility of my leaving them became a preoccupation. Most of my new students had the social skills necessary to initiate a healthy bond with me. However, there were some students who had not yet acquired the skills to sustain a student/teacher relationship. They held on to negative feelings from past disappointments. Consequently, they protected themselves from any possible hurt by retreating behind their walls, their masks.

Initially, most of my students seemed eager to accept me into their world, one where I had not yet earned total membership, yet at the same time, they continued to be reserved for a couple weeks. Eventually their tensions waned. A number of students, however, became threatened by their own vulnerability, afraid to open themselves to the unknown of this new teacher. After approximately a month, some of them started skipping my class; some came to class and refused to work; some picked fights with classmates, and some even picked fights with me.

One student tried to physically attack me. I will refer to this student as Tony. If you could imagine the one student in the school who was notorious for finding trouble, who was suspended more days than he was in school, who was feared by most of the students, and who was shunned by most of the teachers, Tony would be that student. Tony was the school's bully and a member of the school's unspoken Top Ten to Terminate list. By the time that I was hired, the school administrators had exhausted all of their disciplinary options. Tony was headed for expulsion.

One day, as I was ending my direct instruction and preparing my students for their assignments, Tony put his head down on his desk. I immediately reminded him of the class rules, specifically that students had to remain fully engaged in all activities at all times. He waved his hand at me, suggesting that I leave him alone. This reaction surprised me because, up to this moment, Tony had been a little aggressive yet tolerant of my requests. After the class had started their independent work, I went over to Tony to reinforce the rules and to provide him with one-on-one assistance. Once he realized that I was not relenting, his head popped up from his desk, and he yelled out, "Leave me alone! I ain't doing that." Again, I reminded him of the rule that all students had to remain engaged at all times. In an effort to give him some time and space to get himself together, I walked away from him and sat at my desk. Tony got up from his desk, walked aggressively towards my desk and swung his fist to hit me. I averted his hit, jumped up from my desk, and removed him from my classroom. My tone of voice and body language were firm and insistent.

At that moment, Tony, and all of my other students, learned that the classroom rules were non-negotiable and that I was competent enough to uphold them. More importantly, the other students learned that they were important enough to be treated fairly. They had become used to Tony, in other classes, being allowed to break rules. They accepted this unfair practice and opted to keep their opinions about it to themselves for fear of retribution from Tony or from the adult who had allowed him to defy requests for order. My insistence that Tony be required to follow the class rules, like all other members of our class, allowed my students to experience equity. Because these students had been almost forgotten and treated unfairly for so long, they needed to be reminded that equity was their right.

As the year progressed, they experienced other lessons in equality. Tony also gained valuable insight about himself and about me. As a result of his behavior, Tony was suspended from school for ten days. When he returned, I greeted him at the door, as I had always done with all of my students, with a pleasant smile on my face and a compliment or word of encouragement. Tony's reaction to my banter revealed that he was expecting a different response from me. Because other teachers had rejected him, he expected that I would do the same. However, I responded from my belief that children start with a blank slate every day. No matter what may have occurred the day before, the week before, or the month before, students should be greeted with a warm smile and a compliment. My students learned to expect this. They learned that my regard for them was unconditional. It was a given; they didn't need to earn it, nor could they destroy it.

This incident with Tony was only one of many examples in which my students acted out in an attempt to fortify their protective walls against uncertainty and impending hurt. They lashed out against their hope for something better. However, my reaction was still the same. I continued to reinforce the rules for everybody, and I never deprived them of my smiling face and encouraging words. Although it was not always easy, I was there physically and emotionally.

There were days when I faced unexpected circumstances, like a pregnant seventh grader who cried in my arms. There were days when I felt naked in front of their piercing eyes because a lesson had failed miserably. There were days when I wanted to cry because I was so frustrated with not knowing how to reach them. There were even days when I started to second-guess my career option. But I never stopped coming. I kept showing up. I remained my students' constant.

Tiffany, Tony, and all of my students grew to understand that they could trust me. I could have walked into their classroom on that first day in February and declared my trustworthiness. I could have gone to each of them personally and repeated, "You can trust me." I could have written it on a poster board and tacked it to the walls. But I knew that any attempt at building a trusting relationship would be meaningless without immediate and consistent authentic experiences. My students needed to *feel* what it's like to be in a trusting relationship, from nuances of fairness to concrete and unwavering belief in truth. In a culturally responsive environment, when forming caring relationships between students and teachers, trust is one of the most important and impactful aspects of classroom culture. Our culture of trust evolved over the remainder of the school year and into the next.

FOSTERING MUTUAL RESPECT

During this first year as a classroom teacher, I encouraged my students to build trusting relationships with one another, with me, and within themselves. Through activities and experiences, my students learned the importance of fairness and equality. Concurrently, my students and I also learned how to value each other. This was not always easy, as we were from different backgrounds, various cultures, and had innumerable diverse life experiences. Although my ethnicity was similar to that of most of my students, our cultures, though similar in some aspects, were vastly different in others. For example, both my students and I shared a cultural belief that parents were identified as any adult who takes on the financial, emotional, and physical well-being of a child, whether that person was a blood relative or not. However, our cultures splintered in different directions where parental discipline was concerned. I was raised in a family that recognized that your "parent," whoever that may be, was fully responsible for discipline issues. But for the majority of my students, discipline matters were reserved for the parent who was biologically connected to the child in question. Specifically, in the case of siblings, it was commonplace that a sister might be disciplined by a grandmother, but the stepbrother would not be disciplined by this same grandmother because she was not biologically related, although both children lived in the same household. When I needed to call a student's home to discuss matters that could result in disciplinary action, I had to be careful with whom I shared information. Many times, the person on the registration card was not the person that took on the responsibility for the child. And, in some cases, the person listed in the child's records was incarcerated, deceased, or missing. For these and other reasons, it was imperative that I learn about each of my students' backgrounds.

In an effort to fully value my students, I had to respect various attributes of their culture that may have differed from mine. From a book, *Building cultural reciprocity with families: Case studies in special education* (1999), I had learned that teachers should "identify the cultural values that are embedded in [their] interpretation of a student's difficulties or in the recommendation for service" (p. 7). So it was important to my students that I recognize my actions and opinions as embedded in *my* own cultural values and practices, then I could open myself to the idea that my students and their families have *their* own actions and opinions that are culturally-driven. I began to realize that being ever-mindful of this allowed me the space and time to recognize that my truth is not *the* truth. To share this valuable lesson with my students, I allowed myself the transparency to practice this posture of cultural reciprocity with them. To this end, we often had deep classroom discussions. Some examples included whether going directly to college after high school was more important than getting a job right away; whether one should disclose their learning deficiencies to potential employers; and whether people should have to cut their dreadlocks just to get a job.

Through these discussions, some turning into heated debates, my students and I learned to see the world through the eyes of our neighbor. We were less quick to judge a person's actions based on what we thought we were seeing or hearing. Fostering a culture of mutual respect helped my students build esteem and personal pride within themselves and in our class. The bigger challenge, however, became sustaining this sense of pride when it was violated by other teachers and students who were not members of our class. My students had to learn how to transfer these lessons to people and situations outside of the confines of our classroom walls.

I often told my students that it was important for them to walk with their heads held high and their shoulders pulled back as a sign that they had pride and self-esteem. This way, I suggested, others would respect them as well. Furthermore, I would reminded them to never allow negative self-talk, nor allow others to engage in negative opinions about them. These self-affirmations were repeated in my classroom on a daily basis. Initially, esteem declarations came solely from me until my students seemed to get it down into their core and started repeating it to one another. If one student made a derogatory comment about a classmate, the others would jump in with, "You can't say that about him. You don't know what he can do. Just because his [assignment] don't look like yours don't mean nothing!" Having peers hold one another accountable was more significant than any other intervention. Our caring environment began to develop from an intrinsic need to reciprocate respect.

The students were not the only ones having to hold their peers accountable for the esteem of others. I found myself having to correct fellow teachers and administrators for thoughtless comments that were hurtful to my students. One such incident occurred while my students were lined up in the hallway waiting to go to lunch. Another class was coming from lunch. The students in that class were obviously wound up and were not following the directives of their teacher. One student in particular was bouncing in and out of the line, and was completely ignoring the teacher. Out of frustration, the teacher yelled to the student, "Why are you acting like that? Is something wrong with you? You need to be over there" (motioning towards the students in my line). Needless to say, my students were upset. But by this time (I was now in my third year), they had learned when it was appropriate to express themselves and when it was not. Since we were not in the confines of our own class, they knew that they had to do their best to control their emotions.

I did not allow that teacher to get away with his ignorant stereotyping of my students. I needed to teach him and his students that my students deserved better treatment. My anger at the teacher's comment spurred my quick tongue, as I retorted, "No, he can't be in our class. We don't act like that. He would never make it *over here*." I turned away and led my students to the cafeteria. Their smiles spoke volumes about the pride they now felt. I will never forget my delight in seeing how they felt about themselves. At that moment, they knew that my words were not empty idiomatic expressions. They knew then that I really did believe in them and believed that they were deserving of respect from everybody and anybody.

CREATING A SAFE HAVEN

The culture in our classroom was evolving day by day. My students were trusting in the learning process and building self-worth at the same time. They understood the reciprocal nature of respect and held themselves and one another accountable. I, too, was being challenged to eliminate negative self-talk from my vocabulary, as I had not yet built a strong confidence in my abilities as a teacher. Often I just needed to close myself off from the teachers' lounge, from the coffee corner, and from the adult bathroom during high-traffic times. These places were pits of negativity. All types of comments about students, parents, and fellow-teachers were being spewed. In order to grow professionally, I knew I had to find a place where I could express my concerns in a positive and supportive environment. Until I was able to find that place, I remained in my classroom. It became my haven.

Having my own feelings of uncertainties, I was able to recognize these feelings in my students. When I looked in their faces and read their body language, I saw their disappointments in what they found difficult to do and their doubts in what I tried to assure them they could do. They needed a safe place to release these feelings. Out of sheer necessity, a culture of safety was being cultivated in our classroom. My students learned that they were allowed to express any hurts, disappointments, embarrassments, and the like, within the walls of Room 214. Sometimes my children came to class with a need to rant about some personal issue or debate a school-related "hot topic" in a safe, non-threatening environment (ex. the institution of school uniforms), or to cry and sob in my arms or in the arms of a best friend. I allowed them the time and space to speak and be heard. For some of them, this was their only outlet. They also held the great responsibility that we were family and anything that was said in our classroom was family business. Since most of my students were very familiar with not discussing "family business" with outsiders, I was able to take this aspect of our African-American culture and build it into our classroom culture. What happened in Room 214 stayed in Room 214.

Not only did my students and I share the need for a safe space to work out our personal issues, but just as I sometimes felt the need to retreat from areas frequented by the adults in the school building, my students also needed to find refuge from some of their teachers. Their search for quieter waters could have stemmed from a myriad of reasons, including avoiding a substitute teacher, dodging an hour and fifty minutes of sheer boredom, escaping the requests of an "unfair" teacher, or postponing the negative consequences of some unbroken rule. It was not uncommon to hear a knock at my door (although my door remained unlocked, my students learned to respect the learning environment at all times) followed by a phrase similar to, *"Man. . . . Ms. Briggs, I'm trying to stay outta trouble. Let me in, please"* or *"I just got in trouble. They wanna suspend me. Can I chill here, Ms. Briggs?"* Although some of the school administrators or some of my fellow teachers perceived my actions as "breaking the rules", "spiteful", or "wanting to be their [my students'] friend", I generally allowed my students (and eventually students who were not even assigned to me) to come into my classroom to get some relief from whatever was causing their immediate discontent. I simply informed the appropriate teacher or administrator of the student's presence in my room and continued with my lesson.

Allowing my students to retreat to my classroom served several purposes. Obviously, it allowed them to escape from some negative or potentially negative situation to a place of stability and security. Although they knew that they would have to eventually face whatever they were temporarily avoiding, using our classroom to take time out to calm down or to allow some other person, child or adult, to regain their composure provided my students with a physically safe space. Secondly, providing a temporary hiatus from their seemingly constant chaos allowed my students to develop a sense of "psychological safety" and "intellectual safety," as Lisa Delpit explained in an April 2000 interview with John Merrow. According to Delpit, a psychologically safe environment is one that children are "comfortable enough and relaxed enough to learn" (Merrow, 2000). In this type of atmosphere, children feel free to say whatever is on their mind without fear of penalty or retribution from other children or from adults. As I encouraged my students to come to me whenever they felt afraid or out of control, I was fostering a sense of psychological safety in our classroom culture.

A by-product of my students retreating to my classroom for a mental time-out was the development of their intellect. My students were fully aware that the standard for being in my class was full engagement from all students at all times. This included students who were on my roster and those who were not. If this rule was ever questioned by a reluctant visitor, I would chant, "When in Rome…" and my students would finish, "…do as the Romans!" If my students were reading, visitors had to read. If my students were engaged in a class debate, the visitors were expected to join a team and get to work. Even if my students were testing, any student who gained entry into our classroom was required to test as well.

Since my students were not performing at grade level, the double-dip of any learning experiences served as a preview or as a reinforcement of the lessons. Being exposed to the material twice gave some of my students an added feeling of confidence. They would use their first exposure to a topic to learn and gather necessary information. Their second exposure was used to answer any lingering questions or to reinforce what they had learned by teaching other students. This learn-review-reinforce cycle was promoting intellectual safety.

In an intellectually safe environment, according to Delpit (2000), children are encouraged to ask questions and discuss a variety of issues. Through class activities and authentic learning opportunities, they grow an understanding that the world is filled with unanswered questions; there are people on differing sides of an issue with valid and relevant opinions about a particular topic. Children who are intellectually secure are confident in their ability to support their viewpoint while opening themselves up to the views of others. Providing my students with multiple exposures to complex concepts genuinely built their confidence and deepened their enthusiasm. They were able to develop the prowess needed to engage in higher-order thinking activities or in theoretical conversations.

Those who were "trouble-makers or trouble-magnets" in other classes made a beeline for Room 214 where they engaged in relevant and rigorous learning. The school administrators realized that certain students were visiting the office less frequently and teacher referrals were minimized. I capitalized on this opportunity. When schedules were being developed for the next school year, I requested that I be given double blocks of Reading and Language Arts, with the same students scheduled in each block. This schedule arrangement would allow me to see my students twice as much as I would have seen them with a typical schedule. Having them for this extended period of time would afford me the opportunity to cover material in depth and provide an opportunity for my students' full comprehension of concepts. Although it took an added measure to create this type of schedule, my administrators agreed that the benefits outweighed the sacrifice and granted my request.

CONCLUSION

From the very moment I entered my first classroom and looked into the faces of my first set of students, I knew that I was the possessor of something that they desperately needed just as they were the entrusted vessels that safeguarded my deepest need. My students yearned for the opportunity to experience what was rightfully theirs—a quality education in a secure and stable environment. I yearned for the opportunity to nurture and educate children who looked like me, spoke like me, and dreamed like me. And although we arrived at this place from diverse life circumstances, we were all challenged with the similar tasks of building interpersonal and intrapersonal trust, reciprocating respect, and creating and protecting a safe haven.

Culturally Responsive Teaching is a pedagogical concept that guides teachers through a set of practices developed over time to promote student learning using the students' experiences and perspectives. One such practice, developing caring environments and personal connections, helps teachers recognize that children are more academically engaged and invested in an environment where they feel safe and respected. Children also flourish socially when teachers establish personal relationships with them and with their community and culture.

Over the course of my first few years in the classroom, I was sensitive to my students' needs to be "seen" by the adults moving in and out of their classroom. I understood that their initial distrust in me was a consequence of having their trust previously destroyed again and again. In order to teach them, I had to nurture them. In order to nurture them, they needed to know that I respected them, that they could trust me, and that Room 214 was a safe haven for all who entered, including my Tiffanys and Tonys.

REFERENCES

Aud, S., Fox, M.A., and KewalRamani, A. *Status and trends in the education of racial and ethnic groups.* U.S. Department of Education: Institute of Education Sciences. July 2010. p. 48.

Children's Defense Fund (2011). Retrieved from http://www.childrensdefense.org/programs- campaigns/black-community-crusade-for-children-II/bccc-assets/portrait-of-inequality.pdf

Darling-Hammond, L., Austin, K., Lit, I., Nasirwith, N., Moll, L., & Ladson-Billings, G. (n.d.) Session 6—The Classroom Mosaic: Culture and Learning.

Harry, B., Kalyanpur, M., & Day, M. (1999). Building cultural reciprocity with families: Case studies in special education. Baltimore, MD: Paul H. Brookes Publishing Co.

McCarthey, S. (2000). Home-school connections: A review of the literature. *The Journal of Educational Research,93,* 145.Merrow, J. (Producer). (2000, April 15). *'Radio Vault' Podcast—Lisa Delpit: Choosing Excellence* [Audio podcast]. Retrieved from http://learningmatters.tv/blog/podcasts/podcast-lisa-delpit-choosing-excellence/4609/

Smith, P.A., & Hoy, W. K. (2007). Academic optimism and student achievement in urban elementary schools. *Journal of Educational Administration* 45. 5, 556-568.

Section 3: Exploring Wholeness Creates Possibilities for All Our Students to Soar

Please take 5 minutes and write in the space below any passage that particularly grabbed your attention in any of the three articles presented in this section.

_____

_____

_____

_____

After writing that passage, please consider the following activities:

- Join at least four other classmates and discuss each other's passages

- Then, choose one of the group members' passages to write (or create a new one), using a magic marker, in large print on a piece of construction or plain paper.

- Using masking tape, place that paper on the wall above your group's chairs.

- Then as a class individually walk around the room, and read all of the passages on the wall. After reading them all, choose one that particularly appeals or "calls" to you.

- If and when others congregate around that passage, begin to tell each other what experience in your personal or professional life relates to that passage—or any reason that it appeals to you.

- After 4 to 5 minutes of discussion, choose a member from the group who will report back to the class one major idea that was generated from the group's discussion.

- After all groups report, together critique any value you see for this activity in a K-12 classroom.

1. Then watch the 2-minute video listed below and with your partner answer the questions that follow:

   www.youtube.com/watch?v=g9-XX9227ek

- What are some of the main points of this video?_____

_____

_____

_____

- What ethnicities are not pictured in this video? How does that absence create an irony for the theme of this video?_____

_____

_____

2. Now watch the 3-minute video listed below:
   www.youtube.com/watch?v=-cA3t1HW1Ow&feature=related

   ◆ Did this video shatter any stereotypes that you held about special needs children?_____

   _____

   _____

SECTION 4

SEEING THE BRILLIANCE IN ALL OF OUR CHILDREN EXPANDS THE GENIUS OF NATIONS

Image copyright mchaeljung, 2012. Used under license from Shutterstock. Inc.

I still believe the problem is cultural, but it is larger than the children or their teachers. The problem is that the cultural framework of our country has, almost since its inception, dictated that "black" is bad and less than and in all arenas "white" is good and superior. This perspective is so ingrained and so normalized that we all stumble through our days with eyes closed to avoid seeing it. We miss the pain in our children's eyes when they have internalized the societal belief that they are dumb, unmotivated, and dispensable.

—Lisa Delpit, Introduction, Multiplication is for White People:
Raising the Expectations for Other People's Children

CHAPTER 4

INTRODUCTION FROM MULTIPLICATION IS FOR WHITE PEOPLE: RAISING EXPECTATIONS FOR OTHER PEOPLE'S CHILDREN

Lisa Delpit

Recently I was invited by education activist Dr. Raynard Sanders to New Orleans for an educational summit. The speaker, the renowned and controversial Diane Ravitch, had told Dr. Sanders that she wanted to meet me. Dr. Ravitch, currently a professor at New York University, has made headlines with her about-face on many issues related to public education. Ravitch was the assistant secretary of education in the George H.W. Bush administration, where she made her conservative intellectual and political reputation with her staunch support of standardized testing, charter schools, the No Child Left Behind Act, and free market competition for schools. She has now repudiated many of her earlier positions, stated both in public presentations and in her book *The Death and Life of the Great American School System: How Testing and Choice Are Undermining Education*. This courageous scholar has resigned from influential conservative policy groups and has incited many powerful enemies. As a result, in contrast to her former life as a popular conservative commentator, she has now found herself barred from expressing her new views in many popular venues.

Before the speech began, I joined Diane, Raynard, and a few invited guests in an adjoining room. Diane and I talked about the devastation of public schools in post-Katrina New Orleans and how politicians and educational entrepreneurs hawking privatization are claiming the travesty of New Orleans education to be a national model.

Diane asked me why I hadn't spoken out nationally against what was happening. I told her about my work in New Orleans and my modestly successful attempts to engage other African American scholars in the struggle against what was happening there. I added that the sense of futility in the battle for rational education policy for African American children had gone on for so long and that I had come to feel so tired, that I now needed to focus on those areas where I felt I could actually make a difference: working with teachers and children in an African American school. I was so angry from the sensation of butting my head against a brick wall, I told her, that I needed to give my "anger muscles" a rest. Diane looked at me squarely and said, "You don't *look* angry."

I realized two things at that moment. One was that Diane's anger was relatively raw and still fresh and hadn't yet needed to be modulated. It must have been quite a shock to go from being an influential authority whose views were sought and valued in most political circles to being a virtual outcast. While it was undeniably courageous to reanalyze one's positions and come to a significantly different stance, it has to be anger-provoking to realize that the power elite seem less interested in logical analyses for the public good than in maintaining power and profit. Her anger had a different quality than the anger of those of us who have struggled with the same issues for many years.

The second thing I realized was that, yes, I *am* still angry—despite my attempts over the years to calm my spirit and to focus on the wonder of teaching and learning. I am angry at the machinations of those who, with so little knowledge of learning, of teachers, or of children, are twisting the life out of schools.

I am angry that public schools, once a beacon of democracy, have been overrun by the antidemocratic forces of extreme wealth. Educational policy for the past decade has largely been determined by the financial contributions of several very large corporate foundations. Among a few others, the Broad, Gates, and Walton (Walmart) foundations have dictated various "reforms" by flooding the educational enterprise with capital. The ideas of privatization, charter schools, Teach for America, the extremes of the accountability movement, merit pay, increased standardized testing, free market competition—all are promulgated and financially supported by corporate foundations, which indeed *have* those funds because they can avoid paying the taxes that the rest of us must foot. Thus, educational policy has been virtually hijacked by the wealthiest citizens, whom no one elected and who are unlikely ever to have had a child in the public schools.

I am angry that with all of the corporate and taxpayers' money that is flowing into education, little-to-none is going to those valiant souls who have toiled in urban educational settings for many years with proven track records. Instead, money typically goes to those with little exposure to and even less experience in urban schools. I am left in my more cynical moments with the thought that poor black children have become the vehicle by which rich white people give money to their friends.

I am angry because of the way that the original idea of charter schools has been corrupted. In their first iteration, charter schools were to be beacons for what could happen in public schools. They were intended to develop models for working with the most challenging populations. What they discovered was to be shared and reproduced in other public school classrooms. Now, because of the insertion of the "market model," charter schools often shun the very students they were intended to help. Special education students, students with behavioral issues, and students who need any kind of special assistance are excluded in a multiplicity of ways because they reduce the bottom line— they lower test scores and take more time to educate properly. Charter schools have any number of ways of "counseling" such students out of their programs. I have been told by parents that many charter schools accuse students of a series of often trivial rule infractions, then tell parents that the students will not be suspended if the parents voluntarily transfer them to another school. Parents of a student with special needs are told that the charter is not prepared to meet their child's needs adequately and that he or she would be much better served at the regular public school around the corner. (Schools in New Orleans, the "model city" for charters, have devised an even more sinister scheme for keeping unwanted children out of the schools. The K—12 publicly funded charter schools, which are supposed to be open to all through a lottery system of enrollment, are giving preferential admission to children who have attended an affiliated private preschool, one of which charges over $4,000 in tuition and the other over $9,000.)[1]

In addition, the market-driven model insists that should charter schools actually discover workable, innovative ideas, they are not to be shared with other public schools but held close to the vest to prevent "competitors" from "winning" the standardized test race. So now, charter schools are not meant to contribute to "regular" public education but to put it out of business.

I am angry about the hypocrisy rampant in education policy. While schools and teachers are admonished to adhere to research-based instruction and data-driven planning, there is no research to support the proliferation of charter schools, pay-for-performance plans, or market-based school competition. Indeed, where there is research, it largely suggests that we should do an about-face and run in the opposite direction.

I am angry that the conversation about educating our children has become so restricted. What has happened to the societal desire to instill character? To develop creativity? To cultivate courage and kindness? How can we look at a small bundle of profound potential and see only a number describing inadequacy? Why do we punish our children with our inability to teach them? How can we live with the fact that in Miami—and I am certain in many other cities—ten-year-olds facing failure on the state-mandated FCAT test and being "left back" in third grade for the third time, have had to be restrained from committing suicide?

I am angry at what the inflexibility and wrong-headed single-mindedness of schools in this era have done to my child and to so many other children. There is little tolerance for difference, for creativity, or for challenge.

The current use of standardized tests, which has the goals of promoting competition between schools and of making teacher and principal salaries—and sometimes even employment—dependent on tests scores, seems to bring out the worst in adults as well. In locale after locale—including Washington, DC; Georgia; Indiana; Massachusetts; Nevada; and Virginia, to name a few—there are investigations into widespread allegations of cheating by teachers and principals on state-mandated high-stakes tests.

And finally—if there ever *is* a finally—I am angry at the racism that, despite having a president who is half white and half black, still permeates our America. In my earlier days, I wrote about the problem of cultural conflict—that one of the reasons that having teachers and children of different cultural groups led to difficulties in teaching and learning was a lack of understanding about the other group's culture. I now have a slightly different perspective. I still believe that the problem is cultural, but it is larger than the children or their teachers. The problem is that the cultural frame-work of our country has, almost since its inception, dictated that "black" is bad and less than and in all arenas "white" is good and superior. This perspective is so ingrained and so normalized that we all stumble through our days with eyes closed to avoid seeing it. We miss the pain in our children's eyes when they have internalized the societal belief that they are dumb, unmotivated, and dispensable.

Nor can we see what happens to the psyches of young, often well-meaning white people who have been told that they are the best and brightest and that they are the saviors of black children. Most inevitably fail because they haven't the training or the experience to navigate such unfamiliar territory successfully; nor are they taught to learn with humility from parents or from veteran African American and other teachers who know the children and the communities in which they teach. Others burn out quickly from carrying the weight of salvation that has been piled upon their young shoulders. Several young Teach for America recruits have told me that their colleagues frequently run back home or off to graduate school with the belief that the children they went to save are unsalvageable—not because of poor teaching but because of their students' parents, families, or communities.

Yes, Diane, I am still angry. And that anger has fueled the two themes that run throughout this book. The first is the symbiotic interplay between my personal life as a mother and my professional work as a scholar and hopeful activist. Within the chapters of this volume are stories that range from my daughter Maya's first years in elementary school through her admission to college. My concerns for her educational struggles informed my work in schools. Feeling her frustration and pain opened my eyes to the frustration and pain thriving in so many of the classrooms I visited. Reveling in her successes helped me to suggest potential modifications for schools where I saw damaging practices. In fact, Maya has more than once over the years informed me that I wouldn't know half as much about education if I didn't have her! And she's right.

The second theme that runs through the book, from the chapters on educating young children to those focused on college students, is the relevance of a list of ten factors I have formulated over a number of years that I believe can foster excellence in urban classrooms. These factors encapsulate my beliefs about black children and learning, about creating classrooms that speak to children's strengths rather than hammering them with their weaknesses, and about building connections to cultures and communities. I believe that if we are to create excellence in urban classrooms, we must do the following:

1. Recognize the importance of a teacher and good teaching, especially for the "school dependent" children of low-income communities.

2. Recognize the brilliance of poor, urban children and teach them *more* content, not less.

3. Whatever methodology or instructional program is used, demand critical thinking while at the same time assuring that all children gain access to "basic skills"—the conventions and strategies that are essential to success in American society.

4. Provide children with the emotional ego strength to challenge racist societal views of their own competence and worthiness and that of their families and communities.

5. Recognize and build on children's strengths.

6. Use familiar metaphors and experiences from the children's world to connect what students already know to school-taught knowledge.

7. Create a sense of family and caring in the classroom.

8. Monitor and assess students' needs and then address them with a wealth of diverse strategies.

9. Honor and respect the children's home cultures.

10. Foster a sense of children's connection to community, to something greater than themselves.

So, yes, Diane, I am still angry. But I am also still hopeful. Some days I find it easier than others to locate that hope, so I am thankful that I have the opportunity to spend most of my days with the African American children at Southern University Laboratory School. There is nothing to inspire hope like the beaming smile of a kindergartner who has just written her first book or the cool demeanor that can't quite mask the excited grin of a seventh grader who has just mastered quadratic equations or a senior trembling with exhilaration and anticipation as he flashes his first college acceptance letter. No matter how angry I get when I think about what the larger world may have in store for them, I owe my life to children, and I am forever grateful for the hope and joy their smiles and hugs engender.

INEQUITIES IN URBAN EDUCATION

Ruba Monem

What issues of equity and social justice exist in urban educational systems? Because of my life experiences, I have been exploring that question for a while. I have come to believe that society would like for us to assume that the components of our educational system—teachers, administrators, school boards, etc. work in synchronicity; but that belief seems merely an illusion. In reality, in the richest country in the world, educational opportunities for most urban children are obstructed by physical barriers, discriminatory practices, and inferior classroom instruction. I have personally witnessed as a sibling, parent, and teacher the adverse effects of institutionalized Ableism and how educational institutions have stigmatized and marginalized students with disabilities in urban settings. The disparity in educational equality sets students up for subsequent social inequalities. Such inequalities are detrimental for individuals with disabilities and perpetuate stereotypes that allow prejudices about disabilities.

LIMITED ACCESS TO EQUAL EDUCATIONAL OPPORTUNITIES

After reading Jeannie Oakes' research in "Schools that shock the conscience," a story of gross inequities in California schools in the 21st century, I've begun to wonder if we will ever make much progress in the movement for equity in education. In my own state, I have repeatedly observed how students with disabilities in urban systems are set up for failure. In the early 90's, I watched my oldest brother struggle with severe learning disabilities and the torment that ensued from his school placement. He was humiliated on a daily basis by being forced to attend classes in an annex of his high school designated as the "H Wing." The "H" was short for handicapped. Students were bused in from all over the county to attend classes in this very large urban high school with a predominantly African-American and Hispanic population. It was supposed to be one of the best technical schools in the state. However, as soon as the students in special education classes stepped off the bus, they were whisked away and segregated from the rest of the student population. My brother's high school years were an absolute nightmare for him and he dropped out in the 11th grade. My brother's experience definitely jaded my view of education because it went against everything I had ever believed about equity in education. He did not have access to other parts of the school or many of the resources available to other students. The school was ill-equipped to handle its population of students receiving special services.

Unfortunately, not much has changed in the year 2012. Students who are perceived as "undesirable" by educators are intentionally (and unintentionally) isolated from their peers. Is this supposed to be separate but equal? Jeannie Oakes (2010) helped open my eyes and view the problem through a different lens. What if the school served a predominately White population? Would the conditions have been the same? After reading the details of *Williams v. California*, I think that the conditions would have been markedly better if the school served a predominately White population. Because students were bused into a school with a significantly high African American and Hispanic population, the students were discounted. It seems that school officials saw no need to provide adequate instructional materials or qualified teachers. Perhaps school officials believed that such "undesirable" students were undeserving of a quality education, or that these students were "lucky" to attend a technical school, and should, therefore, be thankful that they were even allowed to go to the school. I now see that it was elitist, bureaucratic nonsense. So, how much progress has been made in the movement for equity in education in the past 20 years, or for that matter 50 years? I would have to agree with Jeannie Oakes' assertion that significant changes have been made, but we still have a long way to go.

CULTURAL RECIPROCITY

I was brought up with beliefs and values that were firmly rooted in a culture of ability-based independence and self-reliance. My cultural background played a fundamental role in my family's management of my brother's learning disabilities. The presence of strong-willed, independent-spirited American culture was significant in my upbringing and heavily influenced my view on disabilities. My brother received special education services for most of his academic career. My family never dwelled on his disability. We encouraged him to attend a technical school and pursue a trade of his own choosing. However, his learning environment was not as supportive as we were. There was a direct conflict between the culture of the school and the culture of our home. The culture of the school did not reflect an emphasis on students' strengths; rather it focused on their weaknesses and disabilities. Somewhere along the way, there was a miscommunication that led to a complete incompatibility between the goals set by the school and the goals set by my family.

Although the presence of any one ethnic culture did not play a prominent role in my childhood, the exposure to diverse cultures (Hispanic, Asian, Greek, Turkish) was enough to give me an insight into different attitudes towards disabilities. Many of my parents' friends held drastically different views on disabilities. During their visits to my family's home, I had the opportunity to experience the beliefs and values of different cultures. These diverse cultures were very considerate of people with disabilities. However, some of them held great pity for the person with the disability and the associated "burdens" placed upon his or her family. Thus, some of those friends showered my family with pity and sympathy. These attitudes stood in stark contrast to the independent, strong-willed American culture of my family. We did not view people with disabilities as burdensome.

Had my family's beliefs about academic and social abilities been miscommunicated? Did we fail to convey our beliefs that an individual is only limited by his or her own inner restrictions? Could a mutual cultural understanding have enhanced my brother's learning experiences and bridged the gap between home and school? As Delpit (2010) asserts, learning extends beyond classroom walls. Teachers can better measure the progress of a child when they recognize, respect, and understand a child's home culture. My brother's school failed to consider his personal experiences and connect them to his classroom assignments. In order to accommodate families with diverse cultural beliefs, teachers must be open to educating themselves on how different families view and manage disabilities. Perhaps, once this has been accomplished, schools and families can engage in mutual goal setting that is suitable for the future social and academic needs of the child and is consistent with the families' beliefs (ERIC Clearinghouse, 1999). Could cultural reciprocity have contributed to a successful collaboration between my brother's school and my family? In retrospect, I believe it could have.

In "Culturally Responsive Pedagogies," Delpit discusses marginalized populations, such as special education students. Successful adults, who received special services as students, attributed their successes to their teachers. To me, this is incredibly poignant. Delpit reminds us that we must reflect on our teaching practices and be cognizant of the influence we have over our students. All too often, we watch students enter classrooms that do not reflect their beliefs, cultures, or values. Racially and ethnically diverse students with varying levels of academic achievement are met with teachers, curriculum, and social environments that do not meet their needs. Exacerbating the problem are teachers who feel that students with disabilities are underachievers. These teachers project their attitudes onto their students, resulting in students' negative feelings towards learning.

As professionals who serve marginalized populations, we have the opportunity to empower and motivate our students to succeed. We can accomplish these goals by practicing culturally responsive teaching (CRT). We need to focus on students' diverse cultures, values, and unique personal experiences. We can use individualized information and learning styles as building blocks to maximize student's learning potential and promote positive learning outcomes (Ladson-Billings, 1994; Delpit, 2010). We live in a society designed to thrive on capital, but unfortunately, in our school systems, not all human capital is valued or appreciated. Our complex systems are not set up to place value in diversity or cultural capital. Cultural reciprocity seems too often to be nonexistent. This must change.

SETTING LOW EXPECTATIONS

The beliefs and values I hold about an individual's capacity to learn were solidified when I became the mother of a child with a disability. My son lost his ability to hear around the age of 10 months. His conductive deafness had gone undetected for years. I did not know my son could not hear until he was three years old. He was a curious, responsive, lively child, and there never seemed a need for concern. What we didn't know then was that my son had taught himself to read lips and was able to vocalize words. His speech was not delayed, but it was a bit unintelligible. Medical doctors told me that I should consider teaching him American Sign Language (ASL). In essence, they were telling me to give up on my child's ability to ever produce "perfectly" enunciated words. They set the bar very low and told me that my son's current speech level would be as good as it gets. I refused to let their low expectations crush my spirits. My son's speech was awkward for society, but it was not awkward for him or me. I opted not to teach my son ASL. I went with my gut feeling and decided that he should continue to use his speaking voice to communicate.

Doctors advised me that corrective surgery might improve my son's hearing, but there was no guarantee that he would be able to hear. He had multiple corrective surgeries over the course of two years and slowly regained his ability to hear. When he entered pre-K, he was still in the transition from a non-hearing world to a hearing-world. It was a difficult transition. One day when I picked him up from school, he was crying. When I asked him what was wrong, he answered, "Stop all the noise. I hate it. I don't want to hear." He went on to tell me that the teacher was mean because she would not repeat things for him. She had even yelled at him for following her around the classroom and asking to see her face so that he could read her lips. As a result, he had to sit by himself and look through picture books while the other children were allowed to play and participate in activities. My son felt sad, lost, and left out in class. I was extremely upset and hurt. How could the teacher be so cruel to my child? I comforted him and told him that tomorrow would be a better day. The next day, I scheduled a meeting with the principal. The principal told me that my son was "different" and that the teacher did not have time to focus on his "differences" because she was teaching the "normal" children. Obviously, the meeting did not yield results to my satisfaction; I took my complaints to the school board directors of advocacy and Special Education services. After that, the school was more than happy to provide my child with the accommodations that he required.

My son's hearing impairment was not a cause for sadness. I did not want pity from others. I expected respect and understanding. I believed that my child was capable of achieving social and academic success and I worked tirelessly to maximize his strengths. I felt that the school system was undermining my efforts. When he could not hear, the world was a beautiful place where he could attach his own meanings to the actions he observed. When he was able to hear, the world became an ugly place where people yelled at him and held him to low standards. I never allowed my son to think that he was different or incapable of achieving anything. He did not know there was anything different about him until others pointed out his differences. Fortunately, I made many right decisions along the way. I did not shelter my son and always conveyed high expectations. I advocated for him and refused to let his school suppress his innate desire to learn. The ability of students to succeed and be problem solvers is underestimated, or completely ignored by academic professionals. As such, human potential is not developed. As Parker (2010) points out, parents and communities need to be advocates for quality education. Unless someone raises a question or demands change, academic standards will always fall short of bringing out the best that our students have to offer.

Undoubtedly, different schools take different approaches in their efforts to prepare students for their respective roles in society. The economically advantaged schools provide dynamic instruction in their determination to prepare students for vital positions in a technology driven market. This is in stark contrast to the economically disadvantaged schools which provide scripted direct-instruction geared towards preparing students for lower-tier service related jobs. In *Quality Education as a Constitutional Right* (2010), both Cortés and Parker provide several examples in which professionals discount the quality of education provided to marginalized populations by following curricula that does not draw on creativity, and, even worse, emphasizes an abundance of drill and kill practice exercises. Quality learning outcomes are replaced with acceptance of low expectations and poor teaching practices.

Although legislature has been passed to ensure equality in education, equality begins at the very basic level in each classroom. Cortés and Parker provide evidence for their arguments that marginalized populations are not exposed to quality teachers who deliver instruction beyond mediocrity. My experiences in the field are further documentation for their research and practice. I am convinced that failure to convey high expectations to marginalized students will allow Ableism and other discriminations to persist.

REFLECTION

My decision to become an educator and focus on special education was based on the negative experiences I had with my own child and the poor standard of education that my brother received. Sadly, my brother was reduced to a statistic, a male high school drop-out with learning disabilities. I was determined that history would not repeat itself. I refused to allow negative forces to dictate my son's path. Today, my son is an incredibly intelligent 10 year-old with a 10.6 reading level. In fact, his elementary school library does not hold any books with a readability level high enough to meet his needs. He also has a 12th grade vocabulary level and can hear a pin drop! He has since been exited from speech services. The only extra academic services he receives are the ones delineated on his Gifted Educational Plan, a plan that every child should receive—for all of our children are gifted!

Underpinning my view on teaching practices, family involvement, and communication with diverse cultures is a coupling of personal experiences and the new knowledge I have gained by studying scholars involved in demanding quality education for all of the nation's children. As a result, I have become more highly sensitive to the way I approach methods of instruction and communication with linguistically and culturally diverse families. I have gained a deeper perspective on the importance of setting high expectations and placing emphasis on children's social and academic abilities. I have also gained a deeper respect and appreciation for all familial contributions, regardless of purported capacity. After all, who among us can possibly predict human capacity?

I have also gained a wider understanding of society's barriers and bridges to students' success. It is society that assigns labels to an individual. Consequently, the people around an individual often determine the set of decisions an individual has to make. Therefore, I believe an individual is the product of his or her environment. If we can improve the environment, we can improve the outcome for the individual. School cultures can be toxic. They can either be barriers or bridges to success. The culture of a school plays a pivotal role in the success of a community and its people. A healthy, supportive school culture can empower its students and prepare them to improve the overall outcome of their community. Setting positive expectations and conveying a can-do attitude is essential. Too often, school cultures work against the community instead of working for the community. Should I have caved in when the culture of my child's school expressed to me that my child was lacking in their culture? Was my child inferior because he was not part of the dominant school culture? To me, he was not. To others, unfortunately, he was inferior. That kind of attitude can no doubt impact the lives of students as they transition into adulthood and thwart their attempts at upward mobility.

As I see it, a disability is only a disability when someone tells an individual it is a disability and that individual chooses to accept it. Some of us teach our students about diversity in gender, race, and ethnicity. We rarely discuss diversity in abilities. Students learn about Helen Keller and that is pretty much it. What about Stephen Hawking? What about teaching our students about the Special Olympics? We rarely see teachers or other school site personnel with disabilities. I have never worked with a teacher who had a physical disability or a visual impairment. I believe students can learn a valuable lesson from being exposed to adults with disabilities and other diverse individuals who live successful, fulfilling lives. Perhaps the most important thing I have learned through my personal experiences and through studying scholars and teachers devoted to social justice is that no one should ever doubt the power of the human spirit. When we expect great things, great things will happen. When we tell children they are great, they will be great.

REFERENCES

Cortés, E. (2010). Quality education as a civil right: Reflections. In Perry, T., Moses, R., Wynne, J., Delpit, L., Cortez, E. (Eds.), *Quality education as a constitutional right: Creating a grassroots movement to transform public schools* (pp. 102–114). Boston, MA: Beacon Press.

Delpit, L. (2010). Culturally responsive pedagogies: Lessons from teachers. In Perry, T., Moses, R., Wynne, J., Delpit, L., Cortez, E. (Eds.), *Quality education as a constitutional right: Creating a grassroots movement to transform public schools* (pp. 167–187). Boston, MA: Beacon Press.

ERIC Clearinghouse on Handicapped and Gifted Children. (1991). *Communicating with culturally diverse parents of exceptional children.* (Report No. E497). Reston, VA. (ERIC Document Reproduction Service No. ED333619).

Harry, B., Rueda, R., & Kalyanpur, M., (1999). Cultural reciprocity in sociocultural perspective: Adapting the normalization principle for family collaboration. *Exceptional Children, 66 (1),* 123–136.

Ladson-Billings, G. (1994). *The dreamkeepers: Successful teachers of African American children.* San Francisco, CA: Jossey-Bass.

Oakes, J. (2010). Schools that shock the conscience: What Williams v. California reveals about the struggle for an education on equal terms fifty years after Brown. In Perry, T., Moses, R., Wynne, J., Delpit, L., Cortez, E. (Eds.), *Quality education as a constitutional right: Creating a grassroots movement to transform public schools* (pp. 62–79). Boston, MA: Beacon Press.

Parker, K. N. (2010). Stepping stories: Creating an African American community of readers. In Perry, T., Moses, R., Wynne, J., Delpit, L., Cortez, E. (Eds.), *Quality education as a constitutional right: Creating a grassroots movement to transform public schools* (pp. 116–135). Boston, MA: Beacon Press.

Section 4: Seeing the Brilliance in All of Our Children Expands the Genius of Nations

Please watch the *YouTube* video: www.youtube.com/watch?v=BWf-eARnf6U

After watching the video, with your partner, answer the questions below in the spaces provided:

- ◆ What did you like most about this video?

_____

_____

- ◆ Who seems to hold the most power in this video?

_____

_____

- ◆ What do you see in the video that relates to teaching diverse students?

_____

_____

- ◆ What can you do in the classroom to give more power to students in the learning process?

_____

_____

Please take 5 minutes and compare the readings by Delpit and Monem, selecting any ideas from each article that speak to the brilliance of all children. Write the ideas in the space below.

_____

_____

_____

_____

_____

_____

After writing those ideas, please consider the following:

- ◆ Join at least four other classmates and discuss your answers.
- ◆ Once discussed, choose a piece of music (from a digital device: laptop, cellphone, etc.) that carries a similar theme to anything discussed in either Delpit's or Monem's article.
- ◆ After 10 minutes for finding the piece of music, play the music for the class.

- As a class, critique the value of using music in K-12 classrooms to assist students in learning abstract ideas.

Now that you have worked with a small group, please answer the following questions:

1. Name a strength that you have that contributes to the group's effectiveness. _____

2. Name a quality that you need to learn to help the group be more effective. _____

3. Name a strength of each of the people in your group. _____

_____

_____

4. Name a quality that each needs to learn to help your group be more effective, _____

_____

_____

5. How is reflection a useful tool for all of us in learning new ideas and behaviors? _____

_____

_____

_____

SECTION 5

REFLECTING ON OUR LIVES FOSTERS CRITICAL THINKING IN OUR CLASSROOMS

Image copyright Monkey Business Images, 2012. Used under license from Shutterstock. Inc.

I am raising two children, a son and a daughter. I want them both to aim for the oval office and not the probation office. I shudder at the possibility that one or both of them, as well as count-less other African American children, could end up with cellmates rather than classmates . . . the school to prison pipeline. . . . makes the stakes too high and too grim for many children sitting in our classrooms.

—*Ron E. Miles "Funneling urban youth from schools to prisons"*

CHAPTER 5

WHITE PEOPLE, YOU WILL NEVER LOOK SUSPICIOUS!

Michael Skolnik

Posted March 19, 2012

I will never look suspicious to you. Even if I have a black hoodie, a pair of jeans and white sneakers on . . . in fact, that is what I wore yesterday . . . I still will never look suspicious. No matter how much the hoodie covers my face or how baggie my jeans are, I will never look out of place to you. I will never watch a taxi cab pass me by to pick someone else up. I will never witness someone clutch their purse tightly against their body as they walk by me. I won't have to worry about a police car following me for two miles, so they can "run my plates." I will never have to pay before I eat. And I certainly will never get "stopped and frisked." I will never look suspicious to you, because of one thing and one thing only. The color of my skin. I am white.

I was born white. It was the card I was dealt. No choice in the matter. Just the card handed out by the dealer. I have lived my whole life privileged. Privileged to be born without a glass ceiling. Privileged to grow up in the richest country in the world. Privileged to never look suspicious. I have no guilt for the color of my skin or the privilege that I have. Remember, it was just the next card that came out of the deck. But, I have choices. I got choices on how I play the hand I was dealt. I got a lot of options. The ball is in my court.

So, today I decided to hit the ball. Making a choice. A choice to stand up for Trayvon Martin. 17 years old. black. innocent. murdered with a bag of skittles and a bottle of ice tea in his hands. "Suspicious." that is what the guy who killed him said he looked like cause he had on a black hoodie, a pair of jeans and white sneakers. But, remember I had on that same outfit yesterday. And yes my Air Force Ones were "brand-new" clean. After all, I was raised in hip-hop . . . part of our dress code. I digress. Back to Trayvon and the gated community in Sanford, Florida, where he was visiting his father.

I got a lot of emails about Trayvon. I have read a lot of articles. I have seen a lot of television segments. The message is consistent. Most of the commentators, writers, op-ed pages agree. Something went wrong. Trayvon was murdered. Racially profiled. Race. America's elephant that never seems to leave the room. But, the part that doesn't sit well with me is that all of the messengers of this message are all black too. I mean, it was only two weeks ago when almost every white person I knew was tweeting about stopping a brutal African warlord from killing more innocent children. And they even took thirty minutes out of their busy schedules to watch a movie about dude. They bought t-shirts. Some bracelets. Even tweeted at Rihanna to take a stance. But, a 17 year old American kid is followed and then ultimately killed by a neighborhood vigilante who happens to be carrying a semi-automatic weapon and my white friends are quiet. Eerily quiet. Not even a trending topic for the young man.

We've heard the 911 calls. We seen the 13 year old witness. We've read the letter from the alleged killer's father. We listened to the anger of the family's attorney. We've felt the pain of Trayvon's mother. For heaven's sake, for 24 hours he was a deceased John Doe at the hospital because even the police couldn't believe that *maybe* he LIVES in the community. There are still some facts to figure out. There are still some questions to be answered. But, let's be clear. Let's be very, very clear. Before the neighborhood watch captain, George Zimmerman, started following him against the better judgement of the 911 dispatcher. Before any altercation. Before any self-defense claim. Before Trayvon's cries for help were heard on the 911 tapes. Before the bullet hit him dead in the chest. Before all of this. He was suspicious. He was suspicious. suspicious. And you know, like I know, it wasn't because of the hoodie or the jeans or the sneakers. Cause I had on that same outfit yesterday and no one called 911 saying I was just wandering around their neighborhood. It was because of one thing and one thing only. Trayvon is black.

So I've made the choice today to tell my white friends that **the rights I take for granted are only valid if I fight to give those same rights to others.** The taxi cab. The purse. The meal. The police car. The police. These are all things I've taken for granted.

So, I fight for Trayvon Martin. I fight for Amadou Diallo. I fight for Rodney King. I fight for every young black man who looks "suspicious" to someone who thinks they have the right to take away their freedom to walk through their own neighborhood. I fight against my own stereotypes and my own suspicions. I fight for people whose ancestors built this country, literally, and who are still treated like second class citizens. Being quiet is not an option, for we have been too quiet for too long.

Read more: http://globalgrind.com/node/828497#ixzz1pIlnvFvw

YOUNG BLACK MEN IN MIAMI

Renatto Hernandez

What happened to Miami youth, Trayvon Martin, in Sanford, Florida is a travesty; and the discussions in its aftermath remind me of how dumbfounded I am whenever I learn that people I know believe racism no longer exists. The comment from Fox broadcaster Geraldo Rivera, that the hoodie was as much responsible for Trayvon Martin's death as Zimmerman, seemed to have come straight from the Theatre of the Absurd. Although, contrary to those voices, some role models are taking a different stand. The Miami Heat, for example, took a picture in hoodies that brought media attention to the charade of law enforcement in some places and for some people.

I know this dilemma on a personal level because I have faced racism for being Hispanic at times when I have left Miami, but once I return to the city, that hate for Hispanics vanishes. As a high school teacher in Miami, however, I have heard horror stories from many of my black football players. They seem to face discrimination almost every day in class from authority figures like teachers and outside of class from police officers. The teachers, I had assumed, would be looking out for my players' interests with support and service; instead, however, an attitude seems to pervade the halls where too many adults assume that our black athletes are "up to no good."

I taught an African American recipient of an Athletic Scholar Award whom the police pulled over at least once a month because he drives a green Cadillac that his mother owns. He told me that after getting pulled over repeatedly, he has come to the conclusion that he respects authority figures only after they earn his respect. He also told me that often after being pulled over in the morning for "driving while black," he has lashed out at teachers because the frustration of the earlier injustice got the better of him. I worry that some of the players I teach and coach may one day get fed up with racist authority figures, and when refusing to show submissive slave-like behavior, may end up getting suspended, arrested, or quite possibly killed. Trayvon Martin might easily have been one of my students, too upset to ignore the hostile act of someone following him around in his own neighborhood, simply because he was black and wearing a hoodie in a gated community.

The tragedy of his murder made me again realize how here in Miami, African-American males are vulnerable to racism, not just from white Americans, but from Hispanic/Latino Americans. The denial of the racist culture here that has surfaced as a result of conversations about Martin's death reminded me, too, how important it is that I continue to share with students my story about the moment that changed my perception of dealing with racism in the world around us.

That story begins with my being raised in the projects of New Jersey. Our school and apartment building was a mixture of Hispanics, Indians, and blacks. I usually played outside with the kids in my neighborhood, and they often came to my house for drinks and snacks. When I was 10 years old, my older sister started dating a black man named Mike. Mike was a great guy, he treated my sister like a queen. He also wouldn't mind when my sister brought me along to the movies, or on other dates when she was "babysitting" me. One day I asked her why she hadn't told Mom and Dad about Mike. She said she didn't know how they would take it. I convinced her to tell my parents about Mike while listing all of his great qualities. That night my sister told my parents about Mike, and I was present for moral support. It was at that moment I realized my parents were racists. My parents raised us a certain way, but they did not believe in what they were selling us. My parents forbade my sister to continue to date Mike using the excuse, "What will our family say?" After that day, I never saw Mike again, and I never brought him up to my sister.

Discovering that my parents were "low-down" racists was not only an eye-opening experience but also one that hurt me. My parents allowed me to hang out with my black friends inside and outside of the house, but blacks were not good enough to be part of our family. At that moment I began to think, that if my parents were racists, the whole world most likely was. Trayvon Martin's murder brings all that back to me now.

THE CHILDREN LEAD ME ONE STEP AT A TIME

Alexandre Lopes[1]

I am Brazilian and Portuguese is my native language. I was born into a white, middle-class family, and I grew up in the mountains that surround the beautiful city of Rio de Janeiro.

My parents always valued education, and they went out of their way to provide me with the best one they could afford. They did not trust the Brazilian public education system. Thus, they paid for my many years of private schooling.

I never thought of my family or myself as racist. I am embarrassed to confess, though, that I do not have a single Brazilian friend who is not white. Maybe my limited circle of friendships was due to my being in classrooms with only white classmates during my entire Brazilian academic years. Regardless, however, I am ashamed to admit that until recently, I had never given that detail a second thought. But now I am fully aware that something was wrong with that picture. Moreover, I have a feeling that even back then, I also knew that something was incorrect, yet it was convenient for me to ignore it.

Out of convenience, I chose to live a life of denial. For instance, on the day of my sister's wedding, when Seu Joel made the comment to my father, in front of me, that he was pleased that he had been invited to the party, but that he thought that it was odd that he was the only black person there. My father and I both dismissed Seu Joel's comment. My father gave Seu Joel one of his big smiles and a tap on the shoulder but said nothing. I quickly turned and went to grab a drink and a bite to eat, leaving the uncomfortable situation behind.

Seu Joel, whom my father not only respects as a professional but also as a friend, was then and is now in the construction business and is an expert in his craft. I, too, have respect and admiration for Seu Joel and his work. Every now and then when I return to Brazil to visit family and friends, I still run into him. Well into his eighties now, Seu Joel still imbues his art with the same passion and professionalism as he did when he was a younger man. And I am always happy to see him. However, I now wonder if whenever he sees me, he reads in my eyes the admiration that I have for him, or the shame that I carry for having turned a blind eye to the color of his skin and to that of many others in our community. I am afraid that he will notice that those same eyes of mine that were blind to his skin tone and other non-whites see clearly the privileges that the white color of my skin affords me. Does he see that hypocrisy in me?

At the age of 26, I came to live in the United States as a new immigrant. It was the opportunity I needed to claim my newly acquired non-native status as an excuse to ignore the advantages that my white skin offered me, and I succeeded in believing that my non-native status precluded my privilege as a "white" man. However, that deception did not last long. The truth began to unravel within me that the color of my skin could make things easier for me in America, the same way it could when I lived in Brazil. The only difference in this country vs. Brazil is that, for some perverse reason, white in the United States is also synonymous with "American." So in this country, I knew when necessary, I could simply keep my mouth shut, and I would be assumed to be fully an "American" man. Preventing my accent from coming out, I can still be as white as any "American" and continue to take advantage of the same privileges I had before immigrating to this country. It is sad and demeaning that I have chosen, many times, to betray my own cultural identity in order to fit in, that I gave up my own voice in order to pass for a white, middle-class American and to take advantage of the benefits that come with such status.

I have now lived in the USA for seventeen years. My command of the English language has improved considerably since I first arrived in this country. Nevertheless, until recently, I was obsessed with what I used to call "proper" English and now know better to call it "standard" English. From my arrival into the country, I consumed myself trying to get rid of the smallest trace of an accent in order to speak the "Standard English" I found so appealing. I used to think that my fixation with the English language was related to my interest in the cultural and linguistic aspects of different societies, specifically to the society in which I had chosen to live. However, I know now that, once again, I was trying to deceive myself. I simply wanted to be perceived in this new country as a white American.

I am, indeed, attracted to the culture and language of different societies. However, by believing in a "proper" English and by attempting to discard my accent, I was trying to use English as I had used Portuguese while living in Brazil—to ensure that those who heard me knew exactly to which caste of our society I belonged. It is difficult to admit, but I know now that part of my obsession with "Standard English" is my wanting to fit in and that, in a certain way, it is a reflection of my previous identity in Brazil. It is a desire to establish myself socially and to distance myself from the non-white members of the societies in which I live. I do not think that I consciously desired to create such distance, though. My doing so was nothing but the sad and ugly subconscious reflection of growing up in a society filled with institutionalized racism and then, later in life, trying to fit into a different society plagued by the same pest.

I wish I could say that I had not fallen prey to institutionalized racism. I also wish that I could deny having fallen prey to the structures of oppression that dictate what is proper and improper in our society—yet, I fell prey to both. I fell prey to institutionalized racism and to the structures of oppression present in our society, but not as the victim of those sociological diseases, rather as the victimizer and the oppressor. I wanted to believe that I had internalized, as a victim, the structures of oppression in our society that command that "Standard English" is the only English to be considered "proper"; and, thus, as a Latino man with an accent, I could hide out as a victim of language oppression. I almost fooled myself into thinking that—believing my role as "victim" would make things significantly easier for my conscience. By turning myself into the victim, the oppressed, I thought I might offer myself redemption on a silver platter and seek penance for my own denial as racist in the same comfortable and convenient manner that is so familiar to Latino/Hispanics who share my skin color—stay in denial.

Life has taught me many lessons, though, and one of them is that when you exclude, you, yourself, become excluded. The isolation that I created between so many of my peers and myself ultimately became intolerable, and the burden of my so desired individuality turned out to be unbearable. Nonetheless, life gave me a second chance. Luckily though, from a life of exclusion, forces guided me into an inclusive environment where I teach pre-kindergarten children with and without disabilities.

Some of my three, four, and five-year-olds are white, and some are black. Some of them speak "Standard English," and some do not. Some are language impaired, and some are English language learners. In addition, the school in which I teach is classified as a Title I school, and the majority of the families served by it share a common lower socio-economic denominator. Furthermore, a substantial number of my colleagues belong to minority groups themselves, and I have learned not only to respect them as professionals but also to love them as friends.

I have also learned to value every communication attempt, every dialect in my classroom, in our community, and in the society at large. My students have taught me to take nothing for granted, including my language ability and the color of my skin. I do teach my students Standard English, but not at the expense of their home language and culture (Wynne, 2003). I want them to be able to have both. As Lisa Delpit insists, I want my students to have the warmth and affection of the language and culture they share with their loved ones (Delpit, 2003). On the other hand, I want my precious little ones to have as many opportunities as possible in the lives they choose to lead when they grow up; therefore, while allowing their home languages to fill our room, I, at the same time, am teaching them the standard English dialect.

My students have, indeed, taught me many lessons, and I wish I could say that they caused me to change, but I cannot. What made me change was the courage that I found within myself to look at my reflection in the mirror and recognize the biases that I carry with me for being a white, middle-class male. This I did while I was enrolled in an Ed.D. program, studying issues that children, families, teachers, and communities face in urban schools (Wynne, 2005). I am now aware of the vices to which my white skin has become addicted. Furthermore, I realize that my addiction is not going to easily disappear. I must have the strength to continuously fight it. It is here that my students come in. They give me the inspiration and motivation needed to keep fighting. They give me reason to start over when I go astray; they remind me that, as long as I take one step at a time, I will be okay. Above all, my students always forgive me, and, for that, I am and forever will be humbly grateful.

REFERENCES

Delpit, L. (2003). "No kinda sense." *The Skin that we speak: Thoughts in language & culture in the classroom.* Delpit, L. & Dowdy, J. New York: The New Press.

Wynne, J. (2003). "Who talks right?" *The Skin that we speak: Thoughts in language & culture in the classroom.* Delpit, L. & Dowdy, J. New York: The New Press

_____(2005). "Teachers as leaders in urban education: Testimonies of transformation." *Readers of the quilt: Essays on being black, female, and literate.* J.G. Dowdy (ed). Cresskill, NJ: Hampton Press.

END NOTES

1. Alexandre Lopes was selected Teacher of the Year for his public school district in 2012 and is now a finalist for the State Teacher of the Year.

FUNNELING STUDENTS INTO THE SCHOOL-TO-PRISON PIPELINE

Ron E. Miles

INTRODUCTION

After spending several years studying diverse human cultures, I decided to actively interrogate perceptions of the cultural group with which I identify—African Americans. While having experienced some progress, African Americans as a group are still embattled in a struggle against social, political, economic, and educational inequality, which suggests progress, like quality schools, is not a universally enjoyed reality in the U.S.

Educational disenfranchisement and criminalization of African Americans are personally and professionally unacceptable to me. I am raising two children, a son and a daughter. I want them both to aim for the oval office and not the probation office. I shudder at the possibility that one or both of them, as well as countless other African-American children, could end up with cellmates rather than classmates. So I've come to believe that Colleges of Education and public schools need to overtly address these threats to children's well-being. Teachers everywhere must challenge themselves to create classrooms where learning is inevitable and inviting. Students must have a better chance for success in the classroom than in the streets or in a jail cell. For these students, my children, and for teachers, I share, in this essay, what I have learned about the school to prison pipeline. That pipeline makes the stakes too high and too grim for many children sitting in our classrooms.

This study examines the link between failing urban schools, high rates of incarcerations among African Americans, and the spread of Islam in prisons. The systemic failure of urban public schools to educate and accommodate the learning needs of all students is an essential component of the "school-to-prison-pipeline" (ACLU, 2011). That failure has created a funneling of urban youth, particularly African-American males, out of schools and into prisons. So we must ask: What can schools do to retain African-American students and help them maintain their freedom? Why is it that African Americans comprise over half the total prison population? Why do African-American inmates gravitate to the Islam religion? What aspects of the Islamic faith resonate with African-American inmates? To answer these questions, my study makes reference to ideals from postmodern educational theory and scholarly Islamic literature to provide an analysis of the school-to-prison policies that systematically rob urban youth of their academic potential, life purpose and personal freedom.

SCHOOLING AND SOCIAL JUSTICE

The political "Establishment" of the late 80's early 90's launched a disempowerment and disenfranchising assault on people of color and women in an effort to rescind many of the rich curriculum and freedoms that schools afforded these populations in the previous two decades. As Stanley Aronowitz and Henry Giroux (1991) suggested "the new retributive framework provides a legal mechanism for controlling black and Latino communities" (p. 8). This same framework set the stage for new policies that would also dictate the paths and potential in quality of life that certain groups could enjoy. The unfortunate groups of students, mainly African-American, Latino and other students of color, who could not manage to achieve proficiency on any given battery of tests consequently fail to gain access to the perks and privileges generally available to those in mainstream society. As Aronowitz and Giroux (1991) explained: "A student's failure to meet approved academic standards is tantamount to a sentence from a court of law. The accused is condemned to what some political economists term the secondary labor market" (p. 9). The obvious result has been a steady stream of students into the margins of society, minimizing their possibility of achieving the consummate American dream. The problem, especially for many students of color, is that the standards of learning in school have little to do with the knowledge and experiences that have meaning and value to them. As Aronowitz and Giroux (1991) pointed out: "The poor kids, most of them of color, opted out of school success nearly as much as they were rejected by school authorities for reasons that parallel traditional working-class rejections of school knowledge: to surrender to the curriculum entails more than choosing to acquire cultural capital. That is, school knowledge is loaded with class terms" (p.12).

Such terms are strategically peppered throughout the curriculum to remind students of their place (or at least the one they are meant to occupy) in society's hierarchy. Students who live in poverty or suffer from discrimination often decide to drop out of school rather than face these deplorable reminders on a daily basis. According to the Racial Justice website of the American Civil Liberties Union, if students do not drop out, they are administratively pushed out of school through district level school-to-prison-pipeline policies. "This pipeline reflects the prioritization of incarceration over education" (ACLU, n.d).

When the focus of schools is placed on filling jail cells rather than classrooms with students, it can be easily inferred that America's public education has lost its way. This is why so many unsuspecting young people ultimately lose their way in the hallways, playgrounds and classrooms of America's public schools.

AFRICAN AMERICAN PRISONERS ON THE RISE

Black males are more likely to serve time in jail or prison than members of any other demographic (Kusha, 2009). African Americans have found themselves facing prison sentences for crimes that are not always violent in nature, such as protesting service in the army. According to Kusha, "The inordinately high incarceration rates of African-American males—next to that of Hispanics—has continued with some variations unabated since the 1960s to the present; this constitutes one of the most profound challenges that the American penal system is now facing in the new millennia." Kusha concluded that, "The American criminal justice system does not provide equity as it dispenses penal justice" (p. 67). This sentiment was shared by James (2007) who suggested that, "Of the 2 million plus incarcerated in the United States, 50 percent are people of African descent. Overwhelmingly, this majority is detained (or designated for executions) largely due to racial and economic bias in racial profiling and sentencing" (p. 19). The large percentage of imprisoned African Americans is staggering compared to the total estimated number of African Americans in the United States, which according to the 2010 U.S. census (U.S. Census, 2010) is approximately 12.6% (roughly 39 million) of the total population of nearly 309 million U.S. citizens.

ATTRACTION TO ISLAM

According to Haddad and Esposito (1998), "Islam is the fastest growing religion in America and in Europe. There are, for example more Muslims in America than in Kuwait, Qatar, and Libya. It has been common to speak of Islam and the West, but today any consideration of that topic must include Islam in the West (p. 3). Haddad and Esposito also surmised that, "Islam in America is a mosaic of many ethnic, racial, and national groups. The majority are first- or second-generation immigrants or African-American converts (p. 4). Islam also finds its way to many more African Americans inside American prisons. According to Marable (2009) for "over the past thirty years, Islam has become a powerful force in the American prison system . . . prison officials have allowed Muslim inmates to practice and proselytize relatively freely" (p. 290). However, Islam takes many forms, and it would be a glaring mistake to see the religion and its followers as homogenous in their composition, practices and dispositions. Haddad and Esposito (1998) duly noted that:

The earliest African-American Muslim communities were in fact a response and reaction to the "negro, black, or African-American" experience. Early leaders . . . emerged in the 1920s and 1930s . . . .most influential was Elijah Muhammad and the Nation of Islam. The spiritual descendants of Elijah Muhammad, from Muhammad Ali and Malcolm X to . . . Louis Farrakhan, epitomize the diverse currents that account for much of the African-American Muslim experience (p. 11).

The Nation of Islam and other Islamic orders seemed to offer a counter narrative to being in prison, providing a new path of inquiry for countless African-American males in prisons.

Kusha (2009) suggested that Islam is seen as attractive and relevant to African Americans due in part to "the powerful social justice message of Islam, as well as with the nature of the prison life which is by and large oppressive, violent and dehumanizing" (p. 3). Dennin (2002) understood African Americans to be attracted to Islam because "in most cases conversion to Islam is depicted as a return to the cosmic order. The Muslim sees this as the sine qua non for personal redemption, the road back to virtues obscured by the forces of subjugation and injustice" (p. 6). Marable (2009) supported this notion and explained that, "By embracing Islam, previously invisible, inaudible, and disaffected individuals gain a sense of identity and belonging to what they perceive as an organized, militant, and glorified civilization that the West takes very seriously (pp. 288-289).

One of the more popular conversion narratives appears in the Autobiography of Malcolm X, which was written with Alex Haley. Dennin (2002) described some characteristic reasons for conversion:

The ritual and the narrative theme resolve the historical tensions of African-American society by concluding that liberation from racial domination and spiritual redemption are one in the same. The end goals require an indefatigable dedication to transform oneself and one's fellows. 'Verily, Allah does not change the state of a people until they change themselves inwardly' (Quran 13:12) is by far the most frequently quoted scriptural passage among African-American Muslims (p. 7).

As is the case of anyone who converts to Islam, African-American inmates are looking for redemption, a purpose and a pathway to paradise beyond the walls of prison. Islam demands that all Muslims must follow five core principles in order to gain discipline and direction in the struggle. McCloud (1995) delineated those:

1. the *shahada* or intial acknowledgment of the deity as noted above;
2. *salat* ("formal worship"), wherein believers pray and seek guidance five times daily, while enaging continuously in Qur'anic recitation;
3. *sawm*, a fast wherein believers refrain from food, drink, idle talk and behavior and worldly pleasures from sunrise to sunset for thirty days the month of Ramadan;
4. *zakat*, a constant awareness of what is accumulated during the year so that the excess is taxed and shared with the community at a rate of 2.5 percent at the end of the month of Ramadan; and
5. the *hajj*, a pilgrimage to Mecca, in order to reenact the major events described in the Qur'an that predate and sustain the first Muslim community. (pp. 2-3)

The practice of the above pillars of Islam give incarcerated African-American Muslims a heightened sense of self-respect, freedom and belonging to a global community that serves the will of what they interpret as the one and only almighty, Allah.

RESISTING "WASP" IDEOLOGIES

Many African Americans have gravitated to Islamic traditions for almost a century now. In fact, Islam initially came to the United States on the backs of captured Africans who served as slaves throughout the new world. As Haddad and Esposito (1998) noted, "African-Americans are heirs to a triple cultural heritage: African, Islamic, and Western (p. 12). Traces of the slave plantation system can be seen in the American penal system. Like slavery once did, U.S. prisons continue to relegate African Americans to subhuman status, which challenges their identity as citizens of this nation. The plight of African Americans is a direct result of slavery (Blackmon, 2009) and the subsequent policies that continue to promote racial inequality, social injustice and Eurocentric hegemony. The western, Eurocentric culture abounds in all aspects of daily American life much to the chagrin of many diverse groups, especially African Americans. Islam is there to provide a form of resistance, guidance and protection to all believers of the faith.

DOUBLE STIGMA

Islam has not been highly regarded since people began to pay attention to that religion in the last fifty years or so. The Nation of Islam was a specialized brand of Islam, which really deviated dramatically from the much larger and mainstream Sunni tradition. Non-Muslims may not be aware of the diversity that abounds within and among the various Islamic groups. However, Haddad and Esposito (1998) explained that "Despite the fact that Islam is the third largest religion in the United States and that by now most American Muslims have been born and raised in the United States, the American media continue to view Islam through the prism of the Iranian revolution, regarding it as a retrogressive religion given to extremism and terrorism. (p. 14) The image of Islam has gotten much worse in the last decade following the terrorist attacks on various points in the United States on September 11, 2001. In effect, those attacks prompted the U.S. government to issue legislation and policies that would expand the powers of the policing and penal entities, which some scholars have begun to critique the ways in which "the United States wages war not just against criminals but also against people it constructs as such, i.e., against criminalized peoples" (James, 2007, p. xiv). African Americans have been constructed as criminals under such policies. Of course, Muslim Americans are adversely affected by such policies. And now, African-American Muslims must face stigma on multiple planes. They are not only constructed as criminals, but now they are also branded as terrorists via association with Islam. Yet, experts in the field agree that Islam is not a violent religion and all the people who are affiliated with the religion do not necessarily wish to do harm or enact violence on the United States (Kelsay, 2007).

In the same way that African-American is <u>not</u> analogous for crime, Islam is <u>not</u> analogous for terrorism. Everyone, especially educators, need to do more to combat negative images and begin to provide appropriate opportunities to disseminate truthful information.

DISCUSSION

In some respects, the mainstream American society has begun to view Islam through a similar lens of misunderstanding, fear, and ignorance that historically has been focused on African Americans. Because of the adverse position that Islam and African Americans occupy in relation to mainstream American society, they both have to confront varying levels of social stigma and socio-political attacks. It is in the outer most margins of society, more precisely in U.S. prisons, that Islam and African Americans have begun to discover the mutual benefits in aligning with each other. African Americans, with their longevity and connection to United States, are able to give legitimacy to Islam by helping it to fall under the umbrella of all things "American." Meanwhile Islam provides a more deeply rooted, connection to the "African" cultural identity of African Americans. Dennin (2002) asserts: "Almost 90 percent of the converts to Islam in the United States are African Americans, a trend whose meaning has not been lost to prominent Arab- or Asian-American Muslims who desire to build a political coalition with the goal of enhancing their position in American society" (p. 12). However, Haddad and Esposito (1998) reminded readers that it is not wise to presume the existence of any semblance of solidarity among Muslims.

In summary, all groups place borders around themselves on the basis of perceived difference in culture. Cultural borders can only be bridged through patience, understanding and a desire to accept differences. A major opportunity exists for schools to start this process. Unfortunately, many schools choose to uphold the racist and hegemonic policies and practices that perpetuate inequity in American classrooms and society. As the tenets of the Racial Justice Program suggest, "Children ought to be educated, not incarcerated" (ACLU, 2011). Educators and non-educators alike have a responsibility to challenge the policies and practices within public school systems and juvenile justice systems that make the school-to-prison pipeline a daily ritual all across this country (ACLU, 2011).

Moreover, if greater numbers of African Americans and other minority groups could see themselves and their interests embedded in school curricula and policy, more students might be inclined to stay in school and out of prisons. To achieve equity in American schools, all children, regardless of their socio-economic, ethnic, racial, linguistic, national or religious background should be able to express their cultural heritage, share their voices and experiences and use instructional time to broaden their worldview and that of their classmates. Teachers can achieve these goals by embracing a multicultural approach to education (Nieto, 1992) and allowing all student groups to participate in the construction of knowledge. Experts in culturally responsive pedagogy, like Nieto and Delpit (1997), insist that such practices hold promise to engage disenfranchised students, fostering their desire to stay in school and out of America's prisons. Educators play a vital role in the awakening of the critical voice inside all young people. Educators effectively demonstrating how to value different opinions and perspectives is imperative in the 21st century.

Postmodernism offers educators a number of tools, one of which is border pedagogy that requires instructors and learners to "undermine and re-territorialize different configurations of power and knowledge" (Aronowitz & Giroux, 1991, p. 118). The requires a willingness of educators to steer classroom learning toward themes that resonate with the lives and experiences of their students. Moreover, border pedagogy "also incorporates popular culture as a serious object of politics and analysis, and makes central to its project the recovery of those forms of knowledge and history that characterizes alternative and oppositional Others" (Aronowitz & Giroux, p. 119). While there is an appropriate place in the curriculum for learning about the "great men," appropriate learning spaces should include "other" great men, women, children, histories and cultures (1991). Islam is one of the world's great religions; yet it, too, is often excluded from the curriculum in much the same way that African Americans, Latinos, First Nations and others sidelined by society have been omitted.

CONCLUSION

Education in the United States is designed to promote and reproduce mainstream western ideologies. Anyone who does not fit the white, Anglo-Saxon, protestant mold is most often dismissed. African-American and other marginalized students typically do not see themselves in the dominant curriculum in schools, and they do not see their culture valued in classrooms. Without such vital connections to classroom culture, African-American students may be less inclined to perform at their fullest academic potential. As a result many African Americans reject school, its curriculum and its policies. The lack of motivation can lead to low achievement, poor behavior and consequent expulsion from school. Once students prematurely part ways with schools, their chances for success in life are greatly reduced, especially if they are black. Too many end up entangled in the criminal justice system. How ironic that in the penal system where many African Americans make contact with Islam, they find guidance, relevance and acceptance. But their new connection to the Islam faith adds another level of further discrimination against them.

Teachers and policy makers who want to better understand the (mis)use of school policy and curriculum to systemically suppress the potential, relevance, and benefits of leveraging the diversity of students in American classrooms might study the critical ideas of postmodernists like Aronowitz and Giroux. According to them, the refusal to recognize diversity as an essential approach to enriching student learning is done purposefully and by design. To challenge this precept, some educators have undertaken a pedagogical path that encourages students to evolve from seeing themselves as inactive objects of the schooling process, to envisioning themselves as proactive subjects of their own learning. This transformation, which is rooted in postmodern theory, requires educators to teach students how to cast a critical eye on the existing political, cultural and social structures that shape their experiences in schools, like the tragedy of the school-to-prison pipeline.

REFERENCES

ACLU (n.d.). *What is the school-to-prison-pipeline?* Retrieved from http://www.aclu.org/racial-justice/school-prison-pipeline.

Aidi, H. D., & Marable, M. (2009). *Black routes to Islam* (1st ed.). New York, NY: Palgrave Macmillan.

Aronowitz, S., & Giroux, H. A. (1991*). Postmodern education: politics, education, & social criticism.* Minneapolis, MN: University of Minnesota Press.

Ashcraft, W. M., & Daschke, D. (2005). *New religious movements: A documentary reader.* New York, NY: New York University Press.

Berger, P. L., Berger, P. L., & Harrison, L. E. (2006). *Developing cultures: Case studies.* New York, NY: Routledge.

Birrī, K. (2009). *Life is more beautiful than paradise: A jihadist's own story.* New York, NY: American University in Cairo Press.

Blackmon, D.A. (2009). Slavery by another name: The re-enslavement of black Americans from the Civil War to World War II. New York, NY: Random House, Inc.

Cochran, R. F. (2008). *Faith and law: How religious traditions from calvinism to Islam view American law.* New York, NY: New York University Press.

Curtis, E. E. (2006). *Black Muslim religion in the nation of Islam, 1960–1975.* Chapel Hill, NC: University of North Carolina Press.

Curtis, E. E., & NetLibrary, I. (2002). *Islam in black America [electronic resource]: Identity, liberation, and difference in African-American Islamic thought.* Albany, NY: State University of New York Press.

Delpit, L. 1997. *Other people's children.* New York: The New Press.

Dannin, R., & NetLibrary, I. (2002). *Black pilgrimage to Islam [electronic resource].* New York, NY: Oxford University Press.

Fitzpatrick, P. (1995). *Nationalism, racism, and the rule of law.* Aldershot ; Brookfield, USA: Dartmouth.

Gollnick, D.M. & Chinn, P. C. (2009*). Multicultural education in a pluralistic society* (8th ed.). Upper Saddle River, NJ: Merrill.

Gomez, M. A. (2005). *Black crescent: The experience and legacy of African Muslims in the Americas.* New York, NY: Cambridge University Press.

Haddad, Y. Y., Senzai, F., & Smith, J. I. (2009). *Educating the Muslims of America.* New York, NY: Oxford University Press.

Haddad, Y.Y. and Esposito, J. L. (Eds.). *Muslim on the Americanization path?* Atlanta, GA: Scholars Press.

James, J. (2007). *Warfare in the American homeland : Policing and prison in a penal democracy.* Durham, NC: Duke University Press.

Joyce, B., & Weil, M. (2009). Models of teaching (8th ed.). Englewood Cliffs, NJ: Prentice-Hall.

Kelsay, J. (2007). *Arguing the just war.* Cambridge, MA: Harvard University Press.

Kusha, H. R. (2009). *Islam in American prisons: Black Muslims' challenge to American penology.* Farnham, England; Burlington, VT: Ashgate.

Ladson-Billings, G. & Brown, K. (2008). *Curriculum and Cultural Diversity.* Connelly, F.M.(Ed.), *The Sage Handbook of Curriculum and Instruction* (pp.153-175). London: Sage Publications.

Levtzion, N. (1979). *Conversion to Islam.* New York, NY: Holmes & Meier.

Linzer, L. (1995). *The nation of Islam: The relentless record of hate, march 1994-march 1995.* New York, NY: Anti-Defamation League.

Marable, M., Middlemass, K., & Steinberg, I. (2007). *Racializing justice, disenfranchising lives : The racism, criminal justice, and law reader* (1 Palgrave Macmillan pbk ed.). New York, NY: Palgrave Macmillan.

Marsh, C. E. (1996). *From black Muslims to Muslims: The resurrection, transformation, and change of the lost-found nation of Islam in America, 1930-1995* (2nd ed.). Lanham, MD: Scarecrow Press.

McCloud, A. B. (1995). *African American Islam*. New York, NY: Routledge.

Nash, M. (2008). *Islam among urban blacks: Muslims in Newark, New Jersey: A Social History*. Lanham, MD: University Press of America.

Nieto, S. (1992*). Affirming diversity: The Sociopolitical context of multicultural*

education (2nd ed.). White Plains, New York: Longman.

United States Census Bureau. (2010). *U.S. census data.* Retrieved from http://2010.census.gov/2010census/data/

United States Congress Senate Committee on Homeland Security and Governmental Affairs. (2007). *Prison radicalization : Are terrorist cells forming in U.S. cell blocks?: Hearing before the committee on homeland security and governmental affairs, united states senate, one hundred ninth congress, second session, September 19, 2006.* Washington: U.S. G.P.O; For sale by the Supt. of Docs., U.S. G.P.O.

United States Dept. of Justice Office of the Inspector General. (2004). *A review of the federal bureau of prisons' selection of Muslim religious services providers [electronic resource].* Washington, D.C.: U.S. Dept. of Justice, Office of the Inspector General.

United States Federal Bureau of Investigation. (1999). *Malcolm X [electronic resource].* Washington, DC: Federal Bureau of Investigation.

United States Federal Bureau of Investigation. (2003). *Nation of Islam [electronic resource].* Washington, DC: Federal Bureau of Investigation.

TEACHING BROWN V. BOARD OF EDUCATION IN SEGREGATED CLASSROOMS

Jeremy Glazer

How do you teach kids, in an all African-American class at an all African-American high school, that the *Brown v. Board of Education* decision more than fifty years earlier ended segregation in public schools?

This is not a hypothetical question, but rather a question I remember very clearly asking myself during my second year in the profession.

It was my first time teaching American History and I was in a school in South Phila-delphia that seemed forgotten by time and by everyone else. I had already learned at that early point in my career one of the benefits of being at a school that few cared about was that I could do whatever I wanted. I had almost complete academic free-dom. As long as my kids weren't running in and out of the classroom, I was seen as being an adequate teacher by my supervisors, who rarely opened my door to look in.

So, instead of using the history textbooks the school owned, I spent hours and days and weeks and months crafting my own curriculum, using primary documents, arti-facts, articles, summaries, and all kinds of other techniques to try to teach history in more interesting ways than I'd been taught. The key word in that sentence is *try*. I was *try*ing. I can't say I was often succeeding, but I was trying. (That's what happens in your first few years and don't let anyone tell you otherwise. Good teaching is hard to do and it's a craft that, like any other, takes time to learn.)

But then, as I was planning my unit on civil rights, I was confronted with teaching *Brown v. Board of Education*, and the absurdity of what I was about to attempt dawned on me. There was no way I could teach my students that segregation had ended. They'd end up thinking that either they or I didn't know what the word segregation meant. And an honest consideration of what *Brown* meant in our country was not a hopeful story about law, or government, or progress, but seemed like a particularly cruel lesson in power, racism, and injustice at our still-segregated school. I imagined what it would feel like for my students to hear that, as far as the law was concerned, our daily reality at that school did not even exist.

It was a complicated discussion we needed to have, and I knew this discussion would be necessarily limited by the lack of diversity in our environment. I could not figure out a way as a white, Jewish teacher in an all African-American school to make the discussion feel wide-ranging and productive. I couldn't think around the limits I saw, and I kept returning in my head to the fact that the whole point of *Brown v. Board* was that these kinds of conversations in these kinds of classrooms

94

weren't supposed to happen any more. And yet, there we were. It was truly a lesson in the absurd.

I remember my depression, as I planned the unit, more than I remember the details of how I ended up dealing with the issue in class. I do remember that the concepts of de facto and de jure segregation, of red-lining and other discriminatory practices came up. But what stuck with me for years was my frustration at my inability to do what I thought I needed to do. I could not figure out how to educate my children gently and humanely while being honest, and I could not figure out how to productively incorporate the injustice confronting all of us in that classroom into my pedagogy.

But that's exactly what you need to do when teaching in most of the large public institutions in our nation. So many things about the experience, as we constantly wrestle with issues of injustice, are absurd. You have to figure out how to use the absurdity to further what you are trying to do, which is to get kids to think, to understand, to love learning. Working with the absurdity is part of the struggle.

I only spent one year in that particular school in South Philly. I was privileged in my career to have the opportunity to teach in a wide range of environments—city schools, suburban schools, public schools, and private. And, I was lucky enough to teach a variety of populations, from all black to all white, with a few mixed schools thrown in as well (one, due to a stroke of lucky geography that put it at the intersection of three distinct neighborhoods, was in almost equal parts black, white, and Asian). But I found that truly diverse school populations—and here I'm using the word diverse to mean *different from each other* as opposed to what it has come to mean in code, which is *non-white*—are exceedingly rare. This is a shame for a variety of reasons, the most obvious being that if we are ever going to be a truly multicultural, democratic society, we need not only to know and learn about each other, but also be comfortable with each other, something accomplished only through proximity.

And that proximity, that sharing of *diverse* ideas, doesn't often happen, even in the so-called mixed schools. My last year teaching was spent in a suburban school with significant Anglo, black, and Latino populations. I was teaching a "regular" class. These weren't the AP students, or the honors students, but the lowest level, often called "regs" (yes, the pun on dregs was intended) by my colleagues. It was my first period, and I was supposed to make the kids watch the announcements, which were put on by the TV production class and broadcast over the closed-circuit TV for the last five minutes of class every day.

My students mostly refused to pay attention to the announcements, and I refused to fight with them about it (I was saving my energy to fight with them about reading—I learned after several years to always know which battles are worth fighting.) But, I did find it interesting in an anthropological way why they didn't listen, particularly because they were a generally well-behaved class. I was talking to one of the kids about it one time, asking him why he didn't pay attention to the announcements.

"Those aren't for us," he told me. "Those are for the other kids."

I knew instantly what he meant. The announcements mostly contained news about prom and various other fundraisers and events, the school newspaper, yearbook. All of those activities were populated by the "other" kids—the mostly middle-class white kids in honors or AP classes. They were the ones who put on the announcements as well, so they were talking to each other, not to the "regular" students who weren't involved. The announcements weren't aimed for the *diverse* population, just one level of it.

Segregation doesn't just happen at the level of the school. It happens at the level of individuals. For the growth of students, it's important to push them together, to help them be comfortable with each other, with different ways of seeing the world. And, when we we are in schools with many different groups, it's important to facilitate those collisions. These truly diverse populations are the richest environment for discussions because by their very natures they throw a wide range of spotlights/perspectives on whatever it is you are talking about, be it a political or historical event, a work of literature, even a scientific discussion. When you have many groups who bring in radically different experiences to a discussion, you can't help but emerge with a wide range of questions and critiques. A discussion about *Brown* in a room with a variety of children—rich, poor, black, white, Latino, Asian—is a very different discussion than one in an all black classroom in an all black school.

But it isn't always possible to bring together different students in your school or in your classroom.

As I said before, based on my experience in two of our nation's largest school districts, a diverse classroom population is too rare. So many of our public schools are segregated (a vast majority in both school districts where I taught are over 70 percent of one ethnic group or another). And, even in the schools that are not segregated, classrooms often are. Leveling and other scheduling maneuvers separate, both wittingly and unwittingly, different groups. Segregation is an evil that we have to deal with for the moment. (This does not mean we shouldn't continue to fight and rail against it, to try to open up our classrooms. A colleague and I, she at an all black school the year I was at an all-white private school, had our kids write letters back and forth to at least try to open up discussion. Unfortunately, it never got further than that). But there's a point where you have to deal with the reality on the ground, when you have to deal with the fact that you don't have a diverse population. And it's important to realize that there's opportunity there as well.

It's up to us as teachers to bring some of the beneficial effects of diversity where it doesn't exist—to find ways in to difficult discussion, ways to introduce challenging points of view where they may not otherwise exist. That was my job in teaching a civil rights unit in a segregated school. I needed to find ways to bring all kinds of voices into that discussion, and the experience was depressing for me precisely because I couldn't figure out how to do it, how to have the discussion I knew we needed.

But l learned from that experience and others. I developed as a teacher and became more able to do what I needed to do, and this occurred to me years later when I encountered a situation both strikingly different and strikingly similar to that experience from my second year. And when it happened again, when I was once again forced into an uncomfortable place by segregation, I remembered that depression, the shame in not being able to reframe the experience my students were having in South Philly, and this time I used what seemed like a deficit to my advantage.

This time, I was teaching American Literature in an almost completely white, exclusive private school in the Miami suburbs and we were going to read *Huck Finn*. The book was not my choice, particularly in that setting, but the curriculum had been set before I got there. I figured that if we were going to read this book, I was somehow going to have to figure out how to have an honest discussion about race.

I had seen race come up in previous discussions at the school, both among students and faculty, and such conversations often devolved into a mention of the fact that the handful of black students who were in the school separated themselves by insisting on sitting together in the cafeteria. That was not the kind of narrow discussion I wanted in my class.

I thought back to my experience in South Philly teaching *Brown v. Board* in my all African-American class, and one thing that did stick with me from that whole year was the openness with which my African-American students talked about their views of and experiences with white people. It was an honesty that I found was more difficult to achieve in a mixed school, for obvious reasons. Sure, in South Philly I as the teacher was white, but my students mostly ignored me in discussions anyway. It was like I was visiting from another planet, so they were not shy about talking about white people at all, and seemed to feel comfortable in a way my students the year before, in a class filled with blacks, whites, Asians, and Hispanics, had not.

I remember one particular remark from a South Philly student very clearly. After another in a series of nationally televised school shootings at suburban schools occurred, my student said to me, "White people are crazy! I'd be scared to go to one of their schools."

With my memories of South Philly in hand, I set out once again trying to figure out how to negotiate the absurd, this time in a very different, but similarly limited, environment. How on earth was I going to have a real discussion about race, one that allowed my privileged students to get beyond facile understandings to more problematized notions, in the homogeneous environment of an exclusive private school?

I thought about critical race theory articles I had read, I thought about taking on the notions of why "they," the privileged, sit together in the cafeteria, about reading some Patricia Williams, or Lisa Delpit, or Peggy MacIntosh. But what I wanted was something that would jolt my students into a kind of honesty that analysis may not engender. And finally, I figured out a way to use the fact of segregation as a window in, how to use the disadvantage to my advantage.

I decided to come up with some survey data we would collect on ourselves. I came up with ten innocuous questions, including *How many of you have driven in a car with a friend? How many of you have slept over at a friend's house. How many of you have had a friend to dinner? How many of you have been to a friend's for dinner?* These were questions I knew would be non-threatening and would be answered in the affirmative by almost all of my students. We did the survey in class, I had them count up their yeses and almost every student had ten yeses out of ten.

Then I had them turn their papers over for part two of the survey. I asked all ten questions again, but this time I put black in front of the word friend. Instead of asking for their scores, I asked them to think about the difference in the number of yeses.

It was a jolt, because for almost all of the students, the survey results were vastly different with the word "black" inserted. There was no way to deny it. The data in front of us was clear. It was fact now, this segregated world we lived in, and it was also clear that we were all making some choices in the way we lived our lives that were perpetuating a separation, intended or not. That gave us an opening for discussion. We first could talk about what we noticed, generally, without any individual feeling defensive. We could start to explore how their lives had come to be constructed in a particular way, to help them understand the part they played in what we saw around us. It was an exercise that would not have been as effective in a mixed class, and I simply would not have tried it.

As a class, we opened up a larger discussion of race, we watched Spike Lee's *Bamboozled*, read a few articles, and went on to struggle through *Huck Finn* together, attempting to tackle difficult questions of race and language. And this time, unlike in South Philly, I was not depressed about the absurdity and how I had handled it. I saw some of the students opening up. Several started bringing in articles they had seen, DVD's of shows (like Ali G) to discuss what these representations meant, to think through these difficult issues together. The discussion was rich. Again, not as rich as what can be achieved in a diverse audience, but at least there was the consolation that some students were more honest than they might have been in a mixed class.

I want to be clear that the lesson here is not that a segregated class is better or easier. It's not the ideal for so many reasons, both pedagogical and moral. But, segregated classes are a reality, albeit an absurd reality in the twenty-first century, but one we have to deal with nevertheless. It's just another of the absurd realities confronting our public schools right now.

The lesson is that, within all these absurdities and otherwise uncomfortable realities, you need to use whatever tools you have to challenge students to have the most honest discussion possible.

And so now I think it's time to return to my original question: How do you teach kids in an all African-American class at an all African-American high school that the *Brown v. Board of Education* decision more than fifty years earlier ended segregation in public schools?

You don't, because it didn't. What you do is you try to figure out how to use what you're given, how to take the environment where you teach as an asset that's as much a part of your curriculum as anything. You try to weave the daily experience you and your students have in a way that provokes thoughtful, honest discussion and does what we're supposed to do as teachers: to get kids to think, to understand, to love learning.

Section 5: Reflecting on Our Lives Fosters Critical Thinking in Our Classrooms

Please take 30 minutes and write in the space below your own reflective story about any issue of diversity that is addressed in one or more of the four articles represented in this section. It doesn't need to be a formalized piece, only a first draft of your thinking on these issues.

_____

_____

_____

_____

_____

_____

_____

_____

_____

_____

_____

_____

_____

_____

_____

_____

_____

_____

_____

_____

_____

_____

After writing those ideas, please consider the following activities:

- Choose a partner to share the writing, either read it aloud or ask your partner to read it silently.

- Ask your partner to cite particular ideas that struck her or him as important to your story.

- Ask your partner if he or she finds questions still left to be answered in your story.

- Ask your partner if there is anything missing in your story that might make it clearer.

- Jot down ideas that you now think you should add or subtract from your story to make it clearer for a reader.

- Save this draft as a possibility for a future essay about teaching diverse students.

1. With your class, view the *YouTube* presentation on TED.com of Bryan Stevenson: www.cnn.com/2012/03/11/opinion/stevenson-justice-prison/index.html?c=us

2. After watching the talk on TED.com, choose a partner to discuss any stories and/or ideas from Stevenson's talk that particularly appealed to you.

3. Discuss how the school-to-prison pipeline is created through institutionalized racism.

SECTION 6

LEARNING RESPECT FOR OTHER PEOPLE'S LANGUAGE CAN FREE STUDENTS' MINDS

Image copyright file404, 2012. Used under license from Shutterstock. Inc.

No amount of encouragement from me would prompt them to speak. . . . until that moment, I did not understand how psychologically damaging language biases are. I watched eight students . . . shrink from their brilliance. Here they sat, knowing they had competed . . . and won—yet, at the same time, they felt inferior. They were silenced by language biases born of racism, biases that crippled their inquisitive natures. Their typical bold acts of discovery became impotent in the midst of the majority.

—Joan Wynne "Who Talks Right?"

CHAPTER 6

WHO TALKS RIGHT?

Joan T. Wynne

"The world is richer than it is possible to express in any single language."—*Ilya Prigogine*

It was over twenty years ago, but it could have happened yesterday. I had taken a group of African American high school newspaper staff to a university journalism workshop and awards ceremony. There were about eight students with me that day to learn more about print journalism, and, more importantly, to receive an award for one of the ten best high school newspapers in the metropolitan area.

We were sitting together, in a sea of White faces, listening to one of the media experts talk about ways to improve school newspapers. After he had spoken, he opened the session to questions. My students had several they wanted to ask in their effort to discover new ways of writing creatively for their peers back at school. One of my editors leaned over to me and whispered, "Here are a list of questions we want you to ask him."

I said, "No, you ask him," surprised that my student and his cohort were suddenly shy.

"We don't talk right. You ask him."

No amount of encouragement from me would prompt them to speak. What I now know is that until that moment, I did not understand how psychologically damaging language biases are. I watched eight students, who happened to be some of the brightest young people I have ever taught, shrink from their brilliance. Here they sat, knowing they had competed with other journalism staffs for the best newspaper—and won—yet, at the same time, they felt inferior. They were silenced by language biases born of racism, biases that crippled their inquisitive natures. Their typical bold acts of discovery became impotent in the midst of the majority. And the majority lost a golden opportunity to hear my students' thoughts and learn from their brilliance.

Looking back now, I recognize the full measure of my own mis-education. My schooling had not prepared me, as an English major, to understand the depth and breadth of language oppression. No one had taught me that the language I had grown up loving was used to bludgeon others into submission and feelings of inferiority. But even worse none of my teachers had ever encouraged me to assist these youngsters in creating a psychological sanctuary so they didn't succumb to unfounded language bias when exposed to the dominant culture. In the absence of that instruction, I had made those adolescents vulnerable to the prejudices of the majority, reflected in their own internalized notions of being linguistically inadequate. Nothing had prepared my students or me for that moment of defeat, a moment when they should have been reveling in victorious celebration.

Many years later, during a trip to South Africa, I was once more made aware of the contradictions in perceptions of language prowess between a dominant culture and the "other." While helping to build houses in Alexandria, a black township outside of Johannesburg, I consistently heard from White South Africans how deficient Black South Africans were in their use of language, how they were slow in thinking, and how much "like children" they were. In fact, almost every complaint reminded me of the remarks describing American Blacks that I had heard while growing up in the south. Again, though, those remarks were in conflict with the reality that presented itself to me as I worked in Alexandria. I was often surrounded by young children attempting to help in our construction efforts. Their warmth and friendliness always charmed me, but it was their language facility that totally disarmed me. Those small children, four, five, six, and seven year olds, easily moved from speaking Swahili to Xhosa to English to Afrikaans to Zulu, and several other languages that I can't even remember the names of now. In that small two-mile radius of a township, where over two million people from many different cultures were herded together by the rules of Apartheid, Black children had quickly learned to communicate across the cultural divides. Amazingly, though, despite that gift of language facility, the same insidious myths about language superiority ran rampant. And the myths are destructive. They lie about people's ability to think, and, perhaps, equally as tragic, they prevent the dominant culture from learning from the gifts of "the other."

Sometimes, the lie seems to take on a life of its own. At Morehouse College, the country's premier African American male college, where I taught for fourteen years, I observed intelligent, sophisticated students misled by those myths. There, young men parroted what they had heard mainstream English teachers, like myself, proclaim for years, that the use of standard English was "talking right." In Morehouse classrooms, the students and I would often struggle through discussions on the speech patterns of the children who lived in the housing projects surrounding the college and who were mentored by the Morehouse students. My college students often would argue with me about my contention that those children's language was as valid as theirs. Because the Morehouse students had fallen prey to invalidated linguistic assumptions of the mainstream culture, they had no tolerance for the speech of these children. The mentors assumed that the children's speech indicated not only linguistic, but cognitive deficit. Of course, if we want these children to be socially and economically mobile in mainstream culture, we must teach them standard English; yet, when we reject them because we reject the language they grew up with, we alienate them from the very places where they could learn the standard dialect. And by teaching children that their language is inferior, we teach a lie.

The lasting impact of that lie became clear again only last week at a town meeting of parents in a small southern school district where approximately three to four hundred middle and upper-middle class mainstream parents and working class African American parents met to discuss possible changes in their elementary schools. Out of the twenty or so parents who spoke at the microphone, only one was an African American parent. After the meeting I was told by several of the African American mothers that while they felt very strongly about the issues at stake, they could not and would not speak to the whole group because they felt uncomfortable about their speech in front of those mainstream parents. They had no trouble articulating their ideas to me, but only after I had approached them asking why they had chosen to remain silent. Like my former journalism staff, those parents harbored the mistaken notion that their speech was not good enough to air in front of a majority White audience. Yes, the distortions we teach in schools last a long time. In those places we begin to hush the voices that might lead the way out of the labyrinth of our educational malpractices. That silencing "like a cancer grows" (Simon & Garfunkle, 1966).

TEACHING LANGUAGE SUPREMACY DISTORTS REALITY FOR MAINSTREAM CHILDREN

I believe that the abuses of linguistic oppression toward the children of color are horrendous; the consequences are severe; and the damage to the self-esteem of youths is unconscionable. But, I also believe that there is another dark side to this issue—the severe consequences of notions of language supremacy for the children of the dominant culture.

By neglecting to teach about the beauty and richness of the language of Black America, we do as much damage to White children as we do to our African-American students. If we believe as James Baldwin that all languages define, articulate, and reveal individual realities ("Black English", 1997), then by not recognizing Ebonics, we keep white children trapped in myopic visions of world realities. We give them one more reason to bolster their mistaken notions of supremacy and privilege. If we believe, too, as Baldwin suggests that Black English "is rooted in American history," then, by discounting Ebonics, we keep White children oblivious to significant slices of their own country's history. We deny them the opportunity to look at their own ancestors and history in a way that might help them recognize their collective responsibility for injustices, as well as their collective potential for redemption.

In a nation that is home to a multitude of cultures, and in a world that, through technology, has become a global village, cross-cultural respect and understanding are imperative. Yet if our mainstream children think that their language is superior to others, how can they expect anyone else to believe that they, the privileged, value other people's cultures? With such notions, how will our children, then, ever work collaboratively across cultures to build those bridges of understanding that will allow people to cross the racial divide that separates us as a nation, a world, and a species?

We have learned that prejudice of any kind can stifle our children's growth in critical thinking. In The Open and Closed Mind (1960), M. Rokeach found that:

Persons who are high in ethnic prejudice and/or authoritarianism, as compared with persons who are low, are more rigid in their problem-solving behavior, more concrete in their thinking, and more narrow in their grasp of a particular subject; they also have a greater tendency to premature closure in their perceptual processes and to distortions in memory, and a greater tendency to be intolerant of ambiguity (p.16).

As Rokeach suggests, by fostering prejudice such as language biases, we stifle all students' cognitive development. Thinking their language is a superior language, which is, after all, what too many teachers teach and too many in society believe, White children may become incapable of really hearing other cultures and, thus, learning from them (Allport, 1958; Hall, 1990). For as long as mainstream students think that another's language is inferior to theirs, they will probably not bother to understand it, and therefore, there will be much about the other that they will always fail to understand. Not only will this further widen the cultural divide, but it will prevent the group in power from accessing the knowledge base—and, subsequently, potential solutions to a myriad of world problems—of those deemed "other" by virtue of language form.

Several weeks ago one of my university colleagues explained to me that he had recently tried to listen to a noted African American historian who, during a television interview, continuously referred to every Black person he spoke about as "Brother" or "Sister." This cultural tradition seemed excessive to my friend, annoying him to the point that he felt forced to switch the channel. The seemingly intrusive nature of this different linguistic ritual kept him from hearing the message of a nationally respected scholar of history. For him, and I think for too many of us, our obsession with the familiar form can obliterate the significance of the content. This kind of unconscious intolerance of difference, in my 30 years of experience in the education profession, pervades academia, cutting us off from learning from one another.

What is the outcome of my colleague being so uncomfortable with a cultural pattern of speech that it forced him to "tune out" a speaker whom he knew as a reputable scholar? Might his reaction suggest the serious intellectual consequences of intolerance, cited earlier in Rokeach's study, that if cultural intolerance is strong, it is more difficult to take in new information? Except for those with telepathic gifts, language is the closest way humans know of getting inside another person's head. If our tolerance of language diversity is so fragile that we turn away from those persons who exhibit cultural linguistic patterns different from ours, how can we ever expect to begin to understand each other and, thereby, build a community of learners? If the tolerance is that fragile, how can those of us who are responsible for educating the next generation of teachers, adequately teach them to be sensitive to the language differences of the children they teach or of other faculty members with whom they work?

LANGUAGE SUPREMACY AND THE EDUCATION OF TEACHERS

Recently, I gave a short questionnaire to 15 pre-service teachers at a university asking them their opinions about Ebonics and Standard English. These students are in their last months of their undergraduate program. Because they were not new to the university nor to teacher training, I was surprised at some of their responses. Most of the students responded to the question, "How would you describe 'Standard English'?" with the answer, "Correct English," or "Proper English." When answering questions about the description and use of Ebonics, one intern said, "To me, ebonics is the use of incorrect english. . . . I do not think that allowing children to speak 'ebonics' in the classroom does them a service. I think that 'standard english' is the grammatically correct form of the English language." His response typified the others in the group.

One student response, however, seemed more emotional and dogmatic than the others. "Ebonics," she said, "should not be allowed in the classroom. Our education system should not cater to lower standards of language." She and few of the other soon-to-be teachers seemed to know one of the basic tenets of linguistics: that languages are defined politically not scientifically—and that a "language is a dialect with an army and a navy" (Dorsett,1997, O'Neill, 1997). The responses of the pre-service teachers seemed to reflect no awareness that each dialect and language has an internal integrity unto itself; that one language clearly is not scientifically better than the other, but that one is politically more acceptable than the other—for one dialect belongs to the power structure (Dorsett,1997; Fillmore, 1998; Perry & Delpit, 1998).

As I continued to read the comments of these university students, I wondered why, when language is the major medium of instruction, would we in schools of education give so little time, effort, and attention to teaching our pre-service teachers about the basic assumptions of the realities of language diversity? Why would we choose to ignore the significance of instructing all of our interns, whether they are to teach mathematics, science, language arts, or shop, that language is a political decision and a group experience of a lived reality, not a manifestation of intellectual prowess or language superiority?

In the same semester, in another course of 34 graduate students, most of whom are practicing teachers, I listened to a class discussion about African American children's language. This very heated debate emerged from discussing the question, "What is excellence in urban education?" During the discussion, none of the students addressed the political nature of selecting one dialect as the "standard dialect." The one thing that all participants seemed to agree upon was that all students needed to know "proper" or "correct" English. Many insisted that anytime a student used Ebonics in the classroom, she should be corrected. How is it that we might forget to inform every pre-service and in-service student that all teachers are obliged to honor the many languages we speak? As James Baldwin, Toni Morrison, and many others suggest, language is who we are. If any of us refuse to respect the other's language, it becomes too easy, consciously or unconsciously, to then disrespect the person.

Later, I gave a language attitude questionnaire to five teachers, who were asked to give them to their individual faculties. With very few exceptions, the teachers' responses reflected the same assumptions about Ebonics and "Standard English" as the university pre-service and graduate students. One teacher answered that Ebonics should never be spoken in the classroom because "it sounds ridiculous and illiterate." Without an apparent understanding of multilingualism in any form, another teacher said all children should speak "Standard English" because, "We are a part of the Human Race and Standard English is the common denominator," adding that Standard English was a "neutral and universal language." Even those teachers who voiced some respect for Ebonics speakers, agreed that children should not speak Ebonics in the classroom.

With the research that is now available about the importance of schools accepting a child's home language while still teaching them the standard dialect, too many teachers are astoundingly ignorant of the basic truths about language. The lack of knowledge about language development amongst many of our teachers spoke to a gap in the professional development of these teachers; and, to me, it suggests as well how insignificant many colleges of education may assume that kind of knowledge is.

For someone like myself, who growing up in a segregated south saw "up close and personal" the dangers on the psyches of children who are never given a forum to examine all notions of superiority, this kind of neglect is no small matter. To cavalierly omit, from the education of those who will teach and are teaching our children, discussions of the political ramifications of language use and acceptance is an egregious failure. Teachers without this knowledge will limit White children's worlds and make children of other ethnicities vulnerable to schools' and the larger society's negative views of their cognitive competence.

Again, none of this discussion is to suggest that the Standard Dialect is not to be taught to our students from kindergarten through college—it is after-all the language of power, the chosen form of communication of those who own the missiles, the tanks, the banks, the bombs and the government. It is simply that its importance as a dialect must be put in a context that produces less damage to ourselves and our students. Glorifying Standard English as a superior mode of expression is intellectually limiting.

WHAT SHOULD HAPPEN IN CLASSROOMS?

Nothing short of a revolution in our language instruction will suffice. For, mainstream children and children of color suffer from their linguistic "mis-education." Ironically we, in the dominant culture, do not seem to recognize the contradictions in our attitudes about the language Black people use. We are fascinated with the cleverness of Ebonics, as shown by our incorporation of many of its idioms into our everyday speech. For example, mainstream television personalities such as the Today Show's Katie Couric and Matt Lauer have consistently used such phrases as "Don't 'diss' me like that" and "my bad" during their morning banter. Mainstream advertisers, too, often use expressions and rhythms from African American "Rap" to sell their products. Yet, at the same time, most of our media and educational institutions insist that the language is somehow inferior to the Standard Dialect. Perhaps, we might share those kinds of contradictions with our students as a way to begin our conversations about the political nature of language choice.

The brilliance of the writing of Toni Morrison, a fact well accepted by most people in the mainstream, as indicated by her receiving the Nobel Prize for literature, might also be a great starting place for yeasty discussions of the merits of diverse languages and dialects, of issues of racism, and of the power of story to connect us to our individual and collective history. Using her words to teach African American children the majesty of their home languages and White children the beauty and validity of other languages is a powerful tool for helping to set the record straight about the legitimacy of Ebonics as a powerful language form. When Morrison explains that language "is the thing that black people love so much—the saying of words, holding them on the tongue, experimenting with them, playing with them. It's a love, a passion," she suggests a very different relationship between her people and their language than is portrayed anywhere in the mainstream culture. It's a perspective that pre-service and in-service teachers might explore to counteract the erroneous messages that academia, the media, and other institutions send us about the inferior "dialect" of African Americans.

Linguist, Charles Fillmore, in a speech delivered at UC Berkeley, suggested that educators "offer serious units in dialect in middle school and high school classes throughout the country as a general part of language education" for all children (Fillmore, 1998). Walt Wolfram, another noted linguistic scholar, suggested that activities in such units might enable children to "discover generalizations and systematicities in their own speech and in the speech of others" (Fillmore, 1998).

Recently, hearing "the speech of others" caused a visceral re-awakening in me of the power of language diversity. While attending Al Sharpton's "Shadow Inauguration" rally in Washington, D.C., I heard a dozen or more African American speakers give testimony to the part they, their parents, or their grandparents had played in turning a nation around. They spoke of shattering notions of segregated equality; of dismantling unfair voting laws; and of surviving as a people killings, lynching, attacks by dogs and police—wielding billy-clubs and water hoses. While listening to these stories, I thought about the Southern Freedom movement and of its impact on freedom movements in China, in South Africa, and other parts of the globe (Harding, 1999). I remembered that representatives of only 13% of the population of the United States forever changed the South, the nation, and the world. That day I stood in the midst of throngs of descendents of Africans as they chanted "No Justice, No Peace"; as they sang "Ain't gonna' let nobody turn me 'round;" and "a walkin'. . . a talkin'. . . Marching up to freedom land." The power of the words, of the rhythm, of the cadences of the slogans moved me as we marched in the rain toward the Supreme Court Building to register our disapproval of its justices' most recent decision against voting rights.

I came home with those chants, those testimonies, ringing in my ears. And I couldn't help but wonder . . . .How dare we patronize as an inferior dialect the language of such heroes and sheroes? When I have talked to those now grown-up activists who created the sit-ins of the 60's, who walked in the marches, who survived the jails, they have shared the power of the chants, the songs, the language to keep them alive, committed, and unified in a struggle that no one thought they could win (Conversations, 1988, 2000, 2001; Reagon, 1998; King, 1997). That language and those stories belong in our children's classrooms.

Joseph Campbell, in *The Hero with a Thousand Faces*, (1969) tells us that a hero must assimilate his opposite, must put aside his pride, and in the end must realize "that he and his opposite are not of differing species, but one flesh." We have to educate our White children to understand that we are, indeed, "one flesh." That we are "the other." Then, what a gift to teach them that they are connected to the heroism of those African American students who engaged in "sit-ins" and marches; who against all odds survived arrests and beatings; and who created "a dazzling moment of clarity" for the South and the nation (Curry, 2000). To be taught that they belong not only to the history of the oppressor but also to the history of those who so bravely fought and won those battles for justice is a lesson all children deserve to hear.

What a breath of fresh air it would be for our young people to read about other young people who non-violently took on a violent and corrupt government and won. To use their language and their stories in the classroom might be one of the greatest lessons of empowerment we could give all of America's children. Telling our students of the audacity of ordinary young people like themselves, who dared to think they had the right to shape the world around them, might do more toward creating critical thinkers in our classrooms than any of the other pedagogical tricks that we have up our sleeves.

Alice Walker in *The Same River Twice: Honoring the Difficult* (1996), says that ". . . even to attempt to respectfully encounter "the other" is a sacred act, and leads to and through the labyrinth. To the river. Possibly to healing. A 'special effect' of the soul." Encountering the other is difficult, for all humans, whether it be in language or in ritual; yet, for me, it sometimes seems the only way we will ever make this democracy work. If we, in schools of education, stay silent while others proclaim language superiority, how do we help our students "respectfully encounter 'the other'"? Shouldn't we, who teach teachers, create spaces in our classrooms to explore the political nature of language choices? Shouldn't we in our courses facilitate discussions about the need to value diverse languages, especially in these rocky political times? That we are sending into public school classrooms, teachers whose limited knowledge about language caused them to respond so dismally to a questionnaire about Ebonics suggests that we are failing our teachers' intellectual development, failing their future students' language growth, and failing our troubled democracy. Helping students, in a fragmented modern society, make connections to each other and to a larger world is a respectable outcome (Delpit, 1997; Hilliard, 1997; Palmer, 1998; Wilson, 1998) that many scholars believe can be advanced through the study of diverse dialects and languages. Learning the skills of reading, writing, and mathematics, as well as every other discipline can happen within that context of making connections.

As they learn those skills, our students need a time and space to explore that the interdependence of all of humanity and of all species is a concept that poets and mystics have proclaimed for thousands of years, and is now one that physicists are validating through their study of the universe, from the subatomic level to the formation of the galaxies. Our students need to understand that scientists are continuously discovering the complex interconnectedness of all life, matter, and energy. And all students need to learn that notions of supremacy, whether they come in the shape of superior races or superior languages, do not fit into that grand scheme of things (Bogardus, 1960). Finally, all of us need to remind ourselves of what Prigogine's quotation seems to suggest—that the worship of a single language limits our ability to know and to express that interconnectedness, that "full richness of the world."

REFERENCES

Allport, G.W. (1958*). The nature of prejudice.* Garden City, NY: Doubleday & Co., Inc.

Baldwin, James, "If Black English Isn't a Language, Then Tell Me, What Is?" *Rethinking Schools*, Fall, 1997, Vol. 12, No. 1.

Bogardus, E. S., (1960) *The development of social thought.* New York: Longmans, Green and Co.

Campbell, J (1968), 2ⁿᵈ ed. *Hero with a Thousand Faces.* Princeton: Princeton University Press.

Conversations with Joan Browning, February, 2001

Conversations with Connie Curry, January, 1988; February, 2000; February, 2001

Conversations with Charlie Cobb, Zaharah Simmons, April, 2000

Curry, Browning, et.al. (2000) *Deep in Our hearts: Nine White Women in the Freedom Movement*, Athens, GA: University of Georgia Press.

Delpit, Lisa. "Ten Factors for Teaching Excellence in Urban Schools" Speech at Urban Atlanta Coalition Compact Town Meeting, September, 1997, Atlanta, GA.

Dorsett, C., *Ebonics – 21ˢᵗ Century Racism?* Website: Wysiwyg//62http://members.tripod.com/~cdorsett/ebonics.htm, p. 3

Fillmore, C. (1998) "Speech at UC Berkeley," http://www.cal.org/ebonics/fillmore.htm

Gladney, M. R. (1993). How Am I to Be Heard?: Letters of Lillian Smith, p. 71.

Hall, E. (1989). *Beyond Culture.* New York: Anchor Books edition/Double Day Dell Publishing Co.

Hilliard, A. G. III (1997). *SBA: The Reawakening of the African Mind.* Gainesville, Fla.: Makare Publishing Co.

King, Mary, (1987) *Freedom Song: A personal Story of the 1960's Civil Rights Movement.* New York: Morrow.

Linguistic Society of America, "Resolution on the Oakland "Ebonics" Issue" (1997), http://www/linguislist.org/topics/ebonics/lsa-ebonics.html

O'Neil, Wayne. "If Ebonics Isn't a Language, Then Tell Me, What Is?" *Rethinking Schools,* Fall, 1997, Vol. 12, No. 1.

Palmer, P. (1998). *The Courage to Teach.* United States: Jossey-Bass.

Reagon, B. J. (1998). "'Oh Freedom'": Music of the Movement," *A Circle of Trust: Remembering SNCC.* Greenberg, G. ed. New Brunswick: Rutgers University Press.

Rokeach, M. (1960). *The Open and Closed Mind.* New York: Basic Books, Inc.

Simon & Garfunkle (1966) "The Sounds of Silence," *Sounds of Silence* Album.

Skutnabb-Kangas, Tove, (2000) Linguistic Genocide in Education—Or Worldwide Diversity and Human Rights. Mahwah, NJ: L. Erlbaum Association.

Smith, Ernie A. A Case for Bilingual and Bicultural Education for United States Slave Descendents of African Origin. Fullerton: Department of Linguistics Seminar Series, California State University, Fullerton, 1976.

Smitherman, Geneva, "Black English/Ebonics: What It Be Like?" Rethinking Schools, Fall, 1997, Vol. 12, No. 1.

Smitherman, Geneva, Talkin and Testifyin (1977). The Language of Black America. Boston: Houghton Mifflin Company.

Walker, Alice (1996). *The Same River Twice, Honoring the difficult: a meditation on life, spirit, art, and the making of the film, The Color Purple, ten years later.* New York: Scribner

Wilson, Amos (1998). *Blueprint for Black Power: A moral, Political and Economic Imperative for the Twenty-First Century.* New York: Afrikan World InfoSystems.

HIP HOP CULTURE: THE GOOD, THE BAD, AND INVITATIONS FOR SOCIAL CRITIQUE

Ron E. Miles

From working in public schools, I have recognized the benefits of leveraging Hip Hop to foster a culture of inclusiveness in the classroom. Hip Hop culture is particularly useful for teachers when trying to build relationships, based on respect and decency, with and among students from diverse cultures. Respecting Hip Hop means respecting a cultural phenomenon originated by black and brown African American, Latino, Caribbean youth, a culture of the children typically served in urban settings. Incorporating Hip Hop into the curriculum means inviting black and brown students into the center of curriculum instead of keeping them stuck in the margins. Whether you are a primary teacher searching for a great song for a game of freeze dance or a secondary literature or history teacher looking for a themed selection for students to analyze, perhaps Hip Hop culture can supply the perfect rhythm, beat or lyric that can transform students' perceptions of themselves, their peers, and their schools.

Many of us, at least a decade or older than our students, probably hold lots of reservations about Hip-hop music, language, mores, etc. We hear and see only that which seems destructive in the Hip Hop culture; yet in order to influence young people's awareness of the good, the bad, the ugly, and the profound presented in that culture (as in all cultures), we should first recognize and understand the good and the liberation messages (Alim) found within it. To ease our students toward a more critical stance of investigating those messages, we first need to educate ourselves about Hip Hop. Because it unites youth in a multitude of countries, if we enter the world of Hip Hop with open eyes and ears, we might more effectively connect with multicultural populations in our own classrooms.

GLOBAL TROTTING TO HIP HOP

The global appeal of Hip Hop culture is a phenomenon that few people predicted. Tate (2003) noted that, "the aura and global appeal of hip-hop, lie in both its perceived Blackness (hip, stylish, youthful, alienated, rebellious, sensual) and its perceived fast access to global markets through digital technology" (p. 7). Three decades have passed since Black and Latino youth experimented with spinning turntables and rhyming to a beat back in the mid to late 1970s. Hip Hop culture has given the world critical glimpses at some of the social, political and economic policies that have shaped the disenfranchised experiences of African American, Latino, and other diverse communities in the United States. Now many people around the world have adopted Hip Hop culture as a vehicle to analyze and critique local problems and conditions (Tate). Hip Hop culture could serve as a suitable tool for leveraging discussions, raising consciousness and challenging people's thinking about socially sensitive themes and issues like racism, sexism, classism and sustainability.

Hip Hop culture has criticized the socio-economic dilemmas that have stifled the progress of African-Americans, Latinos and other oppressed groups of people in the United States and abroad. Hip Hop's bold stance to speak out against social injustice has allowed it to jump across borders, classes, nationalities, creeds and ethnicities. Osumare (2005) purported that "Hip-hop culture has become a binding youth subculture that has enabled young people in disparate local communities to share a sense of a common attachment" (p. 267). Hip Hop provides an outlet for alternative perspectives, which are primary for understanding that diverse ways of thinking are needed for problem-solving in a 21st century world.

The true power of hip-hop is readily measured in its financial viability and its worldwide reach (Tate, 2003). The culture boasts a multi-billion dollar presence in the fashion, film and music industries. Its potency is also reflected in its ability to spread outside the confines of urban America into the farthest-reaching corners of the planet. Over the last three decades hip-hop has solidified an economic stronghold and ubiquitous presence. For teachers to forbid it in their classrooms seems an uncreative approach to educating children. Inviting Hip Hop in the classroom door creates a space for students to critique its flaws as well as its virtues.

Born out of the lived experiences and talents of Black and Latino inner-city youth, Hip Hop culture has brought about a certain reverence and appreciation for the plight of diverse groups. As Richardson (2006) explained: "The communicative styles and ways of knowing of the performers can be traced to Black vernacular expressive arts developed by African Americans as resistance and survival strategies. Many of the experiences, such as racism, police brutality, miseducation, and identity imposition, are issues, which are fundamental to the African American and are dealt with in various cultural expressions" (p. 12).

Although some Hip Hop artists are dissuaded from coming across as preachy in their songs, many Hip Hop artists recognize their worldwide audience is watching and listening to them very closely. The latter willingly and deliberately model and teach tolerance, aware that countless young people often mimic the artists' every move, lyric and attitude. Many popular words such as the overused "bling bling" and "shawty" routinely enter and exit the mainstream vernacular via Hip Hop Culture. Ricardson (2006) noted that, "the Hip hop lexicon is largely provided by AAVE (African American Vernacular English/Ebonics) speakers, with some words donated from Spanish, Caribbean English, and from graffiti vocabulary (argot)" (p.11). Since many students from diverse backgrounds can identify with one or more aspects of Hip Hop culture, teachers can easily leverage Hip Hop culture as a teaching tool.

Incorporating Hip Hop culture in the classroom establishes a commonality and connection among all students, allowing them to interact in a meaningful and non-threatening manner. Affording students the opportunity to interact with classmates whom they perceive to be different fosters a greater level of awareness about the vast spectrum of worldviews and approaches to life. Every student has a different collection of lived experiences. For disenfranchised students, those experiences are captured in the Hip Hop culture. In describing those connections, Osumare (2005) used a term called connective marginalities: "Connections or resonances can take the form of culture (Jamaica or Cuba), class (North African Arabs living in France), historical oppression (Native Hawai'i), or simply the discursive construction of "youth" as a peripheral social status (Japan)" (p. 268).

As students begin to understand that being different is something many people share and that difference is not in itself a negative, they may begin to appreciate their uniqueness and that of others. A heightened sense of appreciation for diversity often supports the development of compassion and empathy. Developing such qualities might encourage our students to become more active citizens who aspire social justice not just for themselves, but for all people.

SUSTAINABLE CONNECTEDNESS

American public education is well known for promoting White, Anglo-Saxon, Protestant (WASP) values and perspectives in its curricular and policy decisions (Golnick & Chinn, 2009). Shifting the focus of American education away from the westernized, business model to one concerned with the social and economic wellbeing of students, teachers, administrators, parents and communities can encourage teaching and learning that is transformative and sustainable. Sustainable education, as defined by Sterling (2001), requires a, "change of educational culture towards the realization of human potential" (p.14) and an enhanced concern about the social and ecological interconnectedness of all people and things. Hip Hop culture has made remarkable headway in raising awareness about the linkages between people from diverse backgrounds around the world. Our curriculum and pedagogy might draw upon hip-hop culture's ability to be leveraged in multiple localities while always referencing larger global issues. In each national context, students might analyze how voices from the margins, be they immigrant communities in Europe, indigenous communities in Australia, or political movements in Africa and Latin America, are using hip-hop not only to express themselves and their feelings but also to change their societies, and establish transnational networks. Or students might be asked to examine specific hip-hop cultural norms that seem to reproduce systemic inequalities like sexism and consumerism. Or we might analyze the ways in which hip-hop culture is co-opted by power, including multinational entertainment corporations (Theard).

INTERCULTURAL UNDERSTANDING

Schools and teachers should help students leverage the rich diversity present within their own population. Enhancing students' intercultural knowledge and understanding is a vital step toward fostering greater instances and levels of social tolerance (teachingtolerance.com). Students and teachers who attain a disposition for tolerance become better equipped to advocate for social justice, often understood as the fair treatment of people regardless of perceived differences. The universal fair treatment of all people requires a consensus of what is right and wrong and a steadfast commitment to end prejudice (see socialjustice.com). The more tolerant and fair people behave toward one another the more genuine, fruitful and lasting their relationships are likely to be.

Schools and educators have a major opportunity to teach students about social justice by routinely engaging all students in an equitable fashion and ensuring all students receive equal access to resources that support their academic and social prosperity. One such resource is the student's home culture (Delpit, 2006). Many diverse students claim Hip Hop culture as theirs, which creates a valuable link between students who otherwise perceive themselves as not having anything in common with their peers of another race, ethnicity or religion, or anything that is going on in classrooms. Hip

Hop culture is inherently diverse and speaks to issues that resonate with people from a variety of backgrounds. The best of Hip Hop, when students are taught to distinguish between its best and worst qualities, can support goals of social justice. The exploration of social justice issues in classrooms has implications for the U.S. and the world as new generations of diverse Americans enter the global economy.

HIP HOP CULTURE IN THE CLASSROOM

Hip Hop has become an invaluable tool for critiquing the prevalence of social inequalities, transmitting critical perspectives in a style that is infectious and enlightening (Tate, 2003). Because of its global presence and appeal, Hip Hop culture has influenced the perspectives, attitudes and actions that people from different backgrounds have developed about such social ills as poverty, hate, slavery and war (Osumare, 2005; Hill, 2009), and it serves as a common form of expression for diverse people all over the world (Condry, 2006). The culture has become an instrumental methodology for venting, critiquing and learning. Most young people encounter aspects of Hip Hop in their daily lives, and it seems to dominate the films that the youth watch; the ads shown on television and the fashion of the young. It seems to be everywhere and allows anyone to belong to something that is bigger than their turf, hood or city.

Hip-hop can be an excellent motivating force in a classroom setting for generating discussions about diversity. Open-minded teachers understand that the process of knowledge transfer is most effective when viewed as bidirectional (Nieto, 1992; Ladson-Billings & Brown, 2008). Many of today's new teachers are themselves products of Hip Hop culture. In order to learn about other cultures, it is often useful to have a firm understanding of one's own. Giving classroom space for such a powerful voice of the youth could maximize their learning while helping them critique their own culture and artifacts.

Hip Hop has also been described as an inner-city, minority, youth culture by a number of scholars (Richardson, 2006; Osumare, 2005; Kitwana, 2005). Smitherman (2006) noted that "DMX, Snoop, Ice T, the late Big Pun, 50 cent, Fat Joe, Missy Elliott, and other Hip Hop artists became household names among White youth as Rap Music moved from Black and Latino communities in Chocolate cities to the Vanilla Suburbs of the U.S." (p. 89). One scholarly study (Davis et al, 2001), compiled a list of effective strategies that schools and teachers could use to make school curricula more relevant to the lives of the students they serve (Ladson-Billings, 2004). The study entitled, *The Hip-Hop Project: The Potential of Youth Culture in the Curriculum*, (visit: http://www.tcla.gseis.ucla.edu/democracy/students/labi_hiphop.html) recommended incorporating young people's culture—Hip Hop Culture—into the classroom by:

1. Examining the messages that hip-hop artists are trying to send through their songs to promote discussions among students.

2. Looking at the experiences of the artists and having the students relate to their own experiences.

3. Examining the use of language in hip-hop and how it relates to students' use of language as well as standard English.

4. Comparing Hip-hop music to other forms of music.

5. Offering special courses that reflect student interests. Students in these courses should be allowed to conduct and publish their own research on topics like hip-hop and explore such issues as: why artists use certain language, why themes such as poverty and struggle appear often in the lyrics.

6. Comparing the themes in current rap songs with similar themes in older literary works to help students make the connection between their world and the world of literature.

As did people all over the world, Hip Hop icons and ordinary followers showed support for the victims in the attacks on the World Trade Center on September 11, 2001, Hurricane Katrina of 2005, the 2010 earthquake in Haiti, the Tsunami's in Indian Ocean of 2009 and the more recent one in Japan in 2011 through using its music and its money. Many teachers are unaware of these positive actions and messages of the Hop Hop culture. If we bring these virtues of the culture into the classroom, students may be influenced to pay attention to those virtues instead of the consumerism and sexism that is often associated with Hip Hop.

CONCLUSION

American schools, as institutions of learning and innovation, have the potential to prepare today's diverse students to confront the social, economic and political crises of the 21st century and beyond. Recognizing the limitations of the enduring 19th century model of education is an important first step. Transforming education is a monumental endeavor, as is trying to encourage billions of diverse people around the world to set aside any perceived cultural, geographic and social barriers in order to engage each other and their surroundings in a more sustainable manner. Both goals require the use of a common platform or mechanism for challenging the status quo and disseminating insightful messages about plausible alternatives. One possibility is to leverage the global power and appeal of Hip Hop culture, which has routinely broken down barriers to raise consciousness about various social, political, and cultural problems. Diverse people from around the world now identify themselves as members of Hip Hop culture. If students are offered opportunities to learn the skills in our classrooms to critique the good and the ugly in Hip Hop, then the best messages of inclusivity and justice found in the Hip Hop culture can invite young people everywhere to belong to a global village. By being taught how to critique the bad and the good in Hip Hop, students might be more open to the positive messages which remind them that all people no matter where they exist are human first, equal, and like them have important contributions to make. As a transformative model for diversity education, Hip Hop culture is ecologically and globally relevant; geared toward helping new generations of students find and use their voices; committed to achieving social and environmental justice; and capable of catapulting the American education system to a position of global prominence as a symbol of excellence in diversity education.

REFERENCES

Alim, H. S. (2006). *Roc the mic right: The language of hip hop culture.* New York, NY: Routledge.

Condry, I. (2006). *Hip-hop Japan: Rap and the paths of cultural globalization.* Durham, NC: Duke University Press

Davis, T. et. al. (2001). The Hip Hop Project: The Potential of Youth Culture in the Curriculum, <u>Teaching to Change LA</u>, Winter 2000/2001 vol. 1, no. 1. Available: http://www.tcla.gseis.ucla.edu/democracy/students/labi_hiphop.html (January 1, 2012)

Delpit, L. (2006). *Other people's children: Cultural conflict in the classroom.* New York, NY: The New Press.

Elam, H. J., & Jackson, K. A. (2005). *Black cultural traffic: Crossroads in global performance and popular culture.* Ann Arbor, MI: University of Michigan Press.

Hill, M. L. (2009). *Beats, rhymes, and classroom life: Hip-hop pedagogy and the politics of identity.* New York, NY: Teachers College Press.

Kitwana, B. (2005). *Why white kids love hip hop: Wankstas, wiggers, wannabes, and the new reality of race in america.* New York, NY: Basic Civitas Books.

Ladson-Billings, G. & Brown, K. (2008). *Curriculum and Cultural Diversity.* Connelly, F.M.(Ed.), *The Sage Handbook of Curriculum and Instruction* (pp.153-175). London, UK: Sage Publications.

Nieto, S. (1992*). Affirming diversity: The sociopolitical context of multicultural education (2nd ed.).* White Plains, NY: Longman.

Osumare, H. (2005). *Global Hip-Hop and the African Diaspora.* Elam, H. J., & Jackson, K. A.(Eds) *Black cultural traffic: Crossroads in global performance and popular culture.* Ann Arbor, MI: University of Michigan Press.

Smitherman, G. (2000). Talkin that talk: Language, culture, and education in African America. New York, NY: Routledge.

Sterling, S. (2001). *Sustainable Education:Re-visioning Learning and Change.* Bristol, UK: Green Books.

Tate, G. (2003). Everything but the burden: What white people are taking from Black culture. New York, NY: Broadway Books.

Theard, N. (2012) Syllabus-AFA 4370: Global hip-hop culture. Florida International University.

US Department of Education (2007). *Building on results: A blueprint for strengthening the no child left behind act.* Washington, D.C. Retrieved February 14, 2012, from Department of Education. Web site: http://www.ed.gov:

Section 6: Learning Respect for Other People's Language can Free Students' Minds

Please take 10 minutes and compare the two reading selections of Wynne and Miles, choosing any ideas from each that speak to "freeing students' minds through respect for other people's language." Write your comparison in the space below. _____

_____

_____

_____

_____

After writing those ideas, please consider the following:

- Join at least four other classmates and discuss your answers.

- Once discussed, choose a piece of hip hop music from one of your digital devices (laptop, cell-phone, etc.) that the group thinks carries a similar theme to anything discussed in either article.

- After 10 minutes for finding the piece of music, play the music for the class.

- Then as a class, critique the value of the use of hip hop in K-12 classrooms as a method of assisting students to learn abstract ideas through music.

With the class, watch the video featuring Sonia Nieto addressing "Multi-Lingualism" www.tolerance.org/tdsi/asset/multi-lingualism-asset-not-deficit

1. With your partner, discuss Nieto's premises about the asset of languages.

   _____

   _____

   _____

2. How does her argument compare with the Ebonics debate in Wynne's article?

   _____

   _____

   _____

3. Now watch Michael Eric Dyson on the Today Show video talking about Hip Hop: www.youtube.com/watch?v=GHyRbN6-4wE

- What does Dyson suggest is the good and the ugly of hip hop?

   _____

   _____

   _____

1. Now, please watch Tim Wise speaking about the use of the "N" word: www.youtube.com/watch?v=zmLXZ6_PW9A&feature=related

2. With your partner, discuss the main points that you believe Wise is making in his speech about language and the appropriate use of words. Capture those main ideas in the spaces below:

_____

_____

_____

_____

_____

_____

_____

_____

_____

_____

SECTION 7

RAISING THE VOICES OF YOUTH FOSTERS THE BUILDING OF AN AUTHENTIC GLOBAL VILLAGE

To me young people come first, they have
The courage where we fail
. . . .
The older I get the better I know that the
Secret of my going on
Is when the reins are in the hands of the
Young, who dare to run against the storm

—from "Ella's Song" by Bernice Johnson Reagon

CHAPTER 7

KIDS CAN BE ACTIVISTS OR BYSTANDERS

Craig Kielburger

The following is adapted from a speech by Craig Kielburger, a student from Canada who has been alive in building a campaign against the use of child labor to produce products such as sports equipment, clothing, and handmade rugs. The speech was delivered before the American Federation of Teachers at its 1996 convention.

We have started a movement called Free The Children, a youth group made up of young people mainly between 10 and 16 years of age. Our purpose is not only to help those children who are being abused and exploited, but to also empower young people to believe in themselves and to believe that they can play an active role as citizens of this world.

People sometimes look at me and say, "Well, you're only 13 years old, and 13-year-olds don't do these types of things, and is it normal?" And I ask you, why are people so surprised when young people get involved in social issues?

In other countries, children our ages and younger are working up to 16 hours a day in factories and fields. They are fighting in wars and supporting entire families. Drug dealers don't underestimate the ability of children. So often I find myself believing that the schools and that the adults in our lives underestimate who we are or what we can do, the good that we can do in making this world a better place.

We have been receiving hundreds of copies of letters written by children all over the United States, and I would like to read one of them to you now. This letter is to the president of the Nike Corporation.

"Dear Mr. Nike President: My name is Jamie, and I am eight and three-quarters years old. My Nike shoes are all worn out, but I will buy no more Nike running shoes if you don't tell me that you have no child labor in all of your factories"—and "all" is underlined. "Yours truly, Jamie."

Jamie may only be eight and three-quarters years old, but he's already learning that he does have a voice, that he is important. Jamie is learning to be an active citizen of this world.

It is not often that a young person my age has the opportunity to give his teacher advice—let alone nearly 3,000 teachers. But I believe that in this information age, with its global economy and global human rights, one of the greatest challenges that you as teachers and educators will face is to prepare your students to live in the new global village and to become active citizens of this world. As young people, we are capable of doing so much more than simply watching TV, playing video games, hanging around malls, or simply regurgitating information that is fed to us through schools or the media.

Now, don't get me wrong. I personally love hanging out with my friends and playing video games. But there is much more on top of that that young people can do. Today, young people in North America are more aware, more informed, and perhaps more frustrated than any other generation of youth, for we see all the poverty and injustices in the world. Yet, what role do we play in today's society? Where are the infrastructures, the opportunities which allow us to participate, to give, and to help?

We can either grow up as bystanders simply closing our eyes and becoming immune to what is happening to the people in the world around us, or we can be taught that we can participate, that we do have a voice, that we are important, and that we can bring about a change. And this is why I believe so strongly that service to others, whether at a local—for we have many problems in our own neighborhoods—at a national, or even an international level should be an integral part of our school, of our education.

I say education because when young people are challenged to look at others and to help others, we realize how lucky we truly are. We learn leadership skills and self-respect. We are able to put our energy and enthusiasm to a worthwhile cause. We learn that we can make this world a better place. Some people say that I am exceptional. But to me, the true heroes are the boys and the girls who work in near slave-like conditions to make the soccer balls which your children play with, to make the clothes which your children wear, and who even make the surgical equipment which saves lives in American hospitals.

As educators, you are such a powerful group. You have the power to motivate people, to stand up, and to bring about a change. What will you do to help these children? People, especially young people, live up to those expectations which others draw for them.

Today, if I leave behind one message with you it will be to believe in us, the young people of today. Don't be afraid to challenge us to play a greater role in society, and please, don't under-estimate who we are or what we can do. Our generation may just surprise you.

WE WHO BELIEVE IN FREEDOM CANNOT REST: YOUNG PEOPLE TRANSFORMING THEIR WORLDS

Joan T. Wynne

To me young people come first, they have
The courage where we fail

. . . .

The older I get the better I know that the
Secret of my going on
Is when the reins are in the hands of the
Young, who dare to run against the storm

The above lyrics from "Ella's Song" (Reagon,1981) about the work and words of U.S. Civil Rights Leader, Ella Baker, always remind me that one of our jobs as educators is to get out of the way of the children so they can transform not only their world but also ours. This chapter will examine a national program in the United States, the Young People's Project (YPP); its roots in the Civil Rights Movement; its unique use of mathematics as a pedagogy for transformative personal and civic leadership;its engagement with communities;its partnership with Florida International University (FIU);and the serious implications of this model for reshaping schools and teacher preparation.

HISTORY OF YPP'S EMERGENCE FROM THE ALGEBRA PROJECT & THE CIVIL RIGHTS MOVEMENT

"Without the Algebra Project, Doc and YPP, I would not be in college today. Many of us wouldn't even finish high school," said Whitney Brakefield, a student at Mississippi State University. Brakefieldwas speaking to an audience at an FIU seminar featuring Civil Rights icons, John Doar and Bob Moses. I watched Moses, who seemed to wince at the reference to him, as he listened to a panel of Algebra Project (AP) graduates and YPP participants from Jackson, Mississippi and Miami, Florida.They were part of the "Quality Education as a Constitutional Right" (QECR) national movement first convened at Howard University by Moses in 2005 and later passed to YPP to lead. This particular event was hosted at the College of Law. These students each took their turn to talk about how AP,YPP and "Doc" had changed their lives. It was their mention of

From *Leveraging Social Capital in Schools for Systemic Education Reform*, edited by Ian R. Haslam, Myint Swe Khine and Issa M. Saleh. In press with Sense Publications.

"Doc" that seemed to make Moses uncomfortable. A grassroots leader whose humility is legendary, he prefers to stay in the background of the people he "leads by not leading" (Wynne, 2009). Nevertheless, the students continued their stories, giving the audience a glimpse into the history of these organizations' impact. The students insisted that they intended to continue to be part of this movement toward quality education for all of the nation's children, a seed planted years ago in the sixties.

In 1960, at the suggestion of Ella Baker, Moses travelled the south to begin a dialogue with Black leaders to discover how to support their work for liberation from the Jim Crow South. From the discussions in Mississippi came the "bottom up" campaign for voting rights for all blacks, work led by the Student Non-Violent Coordinating Committee (SNCC) and supported by other African American organizations. Over forty years after those bloody battles and ultimate voting rights' victories and his work organizing Freedom Summer and the Mississippi Freedom Democratic Party, Moses returned to Mississippi to work with those sharecroppers and insurgents' grandchildren and great grandchildren, who were still being denied a quality education in the public schools there and across the nation (Moses & Cobb).

To those children in 1991, Moses brought the Algebra Project, a project he began with his own children in Boston schools. And later through a "Genius" fellowship from the MacArthur Foundation, he expanded AP, designing it as a tool to teach higher level mathematics and critical thinking skills to children stuck at the bottom of the delivery of bad education. He saw access to mathematics as the next civil right. To gain political power in the south, black citizens had to win their right to vote. To win access to college and to economic security in a technology driven 21st century society, poor children will need to become proficient in mathematics. Moses insists that "The absence of math literacy in urban and rural communities is as urgent an issue today as the lack of registered voters was 40 years ago . . . And I believe solving the problem requires the same kind of community organizing that changed the South then. If we can succeed in bringing all children to a level of math literacy so they can participate in today's economy, that would be a revolution" (Mother Jones).

AP uses Dewey's experiential learning pedagogy while at the same time being responsive to youth culture. Neither it nor YPP is afraid to integrate the music, the digital images and interests of the hip-hop culture into its curriculum and methodology to entice the young into the study of mathematics. What seems unique about both programs is their demand for excellence from children at the bottom, a demand that these low-performing students grapple with higher level abstract thinking, and, consequently AP delivers accelerated content and strategies typically reserved for "gifted" programs. Moses further insists that the only ones who can really demand the kind of education they need are the students, their parents, and their community (Moses, 18-21)—a radical idea in educational institutions in the U.S. AP's philosophy puts the power in the hands of the people who are being abused by inadequate education (Moses 2001).

As a veteran educator whose primary focus includes teacher education, exposure to this practice of student and parent demand created an epiphany; and as a consequence, I have included, in every undergraduate and graduate course I teach,discussions of the theory of building student and parent demand. This theory along with the praxis of community and classroom partnering, I consider as necessary indicators of teacher competence.

AP, in addition to insisting on community involvement, asserts that "a real breakthrough would not make us happy if it did not deeply and seriously empower the target population to demand access to literacy for everyone. That is what is driving the project" (Moses 2001, 19). Because of this belief, which is deeply rooted in the Movement, students broaden their context to include not only personally acquiring a quality education, but also sharing it with their community. They begin to see their personal academic gains as an obligation to raise the achievement of others. By 1996 AP had reached some 45,000 pupils, and its instructional materials were being used by teachers in 105 schools across the country (Henry).

ENTER THE YOUNG PEOPLE'S PROJECT

That same year, steeped in the traditions of the Southern Freedom Movement, Moses' progeny, who seemed to have heard the echo of Ella Baker's words, grabbed the reins from the Algebra Project and began to run against the hail storm of inferior education pouring into disenfranchised communities. These youngsters organized a spin-off of AP and named it the Young People's Project (YPP). They have driven the effort to take mathematics into their communities. Founded by two of Moses' sons, Omo and Taba Moses, their friend, Chad Milner, who was a graduate of AP in Boston, and nine 8th grade AP students in Mississippi, YPP explains its mission to be one that:

. . . develops students aged 8-22 from traditionally marginalized populations as learners, teachers, leaders, and organizers through math and media literacy, community-building, and advocacy in order to build a unique network of young people who are better equipped to navigate life's circumstances, are active in their communities, and advocate for education reform in America (TYPP website).

YPP credits the Algebra Project for securing a space for them as young people to organically grow their own organization from the principles they learned from their experiences in AP. The YPP organizers believe that young people can and must significantly alter their own lives as well as the moral life of the nation. They use what they call "math literacy work" as the vehicle to begin that journey of individual and societal change.

In the 16 years of that journey, YPP has evolved from primarily organizing youth to teach math in after-school programs, during Saturday schools, and summer camps to the more daunting work of designing workshops and campaigns to grow the civic leadership and organizing skills of the young to influence public policy. Maisha Moses, after graduating from Harvard, began leading the YPP Professional Development efforts. YPP has also raised funding from foundations as prestigious as the National Science Foundation to advance the research and analysis for documentation. And from school districts, foundations, and organizations within each local site, YPP has raised the compensation to pay the youth as "knowledge workers." In Mississippi they have created a garden on a small plot of land where they hope to one day "create an agricultural training center to help people learn to produce their own healthy foods" (TYPP).

To be such a young organization and to be run only by the young for the young, their successes might surprise us. Annually over 400 High School and College students are trained and employed to do math literacy work. At least 5000 elementary students, family and community members participate in math literacy workshops, events and initiatives each year. YPP employs 20 full and 35 part-time staff. Their median age is 26 and 85% are African-American and Latino. Local sites exist in major cities across the nation from Los Angeles to Miami. They have instituted 3 Local Advisory Boards (Boston, Chicago, and Mississippi) and a National Board of Directors with representation throughout the country. The simple majority of both boards are young people who have been part of the organization (TYPP).

FLAGWAY GAME BUILDS COMMUNITY ENGAGEMENT WITH MATHEMATICS

One of their major vehicles for teaching math to the young as well as their attempts to reach out to the community is a game they call Flagway, a game patented by Bob Moses in 1996. The game is a vehicle to encourage students to see mathematics as fun and as part of their everyday realities, and has been used effectively in several cities to engage students and their parents in math in the same way they enthusiastically engage in sports.

The intent is that, ultimately, through Flagway, students will form Leagues that create opportunities for teams, coached by high school and college students, to compete locally, regionally and nationally. Schools, churches, community-based organizations are invited to enter teams in designated leagues. The underlying purpose of these events is to encourage disenfranchised communities to take ownership of mathematics as an accessible academic discipline and to contradict the notion that, as Lisa Delpit indicates, exists in some black and poor communities of color that mathematics is for white people (Delpit, 2012).

The Flagway Game can be played with students as early as 1st grade and has been enjoyed by adults. In general, the game is played with 3rd–6th graders. During game play students navigate a Flagway or course of radial "paths" based on the Flagway rules (derived from the "Mobius" Function). Speed counts, so as students develop into skilled players several may be running through the course simultaneously, creating dynamics similar to that of a sporting event. Part of the beauty of Flagway is that students can play the game without knowing the rules, allowing all students access to the game and the underlying mathematical principles (TYPP website). YPP in collaboration with TIZ media has created an On-line Flagway Challenge Game so that young people can enter into the world of mathematics no matter their skill level or age. The fundamental structure of the game changes as higher level abstraction is demanded (TYPP).

CAMPAIGN ORGANIZED BY YPP

Another quality of YPP that lends itself to transformative action is its capacity to respond quickly to current realities. Because it is rooted in the Southern Freedom Movement, its MO seems to be one that looks at the realities affecting those at the bottom rung of society's economic ladder, raises the voices of those people, ignores old paradigms that resist change, and organizes to create a new response to the present exigency. It doesn't get stuck in rigid traditions that often cripple large bureaucracies when facing sudden calamities.

One example is YPP's response to the devastation of Hurricane Katrina in New Orleans and the governmental debacle of neglect for its citizens. Over 300,000 survivors had been dispersed across the nation, living in armed camps, housed in churches, auditoriums, living with relatives, etc. Researcher, Elizabeth Fussell, suggests in her report that "Virtually the entire population of the city was displaced and forced to resettle, which some did temporarily and others permanently"(Fussell p.1).

Within weeks after Katrina, YPP began organizing students and young adults from across the south, to "Find our Folks." Along with the New Orleans Hot 8 Brass Band, they went to Atlanta, Baton Rouge, Jackson, Mobile, New Orleans, and Houston to find the hurricane's dispossessed. They networked with community agencies, churches, schools, colleges, volunteers, friends in each city who might support the tour and its work with dispersed populations. YPP organized local meetings and workshops, performing arts events, concerts, media blitzes to find America's citizens exiled to other locations. And through this effort they educated many of us about resistance to hegemony, celebration of cultural histories, music, art and movements, as well as self reflection for healing and growth.

One of the products resulting from the Finding Our Folks tour was a DVD produced by the young people showcasing specific workshops and events from the cities visited, including a visual tour of the devastated neighborhoods in New Orleans. I have used that video as a tool for my pre-service and in-service teachers to explore the power and creativity that young people in and outside their classrooms can bring to the table to democratize us all. Too often my university students feel powerless and are unconscious of their social agency as students and teachers. I have found that this DVD elicits from them serious conversations. During those conversations, they often, from the experiences of the FOF young people, extrapolate a sense of their capacity as teachers to change their professional world. They begin to see themselves possessing social agency.

Reality-based curriculum and Movement pedagogy, reflected in Ella Baker's vision and used by YPP for this tour is a content and strategy that can revolutionize our classrooms and schools. If creative young people grappling with daunting realities, grounded in the wisdom of their elders are given space and time in their local schools and colleges to instruct and inform, might our halls of education breathe new life and become more innovative in meeting the academic needs of their students? In this regard, the legacy of Ella Baker is clear. Giving space, support, and advice when needed, she, like Moses with YPP, stayed in the background as she protected the young in the Student Non Violent Coordinating Committee (SNCC) from being subsumed by the adults in the Southern Christian Leadership Council (Ransby). Baker was committed to a methodology that would allow youth to cultivate their own leadership. She made it possible for SNCC to organize and educate itself, and grapple amongst themselves with the philosophies and methods needed to confront the dangers of the Jim Crow South. Moses elaborates, "What Ella Baker did for us, we did for Mississippi" (Ransby, p. 331); and I would add, what he continues to do for YPP.

In her biography of Ella Baker, Barbara Ransby describes Baker as a "Freirian teacher, a Gramscian intellectual, and a radical humanist" (p. 357). Those qualities seem manifested in YPP whose history also seems inextricably bound to the vision and practices of Baker. Like Freire's philosophy in *Pedagogy of the Oppressed*, both YPP and AP construct an educational space that allows the young to look critically at their lives and surroundings and creatively participate in the transformation of those worlds. And like Freire, they, too, foster resistance to hegemonic systems of thought. In the tradition of Baker, YPP wants the young to think radically. Baker insisted that "For us as oppressed people to become a part of a society that is meaningful, the system under which we now exist has to be radically changed" (Moses, p. 2). Civic Engagement is of paramount importance to YPP. For large populations of disenfranchised students condemned to low-performing schools, radical, transformative thinking seems the only "way out of no way" (Young). For decades, rescue programs that target only the top 10% of the students attending low-performing institutions have never addressed the curriculum nor the pedagogy, as Moses explains, needed to "raise the floor" of academic achievement for students stuck at the bottom; thus, sustaining a "sharecropper" education for most black and brown students in urban public schools (PBS).

FLORIDA INTERNATIONAL UNIVERSITY PARTNERS WITH AP AND YPP

For five years, from 2004–2009, FIU and AP collaborated in the first pilot in the nation of a school-based/university affiliated school reform grounded in accelerated mathematics for low-performing students. While Moses and AP were partnered with the university, the Young People's Project received local funding and started a site housed in FIU's College of Education. The Research & Development work done in Miami by AP, YPP, & FIU in those five years propelled the National Science Foundation to explore the efficacy of this mathematics cohort model in five other cities with African-American, Latino, and White Appalachian populations.

In February, 2011 when the Colleges of Education and Law hosted the previously mentioned QECR forum with Doar and Moses (an event co-sponsored by departments across the campus), community and university responses to this dialogue fostered a renewed partnership between FIU and the Algebra Project with the local community. After the forum, Senior Associate Dean of the College of Law, Michelle Mason, met with Moses, saying "Whenever I'm involved with an event such as this one, I expect a follow-up action plan. So, Dr. Moses, what's our next step?" At that meeting Miami YPP representatives, Moses and Mason and others from across the university campus formed a common vision to drive QECR in Miami. Along with COE, they initiated a plan for a 2011 summer institute on mathematics, civics and rhetorical structures to capitalize on the earlier R&D work with the Algebra Project and YPP. English Professors from the College of Arts & Sciences also joined the effort.

"The intent of the partnership with AP and the institute," Michelle Mason suggested, "is to build a new national model for transforming disenfranchised young people into change agents in their communities" (mtg. 2011).The summer institute was designed also to demonstrate the Flagway game as a tool to get elementary students excited about learning mathematics, while creating a space for FIU law students to teach youngsters' rhetorical and civic skills.

MIAMI YPP LITERACY WORKERS AND AP GRADUATES

For the summer of 2011, six Miami YPP youth and AP cohort graduates chose to teach math to 3rd, 4th, 5th grade students. One of those YPP math literacy workers (MLW), Wilkens Desire, passionately testified in a planning meeting that his cohort was committed "to doing whatever it takes to make sure that all the children in my community receive the kind of quality education that we received from the YPP and the Algebra Project."

These six MLW's agreed to meet for 12 weeks before the summer with a renowned mathematics researcher for 4 hours a day, 4 days a week to prepare the instruction necessary to teach the elementary school students from Liberty City at FIU. During those 12 weeks, two FIU professors, a former local director of the Miami YPP site, and a professor/grant writer from the local community college met also once or twice a week to work with the students on presentation and leadership skills. As testament to their commitment, these students showed up day after day without knowing if enough money would be raised to support them in their professional development or to support the institute. Only one of these students had a part-time job. The other five had no employment. The professors, the director, and the math researcher also met with no compensation.

With budget adjustments and funding from the College of Law and a few donors, ultimately, the program ran for four weeks in the law school. Though there was not enough funding in 2011 to hire a researcher, funding has been currently pledged from the FIU Office of Global Learning Initiative to support research for the 2012 math and civics summer institute.

Education undergraduate and graduate students, professors, law interns and professors (even a courtroom judge), university student affairs staff, Miami Dade College students and professors, and Miami Dade County Public School teachers and administrators, joined this effort to use Movement philosophy and pedagogy to transform the way we educate in universities and public spheres.

INFLUENCE OF THE YOUNG ON PRE-SERVICE AND IN-SERVICE TEACHERS

During FIU's original partnership with AP & YPP, each year for six years, high school students from the Miami cohort made presentations to FIU university students enrolled in education courses, both undergraduate and graduate level. These courses were selected by the professors who engaged with and researched the program. Twice some of these same students also presented at the Annual Research Conference of the College of Education. Several students, who were both AP and YPP participants, presented at national educational conferences sharing their knowledge of mathematics, what it takes to commit to learning mathematics, and what they believe are the qualities that make a good teacher.

In the summer of 2010, six of the YPP students presented their stories of growth and a math lesson to one of my classes. A cohort of teachers, engaged in a Master's Degree Program, were enrolled in this class. When the YPP students told their stories of being transfigured by their experiences as math literacy workers, the graduate students asked them to come to their public school classrooms to tutor and mentor their students. Yet when the YPP students moved to the next piece of their presentation, asking the cohort to participate in a math lesson, the graduate cohort resisted saying they weren't really good at math. The YPP students told them not to worry, that they would make it easy for them as AP and YPP had done for them. Reducing the cohort's anxiety, the newly graduated high schoolers taught the lesson. One graduate student said, "I wish I had learned math that way. I might have done better in college algebra."

As important as the lesson was the conversation with the graduate students after the YPP students left. Many of them talked about how they had assumed that students from that particular high school in the district would not be as articulate, confident, and knowledgeable as these YPP students demonstrated. The breaking down of stereotypes about the capacity of disenfranchised urban children to academically excel is crucial to the instruction of pre-service and in-service teachers. No theory, no pedagogy seems to assault those stereotypes as powerfully as the presence of the young in these classrooms exposing their knowledge and power to learn and to impact their realities.

In sync with the Movement philosophy of inviting the wisdom of the elders into the work, YPP builds networks both nationally and locally, with professionals and communities to share the expertise that can foster the skills youth need to influence their lives and their world. In Miamia COE professor, Maria Lovett, expert in teaching videography as action research, tutored YPP students to use visual media to examine concerns in their schools and communities. During this process students learn to critically examine the media's "mis-representation" of disenfranchised youth, to learn research methods of data collection and analysis, and to disseminate their findings in communities and at professional conferences. The videos produced by the Miami contingent were shown to a COE audience of faculty, students, and some district principals and administrators.

CONCLUSION

If we are to transform our educational institutions, maybe we need to look toward the youth, align with their visions and digital world, raise their voices. In doing that, there still will be time and space for us to share our knowledge which can help build the scaffolds that will support students as they learn to teach themselves and their communities. But to do this, we must disengage ourselves from dominating their learning. As Kahlil Gibran suggests in *The Prophet*, when speaking about the young, "You may strive to be like them, but seek not to make them like you" (p 17).

Gibran insists that the teacher "If he is indeed wise he does not bid you enter the house of his wisdom, but rather leads you to the threshold of your own mind" (p. 56). The vision and practices of Ella Baker, Bob Moses, The Young People's Project seem to embody Gibran's ideal of teaching. They seem to sense that the "houses of wisdom" in this country, the educational institutions, have often become rigid walls of hegemonic, top-down structures that leave most students"to freeze and crystallize and be bound in a mould" (p.4). Yet AP and YPP, operating in integrity with Baker's legacy, consistently turn the reigns over to the young, whether students are grappling with mathematical abstraction, organizing an event, meeting with the community, or learning research and documentation—always there to guide, but never there to dominate.

The organic, fluid nature of these organizations is often misunderstood and undervalued in the context of a Western Eurocentric model of education that dominates U. S. American schooling. The organic takes time. Like food and plants, it cannot be mass produced and retain its whole nutrients, nor can it be quickly assimilated and turned into "scaled up" prescriptive magic bullets. Yet because it is fluid, it can and does respond quickly to sudden shifts in reality as YPP did with the horror of Katrina. YPP demonstrates all of these organic qualities by its insistence on growing its organization from the bottom up via local control. Young people in communities take it, get allies to fund it, and begin to shape it to suit their neighborhoods, their needs, their dreams. In contrast, the Western model traditionally and presently operates from a hierarchal mode of assimilating the young into the culture of the status quo. When shifts occur, they are typically driven by the top for the benefit of the top or driven by marketing rhetoric of the corporatocracy. Russell Berman, President of the Modern Language Association (MLA), in his address at the annual conference remarked:

In this past year, we have seen threats to education at all levels: in many individual institutions, in state capitals, and in Washington, D.C. We have seen a public denigration of humanistic learning, and a culture of shrill hostility toward teachers and teacher organizations. . . . I call on all members to participate in the defense of education under assault" (Berman, p 3).

Only last week, I sat as an observer/facilitator among a small group of faculty where their prevailing theme of conversation was how to more effectively teach students so that their skills are marketable. No one was discussing education for transformation or liberation, only education for the best job. Prior to that discussion, I was on a conference call with university educators and administrators from diverse urban sites to explore themes for panels in an upcoming conference. Two of the themes discussed were "Building a 21st Century Workforce" and "Building Job Skills through Service Learning." The corporate agenda and jargon seems to have become the "new norm" for many public universities.

As a counter to those kinds of experiences, studying and engaging with youth from YPP, an educational experiment that is profoundly rooted in a tradition of radical paradigm shifts, keeps me grounded in the democratic ideals that Moses and Baker espoused. It also helps lessen the desperation that wells up after participating indialogues that seem driven by corporate interests.

While thinking and writing about the roots of YPP in the revolution of the Southern Freedom Movement (Harding), I happened to hear an interview with Wael Ghonim, a major participant and instigator in the Egyptian revolution sparked in Tahrir Square on January 25, 2011. He created anonymous Facebook pages and Twitter messages to advertise meetings and plans for the largest protest in modern Egyptian history. During that "Fresh Air" interview, Ghonim told Terry Gross that the revolution was about the people who risked their lives, "not about google, or facebook." These were just the tools, he said, used to communicate quickly and widely to the brave young who found the courage to act heroically in the face of tyranny. He passionately explained to Gross that he did not want to be the face of the revolution, that he was against "personalizing a cause . . . . definitely against personalizing a revolution. . . . this was leaderless and it should continue leaderless, and no one should be taking the lead after all these people sacrificed their lives" (Fresh Air). Ghonim's words harkened back to the same "leaderless," model of Baker and Moses, one practiced by YPP.

Moses in Mississippi, in spite of beatings, death threats, arrests and jail time, pushed against the limits imposed by those who thwarted democratic, constitutional law; yet he continued to create a space where youth could challenge those who stood in the way of a nation's dream for a real democracy. That space YPP now occupies to "pay it forward."

In considering YPP, I juxtaposed comments from Berman's MLA keynote where he insists that through his contacts in D.C., he believes "A purposeful standardization of education is under way, driven less by a concern with students than with product placement for testing agencies" (p. 8). With that in mind, I wonder if we might reckon with those forces by learning something new about schooling from these serious young people in YPP—these young adults who use every creative tool possible to teach math to children who no one believes have the capacity to learn. I wonder if, like the youth in the FOF tour, all professors in colleges and teachers in public schools flung open their doors and invited the young and community elders into their classrooms to tell their stories, teach their knowledge, share their art, music, theories, might then institutions come alive? With this agenda, might those 50% of college freshmen, who typically drop out of college (Miller), find something in classrooms relevant to their lives, invigorate their interest in learning other wisdom traditions, and get ready to participate in a diverse global society? Might those students condemned to low-performing public schools find a reason to come to school and stay because school no longer would be an alien place that negates their home culture? Do we have the courage to ignore the drill and kill experts, the test mongers building their great fortunes, and the corporate moguls who want public schools to train "worker bees" who will continue to flip their burgers, pick up their trash, and fill their prisons? (Alexander) Can we be honest with one another and suspend our egos as experts, especially when education is under siege, and learn what Ella Baker knew, to turn over the reins to the "young who dare to run against the storm"?

Social activist and singing star, Harry Belafonte, an admirer of the work of Baker and Moses, recently in a speech in Chicago said, "What Dr. King taught us was that without an angry people, without the poor rising up in indignation against their conditions, our leaders will never be pushed to do what they must do" (*Chicago Sun Times*, 2012). Belafonte, a supporter of AP and YPP, also seems to be advocating for students and parents to make their demands upon systems that refuse to provide quality education to their communities.

Quality education seemed to be a subtext of a keynote address given in the College of Education by scholar Marcelo Suarez-Orozco (FIU, 2011). During that address, he said that from a survey used in his research about global immigration patterns, the number one complaint cited about schooling by students across the planet was "boredom." Given that indictment, can we use the experiences and documentation of YPP—-with its history rooted in Movement pedagogy, its mutual respect for the wisdom of its elders and hip-hop culture, its facility with math and the digital world, its capacity to respond quickly to the immediate, and its faith in democratic ideals—to counter the hum drum, mind numbing, low quality, uncreative teaching that is being demanded by phony assessment tools and legislative bodies tied to corporate hierarchy who want to maintain a class of worker who must work for peanuts in order to survive.

As a seasoned educator observing, interviewing, and working alongside YPP participants, I have seen in their founders what Ella Baker must have seen in Bob Moses and SNCC—a group of new intellectuals ready to jump off the page of history into the present world and reshape American democracy.

REFERENCES

Alexander, M. (2012) The new Jim Crow: Mass incarceration in the age of colorblindness. New York, NY: The New Press.

Berman, R. (2012) Teaching as Vocation. MLA Presidential Address. Seattle, WA. http://www.mla.org/pres_address_2012

Cass, J. (2002)The Moses factor. *Mother Jones* (May/June 2002 issue 3).http://motherjones.com/politics/2002/05/moses-factor

Delpit, L. (2012) *Multiplication is for white people: Raising expectations for other people's children.* New York, NY: The New Press.

Freire, P &Macedo, D.(2001) *Literacy: Reading the Word and the World.* London: Routledge.

Fussell, E., et al (2010). Race, socioeconomic status, and return migration to New Orleans after Hurricane Katrina." *Population and Environment*, 31(1-3): 20-42. PMCID: PMC2862006.

Gibran, K. (1923). *The Prophet.* New York: Alfred A. Knopf

Harding, V. (1990). *Hope and history: Why we must share the Movement.* Maryland: Orbis Books.

Henry, N. (2005). 35 Who Made a Difference: Robert Moses, A former civil rights activist revolutionizes the teaching of mathematics. *Smithsonian.com* November 01. http://typp.org/media/docs/2838_05Nov1Smithsonian_35MadeDifference_RMoses.pdf

Ihejirika, M. "Where are their (our) leaders? What's missing is that rage," Belafonte speech, *Chicago Sun Times* February 15, 2012

Lyrics from "Ella's Song," composed by Bernice Johnson Reagon, from her film score created for Joanne Grant's film, *Fundi: The Story of Ella Baker* (Icarus Films, 1981). Used with composer's permission (2012).

Mason, M. (2011) notes from February planning meeting at College of Law, Florida International University.

Miller, B & Ly, P. (2010) College dropout factories. *Washington Monthly.*August. http://www.washingtonmonthly.com/college_guide/feature/college_dropout_factories.php? accessed, Feb. 20, 2012.

Moses, R. & Cobb, C. (2001). *Radical equations: Civil rights from Mississippi to the Algebra Project.* Beacon Press: Boston, MA.

Ransby, B. (2003). *Ella Baker & the Black Freedom Movement: A radical Democratic vision.* Chapel Hill, The University of North Carolina Press.

Suarez-Orozco, M. (2011)Immigration and Education in the Age of Global Vertigo. Keynote, College of Education, Florida International University, Miami FL. Sept. 14.

The Young People's Project website: http://typp.org/ accessed on Feb. 9, 2012.

WaelGhonim: 'Creating a revolution 2.0' in Egypt (2012). Fresh Air from WHYY with Terry Gross, National Public Radio.Feb 9th.

Wynne J., (2009) Grassroots leadership in the 21st century: Leading by not leading. *Transformative leadership and educational excellence: Learning organizations in the information age.* Selah, I. M. &Khine, M. S. (eds.). The Netherlands: Sense Publications

Young, A. (1994) *A way out of no way: The spiritual memoirs of Andrew Young.* Nashville, TN: Thomas Nelson Publishers.

YPP (2007) Finding our folk. DVD. Chicago, Ill: YPP youth.

RUNNING TO THE DIGITAL AGE . . .

Maria Lovett

I met Rae, in 1995 in Seattle. She was a teenage runaway–or homeless youth as she and her friends preferred. "We aren't just running away, we are running to . . . "

Rae and "The Kids on The Ave" as I came to call them, lived in "the squat" an abandoned house off University Way or slept at the Teen Feed shelter. Rae was a passionate writer and illustrator. She and her friends, her street family, welcomed me into their world and began to direct both me and my video camera–through the streets and alleys and into their ideas, aspirations and triumphs. One night, when a homeless teen got upset by the presence of my camera, Grimus, a 15-year-old girl said in my defense "Don't worry man, she isn't Channel 5, we're telling our story here."

As Rae and I walked and interviewed and filmed, I explained to her each decision I was making with the camera. Why a close-up here, why a wide-shot there, how come I chose to film from a low height positioned from where she sat on the sidewalk asking for spare change . . .

"It's not just what you film," I explained, "it is how you frame it."

I gave Rae a still camera and asked her to photograph anything she wanted to with it. She came back a week later, I developed her photographs, and we began to talk about her images and her process.

Rae: Photography is like skateboarding; it changes how you see your world.

Me: What do you mean?

Rae: Well, I skateboard you know, so when I walk down the street I notice every curb, every park bench, every slope in the ground, and I am thinking about skateboarding. There is a jump there, I can ollie over that, ya know . . .?

Me: So what is a barricade to a driver or a pedestrian is a challenging jump to you on your skateboard? An opportunity? Is that it?

Rae: Exactly.

Me: What does this have to do with using the camera?

Rae: The same thing happened–you gave me a camera; you asked me to frame my world, and so when I walk down the street now I think of how I can use the camera to represent my world. How I frame it matters, right? I look at details—like a quarter on the street, or a dumpster, or a cop shooing us off the sidewalk—all of it in a different way.

Me: How?

Rae: It's like skateboarding–it changes how I see. And it impacts how I see. Because I am telling a story and the details all matter. People don't pay attention to the details. And I want to frame it, right.

Me: So you are writing your story with the camera . . . and with your skateboard?

Rae: Yeah, I am.

That was in 1995. I had been teaching youth media production for several years, and I continued to do so. But it was when I started thinking about what the young people I met said about the process that I realized they were not just creating documentaries---they were researching, and they were writing.

Personally, I was always afraid of writing. All my life. I take that back. Except for in third grade with Ms. Cohen. We had "creative writing time" and could write in any form we wanted. We didn't have to use sentences and could even write upside down. So from a young age I loved keeping journals, but when it came to any kind of directed assignment, I froze. I still do. Like writing this article. So instead I pick up a camera. A picture is worth a thousand words right? My first documentary called "Every Kid Counts" was about a youth center in North Philadelphia where I worked. As an undergraduate senior, I had to write a thesis, and I begged and pleaded with my professors to let me make a video. This pre-dated iMovie and cell phones and digital editing but I insisted. I recorded with a large and clunky VHS camera, I struggled through the analog world of videotape, where if you made one mistake or changed your mind in the editing process, you practically had to start all over. Somehow though, I had found my way to "write" the required "paper" that synthesized what I had learned in college. By researching, collecting, recording and re-assembling bits and pieces, details of real life into some form of composition, I shared what I learned, thought, felt and believed. I constructed a visual argument.

That was in 1992. I, now, have worked as a documentary filmmaker and media educator for 20 years. I have taught media production to youth in over a half-dozen cities—homeless and runaways, self-identified gang members, formerly adjudicated teens, dropouts, and private and public school students. Repeatedly, I have witnessed the sophisticated knowledge young people demonstrate in "non-school" environments that are too frequently under-represented by their "in-school" performance. Today, as a professor and researcher in education, I primarily work with students who are pre-service or current teachers. In this arena, I have begun to question if we can make an essential connection between unnecessarily disconnected worlds. In a recent survey conducted at a high school, where I serve as liaison between the school and university, a majority of students "strongly agreed" that the majority of their teachers fail to "connect what students are learning in class to life outside the classroom, and make an effort to understand what students' lives are like outside of school" (2012). Connecting the students' outside life to the inside of the classroom creates an enormous opportunity for making schools relevant to all learners, and especially to struggling readers and writers. Those relevancies also can generate a research based, pedagogical, strategic, transformative, curricular opportunity – one that connects personal and school experiences to knowledge work; our own as teachers and professors, and that of our students. Those connections can make us all wizards of the 21st century, sorcerers stirring pots boiling to the brim with everyone's experiences, wisdom, failures, successes, tribulations and exultations. Cooking up those fragments of real lives, we could percolate pertinent new knowledge to confront the challenges of this century. I and my students might whip in some ingredients and drink from that witches' brew!

That imagined brew, along with my approach to research and pedagogy, has been informed by seeing and listening to the stories of others—a belief that the extraordinary exists in the ordinary. When working as a filmmaker, one literally frames the world—one practices critical perception, finding details that may otherwise be overlooked. Images have a language of their own. As researchers and educators we can make use of a rigorous practice of seeing. It is a critical belief that through absorbing evidence of the everyday---reflecting upon these fragments of information, and acting upon such moments---we can begin to transform the world. Oscar Wilde once said, "The true mystery of the world is the visible, not the invisible." Too often we look but do not *see*, we hear but do not *listen*.

Unquestionably, assorted forms of media culture are a ubiquitous part of the world. Rhetorical messages are increasingly constructed using multiple forms and modes, altering every aspect of communication. Interactions with audiovisual materials have become so pervasive that their influence often goes unrecognized—and unquestioned. Within this hazy landscape, overwhelming stories and images in the media *narrate* the experiences and characterizations of others, but the others never (or rarely) get the chance to *show* their story back.

Education has been slow to seriously realize the burden of control of images for young people. To decolonize media culture, my students become critical consumers of media, negotiating and making meaning from these sources in full consciousness; and most importantly, "speaking back to" oppressive representations, mis-representations and intervening in the construction of messages by becoming media authors themselves. Through their words, their images, and expressions, the youth I've been so fortunate to know, in other cities as well as in Miami, demonstrate that the beautiful, the disturbing, the untold stories and the greatest exaltations reside in the facets of every day experiences. Youth understand a great deal about their world and what they are going through; however, they are often not afforded the opportunity to expose what they know. Not because they have nothing to say, but because too often, the adult world never *asks*.

To intervene in this imbalance and draw from pedagogy and research, and the intersection of both, I initiated a new methodology drawn from the intersection of documentary theory and production with participatory, media and arts-based inquiry and critical pedagogy. I name the method employed Video Action Research and Pedagogy (VARP) (Lovett, 2007).

VARP engages students/researchers in four nonlinear archetypical stages of film and video production: stages: (a) Pre-Production (reflection, research, critical thinking, strategic cognition, and planning); (b) Production (designing, interviewing, constructing and eliciting visual and audio material); (c) Post-Production (editing and assembling material to construct the narrative, reviewing and revising material); and (d) Distribution (announcing and sharing finished material in the public sphere). Particularly emphasized are processes involved in these stages that are useful to essential skills such as writing, reading comprehension, communication and participatory action research. All of which I have explained in a much longer article (Lovett, 2009).

But what I want to leave with the reader of this book is more of a mantra: Get out of the way of your students, who are all sophisticated thinkers, regardless of whether or not you know that to be true. Give them a still camera, a video camera, or a cell phone camera, anything from the digital world, ask *them* to pose the questions and let *them* research, create, critique, write their own lives. Let them present themselves to you and the world with the tools of the 21st century—before the corporate media mis-presents them yet one more time. And if we do–as Rae said, it just might help us change how we see the world and allow us to be "runaways" from the old into the new.

REFERENCES

Lovett, M. (2007). *Creative Interventions: Representing Others through Video Action Reserach*. In McCarthy, C. Durham, A., Engel, L., Filmer, A.A., Giardina, M.D., Logue, J. and Malagreca, M. (Eds.), Globalizing cultural studies: Ethnographic interventions in theory, method & policy. New York, NY: Peter Lang Publishing.

Lovett, M., Katherine E. Gossett, Carrie A. Lamanna, James P. Purdy and Joseph Squier (2009). Writing with Video: What happens when composition comes off the page? In Kalmbach, J and Ball, C. (Eds), *Reading and Writing in New Media*. Cresskill, NJ: Hampton Press.

School District Survey (2012)

Section 7: Raising the Voices of Youth Fosters the Building of an Authentic Global Village

Please take 10 minutes and write about how the Young People's Project's practices of putting the power in the hands of the students differs from the typical instructional practices in many public school classrooms. Write your discussion in the space below.

_____

_____

_____

_____

_____

_____

_____

After writing those ideas, please consider the following activities:

♦ Join at least three other classmates and discuss your ideas about *giving more power* to students in classrooms to make decisions about curriculum, methodology, and learning.

Once discussed, please access the 5-minute *YouTube* production by two students from a former Miami AP/Young People's Project cohort www.youtube.com/watch?v=boeT69PrMRY

♦ After watching the video, discuss with your group any ideas shared by the two students on *YouTube* that might be useful in learning how to educate struggling learners in K-12.

_____

_____

_____

_____

_____

♦ Read with your group the following passage:

Village life requires that most things be done collectively because people are very tightly connected. Tight connection fosters friction. In turn, friction among people deepens their sense of belonging. People bound by community are sure, at some point, to get on one another's nerves. This is not considered a bad thing, but rather a part of the natural human experience.

—The Healing Wisdom of Africa

♦ Discuss with your group any relevance the quote has to your working in small groups

View a few of the student 1-minute videos below; discuss any of the student wisdom that relates to your ideas: **www.whatkidscando.org/featurestories/2012/05_just_listen/index.html**

SECTION 8

LISTENING TO CHILDREN PUSHED TO THE MARGINS CLEARS SPACE FOR EQUITY TO FLOURISH

Image copyright 2012. Used under license from Shutterstock. Inc.

Young people who, like myself, have been disadvantaged because of discrimination, hate, or ignorance need somewhere to turn for help. GLAAD was my life vest, and I plan to be a life vest to as many others as I can. I only want those who face obstacles like mine to know that they are not alone . . .

—Waymon Hudson, from Huff Post blog

CHAPTER 8

CREATING SAFE SPACES FOR ALL OF THE NATION'S STUDENTS

Barbre S. Berris

In a school of 1,000 students, up to 100 will be gay, lesbian, or bisexual; 10 will be transgender; and 1 will be intersex (biologically neither male nor female). If their lives are average, eighty-seven of them will be verbally harassed, forty of them will be physically harassed, and nine-teen will be physically assaulted in the next year, because of their sexual orientation or gender expression. Sixty-two will feel mostly unsafe going to school. Thirty will harm themselves in what may be suicide attempts. Their academics suffer; social and emotional needs go hand in hand with educational needs, and nervous students don't learn easy (Young, p. 1, 2011).

As exemplified in the above passage, lesbian, gay, bisexual, transgender, and intersex (LGBTI) students encounter immense challenges during their school experiences both on and off campus. These experiences have been negatively linked to their physical and mental well-being and academic success. Research has shown that LGBTI students face problems such as low self-esteem, feelings of alienation, depression, anxiety, substance abuse, self-destructive behaviors and even suicide throughout their entire education experience (GLSEN, 2009; Rackin, 2003; Ross, n.d., Vaccaro, 2006). In many cases, these problems are not a result of someone identifying as LGBTI, but rather a result of actions and speech of intolerance and discrimination by peers, parents, teachers, clergy and strangers (Young, 2011). LGBTI students across the country have reported incidents of insensitive teachers who allow gay slurs to go unanswered and sometimes teachers make slurs themselves. Kosciw and Diaz (2006) found "even when faculty or other school staff were present, the use of biased and derogatory language by students remained largely unchallenged," and teachers and staff who witnessed homophobic remarks intervened only 16.5 percent of the time (p. 17).

I became interested in LGBTI issues in high school when my best friend "came out" to me. Because he lived in a small town that did not support homosexuality, in fact viewed it as a sin, I was one of the first people that he told he was gay. Upon learning this information, it never crossed my mind to treat him any differently because he was gay. However, I quickly learned that not everyone was as supportive and open-minded about gays. Witnessing the hardships my friend went through after he "came out" made me interested in learning more about LGBTI issues. Since embarking on this journey, many LGBTI individuals have welcomed me to be a part of their community without question. If they are so welcoming and open to me, how can I not want to be just as open with them?

Everyone needs to feel accepted and supported and often the LGBTI community does not receive the acceptance and support they need and, more importantly, deserve. It is not my place to judge the choices of anyone, I can only be a supportive person and professional.

Because of my various roles in Student Affairs positions on university campuses, my professional experience with these issues has been primarily on the college level. In addition to initiatives geared towards LGBTI students, many of these institutions are working to educate the campus community to be allies and a safe space to form an inclusive, non-violent environment for LGBTI students to thrive, learn, and be accepted. Often this acceptance can make the difference between whether or not the student will drop out or graduate (Ross, n.d.). Young (2011) found when LGBTI students are able to connect to an accepting and supportive adult in their school, they learn more, make better grades, and have enhanced emotional well-being. One such program initiative for campus communities is the Safe Space program.

It is unclear where the idea for "Safe" programs for LGBTI individuals began, the earliest documented program is Ball State University's Safe on Campus program (Poynter & Tubbs, 2007). Since their development, names for programs vary, including such titles as Safe Space, Safe Zone, Safe Harbor, Safe on Campus, and Allies (for this section, Safe Space will refer to these programs) and the target population has broadened to include queer (a once derogatory term, but now a term used with pride) and questioning individuals; however the goals of the programs are similar. All are geared to improving campus climate for LGBTQQI individuals, common goals include "increasing awareness, enhancing conversations around LGBTQQI issues, providing safe spaces, educating and providing skills to members to confront homophobia, transphobia, biphobia or heterosexism" (Poynter & Tubbs, 2007, p. 122). Furthermore, these programs are based on a need to identify, educate, and support campus members about the needs of LGBTQQI members. Participants in Safe Space programs are often identified by displaying a "safe symbol" sign, typically incorporating a pink triangle, rainbow and/or the word ally on a sign displayed on one's office doors or living space (Ballard, Bartle, & Masequesmay, 2008; Evans, 2002; Poynter & Tubbs, 2007).

Safe Space programs are similar in that they share common goals and reasons for development; however, these programs can differ greatly in their structures. The greatest difference is whether training is required to receive a "Safe Space" sign. To reach a greater population of participants, some campuses do not require training (Ballard, Bartle, & Masequesmay; 2008; Evans, 2002; Poynter & Tubbs, 2007) to create a space designated as a "Safe Space" by the sign. In those instances, once an interested individual has requested a sign, he/she is provided with informational material about the sign and guidelines they must follow to display the sign. Even for campuses that require training, structures vary and depend on the goals and assessed needs of the program on a particular campus. One drawback to requiring training is that fewer campus constituents may participate; however, in many cases those who do participate may be more committed as they have taken the step to attend workshops (Poynter & Tubbs, 2007). Controversy exists over whether training should be required for individuals wishing to display a Safe Space sign (Ballard, Bartle, & Masequesmay, 2008). Research has found that the benefits of training outweigh the possibility that fewer people may participate for several reasons (Ballard, Bartle, & Masequesmay, 2008; Evans, 2002; Poynter & Tubbs, 2007). First, training allows participants the opportunity to learn how to overcome conversational barriers that may arise when interacting with LGBTQQI individuals. Poynter and Tubbs (2007) noted, "posting a Space Safe sign or symbol is helpful in communicating nonverbal support but not all persons who post a sign or display a symbol are able to communicate effectively when conversation [about LGBTQQI issues] ensues" (p. 125). Second, training can reduce the possibility of individuals only posting signs because they feel that it is "cool, "politically correct," or the "right thing to do" without possessing the knowledge or skills to adequately address real-life issues faced by LGBTQQI students (Ballard, Bartle, & Masequesmay, 2008). Third, while training may not guarantee LGBTQQI-cultural competence immediately, it does provide an outlet to learn more and interact with individuals interested in learning further about the topic (Poynter & Tubbs, 2007). Similar to programs where training is not required, participants of the training models are provided guidelines, typically in the form of a contract or values statement to execute, before being allowed to display the sign (Ballard, Bartle, & Masequesmay, 2008; Poynter & Tubbs, 2007). Additionally, Poytner and Tubbs (2007) found even with a training program, ongoing educational opportunities should be required for participants to remain active in a Safe Space program. They found continued development helps individuals better understand and learn additional resources to assist them in their advocacy.

STEPS TO CREATE A SAFE SPACE PROGRAM

Once the decision has been made to create a Safe Space program at an institution, many strategic considerations must be discussed, including: identifying who will organize and administer the program over time; ensuring that all university stakeholders, including campus administration, faculty/staff and students, are aware and accepting of the program; and determining what resources are available for program creation, what will be included in the program, and how the information will be distributed to program participants.

For campuses with professionally staffed LGBTQQI resource centers, Safe Space programs are typically initiated by these centers; however, when campuses do not have such resources, the implementation of a Safe Space program is coordinated by faculty/staff and/or student organizations. Many schools utilize an advisory committee consisting of faculty/staff members and students to design and implement the program. This model is advantageous due to the expertise and knowledge of faculty/staff organizers and the energy and empowerment of student organizers. In addition to the advisory committee, campus offices and/or academic departments including women's centers, multicultural centers, Greek affairs, residence life, counseling and psychological services, health education, student activities, Women's studies, academic advising, human sexuality, etc. may have an interest in helping launch the program and should be consulted in the formation of the program (Poynter and Tubbs, 2007).

Once a committee is created, the next step is to determine the goals and objectives of the program. An example of these goals and objectives is: "The goal of X University's Safe Space program is to provide a network of students, staff, and faculty committed to providing support to lesbian, gay, transgender, queer, questioning and intersex (LGBTQQI) individuals and their allies at X University and beyond". The Safe Space program aims to (1) identify and mobilize a network of people who are empathetic and knowledgeable about LGBTQQI issues and concerns, (2) emphasize knowledge about campus and community resources as well as counseling and helping skills, (3) provide evidence of LGBTQQI support by displaying a sign as a visible symbol of personal commitment, and (4) reduce the fear and discrimination of LGBTQQI persons within the X University community.

A program's goals and objectives will impact its structure, which is the next step in the implementation process. The structure includes the resources that will be provided to participants, whether or not training will be required for participant's to be deemed a safe space, and a contract for participant's to sign as an agreement to provide a safe space for individuals facing sexual orientation or gender identity issues. Because there is no universal, standard format for Safe Space programs, the structure varies based off of the needs of individual institutions; however, there are common components that all programs possess. Program participants should be provided with educational materials about the LGBTQQI community. This material is typically provided to participants in a binder divided into the following sections: introduction of the Safe Space program including purpose, goals, objectives, and facilitator information; overview of lesbian, gay, bisexual, transsexual, queer, questioning and intersex (LGBTQQI) basics including definitions and theories; the coming out process including theories of coming out, ways to prepare for coming out, and information when a person comes out to the participant; and ally resource tools including how to use the resources, benefits of being an ally, ways to create a non-homophobic campus environment, and when to refer a student to a mental health professional.

When the educational materials have been created, the next step of training is to provide lessons for determining the structure. During training, participants should also be provided an overview of the purpose of the program, information on issues that LGBTQQI individuals may be facing, and information on further resources and how to make referrals. Additionally, time should be allotted for introduction, discussion of terminology, a panel of LGBTQQI individuals and allies to speak, and activities, such as case studies and role plays to apply information learned. For training to be successful, it is also important to set ground rules in the begging of the session to set the stage for a safe space where participants are comfortable sharing dialogue, to respect each other's opinions and to maintain confidentiality of personal information shared (Poynter and Tubbs, 2007). At the conclusion of the training, participants should be provided with the opportunity to sign a Safe Space contract. By signing the contract, participants agree to provide a "safe space" for anyone dealing with sexual or gender orientation issues and to uphold the expectations and responsibilities of being an ally.

Being involved in Space Safe initiatives and conversations has taught me huge lessons. One of the biggest lessons is probably that of acceptance for all people, regardless of their perceived differences. As a privileged white woman, I never felt the profound impact of extreme societal rejection, nor the power of what it means for socially rejected people to find alternative places where they know they are accepted. I think this lesson surprised me the most when my husband and I were once with friends at a gay night club. After being at the club for about an hour, we had a mutual acquaintance of ours come over and hug us both. We asked what the hug was for and he looked at us and said "Thank you." When we inquired further as to why he needed to thank us, he said, "for wanting to spend your Friday night in a gay establishment and feel completely at ease." He added that it was not often that a heterosexual couple is open and accepting enough of the community to come to its established place for social gatherings. His comments taught me that it only takes a few minutes to make a difference in someone's life. Having the opportunity to do so through LGBT outreach and initiatives, such as safe space programs, is just a little piece of something I believe that I and others can do to make a difference in student lives.

Support, acceptance and outreach is needed at all levels in education. Whether it is a mentoring program in elementary and middle grades or a gay straight alliance program in high school, it is important that this population is reached. In light of increased incidents of bullying in K-12 education and suicide rates of this population, forming programs, such as safe space, in all educational institutions is important so LBGT students can learn where they can find a haven, free of worries about being treated as different, and can, therefore, be accepted for who they are.

REFERENCES

Alvarez, S. D. & Schneider, J. (2008). One college campus's need for a safe zone: a case study. *Journal of Gender Studies,* 17(1), 71–4. Retrieved from EBSCOhost.

Ballard, S. L., Bartle, E., & Masequesmay, G. (2008). Finding queer allies: The impact of ally training and safe zone stickers on campus climate. Retrieved from EBSCO*host*.

Evans, N. J. (2002). The impact of an LGBT Safe Zone project on campus climate. *Journal of College Student Development,* 43(4), 522–538. Retrieved from EBSCOhost.

GLSEN. (2009). The 2009 national school climate survey: Executive summary. Retrieved from http://www.glsen.org/binary-data/GLSEN_ATTACHMENTS/file/000/001/1676–4.pdf.

Kosciw, J. G. & Diaz, E. M. (2006). The 2005 national school climate survey: The experiences of lesbian, gay, bisexual, and transgender youth in our nation's school. Retrieved from http://www.glsen.org/binary-data/GLSEN_ATTACHMENTS/file/585–1.pdf

Poynter, K. J. & Tubbs, N. J. (2007). Safe zones: Creating LGBT safe space ally programs. *Journal of LGBT Youth,* 5(1), 121–132. Retrieved from EBSCOhost.

Rankin, S. R. (2003). *Campus climate for gay, lesbian, bisexual, and transgender people: A national perspective.* New York: The National Gay and Lesbian Task Force Policy Institute. Retrieved February 20, 2012, from www.ngltf.org

Ross, F. (n.d.).Supporting GLBT students through mentoring. Retrieved February 20, 2012, from http://www.naspa.org/programs/nufp/resources/Supporting GLBT Students.pdf

Vaccaro, A. (2006). Gay, lesbian, bisexual & transgender students. In L. A. Gohn & G. R. Albin (Eds.), *Understanding college student subpopulations: A guide for student affairs professionals* (pp. 349–386). United States: National Association of Student Personnel Administrators (NASPA), Inc.

Young, A. L. (2011). *Queer youth advice for educators: How to respect and protect your lesbian, gay, bisexual and transgender students.* Providence, RI: Next Generation Press.

A WEALTH
OF WHAMMIES
FOR YOUTH
IN POVERTY

Paul C. Gorski

It is unjust enough that scores of young people in the United States are denied basic human rights; that even in a country which paints itself as a global model of human rights, kids go without food, safe and affordable housing, equitable schooling opportunities, and healthcare. Heck, in a country with the level of resources the U.S. has, the very existence of homelessness, hunger, and poverty in the face of growing corporate profits is inexcusable. In this way, the U.S. *is the very definition of systemic classism*: a country in which poverty rates, income inequality, and corporate profits often grow simultaneously.

What's worse, though, is that poor youth bear the brunt of this injustice. They are denied opportunity themselves, piled, as they often are, into over-crowded and under-resourced schools in which they are offered less rigorous curricula and pedagogies and more skilling and drilling than their wealthier counterparts. But they also carry the burden of their families' disenfranchisement, suffering society's refusal to provide their parents or guardians with living wage work or decent healthcare. It's a sort of double-whammy of economic injustice.

Make that a triple-whammy. Because even while poor kids and their families suffer these injustices, they are blamed, not only for their own poverty, but for the very economic conditions that press upon them most vigorously. It's been maddening to watch Reagan's "welfare queen" rhetoric reappear in the midst of the economic crisis (as if the economy hasn't always been in crisis from the perspective of poor people) in a new "entitlement class" discourse. Both terms serve the same purpose: to deflect collective attention from gross economic injustices driven largely by corporate greed and to aim it, instead, at those people with the least amount of power to popularize a counter-narrative. But, what's more, it's been horrifying to observe mass compliance with this deflection. The result: Republicans return to office en masse, where they no doubt will attempt to extend Bush's tax cuts (read: welfare) for the wealthy while continuing to kill those social programs meant to aid poor families. Classic deficit ideology in motion.

Symptoms and scars from this compliance abound. For example, I have watched in utter disbelief as those once infuriated to action by *Savage Inequalities*, Jonathan Kozol's tome describing the proverbial shafting of poor students in the form of school funding inequities, similarly embrace Ruby Payne's A Framework for Understanding Poverty, a book which is, itself, both regression and shaft. The former forced us to take on systemic injustice against youth head-on, identifying the "problem" to be solved as existing within an unjust system, as one pressing upon our country's most disenfranchised families. The latter gave us an "out"; it permitted us to ignore injustice altogether and to imagine ways we might redress poverty by fixing poor people rather than by fixing that which necessitates the existence of poor people in the wealthiest country in the world.

At last count, Payne and her stable of trainers have found their ways into upwards of 70% of school districts in the U.S., making millions of dollars a year by telling us how badly poor kids need to learn to act like middle class kids, while federal education policy continues to demonize poor students (as well as students of color and ELL students) and the teachers who teach them. Ugh. Make that a quadruple whammy.

Meanwhile, in those same schools, the very students who are denied opportunity because they are poor simultaneously are learning the Great Lie: that the U.S. is a meritocracy, that they can be Oprah Winfrey or Bill Gates if they just work hard enough. If *they* just work hard enough. This is a set-up. Because, on average, it makes no difference at all how hard poor kids work. Some will find their ways into higher socioeconomic brackets than their families, but a vast majority of them won't. And it's not a matter of merit. Not mostly, at least.

People often ask me what I propose to do about all of this. It's a fair question, I suppose, although I think the eagerness for practical solutions even when we don't fully understand the problem is what leads us down the Ruby Payne path. If we find ourselves committed to understand and then act, I have found a few reflection-and-action steps to be a good place to begin.

First we should ask ourselves, *Why are poor people poor*? In a capitalistic and classist society, social conditions exist because somebody profits from them. Who profits from poverty?

Secondly, we should ask ourselves, with the previous question in mind, *What were we socialized to believe about why poor people are poor?* Part of understanding a problem, after all, is in understanding how we are encouraged to misunderstand it and, of course, to misunderstand who profits from our misunderstanding.

Thirdly, we should resist the temptation of deficit ideology, which locates the problem of poverty within supposed deficiencies of poor communities rather than in that which disenfranchises poor communities. This also means rejecting solutions to classism aimed at youth (and adults) that are meant to fix poor people rather than fixing economic injustice. (And who, by the way, profits from deficit ideology?)

Fourthly, we must realize that fixing classism means fixing economic injustices and that this requires attention to systemic concerns. The worst classism is not peer ridicule or biased media, although certainly these contribute to a larger process of hierarchy-maintenance. The hierarchy won't crash with the mitigation of teasing or even with more programs to feed, clothe, and house poor people (as important as these programs are). So rather than focusing on mitigating classism or sustaining poor kids in poverty, fight the conditions that necessitate or recycle poverty, such as the scarcity of living wage jobs, the dissolution of labor unions, the neoliberal shift of welfare from the poor to the corporate elite, and the influence of corporate lobbies on local, state and federal policy. I know these actions sound big, so connect with groups, like United for a Fair Economy, which already are organizing around economic justice and taking on those who profit from these conditions.

It's a long road—social reform. So let's commit, at the very least, to not making it longer with diversions.

Section 8: Listening to Children Pushed to the Margins Clears Space for Equity to Flourish

Please take 10 minutes and write about any people you know or have known who have been part of the LGBT community. What qualities about that person do you admire? What struggles has he or she endured because of his or her "coming-out"? If you do not know anyone from that community, please write about your belief system in regards to LGBT issues.

Please write your discussion in the space below.

_____

_____

_____

_____

_____

_____

_____

After writing those ideas, please consider the following activities:

- Choose a partner and share your written discussion. How do your ideas compare and contrast with any of the ideas represented in the articles read in this section?

_____

_____

- Why do you think that these particular students are pushed to the margins in schools?

_____

_____

- After reading Gorski's article, what ideas about poverty do you think teachers should consider when teaching children who live in disenfranchised communities?

_____

_____

_____

◆ What are some of the biases in schools leveled against children living in poverty?

_____

_____

_____

◆ What kinds of actions can teachers take to rid schools of those beliefs and behaviors?

_____

_____

_____

After your discussion, please view with your classmates the short *YouTube* production www.youtube.com/watch?v=_B-hVWQnjjM (1 min. 46 seconds)

1. After watching the video, discuss with your group any ideas that you think would be useful in assisting K-12 students to develop inclusive attitudes in and outside classroom spaces.

_____

_____

_____

_____

_____

_____

2. Read Waymon Hudson, "Gay Georgia teen starts group to help LGBT youth" on website:

www.huffingtonpost.com/waymon-hudson/gay-georgia-teen-starts-g_b_649042.html

3. Discuss with your partner or a small group how Waymon's article might be helpful to any of your students in educating themselves about the issues of LGBT civil rights. After your discussion jot down your group's ideas in the space below:

_____

_____

_____

_____

_____

4. How might his column be used to counter homophobia in schools?

_____

_____

Watch the video, *It gets better:* http://www.youtube.com/watch?v=OCSUfFStTQE

- ◆ Discuss with your partner any concepts that you found to be significant concerning issues of children and diversity. Then, please write below describing your discussion with your partner.

SECTION 9

CREATING DEMOCRACY REQUIRES YOUTH PARTICIPATION IN THE CLASSROOM AND OUT

Image copyright Thomas M Perkins, 2012. Used under license from Shutterstock. Inc.

I've witnessed very young children learn to function as democratic citizens, not as obedient robots. And through the veteran teachers' enthusiasm for exploration and change, I continue to realize that no matter how long I teach, I will always have something to learn from children. But especially I have found in this supportive environment that classrooms for all children must be spaces for discovery and joyful noise!

—Ceexta Hall

CHAPTER 9

THE ETHICS OF MOVING FROM DEFICIT RESEARCH TO YOUTH ACTION RESEARCH

Joan T. Wynne

Abstract: *Research practices in US urban neighborhoods often seemed stuck on discovering the deficits of students and families of color, living in poverty. This propensity has created in urban communities a deep suspicion of research. In this paper, I will use stories from African American and indigenous people's history, people who have been pushed to the margins, as a backdrop for examining youth action research as an ethical alternative to "deficit research practices." After offering a bit of a satirical scenario of where deficit theories can lead us, I will introduce the work of two young scholars who are developing youth as participant action researchers. And through those stories, pose possibilities for looking beyond deficit thinking and toward the young people who are leading education for liberation in their communities.*

INTRODUCTION: STORIES THAT VALIDATE THE NEED FOR YPAR

"We are the creature of questions and consciousness, and the creature of storytelling, the creature who addresses other creatures with words, with stories. So I think that stories and pictures address the fundamental basis of who we are, and they're in that sense the most existentially penetrating aspect of teaching."

—*Robert Coles in Teaching Tolerance*

Because I am a former teacher of literature, I have, like Robert Coles, a penchant for the belief in the power of story. And story, for me, undergirds all research, whether it is told in numbers or narratives. Yet, in research, whose story gets told and who tells that story becomes as important as the story itself. Researchers from dominant cultures for centuries have been telling the story of indigenous people from a mainstream lens and within a context of dysfunctional, deficit presuppositions (Smith). I have found that practice to be also true when research stories are told about parents and children living in urban or rural poverty in the U.S. And it is in these contexts that Youth Participatory Action Research (YPAR) offers a counter narrative, an ethical alternative.

Before exploring the value of YPAR, I want to offer a piece of southern American history as the background story for considering YPAR as a challenge to colonial or deficit methodologies, moving teacher education programs away from their often "missionary" style research.

Robert Coles, a child psychiatrist and researcher during the U. S. Civil Rights Era, in his narratives about working with children assumed to be traumatized by violent racist attacks, offered a contrast to the typical modern portrayal of people at society's bottom. He went to the south, he said, expecting manifestations of psychopathology in black children desegregating schools, but found, "remarkably little psychiatric illness . . .despite their trials" (1972, 8 & 26). He further found in the behavior of these children immersed in the battle for civil rights, a "moral capacity, moral spirit, moral leadership" (1986, 26–27). By telling the stories from the children's perspectives, Coles was able to look beyond his mainstream lens and see strength and courage where many, trapped by their dominant constructs, saw only victims.

Researcher Charles Payne in *I've got the light of freedom* (1995) found those same positive qualities while raising the voices of those at the bottom to explain the complexities and triumphs of the Southern Freedom Movement. In his book, an African American sharecropper, Fannie Lou Hamer, talks about the struggles of oppressed people in the south who demanded their rights as democratic citizens, a collective challenge that shaped the destiny of the nation. While jailed for her audacity to register to vote, Hamer was brutally beaten, losing an eye, yet forgave her torturers. Her report of the narrative of another victim, Annell Ponder, illumines that same quality:

And I could hear somebody when they say, "Cain't you say yessir, nigger? Cain't you say yessir, bitch?" and I could understand Miss Ponder's voice, She said, "Yes, I can say yessir." He said, "Well, say it." She said, "I don't know you well enough." She never would say yessir and I could hear when she would hit the flo', and then I could hear them licks just soundin'. . . .but anyway, she kept screamin' and they kep beatin' on her and finally she started prayin' for 'em, and she asked God to have mercy on 'em, because they didn't know what they were doing. (Payne, p. 227)

Like the people from Cole's research, these sharecroppers demonstrated a sophisticated ethical belief in the redemptive quality of the human spirit. Many, instead of hating the oppressor, chose to believe in his potential for recovery. Hamer and Ponder, and thousands of other Black activists like them, understood "whites as trapped in their own history" (Payne, p. 310). These principled sensitivities mirrored in the stories of those thousands stood in stark contrast to the moral depravity of the Jim Crow South. Those narratives were part of the Civil Rights Movement which Richard Rorty explains as "an expression of naked moral outrage at unnecessary human suffering. It was the great, inspiring moral event of our lifetime" (1995).

Through learning about the stories of black people in Mississippi forced to live in poverty, urban researchers might gain a broader understanding of the historical context of the lives of those students and families they are investigating, a context that lies beneath and belies the mainstream researchers' stories. For researchers to become stuck in discovering the deficits and dysfunctions of people forced into poverty, these victims of failing schools, seems unproductive in the light of their ancestors' narratives. Their history of liberation practices, reflecting an ethic highly tuned to the possibility for the oppressor to deliver himself from evil deeds, demands a less simplistic research agenda for studying the education of their progeny.

That redemption ethic resounds also in the stories told by Lilla Watson, an Indigenous Australian activist and artist. During a 2007 radio interview, she shared a story about her Aborigine father who as a young boy was "chained like a dog," left for 3 days without water, escaped, then was beaten for having escaped. Yet, she insists, "My father was never bitter about white people. That is one of the strengths of Aboriginal culture. We can still see the people, the colonial oppressors as human." The interviewer, Phillip Adams, remarks that the Aborigine's capacity to forgive surprises him. "Yes," she said, "I only wish that white people could understand that quality as a strength and not a weakness." So, it would seem, if we come as researchers to find the deficiencies within the communities that receive bad education, we're missing the point.

At a United Nations Conference in 1985, Watson invites another challenge. She said, "If you have come to help me, you are wasting your time, but if you have come because your liberation is bound up in mine, then come let's work together." While working in schools, I have found her insight to be a profound paradigm shift for me and many others in mainstream culture. As educators and researchers, we often seem to gallop into the urban arena with a missionary zeal, with pre-conceived questions and interventions to "fix" all those children, families, and schools. Understanding that our "liberation is bound up with theirs" is rarely understood, yet taking hold of that principle might be instrumental in the ethical emancipation of the dominant culture.

FROM PAST TO PRESENT

Today, research still abounds that blames parents and poverty as the causes of children's lack of success at low-performing schools. Many other schools, however, have been documented where poor students academically soar. The late scholar and activist, Asa G. Hilliard, III, called these schools "Power Schools" because the people there create a culture of belief in the genius of all children, regardless of socioeconomic circumstances. And their teachers, Hilliard insisted, not only believe it, they demand it from the children, while putting support systems in place to foster excellence. We know from the Mississippi Freedom Schools, operated during the sixties, that with minimal to no resources, college students taught sharecroppers to read and understand the U.S. Constitution so they could demand their right to vote (Payne, 1995). We know from Paulo Friere's work in Brazil that socioeconomics does not keep adults living in poverty from learning and using knowledge to transform their lives (Friere 1970). We know from Bob Moses' NSF research agenda that children scoring at the bottom quartile of academic tests, can, indeed, learn algebra, trigonometry, calculus, etc. (Wynne, 2010). And not only do they learn it, but also teach it to younger children. Shouldn't we be focusing, as Hilliard suggests, "on the quality of the service rather than on the analysis of children and their families" (2001). I've grown weary of research that dominates the field on the dysfunctions of children and parents living in poverty, that insinuates their low SES is the culprit that keeps them from learning. Those stories are from an old paradigm, and we need to stop telling them. They lead schools nowhere.

Most Critical Race Theorists (CRT) assume, as I do, that hegemony is a major reason that poor people aren't given the schools and teachers that can effectively assist them in achieving academically. African American and Indigenous Women's scholarship probably lead the intellectual discourse about the impact of "the interlocking relationships between race, gender and class" on the research concerning people of color and children of the poor across the globe (Smith, p. 167).

During the last decade, a U.S. federal judge validated these scholars' assumptions about the nation's intent to ill-serve its marginalized citizens. On June 25, 2002, Justice Alfred T. Lerner reversed a NY state court's ruling that had vindicated parents who had sued the state for failing to adequately educate their children. In his decision in *Campaign for Fiscal Equity v. New York,* he declared that New York students were only entitled to an eighth-grade level education and low-level job preparation. When the national courts sanction a system of apartheid schooling, we as educators should speak clearly and often about how notions of power and privilege can contaminate our research agendas. Further "deficit" research studies investigating what parents and children living in poverty do or don't do at home seems a waste of our professional time.

One of those studies, popular in the U.S., was designed by Hart and Risley (2003) who with all of the best intentions wanted to better understand how to close the language gap between poor and middle-class children. Through 2-1/2 years of visiting 42 American homes, they claim to have discovered that a child from a professional family would hear 8 million more words during a year than a child in a welfare family—finding, I suppose, that middle-class families certainly use a lot of words. Again basing assumptions on a deficit model for research, one of their prescriptions for resolving the language gap was to teach parents and care-givers to talk more to children living in poverty.

While regarding Hart and Risley's study, it might be constructive to consider a contrasting study by a white journalism professor in Texas, "The morally lazy white middle class," published by the Poverty & Race Research Action Council. In that study, Jensen (p. 12) said, "In both domestic and international policy, it is the self-interested behavior or the inattention to injustice on the part of the white middle class that makes possible the oppressive policies of the U. S.—the attack on labor unions and working people, the coddling of big business that produces obscene gaps in wealth and privilege, the abandonment of the poor, and the assault for five decades on any third-world movement that dared to strike out on an independent course."

A LOGICAL PROGRESSION OF DEFICIT THEORY: AN ETHICS GAP

Now if we juxtapose those two studies, while considering Lerner's decision, CRT's assumptions, and Movement stories of resistance, we might be led to consider as a logical progression a research agenda that puts Hart & Risley in the homes of only the elite. While many have investigated the language gap & the so-called "achievement gap," maybe other researchers could start examining the ethics gap.

But to begin a conversation on the ethics gap, it might be useful to set the context by telling another story from Coles research about the people on whom most deficit theorists base their research. In *The Moral Life of Children*, Coles reflects on the life of six-year-old Ruby Bridges, who first integrated a white school in New Orleans amidst violent protests and had to be escorted to school by Federal Marshalls for protection each morning. Ruby's mother told Coles that every night Ruby prayed for those in the mob who threatened and harassed her (1986, 26–27). That kind of moral spirit, superior ethical behavior, might be used as a standard for measuring the ethics gap. If we contrast this story against the deficit model of research, proliferated by studies like Hart & Risley, Ruby Payne, etc. then the research agenda might look like the following: Researchers would:

◆ Visit privileged white families' homes to investigate what happens or doesn't happen in those homes that cause their children to go into suburban schools like Columbine and randomly kill other children. What deficit exists in those homes? In those literacy rich environments, which of those multitude of books fosters such behavior?

◆ Or visit those suburban homes to investigate why the majority of drug users are their children—and the majority of drug dealers are their parents (NIDA, 2003). What doctrine in all of those books on their shelves promotes that kind of unethical behavior?

♦ Or investigate why their grown up children secretly sell arms to other countries, perpetrating violence while calling it free trade—or engage in double-speak about the horrors of weapons of mass destruction while sitting on the largest arsenal of WMD on the planet. What books do they make their children read that create a love for duplicitous language and behavior? What is missing in their home education that hinders their moral and/or cognitive development? Maybe we should disaggregate the dysfunctions of those families?

♦ Or investigate which of those multitude of words and books used in these homes makes their adult children either so ethically bankrupt and/or cognitively under-developed that they can't discover why the richest nation in the world can't feed 12 million of its children who live in poverty—or why that same nation cannot make sure that all of its children have health care? or why that nation spends more money on bombs than they do on education? What are those parents feeding their babies that cause them to grow-up blind to the laws of justice and equality for all—Is there something their parents say with all of those words at their disposal that encourages their adult children to become addicted to greed? Do their addictions to money and power cause their brains to shrink? Does being stuck in denial of their wrong-doing foster the notion that creative problem solving means whoever has the biggest bomb is the most civilized? Are their mothers using too many words so that their children get too confused to wonder about these ethical issues?

♦ And just where were the appropriate adult role models for their young teens? Were their absentee fathers, too busy amassing great fortunes, buying boats, cars, mansions to develop moral character in their sons and daughters? Is there a correlation between number of hours played on a tennis court or golf course by parents to numbers of times their adult children lie, cheat, steal from the public coffers? Does too little time in prison for parental white-collar crimes keep their children from learning truth or consequences? Well, you see, the questions are infinite for the researcher.

"WHERE DO WE GO FROM HERE?"

Using these questions that seem a logical progression from deficit research methodology, then researchers might go beyond investigating the families of the elite. They might begin studying these families' schools, their suburban schools—and, then, their colleges like Yale, Harvard, Princeton, Stanford—those schools that have fostered an education which graduates people who produce companies like Enron, Tyco, Arthur Anderson, Haliburton, Goldman Sachs, Blackwater, Citibank, Bank of America, etc. who profiteer from war, rob taxpayers with bloated contracts, rob people's pension funds, bankrupt small businesses, sell bad loans to homeowners. What is deficient and dysfunctional in those schools? Was their curriculum watered down? Were their standards too low for teaching critical thinking in ethics courses? Do their accounting courses teach nothing about the integrity needed to handle national budgets? Shouldn't these schools be held accountable when one of their graduates and former president of the nation thinks that taking a 2 billon dollar surplus and changing it into a 9 trillion dollar deficit is good economics? But even larger, shouldn't these schools be accountable for hiring unqualified teachers who either could not or did not model or teach integrity, compassion, and service to all of humanity? In other words, in those families and schools how do we close the ethical achievement gap? Have we been focusing too much of our research on the wrong families and the wrong schools. Might we as researchers be asking the wrong questions?

Might we ask a question spoken years ago by Martin Luther King, Jr. who said, "Where do we go from here?" (King 1968) For me, that question is at the crux of the raison d'etre of all research. In examining any topic, don't the discoveries always lead us to ask King's question?

And, if we put that question in the context of the deficits and deficiencies of elitist education, then we might be led toward King's later assumption that in order to know where we go from here, "We must first," he says, "honestly recognize where we are now . . . .The plantation and the ghetto were created by those who had power . . . Now the problem of transforming the ghetto, therefore, is a problem of power" (King, p. 37) Again, if we put King's quotation in the framework of ethical urban research, I think we might spend as much time looking honestly at that "problem of power" as we do focusing on the victims of that power. Maybe in our public schools, institutions, and communities, the power elite keep us focused on the purported abnormalities of the "huddled masses" so that we don't focus on the moral dysfunctions and deliberate chicanery of those privileged few.

CREATIVE SCHOLARS' ANTIDOTE TO DEFICIT RESEARCH AND PRACTICE

King's concerns about the abuses and toxic residue of power are addressed in the stories of two young scholars who are radically engaged in YPAR, offering a counter to deficit research agendas. They both use YPAR methodology to capture the imagination of their pre-service and in-service teachers in exploring the multi-facets of power issues in schools. Yet more importantly, these two researchers, Maria Lovett and Louie Rodriguez, help develop urban public school children into research practitioners, lifting their voices, sparking their creativity, and all the while, demanding excellence from these students. That demand is possible because both professors are building scaffolds for those youngsters to deconstruct the epistemologies that have trapped them and their ancestors for a century into inferior schools. They both as Lovett suggests, use the "rigor of academic research to open dialogue on silenced issues, to re-expose concealed oppressions, and to mobilize action." And like Coles and Payne, they believe in the capacity of children, abandoned by society, to excel. Derrick Bell, in an interview with NPR in 1992, said:

"In all my courses, I really have to teach the basic messages of my life... that the rewards, the satisfactions, are not in being partner or making a million dollars, but in recognizing evils, recognizing injustices, and standing up and speaking out about them even in absolutely losing situations where you know it's not going to bring about any change—that there are intangible rewards to the spirit that make that worthwhile."

Both Rodriguez and Lovett, I believe, emulate Bell's message. Both know that their research focus is typically devalued by tenure & promotion committees; yet having received those warnings and knowing the risks to their academic careers, they soldier on bringing their expertise into urban communities, raising the voices of young students, and helping to empower them to work toward liberating their communities from the layers of injustices perpetrated by racist and classist policies and politics.

Their work also reflects the call by Bob Moses, President of the Algebra Project (AP), MacArthur Genius Fellow, and Civil Rights icon, to organize the people at the bottom to demand what the rest of the nation says they don't want—a quality education. Moses insists that if our intention is to radically change an oppressive system, then "embedded in this work" of education is the concurrent building of a demand for positive change by people at the bottom. In most current urban educational systems, student voices sit at the bottom of the hierarchal chain of school-speak. Yet Moses continuously reminds us that "Young people finding their voice instead of being spoken for is a crucial part of the process" (Moses, p.19). Underneath his practice of raising those voices "is the idea that if you can really bring about any kind of change at the bottom, it is going to change everything" (Moses 2001, p.188). Our work, like Moses' and Freire's, is grounded in a belief in the power of the disenfranchised to transform their worlds (Moses 2001; Freire 1970; Rodriguez 2009).

RODRIGUEZ AND YOUTH PARTICIPATORY ACTION RESEARCH

Rodriguez uses YPAR practice to encourage young people in low-performing urban schools to examine the challenges that they face as a consequence of being denied an equitable space in the world of power and privilege. And one of its most vital components is its insistence on leading students to examine the resources and talents present in their own communities. Additionally, those examinations typically propel student participation in civic engagement. Rodriguez explains that:

In this work, a culture of dialogue is initially established because given the policy environment . . . most marginalized youth aren't used to speaking with one another . . . about social injustice in school. So, developing a dialogical culture is key. Then I provide a brief history of educational inequality for all the major communities of color in the U.S.— African Americans, Latino, and Native Americans and women. We engage in a series of dialogues about inequality and the conditions we face in our own schools. We organize themes and topics . . . then the youth assign themselves to a group. From there, youth are taught research methodology . . . . After data collection and analysis, youth put together presentations and disseminate their findings to anyone who will listen in the hopes of transforming policy and practice at all levels (Rodriguez, personal e-mail, April 19, 2010)

While in Miami, Rodriguez taught Moses' AP high school cohort. He guided students into dialogues, and students presented their research at the end of each summer experience, demonstrating their growth from disengaged students to pro-active, confident activists. Our instructional plan during the summer was driven by Moses and Freire's beliefs that education is never politically neutral; it either supports the status quo or it fosters a journey toward individual and societal transformation (2001).

Part of that journey for us is to tie our work in the public schools to our university teaching. Algebra Project high school students presented their work to FIU undergraduate and graduate classes. These sessions were powerful to witness as stereotypes about urban children held by university students inevitably bubbled up in discussions and were addressed. During one of those sessions, a high school student was explaining that she hated hearing teachers say to her, "I got mine; you get yours." To emphasize her frustration about those kinds of comments, she said she felt like throwing a chair at teachers when they uttered those words. After she talked, she overheard a college student mumbling, "That's why we don't want to teach at schools like yours." When the high school student challenged the college student about his comment, a good discussion ensued between the two groups about the fear and myths that pre-service teachers harbor about urban schools (Wynne, 2010).

Rodriguez suggests that these sessions, along with the other YPAR components, "create a way to bridge universities with communities by truly living up to Bob Moses' idea of 'school-based, university affiliated' projects" (e-mail). Moses modeled for all of us in Miami a conviction that real reform for urban schools will succeed when the university leaves its ivory tower and comes to the school house. Moses brings research mathematicians into high school classrooms to work with the students at the bottom.

One high school participant in the project, Tranette Myrthil, received the Princeton Prize in Race Relations for 2009. In a recent article in *Teaching Tolerance*, Tranette's work with Rodriguez and her social studies teacher was featured as a demonstration of the deep implications for student voice, power, and academic success that are consequences of YPAR methodology. Tranette had also participated in Moses' AP residential Academic Summer Institute at FIU, where, under Rodriguez's tutelage, she deepened her understanding of his philosophy of education for liberation and his critical pedagogy.

Rodriguez insists that crucial to his YPAR work with youth is the use of power. "We use power with, rather [than] over youth to foster relationship building, collaboration among students and ourselves, and to create the contexts for rigorous and engaging inquiry-based learning" (Rodriguez 2009). Underlying that practice of inquiry is Rodriguez's conviction that urban youngsters can and do, using equity and justice as their cauldron, re-shape their lives and the society that seeks to exclude them. As a result of his work with Moses, Rodriguez and his students have joined a national dialogue about Quality Education as a Constitutional Right. To engage in that movement, he explains that he uses his "classrooms in ways that attorneys [during the Southern Freedom Movement] used courtrooms" (2009).

LOVETT, VIDEO ACTION RESEARCH AND PEDAGOGY

Sharing that passion for youth action research, Lovett, guides students to use digital media to explore their world. Her mastering of videography as a research tool immediately captivates the students' attention. She leads them from simple fascination with the tools (cameras, laptops, software and hardware, blogs, wikis, etc) toward questioning how those tools can be used for and against them. She explains that: "To decolonize media culture, my work advocates for our students to become critical consumers of media, encourages them to negotiate and make meaning from these sources, and intervenes in the construction of new messages. Thus, the work includes not only intervention by deconstructing such images (and media spaces)—but also producing and sharing new knowledge, their knowledge." Like Rodriguez, Lovett, teaches university and high school students to look at their world with a new critical eye. Through her work at the FIU summer institutes, disenfranchised high school students began to use diverse forms of media production to critique their school and community realities. They began to use the web to search history for clues into the origins of their present struggles; to secure historical photographs, music, government documents, etc. as evidence to integrate into their digital research.

She taught these technologies to an AP cohort and the Young People's Project (YPP) students, who worked after-school, tutoring elementary students in mathematics and reading. The adolescents documented their venture into knowledge work with the children and taught them to use digital media to explore issues that interested them. Lovett indicates: "The method values process as much as product. Students pose-problems, research their topics, and create counter-stories to challenge dominant narratives. Students are challenged to study representations that frequently exist and are promoted—and then "speak" back. They are empowered with the task of re-presenting" (e-mail).

In the beginning of her work with Moses' AP students, this process took time. She used her first summer at the institute to introduce these urban students to equipment, software, techniques, etc. that they had previously never been exposed. Undaunted, though, Lovett continued the process during the students' mentoring experiences in their YPP after-school and Saturday sessions. By the time of the second year of the after-school program, several students had begun editing serious short documentaries that they had co-created, and some of these were presented to a COE faculty assembly.

Lovett's and Rodriguez's critical pedagogy creates opportunities for teachers and public school students to deeply reflect about the hegemonic structures that often stifle students' intellectual pursuits and dreams. And the products of those reflections can become imaginative flights into theatre and art; into critical and visual depictions of transforming their worlds.

We need to use our students' and our own imaginations to build a research agenda that deals with the problems of schools and solve those. From there our students will begin to build the confidence that they can solve the challenges they face in their neighborhoods. A unique value YPAR offers the researcher is an opportunity to collaborate in the excavating of the wisdom of the people most at stake in K-12 institutions, the students. That value turns traditional research upside down by giving legitimate voice to those perpetually silenced in schools.

But whenever partners work together in research, whether it be university researcher with youth, teacher, or community organizer, our earlier question of "Whose story is being told and who is telling that story" is always significant and sensitive. The old paradigms of power relationships complicate the process. Michelle Fine, who directs the Institute for Participatory Action Research and Design at City University of New York, describes its precarious nature: "Before, during and after the PAR project, whether in prison, in schools or in communities, the ashes of vulnerability—no matter how hard we try to anticipate—fall unevenly. Because of these delicacies, throughout these projects, epistemological and ethical deliberations must be deep, continuous— bold and cautious at once—about who pays for speaking truth to power" (2010). People at the margins of society for millennium have sacrificed both life and limb for speaking truth to power. Thousands of stories from across the globe could be told to illuminate that sacrifice and the dramatic shifts in governing bodies that came as a result of that heroism. Using research to uncover those narratives, as well as to create new ones, alongside young people and their teachers, aligns us with what Coles explains as the "most existential penetrating aspect of teaching." For, instead of seeing students as 'the problem,' through YPAR we take up King's challenge to transform society by having our young examine power as 'the problem.' In doing that, students change the power differential; they become the researchers instead of the objects of research. Moreover, when youngsters find their authority through the meticulous use of research protocol, they build their capacity to offer their communities alternatives to conventional beliefs of what constitutes "expert knowledge." And as Bob Moses suggests, by changing the bottom, they change everything.

REFERENCES

Aboriginal lives: Lilla Watson & Tiga Bayles, (2007) ABC Radio National, Australia. http://www.abc .net.au/rn/latenightlive/stories/2007/1926234.html

Campaign for Fiscal Equity, Inc. v. New York, 744 N.Y.S.2d 130 (2002). Press Release, Campaign for Fiscal Equity, Appellate Court Strikes Down CFE Decision (June 25, 2002) available at http://www .cfequity.org/appellatecourt7-25-02.

Coles, R. (1986). The Moral Life of Children. Boston: Atlantic Monthly Press.

Coles, R. (1972). *Farewell to the South*. Boston: Little, Brown and Co.

Drug abuse and addiction research: The sixth triennial report to Congress. (2005) National Institute on Drug Abuse. http://www.drugabuse.gov/STRC/Prevalaence.html

Fine, M. (2010) web description A brief history of the Participatory Action Research Collective. http://web.gc.cuny.edu/che/start.htm

Freire, P. *Pedagogy of the oppressed* (1970). London: Continuum Publishing Company.

Freire, P & Macedo, D.(2001) *Literacy: Reading the Word and the World*. London: Routledge.

Hart, B. & Risley, T. (2003). "The Early Catastrophe: the 30 Million Word Gap," *American Educator*, 27(1) pp. 4–9.

Hilliard, A.G. III (2001). Moving Beyond Standards To Provide Excellence and Equity in the African-American Community. Speech, Howard University. http://www.africawithin.com/hilliard/standards_movement.htm Hilliard, A.G. III & Sizemore, B. (chief consultants) *Every Child Can Succeed*. Television series. Bloomington, IN: Agency for Instructional Technology.

Interview with Robert Coles (1992). *Teaching Tolerance*. Montgomery: Southern Poverty Law Center. Number 1.

Jensen, R. The morally lazy white middle class. *Poverty & Race*. Poverty & Race Research Action Council. November/December 1999, p. 12.

King, M.L., Jr. (1968) *Where do we go from here: Community or Chaos?* (1968). Boston: Beacon Press.

Kozol, J. (2005). *The shame of the nation: The restoration of apartheid schooling in America*. New York, NY: Three Rivers Press.

Lovett, M. (2007) "Creative Interventions: Representing Others through Video Action Research. *Globalizing Cultural Studies: Ethnographic Interventions in Theory, Method, and Policy*. McCarthy, C. et. al. (ed). New York: Peter Lang Publishers

Lovett, personal e-mail, April, 19 2010.

Moses, R. & Cobb, C. (2001). *radical equations: Civil Rights from Mississippi to the Algebra Project*. Boston: Beacon Press.

Payne, C. M. (1995). *I've got the light of freedom: The organizing tradition and the Mississippi freedom struggle*. Berkeley: University of California Press

Rodríguez, L. F. & Brown, T. M (2009). Engaging youth in participatory action research for education and social transformation. *New Directions for Youth Development, 123*.

Rorty, R. (1995). Color-Blind in the Marketplace. Book Review. *New York Times*, September 24.

Shah, N. (2009) What can this student teach you about the classroom? *Teaching Tolerance*. Montgomery: Southern Poverty Law Center. 36, fall. Retrieved from: http://www.tolerance.org/magazine/number-36-fall-2009/what-can-student-teach-you-about-classroom

Smith. L. T. (1999). *Decolonizing methodologies: Research and indigenous peoples*. London: Zed Books Ltd.

Watson, L. (1985) United Nation's Decade for Women's conference, Nairobi. http://en.wikipedia.org/wiki/Lilla_Watson

Wynne, J. & Giles, J. (2010) Stories of Collaboration & Research within an Algebra Project Context: Offering quality education to students pushed to the bottom of academic achievement. *Quality education as a constitutional right: Creating a grassroots movement to transform public schools*. Boston: Beacon Press.

WHEN I LEARNED HOW TO TEACH IN A CONTEXT OF DEMOCRATIC PROCESS

Ceexta Ren Hall

When I was a child I knew that I wanted to be a teacher. I loved the idea of having my own classroom and having children come every day just for me to teach whatever I knew. I remember placing my dolls in a straight row in front of my small chalk board. I would have a ruler in my hand to point at the dolls that were not following directions. I had the commands "All eyes on me, no talking, sit up straight, no helping others" all down perfect. Back then my perception of a teacher was someone who told you what to do and how to do it. It was not until I got into a classroom myself as an intern that I learned what really makes a teacher and what does not.

My learning how to and how "not" to teach started when I was in the 12th grade. I had been taking Early Childhood Education classes for my whole high school career; I had learned how to take care of children. I learned the rules required for a classroom, according to the state regulations. One day my teacher told me that I was ready to volunteer at a local daycare for 30 hours out of the week in order to reach my requirements to pass the class. I was so excited about the possibility of being placed in a real classroom to put into practice everything I had learned in my high school education classes.

All week I waited for my teacher to find a placement for me. Then the day came, and I got the news that I was assigned to a daycare near the high school that was attached to a church. I was on the first bus to the day care the next morning. I arrived there about 30 minutes early. I was the only one there so I decided to walk around the school. I saw signs everywhere. In the hall way a sign said "Straight Line." I saw another sign in the front of the church door that read "Be quiet in the house of God." I saw worn down floor tiles where the children walked. I walked back to the front where I eventually met the instructor I would shadow. After telling the history of the school and an overwhelmingly long list of rules, she invited me to follow her to her classroom, where I learned that she had been teaching for 15 years.

Immediately, she began preparing the lunch for the children while they were glued to the TV. Later she turned on the lights, like robots they got up and sat in their chairs. When the food was placed in front of them, they ate, and when finished, they walked to their mats that the teacher had prepared during lunch time. Before they rested, they were read a book and like clockwork by the 5th page every child was asleep. They and

I went through this same routine for a year. I kept wondering where was the laughter? Where was the creativity? Where was the learning?

I talked to the teacher, and her words still haunt me. She told me that the school was preparing these children for public school. She told me she had wanted to be a teacher her whole life, but this place had taken away her dreams. She complained that she was so tired of always cleaning and "doing" for the children and that she was planning on finding other work. She told me she remembered when she was like me, enthusiastic about teaching. But what scared me most was that she had lost her love for learning and teaching. And as an African-American/Carribean woman, I was horrified because too many of the children in my community were in classrooms with people who had lost their love for teaching.

At the end of the year, I was offered a teaching position to replace the teacher I had been assisting. It took me no time to refuse. I would not be a person who sucked opportunity out of children. So after that discouraging experience when applying for college, I didn't know what I wanted to do. I had wanted to be a teacher but my experience at the day care had shattered my dreams. Therefore, on my application I checked "undecided" in the box marked "major."

But then one day, when searching on my university's job site, I saw it—an advertisement to work at a Learning Center. I was so drawn to this listing because of the word "Learning." The name itself seemed to indicate a day care where children were not just being taken care of, but also were being offered educational experiences. I completed my application in hopes that the passion I once had for being a teacher would be restored in this place. My dream was that it would not be a place for children to be told what to think, rather invited to think.

I remember it as though it were yesterday. When I was called into my interview, the first thing I heard was children's laughter. As I was invited to spend the day touring the school, I saw in every classroom, children learning new skills through manipulatives. Hands-on learning seemed the major instructional strategy. The children were not being told how to learn. They were given the freedom to explore and create. Each classroom had separate learning stations, where children chose their interests at a particular time. I listened as children were invited to express themselves about mathematics or science or reading. They shared with each other what they were learning. If misbehavior occurred the student was invited to sit at a learning station alone and reconsider her behavior, and, then, come back to a small group space.

By the end of the tour, I knew this was where I needed to be. There were no signs in this school. The only things displayed on the walls were pictures that the children had created. There were no TV's playing to dull the children's participatory spirit. There were no disengaged, disgruntled teachers. Many of the instructors had been there for twenty to thirty years. They loved their students and their work. Like their students, the teachers were given the freedom to explore and create.

The model being used seemed congruent with a philosophy of developing in the youngest of children a democratic process for learning. The founder of the school had been teaching for 30 years and had the energy of a person who had been teaching for only a couple of hours. At the end of the tour and the interview, she asked if I had any questions. But I had no questions. The children's laughter and energy in this Learning Center had already supplied the answers to every question.

This is my second year of teaching at the Learning Center. I could not imagine being in another place to learn how to teach. I learn every day from the children the ways of teaching. And it's not about asking them to stand in straight lines nor to yell commands at them. It is giving them the tools to learn as much as possible on their own. Helping them uncover their particular way of expressing their feelings and, then, learning how to communicate effectively with others. It is giving the children the love and support that a teacher should give. I've learned at this place more than I have learned in many of my education courses. I've witnessed very young children learn to function as democratic citizens, not as obedient robots. And through these veteran teachers' enthusiasm for exploration and change, I continue to realize that no matter how long I teach, I will always have something to learn from children. But especially I have found in this supportive environment that classrooms for all children must be spaces for discovery and joyful noise!

Section 9: Creating Democracy Requires Youth Participation in the Classroom and Out

Please take 10 minutes and write about the following:

1. Your views of what a real democracy would look like in schools. Be as specific as possible.

_____

_____

_____

_____

_____

2. After having read the selections of articles for Section 9, what kinds of activities would you suggest students should be allowed to do in schools that would develop them as active democratic citizens?

_____

_____

_____

3. How can teachers empower themselves to be active in policy decisions that impact schools and communities?

_____

_____

_____

After writing those ideas, please consider the following activities:

- Choose a partner and share your written discussion.

- Join another set of partners and generate a list of activities that students, teachers, and parents can engage in to demand quality education for everyone's child.

- Write those activities in large print, using a magic marker, and use masking tape to put them on the wall.

- Discuss those activities with the entire class.

Watch the video: www.youtube.com/watch?v=AMjR6Htckdc "Silenced Voices."
After watching the video, please discuss with a partner the major points the students were making about the quality of teachers that taught in their schools and write about your discussion.

_____

_____

_____

Describe any differences about how the media portrayed the students and how the students present themselves on the video.

_____

_____

_____

_____

Discuss below anything in the video that surprised you.

_____

_____

_____

_____

How could your students use digital cameras and other digital tools in the classroom to examine issues that concern them?

_____

_____

_____

_____

_____

SECTION 10

TEACHING WITH IMAGINATION AND COURAGE UNSHACKLES OUR SPIRITS

Image copyright FreeSoulProduction, 2012. Used under license from Shutterstock. Inc.

I can't teach you if I don't know you, if I am not standing where you stand and touching the world through your fingertips. I cannot be you, but humans have imagination, and I must use every flyspeck of my brain's creative and empathic aptitude to truly hear you.
—Cindy Lutenbacher "A Mother's Journal"

CHAPTER 10

SO YOU REALLY WANT TO BE A TEACHER?

Carlos Gonzalez Morales

Don't do it. If you are reading this, you are probably in an education class and you are either studying to be a teacher or are already one and working on your graduate degree. For those of you in the belly of the monster we call schools, I am truly sorry; it probably is too late for you. For those of you who are not teachers just yet, there's still time to get out.

If you are doing it because you say you love kids, get out. There are other ways you can love kids. Volunteer with Big Brothers and Big Sisters. Have some. Adopt some. Take care of the neighbor's.

If you are doing it because you want to make a difference, get out. You can make a difference working as a banker, politician, or real estate developer. There are options for you. Join law enforcement; become a lawyer; but by all means don't be a teacher.

Teaching is not the career they tell you about in your college courses. As a matter of fact, your professors are mostly lying to you, setting you up for a life of professional misery and frustration. So-called schools of education are there to perpetuate themselves and an agenda that has little or nothing to do with teaching or learning. By the way, everything they tell you about classroom management is useless when you find yourself in a room with 30 or 35 kids and a completely scripted curriculum; where when you breathe is carefully choreographed to coincide with the latest test taking success strategy, the one that will save your school from sinking into the shame of being graded less than satisfactory.

I mean it. Run while you can. Drop your class and this book. Find something else to do with your one precious human life. No one around you will think less of you. As a matter of fact, most people around you have very little respect for teachers and teaching. If you think I'm exaggerating, listen to the political discourse around teaching and the loss of learning that has taken place as a result of high stakes testing and the correlated repressive policies of No Child Left Behind. Do you think that could have happened if our political leaders had asked classroom teachers? Of if legislators and others in power had any respect for the profession?

If you are still reading this and are still holding out, I will say this. Prepare yourself for the struggle of your life. You are entering a world where the only way to survive with some integrity is to learn quickly how to sabotage, undermine, and persistently resist the machine of factory education. To do so you will need help; you will not be able to do so on your own. The first thing that you will need is to create a community of resistance, one that runs parallel to the official structures, one that for the most part remains invisible to those same structures.

Creating this community is not easy. Everyone around you will be in survival mode: overworked, scared, and for the most part compliant. (Pretty much the same way your college classes are organized by your professors. All of those projects and papers are typically mandated by others and for the most part mere distractions from the real work that could help you survive and thrive.)

Being a teacher is nothing less than being a cultural guerrilla. To teach is to question and to question is to undermine. If you do it in the open, you will eventually be stopped, made an object of derision, and marginalized. Once you get hired, you will need to look around and notice who has survived the place and still has some heart and passion left in them. You can tell who those folks are. They seem happy when everyone around them is often clocking in and out. They don't blame their students. As a matter of fact, when you hear them talk about their students, there is a glow and a passion that has an infinite depth. Get closer to those few; more likely than not, they will be closeted cultural warriors, ones that have quietly found a way to monkey-wrench a system that works on fear and most significantly oppressive apathy. To create community with such human beings is to create a world within many worlds, an air bubble in an otherwise toxic atmosphere that will leave you gasping for life.

If you can't help but teach, even when you know all of this, I say prepare yourself for the most exciting and amazing of experiences. You are up against a monolith of a system that takes curious and creative human beings at age five and spits out for the most part eager, compliant consumers by age 22—often with debts that will further trap them into never questioning the very premise of an education that annihilated the wonder of living out their dreams and passions.

If you can't help but teach under these conditions and circumstances, then you may be one of the knowledge/wisdom workers who with other such people are creating the soul sustaining creative bubbles that will provide the space for us to survive until the machine has been stopped or runs out of destructive fuel to continue.

So here's to community, cultural guerrillas, creative bubbles, soulful spirits, and to YOU, if you have the courage to teach!

A MOTHER'S JOURNAL: HOW DO WE FILL OUR SCHOOLS WITH GREAT TEACHERS?

Cindy Lutenbacher

> *For the African teacher, teaching is far more than a job or simply a way to make a living. Students are not "clients" or "customers." Our students and parents are our family. No sacrifice is too great for that family, for its growth and enhancement.*
> —Asa Hilliard (2002), "To Be an African Teacher"

> *In order to teach you, I must know you.*
> —Native Alaskan educator, (cited in Delpit, 1995, p. 183)

TEACHER ONE: Second Grade Teacher, NHE School, August 30, 2007

It was my first day to volunteer in the second-grade class at my neighborhood public school. So, I was excited and a little nervous. Signed in at the office and got my visitor's sticker. Down the hallway, past the empty cafeteria/auditorium. Smiled at the women who work in the cafeteria, and they smiled back. Clean hallways. Posters and bulletin boards everywhere, a bizarre cacophony of "Welcome, Students!" and "All About Me: Respect, Integrity, Citizenship, Compassion, Self-Discipline. . ." and "No Bullying Zone" and "School Safety Zone" and "Having Weapons in School is a Felony" and "Strategic Plan for Neighbor Hills"" and "Neighbor Hills Shines in Georgia Performance Standards," the last with a multi-page list of all the "Georgia Performance Standards" for each grade.

When I arrived at Mr. Smith's class, I heard him speaking to the children. Okay, he was shouting. "GET QUIET OR GET OUT!!! THERE IS NO TALKING IN <u>MY</u> CLASSROOM! YOU CAN GET QUIET OR GET OUT, *NOW*!!!"

I knocked on the door, and let myself in. Mr. Smith smiled at me, and I said, "I'm here to volunteer." He nodded his head, and I started toward the children, who were mostly seated in their desks, with the desks arranged in four rectangles of four desks per rectangle, facing inward. A little guy popped up and ran to me. "Are you Muslim?" he asked.

"No," I said, "are you?"

"Yes!"

"Cool. I'm a teacher and a lot of the students in my classes are Muslim, too." He popped back to his seat. "What's your name?" I asked.

"Zakariyya."

"Cool. I'm Nikki's mama."

I went to Nikki and put my arm around her. "Hey, Babe," I whispered, and she grinned like no tomorrow. I stooped down beside her to listen and get with the program.

Mr. Smith was amid a lesson in grammar. "At the end of every sentence, you have to have a punctuation mark. But there are different punctuation marks, depending on the sentence. . ." On and on.

The kids were like super-heated molecules, bouncing in space. One cluster of molecules was only tuned in to each other, as two of the girls were laughing and doing a playful dozens with one another. At another cluster, one little boy was dropping things on the floor so he could go beneath his desk. Another little boy got up to sharpen his pencil. Occasionally, I saw one or two children looking at Mr. Smith. Primarily, there were wiggling bodies, laughter, chatter, kids focused everywhere but on Mr. Smith.

Smith went on. "So, suppose you say, '*The house is on fire!!!*' and you are really excited. What comes at the end of this?"

"OOOOwee! Call 911!"

"Get out! Everybody run out!!!"

"My Nana can't run."

"STOP THAT!" yelled Smith. "You put an exclamation mark there. What if I said, 'The house is on fire?' like that? What would you put?"

"Water! Put water on it!"

"Naw, man, get out and call 911!!!"

Well, at least he got their attention for a quick minute. Next, he wrote ten sentences on the board for the children to copy and then decide what kind of punctuation should go at the end. As far as I could tell, he was clueless that he had not only just negated the possibility of a reasonable response to the assignment, but had also missed the kids' world by a south Georgia mile. That is, he had just told the children that the kind of end punctuation one chooses depends upon how the sentence is said and what the speaker intends.

In order to teach you, I must know you.

PREFACE

I know, I know. Prefaces are supposed to come first. Sorry.

I am a mother of public school children. I have also been a teacher my entire life, the last twenty-two years of which have been spent at Morehouse College, where I teach English—mainly comp, which I love.

In school year 2007–2008, I volunteered a day a week in each of two different public schools; the story of how those two days a week came to be doesn't merit taking your time, but the heart of the matter is the fact that my youngest daughter, seven years old that year, has special needs—classified that year as significant, global, developmental delay of unspecified origin. She has since been diagnosed as MID, or mildly intellectually disabled. Her first-grade year in an LD (learning disability) class was a nightmare of galactic proportions. Ostracized, bullied, and otherwise tormented by the six boys in her class for her pants-wetting accidents (the only other girl was severely autistic), Nikki was becoming the "problem" kid, the one to inspire daily notes home to me from her teacher and assistant teacher. Daily, her bad behavior, her oppositional ways, her disobedience. Refusing to give up the book she was reading when it was math time.

Giving the teacher the finger. Using vulgar language, the meaning of which she knew not. Kicking at the boys. "I hate those kids," she said.

Despite my best efforts to communicate, to participate in the classroom, and to help solve some of the conflicts, I could see that Nikki was in danger of being routed into the storm drain of Bad Kid, the one who ends up being "pushed-out" of a school so that the school's AYP (Adequate Yearly Progress) won't suffer. Sweet, funny, often lost, often unyielding-as-Gibraltar Nikki was perishing.

Never again, I swore.

I needed to be with Nikki in her school, whatever school or classroom or special ed model that might be.

//////////////////

"What is the matter with you!!" Smith yelled at Pencil Dropper.

Nikki began to try to copy the sentences. Her writing is quite slow and she's not clear yet about the need to leave spaces between words. Other children at her desk group were much faster, but Nik did not notice. She just trudged away at it. Sakaría was done in a zip and started to wander the classroom.

I, too, began to wander around the room as Mr. Smith wrote on the board. Some children were writing, but most were just enjoying one another. The names of the children were on banner-board in large letters, plastered on their desks. I stooped down next to one little chatterbox. "KiyEEsha?" I asked. "Did I get that right?"

"Yeah," she smiled.

"Say my name!" another girl said.

"Hmm. . .I want to get it right. . . Let me see. . ."

When Mr. Smith finished the sentences, he moved on to the next part of his lesson plan, which was, apparently, to continue to berate and yell at the kids. "There is NO talking in MY class!!! Ever!!! You do NOT get out of your seats, even to sharpen your pencil!"

Smith had already missed any number of to-know-you moments. Names and religion and the delicious literal-ness of little ones.

"The trouble may start in schools of education, where preservice teachers in many states spend very little time learning about learning, relative to the time devoted to subject-matter content. Worse, when teachers these days are told to think about learning, it may be construed in behaviorist terms, with an emphasis on discrete, measurable skills. The point isn't to deepen understanding (and enthusiasm) but merely to elevate test scores." (Kohn, 2008)

Smith was getting angrier and more frustrated by the minute, and he strode over to the little guy who was dropping things under his desk and rapped him on the head with his pen. "Get up! Get up, <u>now</u>!!" He grabbed the child by his arm and yanked him into his chair.

After a little more lecture, he told the kids to open their grammar books to work on the exercise on page 25. It was sentences with the words out of order. "bird saw I the a in tree." Nikki began to copy the sentences directly as they were in the book. "bird saw I the a in tree." She had no idea what was expected. no She expected had what idea was.

"Stop talking! Stop talking right NOW!!" Mr. Smith yelled at Kyesha, all up in her face. "You haven't done anything but talk this whole time!" He was right, but also way, way wrong. And what a loss for Mr. Smith as a teacher and the kids as. . .kids. I wonder if it ever occurred to him to just *listen* to them. What might he have learned?

I am thinking of another classroom on another day. First-graders were making books and including pictures. Dalila got interested in the fact that the scissors had become magnetized.

"Look!" said Dalila. "The scissors is killing the paper clip. Agggggghhh!"

Khin responded quietly, "Killing is. . .bad. We don't like killing. My grandma was killed. In Burma. Grandpa, too."

"My grandma is alive. Well, one is," said Thuya.

Smith slapped Kyesha lightly, but with anger, on her shoulder.

Again, I roamed the rectangles to help. One little crew was struggling, but a girl was on it. When she said, with a question mark at the end of her voice, "I saw a bird in the tree?"

"Awesome!" I gave her five and did a little dance. The kids were delighted and quickly went to the next problem. When they solved it, I danced for them, again. That became our relationship for the day. They work and solve, and I dance.

I suppose you should know that I'm a terrible dancer. My twelve-year old daughter won't speak to me if I dance, either at home or in public.

One thing that struck me is the fact that Mr. Smith and I are white. And, if appearances are instructive, all of the 17 children in the class are African American or of African descent. Yes, that includes Nikki, my daughter.

I know too many white folks who think race *doesn't* matter, too many white teachers who claim, "I don't even *notice* race." But I believe that race and racism affect everything. Really. Everything.

In the two hours that I was in the classroom, the only positives I heard Mr. Smith proffer were literally a handful of "Good" as responses to the "correct" answers to the problems. In the two hours that I was there, I heard him use only one child's name, once. In the two hours, the children did nothing but grammar and were expected to stay in their seats the whole time, not even if their pencil points broke. In the two hours. . .well, I wanted to cry.

Early on in my short time there, Ms. Parker came into the room, saw me and immediately came to give me a hug. Ms. Parker is the Special Ed teacher with whom I've had the most contact. She is young, energetic, African American, warm, and extremely smart. Nikki perks up whenever she's around.

"Aliya!" Ms. Parker said. "Sit up and pull your dress down over your knees, young lady!" Aliya responded almost immediately, and I found myself comparing Ms. Parker's voice with Mr. Smith's. Both raised their voices, both were direct, both were nononsense. But when I think of Ms. Parker getting Aliya to do what she needed, I hear the voice of a mother who wants her child to *make* it in this world and in *one piece*. When I think of Mr. Smith. . .well. . .I'm having a hard time finding an image other than *overseer*. His fury is his whip.

TEACHER TWO: Yang Liu, International Community School, a public charter school for children who are refugees (and for local children, too)

JANUARY 15, 2008

It was my second day to volunteer in Yang's class. The kids were busy in their first-second grade groups, but with individual tasks: begin working on a story. Yang had given the kids worksheets with large circles in which they could brainstorm ideas for a story.

After Writers' Workshop, the groups split and returned to first and second grade rooms. Yang gathered the first-grade kids in a circle to talk about Dr. King. I came to see that the entire day's lessons in almost every subject were planned around Dr. King.

"So, today is birthday of Dr. Martin Luther King, Jr. Who can tell me something about Dr. King?"

"I see teevee," said Ghedi from Somalia.

"Good! And what did you learn?"

Ghedi began to search the room with his gaze. "I remember only a few thing, but I remember other thing."

"Good start. Can you tell us something?"

"Birthday cake!"

"Okay, then. It's Dr. King's birthday, but it is much more than birthday cake, yes? Children, I have to tell you something. Dr. King is one of my heroes. When I was growing up on the island of Mauritius, we thought the United States was great. When we heard of the terrible things that were being done to African American people here, we thought *What? What can this be?* So I learned about Dr. King and the way he was trying to get things to change. Peacefully. He is my hero."

"He's everybody's hero," said Dalila.

"That's right. Everybody's hero. First, does everyone know what a hero is?" A quick vocabulary lesson—that's Yang's way. Always from context and always inside whatever is going on in the class.

The kids looked at one another before Abby offered up, "Someone who saves lives? Who helps other people?"

"Yes, Abby. Dr. King was helping all people because he was trying to teach us to live together peacefully."

Sajat from Afghanistan piped in. "Because all the grown-ups fight, and that's why he was a nice man."

"Good, Sajat. Tell me, Sajat, is fighting a good thing?"

"No, no, he say not to fight."

"What is fighting, children? Is it like war?"

Yang Liu does what many U.S.ian teachers are afraid to do: she talks about things that may be very painful, but they are things that the children have experienced. And many if not most of the kids in her class have themselves seen war. She seems to have such a profound belief in healing. And a profound belief in the ability of humans to find and create love in their hearts.

I remember one time in Saturday School (English classes for families of the students at ICS) when I was helping with the adult English class. On that day, there were only women there, and we sat on the same floor, same rug as the first-graders in Yang Liu's class. I was new to the class, so Yang used the opportunity to ask each woman to introduce herself to me in English, telling name, country, children and ages, and I don't remember what else. Excellent exercise, for the women knew each other well and would laughingly correct each other's English. They're tight, truly tight. Caimile, a grandmother from Somalia told of her three grown sons, one of whom lives here, but two of whom are trying to emigrate. I noticed that Bebegol, grandmother from Afghanistan, began to silently weep.

"Bebegol is sad, yes?" said Yang. "You are sad because your sons were killed in Afghanistan." Yang went to Bebegol and knelt before her, held her in her arms, and gently rocked her. "It hurts so much, so much to say goodbye to children." For a few minutes, Yang just held and rocked her, and the rest of us sat with tears falling from our eyes. When Bebegol had cried enough for the moment—how can there *ever* be enough tears for a child killed—Yang stopped hugging her and just held onto her arms. Then Yang turned to the group and said quietly, "War is so terrible. Such terrible things happen. That's why we work for peace. "

I don't remember exactly what else Yang talked about, but we went on to finish introductions, and then, Yang said, "Oh, Bebegol, you promised you would show us how to dance like you do in Afghanistan!" And then, Bebegol stood, we all stood, and she began a kind of slow Hora-like dance. We all tried to imitate, and within moments, we were laughing and teasing one another. Including Bebegol.

I remember the time that I asked my friend Linda about her younger brother who had died of leukemia when he was 14 and Linda, 17. I asked, "How do parents ever get over the loss of a child?"

"They don't," said Linda. "They can only learn to live with it."

Bebegol will never get over the loss of her sons. No one can. But she may be able to live with the infinite chasm that is a mother's grief. If there is enough Yang Liu to go around.

"Children, what is the opposite of war?"

"Peace!" they shouted.

"Yes, and Dr. King said that peace is what we want. What we need."

Yang gave me a book about MLK to read and discuss with the children. I confess I don't recall the book, but I know I talked with them about racism, the concept that people with lighter colored skin were somehow "better" than people with darker colored skin. I used my own skin to exemplify the lighter colored, and most of the children's as darker. I talked about remembering separate water fountains and bathrooms in my home of Louisiana, about restaurants and schools and school books. I kept asking them, "Is that right? Is that okay?" and always, they could easily see that racism was wrong.

When I finished, Yang took over the discussion. "And it's more than just an idea. It's something that is very real because there were very bad laws to try to keep people apart, and to keep brown-skinned people down. Do you know that if we were living when Dr. King was alive, I would not have been able to be your teacher? You could not all be in the same classroom? Ms. Azizi could not be your teacher?" The kids were struck—eyes large, mouths open, brows a trough of disbelief. "Those were some of the bad laws that I'm talking about. It's not just some bad idea floating about the sky; it's real laws that were made. What's a law?"

On we persevered for just a few more minutes about bad laws and good laws and the impact of Dr. King on the laws. It had been about twenty minutes and Yang could see the kids were getting restless, so she got them on their feet to walk as if they were part of Dr. King's march. We sang "We Shall Overcome" as we walked.

"We learned that last year with Ms. Htue-Htue!" several kids exclaimed.

"Good! Yes! You know Ms. Htue-Htue is my friend. I lived six months in her apartment with her family. Who is from the same country as Ms. Htue-Htue?"

Benjamin raised his hand, and Yang said, "Good. And Khin, Thuya, raise your hands. Sandi,. . . . Yes, that's right. In Burma, the government wants to control the people, so they have made bad laws that hurt the people. Another of my heroes is Aung San Suu Kyi because she has worked for many, many years to change the government and their bad laws. She has been in prison in her house for many, many years. She cannot go outside to feel the sun or walk in the grass."

The children were enraptured. Burma was the home of about a fifth of the class, and all the kids were getting a short civics lesson in a very short span of the day.

Time for recess, so Najiba asked the children individual questions about Dr. King in order to line up and get coats. After recess, time for math with cubes and sticks and understanding one and ten columns. I remember Yang asked Trey, "How would you solve the problem?" and I loved his answer.

"I don't know yet, Ms. Liu." It was the "yet" that caught me; everyone is a learner, and if we don't know answers to questions, we can learn. We can learn.

At lunch, I ate with Yang and we talked of racism. "I remember a time when my son was in college, standing in line to register for classes," she said. "A girl was yelling, and he looked around to see who she was yelling at. He finally realized it was him. She thought if she yelled, he would understand English better. He told her, 'I'm as American as you.'"

Once again, I heard Yang speak to her wish that the teachers would become "more radical" and not so concerned over "silly things." When she went to empty her plate, I stopped her. "Wait! Let me have your fish sticks. I'll give them to my kids!"

"Ah, if only I could fill my plate, I would be able to take only what I can eat," replied Yang.

After lunch and recess, it was reading time, so we gathered on the circle rug. Yang wanted me to read the MLK book written by his sister *My Brother Martin*, and I had brought three books. We had time for the book about Dr. King and only one of the three. "Children, Ms. Cindy has brought three books, but she can only read one of them today. She'll read the others another time. So, to choose which one we want, we are going to be a democracy. Each one will get one vote." She was handing out sticky-notes to each child as she talked. When she got about six children from me, she said, "Okay, now what if I don't give a vote to the rest of the children who are near Ms. Cindy. They don't get to vote on which book we would like to hear. What do you think of that?"

The children without votes were crestfallen, slightly fearful I think. But immediately the whole class began saying, "No fair! That's not right! NO!!"

"You've got it, children. You understand. It's wrong if everyone doesn't have the same rights."

Then, with no child left out or behind, each kid went to place his or her sticky-note vote on the rug in a line beneath his/her book of choice. In this way, Yang made a bar graph to show which of the three books got the most votes. She did a few more math problems (How many more votes did *Anansi Goes Fishing* get than *Tiger Soup*? Etc.), and I realized that in a short few minutes, the kids had received a history lesson, a civics lesson, a math lesson, and a lesson in equality, all stirred into one soup of a moment.

"This is a point the Standardistos don't seem to grasp: you develop mathematicians by helping children find the marvel of mathematics, not by issuing high-stakes testing threats." (Susan Ohanian, 2003")

Then I read *Anansi* and *My Brother Martin*.

The book concluded with the statement, "And so my brother Martin did turn the world upside down." Tyuma smiled and giggled a little.

"What is funny, Tyuma? What are you thinking about?" asked Yang.

"I think that if the world turn upside, our head come through the cloud." The class laughed at that image, and Yang and I joined in. *I cannot teach you if I do not know you. And how can I know you if I do not listen to you?*

"I like that picture, Tyuma," said Yang. "Who knows how to spell 'cloud'?" And together, they sounded and guessed it out. "There's a phrase 'head in the clouds,' isn't there, Ms. Cindy? Will you tell the children what it means?" Another language lesson, woven in.

Yang continued. "Children, you see that poster over there? Dr. King made a very famous speech called 'I Have a Dream,' and his dream was that all children would have what they need and that all people would be treated equally and live together in peace. I have a dream, too, and it is that all people would have the health care that they need. Everyone needs to be able to get the medicines and the help that they need when they are sick, yes? What are your dreams? What do you wish for all people?"

"Teaching is mostly listening, and learning is mostly telling." (Meier, xiii)

So I scribed their responses on the easel-born dry-erase board:

I have a dream. . .

- There is a job for everyone
- Everyone has freedom
- Everyone's needs are taken care of
- No more wars

- No passport is needed to visit another country
- Everyone makes peace
- Everyone in different countries will be friends
- (Mine) Every child will have teachers who love him or her as much as Ms. Liu and Ms. Azizi do
- Skin color does not matter
- Everyone is healthy
- Everyone has a home
- No hunger—everyone has enough food to eat and money to use
- (And last, Alethia) Every child has love

The kids got to work on making a picture for one of their dreams, and I left to go get Nikki from Neighbor Hills and to spend a few minutes alone with the dreams of children.

METHODOLOGY

Thanks to the late Dr. Dwight Conquergood of Northwestern University, I have knowledge of what anthropologist Clifford Geertz (1973) dubbed "thick description," observation that was rich with authenticity and detail and included the context of culture and its study, as well as the voice of the observer. Geertz was less interested in accuracy of interpretation than in furthering and deepening discussion and in challenging perceptions. He cared less about a "perfection of consensus" and more about "the precision with which we vex each other" (p. 29). The methodology of participant-observer engaged in thick description is what I have used in my work. I volunteered one full day each week in the two public school classrooms, helping with one-to-one tutoring, small group activities, story-reading and enactment, and generally doing whatever the teachers asked of me or whatever seemed to need doing. Throughout the days, I made notes of what I observed and then came home to immediately turn my notes into prose, or thick descriptions. In the path of Geertz, I write with provocation in mind. I write in order to vex myself as I invite others to be so troubled. . .especially and ever more deeply vexed with questions surrounding what we know to be important in any learning environment—the power of the teacher and his/her connection to students.

DISCUSSION IN CONTEXT

These snapshots of two teachers—and they are only snapshots—represent something of the extremes in teaching, and as such, may appear almost as caricatures. I suspect that we all have our own stories of these extremes, as well as everything in between. And if our goals in education center upon nurturing young people who are critical thinkers, questioners, creative problem-solvers, community-minded citizens, and . . . then we do know a great deal about what makes a great teacher (life works of Asa Hilliard, Marilyn Cochran-Smith, Linda Darling-Hammond, Lisa Delpit, Alfie Kohn, Gerald Bracey, and many more). Furthermore, research has given us much to consider in terms of "raising up" such teachers via excellent schools of education (Darling-Hammond, 2006; Hilliard, 1995) and how to support great teachers with structural and policy choices that include factors, such as teaching communities that give teachers time and opportunity to collaborate and learn from one another, lighter teaching loads, and time with successful teachers (Hilliard, 1995; Rothman & Darling-Hammond, 2011).

Progressive educators have also learned much about the impact of external factors on children and their learning, factors such as poverty (Krashen, 2005 and 2011; Ravitch, 2010a and 2010b; Baer, et al.; 2007), access to a good variety and quantity of books (Krashen, 2008), the "savage inequality" (Kozol, 1992) of public school expenditure, inferior and biased curriculum (Hilliard, 1998), and, of course, more recently, No Child Left Behind. Yet, while fully understanding these factors, the late Dr. Asa Hilliard (1998) also always acknowledged and celebrated those whom he called "power teachers"—teachers who have thrilling classrooms and highly successful students, regardless of these external factors. Hilliard gave much of his life's work to showing the ways that such teachers trounced every stereotype and perceived obstacle, as the "at-risk" children in their classrooms soared in every way. "Just as there is a vast untapped potential, yes, genius, among the children, there is also a vast untapped potential among the teachers who serve the children" (Hilliard, 1991). I think of what Yang Liu once said: "Give me a tree and some students, and we will have a school." For me, the vex becomes the struggle to change the external factors while simultaneously recruiting, nurturing, and supporting power teachers. Neither side of this vexation should be used to cancel or contradict the impact of the other.

I am also thinking: *I can't teach you if I don't know you, if I am not standing where you stand and touching the world through your fingertips. I cannot be you, but humans have imagination, and I must use every flyspeck of my brain's creative and empathic aptitude to truly hear you.* That embrace by a teacher is made complex by many elements of the relationship, not the least of which is found in the statistics concerning race and my own state of Georgia: although 80% of all public school teachers are white (Freeman, Scafidi, & Sjoquist, 2002), but 54% of all public school students in Georgia are children of color (Suitts, 2010). Have those eighty percent of the teachers done their 24/7 homework to understand and combat racism in order to embrace a critical region in the lives of their students of color? This is not to say, for example, that all African American or Latino teachers have a handle on racism and the internalized self-hatred that is the steady diet of racism. Nor is it to say that white students don't need teachers who are actively anti-racist. But I am certain that without a lifelong, intensive struggle and commitment, white teachers don't get it. We just don't. As Beverly Daniel Tatum notes, "Most teachers in the United States are White teachers who were raised and educated in predominantly White communities. Their knowledge of communities of color and their cultures is typically quite limited" (2007, p. 71). We can make a good start if we are willing; Tatum describes a two-year professional development course that required teacher participants (85% White) to deeply examine racism within their own lives and schools and to develop proactive plans for dealing with racism. The study of the impact of the course showed significant gains attitudes and aptitudes made by the teachers, all of whom had volunteered for the course (2007, pp. 72–79). Would the same result be achieved if teachers were required to take the course? As a white southerner, I have concerns that far too few of my white colleagues even recognize that there is a problem and that they/we have an internal problem, or far too few are willing to take active steps in their lives and classrooms to combat racism. For myself, I fully expect to battle the unconscious racism I consciously find in my mirror until the day I die. And then some.

And racism is but one facet, albeit one of the most profound, that impacts teachers' abilities to deeply *know* their students, to connect with them, to teach.

I am thinking of colleges of education and of some of the brilliant teachers in those institutions, teachers like Asa Hilliard, Lisa Delpit, Joannie Wynne, Theresa Perry, Vera Stenhouse, and Mari Roberts. But I am thinking also of my own certification process and the history-of-education teacher whose name I have mercifully forgotten, the one who required us to read Horace Mann's soporific biography. Nothing else; that was it; that was the course.

Are colleges of education where the hope lies? Can professors of education make enough of a difference in the lives of pre-service teachers in order to people our schools with Yangs? And perhaps even more so, how do we make sure that the colleges of education are filled with Dr. Hilliard and not Dr. Nameless? Can colleges of education tell their almost graduates, *Sorry, but you aren't far enough along the journey of facing your own racism/sexism/classism/xenophobia, etc., so you'll have to choose another career or take another year or decade of opening your heart and training your mind before we'll entrust our young ones to you?* But how can we entrust our young ones to teachers who haven't done their internal homework, who aren't committed to lifelong tilling of the soul? NCATE has "disposition" standards, but these are only goals and not strategies of the soul. Leslie Coia, teacher of education at Agnes Scott College sums the matter concisely: "We've tried and tried and we've come up with more and more instruments. But it's just not working" (Personal communication, March 5, 2011). "The fact is that real learning often can't be quantified, and a corporate-style preoccupation with "data" turns schooling into something shallow and lifeless" (Kohn, 2008).

Can colleges of education say, *Sorry, but there's not enough love in your heart? You aren't dedicated enough?* I know of no checklist of love that isn't grounded in interpretive observations and measures, and such interpretations are profoundly rooted in the souls of the observers.

My mother always said, "Can't fool kids and dogs. They know who loves 'em." But we sure can fool adults and rubrics.

I agree with Darling-Hammond (2006, ix) that teachers are made, not born, but I also agree with my former acting teacher Diana Lee who once said, "Anyone can be a phenomenal actor. The question is whether or not you can get there in one lifetime." In other words, I believe that great teaching is part superb training and part determination. For me, the real question is how we construct a system that fosters/nurtures the teachers who have a deep enough commitment to be able to push their gifts hard enough to get there in one lifetime. And if the most important attributes of the genius of teachers are things that rely so much upon the interpretation of those in the position to evaluate teachers, how do we evaluate the evaluators?

I don't know if I am troubling you with my questions, but I certainly have vexed myself.

POSTSCRIPT

After about two more visits to Mr. Smith's classroom, I gave a copy of my journal to the school principal—and in the presence of another teacher. Because the journal included noting that Mr. Smith had struck a child, albeit not very hard, the principal had to do something. He passed the journal along to the "proper school authorities." In another week, Mr. Smith was transferred to another elementary school. I later learned that after a week or so at this other school, he had behaved in a way similar to what I described and was put on indefinite leave. In the late winter, I and a number of other faculty and staff members were subpoenaed to appear in a hearing about him. Apparently, the county wanted to fire him, but he was going to fight it. The hearing kept getting postponed until it disappeared entirely. One of the teachers and I surmised that once he saw the list of those called to testify, he gave up. We'll never know. The teachers all tell me that having a recorded journal from a *parent* is what made the difference. The year prior, his teaching assistant had observed Mr. Smith doing all the things I noted in my journal, and more. She spoke with the principal, assistant principal, school counselor, and everyone in any position at all at the school; nothing was done. In my county, a Black assistant teacher can be ignored; a white parent cannot.

And Yang? She went to China to teach, but returned to Atlanta, fall of 2009, to be one of the two central teachers for a tiny and free school for girls that a bunch of us are creating: The Global Village School. The thirty students are all teenage girls who are survivors of war and who experienced either no schooling or severe under-schooling because of having to spend their childhoods surviving in refugee camps or making carpets in Pakistan or simply fleeing. My county gives them a few months of ESL and claims they'll be fine in high school.

Step by step we go. Step by step.

REFERENCES

Baer, J., Baldi, S., Ayotte, K., & Green, P. (2007 Nov.). The reading literacy of U.S.fourth grade students. *Institute of Education Sciences of the National Center for Education Statistics, U.S. Department of Education.* Retrieved from http://nces.ed.gov/pubs2008/2008017.pdf.

Daniel Tatum, B. (2007). *Can we talk about race? and other conversations in an era of school resegregation.* Boston: Beacon Press.

Darling-Hammond, L. (2006). *Powerful teacher education: lessons from exemplary programs.* San Francisco: Jossey-Bass.

Darling-Hammond, L, (2007). A good teacher in every classroom: preparing the highly qualified teachers our children deserve. *The entity from which ERIC acquires the content, including journal, organization, and conference names, or by means of online submission from the author.Educational Horizons, 85.2,* 111–132. Retrieved from http://www.eric.ed.gov/PDFS/EJ750647.pdf

Darling-Hammond, L. (2008). Creating excellent and equitable schools. *The entity from which ERIC acquires the content, including journal, organization, and conference names, or by means of online submission from the author.Educational Leadership, 65.8,* 14–21. Retrieved from www.eric.ed.gov

Delpit, L. (1995). *Other people's children.* New York: New Press.

Freeman, C., Scafidi, B. & Sjoquist, D. (2002). Racial segregation in Georgia public schools 1994–2001: trends, causes and impact on teacher quality. Retrieved from Georgia State University, Andrew Young School of Public Policy: http://aysps.gsu.edu/FRC2002report77.pdf

Geertz, C. (1973). *The interpretation of culture.* NY: Basic Books.

Hilliard, A.G. (1989). Public support for successful instructional practices for at-risk students. Retrieved from www.eric.ed.gov

Hilliard, A.G. (1991). Do we have the will to educate all children? *Educational Leadership, 49.,* 31–36 Retrieved from www.eric.ed.gov

Hilliard, A.G. (1995). Teacher education from an African American perspective. Paper presented at Invitational Conference on Defining the Knowledge Base for Urban Teacher Education.(Atlanta, GA, 11 Nov. 1995). Retrieved from http://www.eric.ed.gov/PDFS/ED393798.pdf

Hilliard, A.G. (1998). *SBA: reawakening the African mind.* Gainesville, FL: Makare Press.

Hilliard, A. (2002). To be an African teacher. *Kintespace.* Retrieved May 23, 2009, from http://www.kintespace.com/kp_asa0.html

Kohn, A. (2008). It's not what we teach; it's what they learn. *Education Week,* 10 Sept. 2008. Retrieved from http://www.alfiekohn.org/teaching/edweek/inwwt.htm

Kozol, J. (1992). *Savage inequalities: children in America's schools.* New York: Harper Perennial.

Krashen, S. (2005). The hard work hypothesis: is doing your homework enough to overcome the effects of poverty? *Multicultural Education* 12 (4), 16–19.

Krashen, S. (2008). The case for libraries and librarians. Invited paper, Obama-Biden Education Working Group. Retrieved from: http://www.sdkrashen.com/articles/case_for_libraries/index.html

Krashen, S. (2011). Protecting students against the effects of poverty. *New England Reading Association Journal (in press)*. Retrieved from http://www.sdkrashen.com/articles/protecting_students.pdf

Meier, D. (2002). *The power of their ideas: lessons for America from a small school in Harlem*. Boston: Beacon Press.

Nieto, S. (2006). Solidarity, courage and heart: What teacher educators can learn from a new generation of teachers. *Intercultural Education, 17(5)*, 457–473. Retrieved from: http://www.jcu.edu/education/ed350/Solidarity,%20courage%20and%20heart_Sonia_Nieto.pdf

Ohanian, S. (2003). Capitalism, Calculus, and Conscience. *Phi Delta Kappan, 84 (10)*, 736–747. Retrieved from http://www.kappanmagazine.org

Ravitch, D. (2010). *The death and life of the great American school*. New York: Basic Books.

Ravitch, D. (2010). Diane Ravitch responds. *Economic Policy Institute*. Retrieved from http://www.epi.org/analysis_and_opinion/entry/diane_ravitch_responds/

Rothman, R. & Darling-Hammond, L. (2011). Teacher and school leader effectiveness: lessons learned from high-performing systems." *Alliance for Excellent Education*. Retrieved from: http://www.all4ed.org/files/TeacherLeaderEffectivenessBrief.pdf

Suitts, S. (2010). A new diverse majority: students of color in the south's public schools. Atlanta, GA: Southern Education Foundation. Retrieved from http://www.sefatl.org/pdf/New%20Diverse%20Majority.pdf

HOW DO WE DISCERN BETWEEN APPLES AND MATH, AND TEACHING FROM TESTING?

Fernanda Pineda

Holding her Ministry of Education Math textbook open, the teacher from the city asked the rural Quintana Roo first grade students: "Two apples plus two apples are. . . how many apples?" The Mayan children looked at her with puzzled eyes. The teacher asked again with a louder voice, "How many apples?" The children sat silent. And the teacher for the third time, with a curled lip, asked the same question with a resounding boom. She, it seems, was unconscious of the students' real dilemma. She thought the students were slow in mathematics, but because apples did not grow naturally in these students' community, they were stuck not on the numbers, but on trying to decipher what apples were. Adding "two plus two" was just the next step in solving the mystery of their teacher's questions. And as teachers often do, she had misread the students' silence.

This incident is fairly typical of the misunderstandings that occur when educators are disconnected from their students' culture, community, and ways of knowing. Unfortunately many of us in classrooms are unfamiliar with what our students' lives are like outside the classroom. And too many of us do not know enough about how to engage in culturally responsive teaching (CRT) (Chan, Lam, & Covault, 2009 and Luciak & Liegl, 2009; Delpit, 1997) so that we can move through these misunderstandings without curling our lips. CRT instructional strategies encompass teaching the whole child using cultural referents in a classroom environment that empowers, transforms, validates, and emancipates (Gay, 2000; Ladson-Billings,1992). Sounds lofty, but simply put, within such a frame, teachers begin by asking their students what they know before they decide what they need to know. Especially teachers, whose culture is not the same as the students they teach, should use every strategy they can muster in order to become familiar with the mores, knowledge base, and wisdom traditions of their students' communities.

Additionally, teaching "other people's children" (Delpit) requires an understanding of power, privilege, and knowledge biases, and how these relate to teaching and testing. As the world becomes increasingly interconnected, teachers should be at the forefront of exploring how power and privilege (Hovland, 2005) complicate and often distort appropriate pedagogy. Interest groups who hold the most power and privilege within a society are more likely to influence curriculum development (Apple, 2000; Levin, 2008), and often these groups are not the same ones represented in culturally diverse classrooms. So as teachers we need to even the odds by demanding of ourselves the constant intellectual exploration of all that is different so we can actively counter the distortions created by the privileged within each society about disenfranchised children.

Levin (2008) reminds us that a curriculum is an official statement of what students are expected to know and to be able to do. If the curriculum is "official," then teachers of diverse populations must endeavor to understand who is determining what is considered 'knowledge' and what will be tested. This understanding is particularly significant because testing and accountability currently guide curricula development (Spring, 2008) and educational policy (Kamens & McNeely, 2010) more than ever. Teachers of students from diverse populations and lower socioeconomic status must be especially vigilant for cultural biases in curricula and testing. Awareness of language usage, context, and references unfamiliar to students outside of the cultural mainstream should become a constant quest of critical pedagogues.

Because I am from Mexico, examples of our educational dilemmas most often come to mind. For instance, in Mexico Sylvia Schmelkes (2009) analyzed test scores of indigenous students in higher education and found that they scored significantly lower than the national mean and even lower when compared to the private school mean. Because test scores represent the path to higher levels of education, this disparity should not be ignored by our teachers and policy makers. Those of us who believe in a just society and who serve students in classrooms are obligated to address these inequities on a consistent and significant basis. Otherwise we operate in a context of mis-information with limited professional skills and knowledge.

As in Mexico, schools in the U.S. suffer the same kinds of urban, rural, suburban disparities in quality of educational curriculum delivered and gaps in testing results (Au, 2010). Despite the many gross testing limitations, though, I am not arguing against assessment. Assessment is useful to increase accountability for more effectively teaching students who typically are failed by schools, to improve application of standards, and especially to inform teaching methods. And appropriate assessment can be used to help teachers create baselines to better inform families of their child's progress, using several sources of evidence. Nonetheless, the unprecedented standardized testing movement worldwide - observable in Mexico since the 1990's (Benveniste, 2002)—has some worrisome traits denounced by many authors (Gabbard, 2000; Mathison & Ross, 2008; Schmelkes, 2009; Treviño, 2006). Some of the typical traits of these assessments are the biases against cultural and linguistic minorities, students in rural areas, or of low-income families (Pineda, 2010; Schmelkes, 2009; Treviño, 2006). These biases are visible throughout Latin America, where standardized testing shows strong disparities in favor of the urban and more affluent populations (UNESCO, 2008).

A particular case of children from one of the poorest municipalities in Mexico called Metlatónoc, is another good example of testing gone awry. In Metlatónoc, where over 50% of the population speaks an indigenous language, the schools in 15 of 24 villages scored "0" in the national standardized tests. ENLACE, the Mexican national exam, tests "knowledge" using passages about pets with passports (p. 8), and talking rhinoceros (p. 1) for reading comprehension, and the people-counter device at the zoo's door (p. 3) for demonstrating math skills (ENLACE, 2009). These passages are easily understood by children from the cities who are familiar with zoos and with information accessible through books and other resources. But for the Metlatónoc children, these "knowledge" contexts are totally unfamiliar and the educational resources of the city population are unavailable in this region.

Very likely the children in Metlatónoc can tell time without a watch, differentiate the seasons of the year with great detail, and describe animal reproduction in ways that other children cannot. However, I believe (Pineda, 2010) that these abilities are rarely if ever assessed on the all-important standardized tests. Yet this knowledge is valuable and necessary in these children's lives. By failing to account for cultural differences, these tests manifest the subjective nature of the knowledge measured, illustrating the failure of the testing mechanism, not the failure of the child.

Even though Mexico has implemented numerous programs to reach "dispersed rural communities and. . . migrant and indigenous populations" (UNESCO, 2008, p. 107), the road is still long and arduous. To further the goals of educational equity and culturally responsive teaching and assessment, teachers should be perpetual advocates against standardized testing biases. We should be advocating for different assessment practices, more pragmatic portfolio assessment, performance and self-reflection evaluations, peer reviews, etc. to achieve the goal of learning where the students are, so we can expose them to what they might need in order to get where they want to go.

When assessing testing design, multicultural educators should constantly question the implications in the test design for minorities (Carney, 2008), and for whose knowledge is being subjugated (Rahnema, 2001). Teachers need to be relentless in driving testing companies to raise their standards of evaluation to include these considerations. Passivity by practitioners on these issues allows students to be at the mercy of profit-driven assessment companies. Educators should not allow passivity to disconnect us from our children's culture, heritage, and ways of knowing.

Some practical suggestions for educators to know enough about their students to adequately assess what they know and don't know might include visiting community gathering centers such as temples and markets to establish contact with people who are culturally different; visiting the homes of our students; calling parents to ask for guidance instead of offering criticism of their child's behavior; and, of course, traveling to our children's countries of origin would be ideal, though maybe not so practical. Nonetheless, we should volunteer to serve on test-design committees, and be active in our civic duties such as voting for diverse population-friendly propositions and amendments. The process might be intimidating at times, but as Grant and Brueck (2010) remind us, "It is often at the edge of our comfort zones where the excitement of real development, true growth and meaningful transformation lies" (p. 10).

Most importantly, though, we must first learn what our students already know before we can begin teaching them what we think they need to learn. We can do this easily by listening to our students' and their parents' stories. Learning and respecting the wisdom and traditions of our students' culture is an imperative component for quality education. Knowing and valuing cultural differences, addressing the forces of high-stakes testing, and keeping an open mind to ethnic and social nuances create a powerful combination for teaching diverse populations in a world wrestling with injustices. When sitting in our classrooms, this combination may help us all discern between questions of apples and questions of mathematics, and between teaching and testing.

REFERENCES

Apple, M. (2000). Official knowledge: Democratic education in a conservative age. (2nd ed.). New York: Routledge.

Au, W. & Temple, M. (2012) *Pencils down: Rethinking high-stakes testing and accountability in public schools.* Milwaukee, WI: Rethinking Schools, Ltd.

Carney, S. (2008). Learner-centered pedagogy in Tibet: International education reform in a local context. *Comparative Education, 44*(1), 39–55.

Chan, K. C., Lam, S. and J. M. Covault (2009). White-American pre-service teachers' judgments of Anglo and Hispanic students behaviors. *Intercultural Education, 20*(1), 61–70.

Delpit. L. (1997). *Other people's children.* New York, N.Y.: The New Press.

Evaluación Nacional del Logro Académico en Centros Escolares. (2009). *Descarga las pruebas aplicadas en formato PDF (sample of 3rd grade ENLACE online)*. Retrieved from http://enlace.sep.gob.mx/ba/docs/2009_p3.pdf

Gabbard, D. A. (2000). Accountability. In: D. Gabbard (Ed.), *Knowledge and power in the global economy: Politics and the rhetoric of school reform* (pp. 53–61). Mahwah, NJ: Lawrence Erlbaum Associates, Publishers.

Gay, G. (2000). *Culturally Responsive Teaching: Theory, Research, & Practice*. New York: Teachers College Press.

Grant, C. and S. Brueck (2010). A Global Invitation. In C. Grant and A. Portera (Eds.), *Intercultural and Multicultural Education: Enhancing Global Interconnectedness* (pp. 3–11). New York: Routledge.

Hovland, K. (2005). *Shared futures: Global learning and social responsibility*. Washington, D.C: AAC&U.

Kamens, D. and C. McNeely (2010). Globalization and the Growth of International Educational Testing and National Assessment, *Comparative Education Review, 54*(1), 5–25.

Ladson-Billings, B. (1992). Reading between the lines and beyond the pages: A culturally relevant approach to literacy teaching. *Theory Into Practice, 31*(4), 312–320.

Levin, B. (2008). Curriculum policy and the politics of what should be learned in schools. In F. M. Connelly, M. F. He, and J. Phillion (Eds.), *The SAGE Handbook of Curriculum and Instruction*. Los Angeles, CA: SAGE Publications.

Luciak, M. and Liegl, B. (2009). Fostering Roma students' educational inclusion: a missing part in teacher education. *Intercultural Education, 20*(6), 497–509.

Mathison, S. and E. W. Ross. (2008). The Hegemony of Accountability: The Corporate-Political Alliance for Control of Schools. In Gabbard, D. and E. W. Ross (Eds.). *Education Under the Security State: Defending Public Schools* (pp. 91–100). NY: Teachers College Press.

Pineda, M. F. (2010). Standardized Tests in an Era of International Competition and Accountability. In Wiseman, A. (Ed). *The Impact of International Achievement Studies on National Education Policymaking*, Volume 13, International Perspectives on Education and Society Series (pp. 331–353). UK: Emerald Publishing.

Rahnema, M. (2001). Science, universities and subjugated knowledges: A "third world perspective." In R. Hayhoe & J. Pan (Eds.), *Knowledge across culture: A contribution to the dialogue among civilisations* (pp. 45–54). Hong Kong: Comparative Education Research Centre, The University of Hong Kong.

Schmelkes, S. (2009). Intercultural universities in Mexico: progress and difficulties. *Intercultural Education, 20*(1), p. 5–17.

Treviño Villareal, E. (2006). Evaluation of the learning of indigenous students in Latin America: Challenges of measurement and interpretation in contexts of cultural diversity and social inequality. *Revista Mexicana de Investigación Educativa, 28*(11), 225–268.

United Nations Educational, Scientific and Cultural Organization. (2008). *EFA global monitoring report 2008: Education for All by 2015, will we make it?* Oxford, UK: Oxford University Press.

Section 10: Teaching with Imagination and Courage Unshackles Our Spirits

Please take 10 minutes and write about the importance of building relationship between teacher and students and between students and students. As you write, consider Parker Palmer's passage from his book, *To know as we are known*[1]:

> *What scholars & good teachers have always known—is that real learning does not happen until students are brought into relationship with the teacher, with each other, and with the subject. We cannot learn deeply and well until a community of learning is created in the classroom.*

Please write your thoughts in the space below.

_____

_____

_____

_____

_____

_____

_____

_____

After writing those ideas, please consider the following activities:

• Join at least three other classmates and create a "relationship-building" activity that is relevant to learning any subject and that is useful in connecting students with students and with the teacher within the classroom.

• After 15 minutes of designing the activity, each group might present the activity to the class so they can participate in it.

• Then discuss as a class why you think the three authors in this section insist that to be effective in classrooms, teachers must "know" their students.

1. Please watch the brief videos below and answer with your partner the questions that follow: www.tolerance.org/tdsi/asset/showing-caring-while-having-high-expecta

2. What does Sonia Nieto suggest that teachers of Latino children should do for their students?

_____

_____

_____

3. Now watch: www.tolerance.org/tdsi/asset/know-your-students-well

_____

1 Palmer, P. (1993). To know as we are known: Education as a spiritual journey (p. xvii). San Francisco: Harper.

4. What specific strategies does Victoria Purcell-Gates suggest are necessary for teachers to be effective when teaching children from different cultures and backgrounds?

_____

_____

_____

_____

_____

_____

_____

SECTION 11

LIBERATING SCHOOLS FROM HEGEMONY INSPIRES TEACHERS AND STUDENTS TO EXCEL

Image copyright djgis, 2012. Used under license from Shutterstock. Inc.

Connections and context. I learned a lot about research and I learned a lot about myself while I was in Alaska. One of the monumental lessons I learned was to reconsider my role on the earth, to understand that I could not be a distanced observer and controller of the world as academic research would have me believe. Rather, I was but one component of the world, connected to and no more important than all other parts. . . . an older Aleut friend said, "When you see the mountain, say 'Hello, Grandfather.'"

—Lisa Delpit, "Hello Grandfather"

CHAPTER 11

"HELLO, GRANDFATHER": LESSONS FROM ALASKA

Lisa Delpit

Much scholarly research and writing focuses on disconnection. Traditional bastions of academe distance people from one another as they create power relationships whereby one group maintains the power to "name" the other. They decontextualize people as their research subjects are scrutinized and analyzed outside of their own lives. As one American Indian friend says, "I wonder how many people, as they tell stories around their campfires, know that their lives are sitting far away on someone's shelf gathering dust."

Connections and context. I learned a lot about research and I learned a lot about myself while I was in Alaska. One of the monumental lessons I learned was to reconsider my role on the earth, to understand that I could not be a distanced observer and controller of the world as academic research would have me believe. Rather, I was but one component of the world, connected to and no more important than all other parts. Once, when I was going to Denali National Park to sightsee (Denali is the Indian name for Mt. McKinley), an older Aleut friend said, "When you see the mountain, say Hello, Grandfather.'" That statement stopped me in my tracks: I had been going, as the superior human, to look at the lifeless, inanimate mountain. She reminded me in that brief lesson—and it was a lesson—that the mountain and I were part of the same world, that it had lived infinitely longer than I, that it would "see" me, even as I thought I was looking at it, and that I must then approach this grandfather with due respect, a respect deserved for all that it had seen.

This lesson was only one of many I received on learning to be a part of the world rather than trying to dominate it—on learning to see rather than merely to look, to feel rather than touch, to hear rather than listen: to learn, in short, about the world by being still and opening myself to experiencing it. If I realize that I am an organic part of all that is, and learn to adopt a receptive, connected stance, then I need not take an active, dominant role to understand; the universe will, in essence, include me in understanding. This realization has proved invaluable as I, an educational researcher, pursue learning about the world.

These lessons were not entirely new to me, for I come from a culture steeped in connectedness. Learning them, however, did push me to make explicit to myself aspects of my home culture, which previously had been an unexamined backdrop for everyday living.

My years of growing up fostered connectedness, as well as an understanding that things are never as they seem at any one "level of analysis." I learned early that Miss Pat, of Romper Room—no matter how much I looked into her magic mirror and no matter how good a "Do-Bee" I was—would not let me join her television classroom. "That's only for white kids," my mother explained. Things weren't as they seemed on television. She had to explain the connectedness of things initially beyond the grasp of my four-year-old, home-centered mind: somehow my "nappy" hair and my family's brown skin (I had yet to understand that my own "lighter" skin was irrelevant as long as it was embedded within a brown family) was connected to the workings of the larger world in ways that prevented me from sitting in Miss Pat's circle or from going to the bathroom while shopping downtown—and prevented my mother from trying on hats in a department store or from getting a teaching job closer to our house.

I also learned early on that my fate was irrevocably connected to that of other black people: if ever, heaven forbid, an actual or imagined crime was committed by a black person against a white person, then the well-being of all black people was at risk, often serious physical risk. We children in our segregated schools were constantly admonished about being proper "representatives of the race." The white population saw us as one undifferentiated mass, and so, perhaps, we learned to see each other that way as well. On the positive side, we therefore learned to feel like one family whether we knew each other or not, to take responsibility for caring for one another, and to take great pride in the accomplishments of our race. The sociologists and the anthropologists call it "fictive kinship"; we just called it living right. Alaska taught me to understand what I had lived.

Another lesson I learned in Alaska was the importance of context. In education, we set about solving educational problems as if they exist in a vacuum. We isolate the problem and then seek technical solutions. I was a professor of literacy in Alaska, so I was well aware of the traditional solutions for the "literacy problem" among people of color and people in the Third World. Children and adults in Alaskan villages were spoken of in much the same way as children in inner-city communities: illiteracy was high among adults, children weren't reading on their grade level (indeed, they weren't reading much at all outside of school), there was a "literacy crisis" that had to be addressed. The call for technical solutions abounded—"change the instructional methodologies": more phonics; less phonics; flood households with books, magazines, and newspapers; teach adults to read; teach parents to read to their children; encourage children to read to their parents; and so on, and so on, and so on.

Certainly some of those solutions might promote reading and writing, but I knew from my own experience that the "problem" might be deeper, related to more than the technical skills of literacy. Understanding the nature and importance of context was helpful to me not only in terms of shedding new light on the "problem"; it also helped me to understand some of the underpinnings of the Western worldview.

In our Western academic worldview, we assume that literacy is unequivocally good, and that everyone should aspire to be literate. Most of us have not taken the time to think about possible drawbacks or political implications of this ideology. Literacy can be a tool of liberation, but, equally, it can be a means of control: if the presses are controlled by the adversaries of a community, then reading can serve as a tool of indoctrination. Governments may want more people literate so that they can be held accountable for upholding laws—whether or not those laws are in the best interest of a particular community.

The practice of literacy, typically a solitary endeavor in academically oriented Western societies, can also promote alienation in communities that value collaboration and interaction. Growing up, I remember being admonished to "put that book down and go outside and play with your friends." Alaskan villages similarly value interaction and community more than individualism and solitary pursuits.

Sometimes, when I visited village classrooms I saw such conflict enacted before me. The then-accepted "best practice" in reading instruction was to abandon what many of us grew up with, "round-robin reading"—having each child read aloud in turn from a text. The savvy Anglo teachers frequently adopted these newest methods and had children read silently instead. The Native Alaskan* teachers usually adopted strategies their progressive administrators thought were outdated: they continued to have children read texts aloud as a group. Since my role as literacy instructor was to update teaching techniques, several school principals suggested that I try to get the Native teachers to change their instructional practices.

Having learned, however, the necessity of learning from the people I was supposed to teach, I presented my "suggestions" by initiating a discussion. The comments of the Native teachers were enlightening. They let me know that in order to engage their Native students and to ensure understanding of what was often a text about foreign concepts, they found it vital to read as a group. They believed that students could eventually be led to reading on their own, but that first they needed to introduce them to the new skill and the new concepts in contexts they already found familiar, namely, interactions with people rather than with books. Connectedness was an issue once again.

Their insights reminded me, too, of work of sociolinguists and educational anthropologists such as Shirley Brice Heath, who observed a distinction between many African-American communities and middle-class white communities. *In the latter, a baby's crying resulted in someone bringing a toy for the baby to play with. In the African-American communities studied, where households tended to be more people-rich than toy-rich, someone would inevitably pick the baby up. Thus, the African-American babies early on expected people to solve their problems, while the white middle-class babies grew to connect appeasement, at least in some contexts, with objects.

When I found myself wondering how to pursue investigating whether that preference might persist as babies grew up, I asked a teacher of a multicultural group of middle-school children in Fairbanks to have her students answer a brief survey on how they would most like to learn something new. They were to rank learning from a teacher they liked, learning from a book, learning from a friend, learning from a teacher they didn't like, and learning from a computer. Sure enough, in that classroom, a higher percentage of white children preferred learning from computers and books while the African-American and Native Alaskan kids preferred human teachers. Although the sample was too small and the procedures too unscientific to come to any real conclusions, I did find the results intriguing, especially now, in light of recent recommendations to improve education in inner-city schools by shifting completely to computer-based instruction. We risk failure in our educational reforms by ignoring the significance of human connectedness in many communities of color.

Spending time in Native Alaskan villages and talking with Native Alaskan teachers brought me face to face with the question of just what it takes to be successful in Western-oriented schools. How do academically oriented families train their young to be successful? How do schools reinforce and sustain what academically oriented families teach their children at home? Through readings about literacy and through my Alaskan experiences, I came to what were for me some breakthrough insights. To explain, though, I must take a rather circuitous path.

Many scholars who have studied literacy (including David Olsen, Walter Ong, Ron and Suzanne Scollon, Jack Goody and Dan Watt) have contrasted literacy with orality. Literacy communicates a message solely through a text, through the *word*. Orality, by contrast, has available to it other vehicles for communication: not only is the message transmitted through words (the text), but by factors such as the relationship of the individuals talking, where the interaction is taking place, what prior knowledge and/or understanding the participants bring to the communication encounter, the gestures used, the speaker's ability to adjust the message if the audience doesn't understand, intonation, facial expressions, and so forth—the *con*, (meaning "with,") in *context*.

Think about the difference between learning to play chess from your grandfather or learning from a book. The best part about learning from a grandfather is that there is presumably a relationship to build the learning on and, because he is there with you, he can adjust the instruction according to what he sees that you need. The problem with depending on a grandfather is that you might not have one when you need one. A book, on the other hand, transcends the necessity of the "teacher" sharing your time and space: you are in control of when you learn, even from a teacher who might be long dead. Given the hectic lives we lead in most industrialized societies, books are much easier to schedule than grandfathers.

As we pursue the increased demands and the often scheduled isolation of the modern world, there are more and more forces pulling away from sharing time and space with those we might want to learn from or communicate with. The "modern consciousness," as the Scollons would say, and its move toward greater and greater dependence upon literate communication, inevitably moves us toward a focus on "text" rather than on "context," on words rather than on all the phenomena surrounding the words.

David Olsen suggests that when children are taught to read in school, they learn both to read and to treat language as "text." Over the years, they learn, in other words to rely less and less on contextual data and more on the decontextualized word. Jenny Cook-Gumperz says that teachers have even developed an oral style to guide children to becoming literate. By teaching children to pay attention to exact wording more than to contextualization cues in following instructions, they work toward developing skills in decontextualization that are perceived as necessary to literacy. (Even such seemingly pointless rituals as taking points off for putting one's name in the upper-left corner of the paper instead of the upper-right corner has a purpose when viewed in this light.) In schools, then—some would say in the "modern world"—the decontextualized word reigns supreme.

Not so in communities like Alaskan villages, which are more "connected" than our modern communities, and less dependent on literate means of communication. Grandfathers are usually nearby, so learning from them is more practical than learning from books. Schedules, far from isolating individuals, bring community members into frequent contact. People who work together never have to resort to memos to communicate. And news spreads from household to house-hold without the need of newspapers.

In such communities, the *context* of a message is at least as important as, and often more important than the text of the message. It's not just what is said, but who says it, who is present when it is said, the intonation of the speaker's voice, how he or she looks when it is said, what else is happening at the same time, what happened yesterday or last week or last year.

These two contrasting communicative styles became quite evident in my own life when I moved from a predominantly white university to an historically black institution. At the white university, people tended only to listen to what you *said:* you could feel quite confident that no one would be the wiser if you expressed an entirely different message through facial expression, body language, or intonation. At the historically black university, however, I had to relearn quickly how to behave exactly as I had in my home community. People *watched* what was said as much as they listened to what was said. As a child, I could get punished for saying "yes, ma'am" while subtly "rolling" my eyes. At this institution, any gesture, any change in intonation, any slight facial expression could communicate to an audience an entirely different message than my words would suggest. Like Native Alaskans, African-Americans placed the value of context far above that of decontextualized "text."

Looking at what happened with Native teachers and children in classrooms, where the expected and approved instruction often ran counter to community expectation, helped me better understand some points of classroom cultural conflict. Jerry Mohatt, a psychologist who has worked and conducted research in many Native American communities, has captured on videotape an interesting set of interactions contrasting an Anglo teacher in a classroom of Native children, and a Native American teacher in a similar setting. What's interesting to me is the frequency with which the Anglo teacher's words do not match his actions: he frequently directs the children to do something while he is physically engaged in a completely different task himself. For example, he says, "copy the words from the board" while he is away from the blackboard looking through his desk for something or other. The Native teacher, by contrast, almost always matched her words with her actions: if she says, "copy the words," she is at the blackboard pointing. The Anglo teacher asks that the children attend to what he *says*, not what he does; the Native American teacher, on the other hand, supports her words in a related physical context. What gets *done* is at least as important as what gets said.

It would be easy to suggest that the Anglo teacher should be more consistent, but in truth he may well be unconsciously preparing children for their future schooling where they will be expected to attend to the words and not the surrounding context. Yet, if they learn what he teaches, they could find themselves in conflict with what they learn at home.

A Native Alaskan teacher commented to me that one of the most senseless rituals of schooling was the roll call: "We ask the children if they are here while looking at them!" But, of course, that conforms to the decontextualizing rituals of school: we insist that children assert their existence through the *word*, their actual presence is insufficient.

This teacher, however, developed a different kind of ritual:

What I do is to greet all the children in the morning and talk to them. I ask them how they slept and what they had for breakfast. I also ask them what they saw on the way to school. "Did you see any clouds? Was the ground wet? Ooh, was it really cold out?" Every day I ask them about what they saw and pretty soon they begin to notice more and more because they know I'm going to ask. Then I can lead them to make connections—to learn that when a certain kind of feel is in the air then it will snow, or that when a certain kind of cloud is in the sky then the weather will change. They'll learn to learn from everything around them; they'll learn how to live in their place. And since I'm talking to them anyway, I'll mark them present!

Another example of the decontextualizing ritual often enacted in schools is our insistence that children verbally mediate any action. The action itself is not evidence of its existence—it must be put into words. Native teachers often told me that one of their greatest frustrations was to have one of their instructors in school insist that they explain how they solved a problem. Doing it was not sufficient; unless it was accompanied by words, it didn't count. How many times do we insist that children talk through some problem they have already solved? We think we are "checking for understanding," but could we merely be helping children to learn to ignore context? Could we be asking them to ignore knowledge they've acquired through a variety of nonverbal sources and to limit their understanding of the world to the word?

Ron and Suzanne Scollon, in their book *Narrative, Literacy, and Face in Interethnic Communication*, talk about their surprise in discovering how they had programmed their own daughter to focus on the decontextualized word.[1] As many linguists do, they had begun chronicling on audio tape their daughter's language development from her infancy. When they listened to the tapes they were more surprised by what *they* said than what *she* said. At one point, when the baby falls down and begins to cry, her dad scoops her up to comfort her with the words, "Aw-aw poor kid. . . What tripped you, did you see what tripped you?" Although the little one is not yet able to talk, she is already being taught implicitly that crying, or any reaction for that matter, is inappropriate unless it is accompanied by a verbal explanation. The Scollons discuss how so much of what just seems ordinary to academically oriented parents is really training children to respond to the world in very specific ways. While these modes may be reinforced in school, they are foreign to many children growing up in families not of part of an academic culture.

Along with valuing context, Native Alaskan communities value children in ways that many of us would find hard to fathom. We non-Natives tend to think of children as unformed future adults. We hear about the birth of a child and ask questions like, "What did she have?" "How much did it weigh?" and "Does it have any hair?" The Athabaskan Indians hear of a birth and ask, "Who came?" From the beginning, there is a respect for the newborn as a full person.

I often heard Anglo teachers in villages complain that parents don't care about their children. Nothing could have been further from the truth, yet these teachers could not see how care was manifested. They complained that parents didn't make their children come to school, yet parents believed so strongly in the necessity of respecting children's thinking that they would say that if the child did not want to come to school, then the school must not be a place that welcomed the child. The teachers said that parents didn't make the children do homework, but the parents believed that if the teacher could not present the work so that the child understood its value, then the work must have had no value. In the parents' view, children were not to be coerced with authority, but were to be treated with the respect that provided them with rationales, stated or unstated, to guide them to make decisions based on their own good sense.

During my first few years in Alaska, I was confused by a statement I heard over and over in many villages. When parents found I really wanted to hear what they had to say, they would tell me in a tone of quiet desperation, "They're making our children into robots." I accepted what they said and tried to be as sympathetic as I could while trying to understand exactly what they meant.

It wasn't until I came back to the university and talked to Eliza Jones, a gifted Athabaskan linguist, that I began to understand. Eliza, wise and educated, although not in the formal, schooled sense, told me a story—the Athabaskan way of teaching that I learned to cherish.

A little boy went out with his grandfather and other men to hunt bear. After capturing a bear and placing it in a pit for skinning, the grandfather sent the boy for water to assist in the process. As the boy moved away from the group, his grandfather called after him, "Run, run, the bear is after you!" The boy tensed, started to run, then stopped and calmly continued walking. His grandfather called again, louder, "Run, run I say! This bear is going to catch and eat you!" But the boy continued to walk. When the boy returned with the water, his grandfather was very happy. He had passed the test.

The test the boy passed was to disregard the words of another, even those of a knowledgeable and trusted grandfather, if the information presented conflicted with his own perceptions. When children who have been brought up to trust their own observations enter school, they confront teachers, who, in their estimation, act as unbelievable tyrants. From the children's perspective, their teachers attempt to coerce behavior, even in such completely personal decisions as when to go to the bathroom or when to get a drink of water. The bell rings, go to lunch; the lights blink, put your work away, whether you are finished or not. Despite the rhetoric of American education, it does not teach children to be independent, but rather to be dependent on external sources for direction, for truth, for meaning. It trains children both to seek meaning solely from the text and to seek truth outside of their own good sense—concepts that are foreign and dangerous to Alaskan village communities.

I wonder, too, about the effect that this dependence on the decontextualized word has had on our general society. The word has the potential for becoming more and more disconnected from its surrounding context, more and more disconnected from actions. Sometimes it sees that we are moving closer and closer to the "doublespeak" of Orwell's *1984*, in which the Ministry of Love conducts war and the Ministry of Truth creates propaganda. During recent administrations the Department of Environmental Protection was led by toxic waste producers, and an era that was supposed to result in a "kinder and gentler nation" ended with more people homeless than I had ever seen in my lifetime.

In *Drylongso*, a collection of life stories from "ordinary black folks," one of the informants says to author John Gwaltney, "How can white folks talk so good and do so bad?" The informant goes on to tell a story about how a group of white cops accosts him and beats him silly. Afterward, one of them announces, "We have to get this man to the hospital." Not only is he injured and mad, but now he has a $109.50 hospital bill he can't afford to pay![2]

I do not wish to suggest by these stories that children from communities of color cannot or should not learn to become literate. Rather, I propose that those of us responsible for teaching them realize that they bring different kinds of understandings about the world than those whose home lives are more similar to the worldview underlying Western schooling. I have found that if I want to learn how best to teach children who may be different from me, then I must seek the advice of adults—teachers and parents—who are from the same culture as my students.

D., a Native teacher, told me a story about being a bilingual aide in an Anglo teacher's classroom. The teacher wanted to bring the children's culture into the class. She asked D. to write the directions for making an animal trap on the black-board so the children could make traps in class during their activity period. D. told me she had a hard time writing up the directions, but struggled through it. The kids, however, were the ones who really had a hard time. They found the directions impossible to follow. Finally, in utter frustration, D. went home and got a trap. She took it apart and let the children watch as she put it back together. Everyone made his or her own trap in no time.

Learning solely through the decontextualized word, particularly learning something that was so much a part of their home culture, was simply too foreign for the children to grasp without careful instruction about how to make the transition. Another Native teacher told me that she handled making this transition by having the children practice writing directions to go to or from a certain place in the village. When the children finished, she took the class outside. Of course, the students wrote in ways that assumed a great deal of insider, contextual knowledge. This teacher had them laughing and trying harder and harder to be more explicit as she pretended that she was an outsider, a *gussak* (white person) trying to get her knowledge solely from the text. They soon understood that they had to use words in a different way in order to get their message across.

She repeated the exercise with other familiar activities over the year, such as having the children write down how to make different Native foods and then having them watch her attempt to follow the directions. After a while, the children learned that they could make use of decontextualized literacy when they needed to. They did not learn, however, that they had to give up their own contextual way of experiencing the world.

Other Native teachers made literacy learning a group rather than a solitary endeavor. There was much time spent talking and discussing what was read, particularly when the text presented concepts foreign to the children's physical setting or to their background knowledge. Many Native and sensitive Anglo teachers also devised reading and writing activities that would in some way contribute to the well-being of the community. Some had students write letters to senators about the Native Land Claims Settlement Act or to the Fish and Game Department about some new ruling that was adversely affecting the village subsistence economy. In short, the successful teachers of Native Alaskan children found ways to contextualize the literate endeavors and to celebrate, rather than to limit, the sense of connectedness which the children brought to school.

Unfortunately, most Native Alaskan children do not have Native Alaskan teachers, just as most children of color throughout this country do not have teachers from their own cultural group. A young Athabaskan Indian boy once looked at his teacher and asked, "When are we going to die?" The teacher to whom he addressed the question was surprised, but answered, "Well, none of us know when we are going to die, that is for a power beyond us to decide." The young boy looked away and said softly, "Well, if we don't know when we are going to die, then why do we have to go to school? Why can't we just be happy?" That Native Alaskan teacher later said to me with tears in her eyes, "Why can't we figure out ways to make that child happy in school?"

Touched by those comments, I have carried around the question of that child and that teacher for many years. Why do we have such a hard time making school a happy place for poor children and children of color? A few years ago, I asked Oscar Kwageley, a friend, teacher, Yupik Eskimo scientist, and wise man, what the purpose of education is. His response startled me and opened my eyes even more: he said, "The purpose of education is to learn to die satiated with life." That, I believe, is what we need to bring to our schools: experiences that are so full of the wonder of life, so full of connectedness, so embedded in the context of our communities so brilliant in the insights that we develop and the analyses that we devise, that all of us, teachers and students alike, can learn to live lives that leave us truly satisfied.

END NOTES

1. "Native Alaskan" and "Alaskan Native" are terms self-selected by the indigenous peoples of Alaska to represent themselves as a political group in land claims negotiations with the federal government.

2. In no way should these examples suggest that all white people or all black people are the same. There is a great variance within any group. For example, African-American families whose lifestyles are more similar to middle-class white families have adopted more of the latter's child-rearing practices.

THE IMAGINATION BUBBLE: WORLDS WITHIN WORLDS OF RESISTANCE AND FREEDOM

Alex Salinas

After ten relatively drama-free, productive years of enjoying my status as a respected faculty member, it was the second time in less than six months that I was looking at a document threatening to fire me. A student who belongs to the service club I advise had my office key to gather supplies for a campus fundraiser while I was in class. When I met him after class to get it, he told me an administrator had seen him opening my door, confiscated the key, and left a message saying I was to go to his office in person to retrieve it. When I got there, the receptionist said the administrator wasn't available, but had left a message that I could have my key back. She also reported, however, if I did that again, he said, I wouldn't be getting another key.

I was shocked, considering that giving students keys to retrieve supplies is a common practice among faculty. The receptionist also handed me a 9-page document entitled "Manual of Procedure" and referred me to a highlighted section in the middle: causes for "summary termination," which included "loaning or permitting duplication of College keys."

Absurd, I thought. It's just a key. How can this be a rule? Soon, though, the annoyance heated into anger. The message as well as the impersonal document filled with passive-aggressive administrator-ese became offensive. I emailed the administrator asking him to clarify the key policy and the subtext of his warning. His response was evasive. When I saw him in the hall a few days later and tried to impress on him the slap-in-the-face quality of his message, he seemed puzzled, almost as if nothing meaningful had happened. "Key-Gate" was a minor incident in a long line this past academic year that made the work of being an educator painful.

Two other more serious incidents occurred. One happened the second week. I received an email notifying me of an official investigation into whether I had inappropriately applied for a grant, saying that depending on the results, I could lose my job. After a year of tense waiting, dozens of meetings with my faculty union, and a few awkward "interviews" with the administrator whose duty it is to investigate faculty, I was cleared of all charges.

A month after the investigation began, a supervisor deducted points from my performance review because of students complaining they were being forced to complete a particular service project, a misunderstanding that contradicted what I had said in class and had written on the syllabus. I had spoken with the administrator and students about the complaints when they first arose, to everyone's apparent satisfaction, but the document, which I refused to sign, implied I had ignored the feedback and was continuing to engage in the bad "service-learning practices" that had been misconstrued in the first place. After a long appeals process, the administration dismissed my objections, declining to even acknowledge my side of the story in the language of the review. The bottom line was that in both the grant and performance review actions, my bosses were implicitly calling me a liar, and I was fed up.

Walking back to my office with this mountain of aggravation suddenly compressed into the small weight of the key in my hand, I reflected on the symbolism of the moment. I felt locked out—of the inner circle that made decisions about this fundamental part of my life called being a teacher. And I recognized that all of these incidents could have been resolved with quick dialogues carried out in good faith before they escalated into disciplinary attacks; instead I got mostly forms, perfunctory meetings and blank stares.

I also felt locked in—trapped in a system, in a building, that at times made it hard to breathe. As teachers, we can't help but feel this way occasionally; yet one of the surprises for me was that in my ten years as a professor, I had never questioned the proposition of being part of an oppressive "educational system" in such a persistent way. And suffering over it.

The nuances of these particular incidents are not that important, nor through them am I suggesting that my administration—and administrations in general—work from basically malicious intentions. But I do believe that because of the nature of institutions, those of us who question basic assumptions might meet resistance in punitive incidents like these; and that those flagged with labels like "trouble maker" might suddenly find one incident building into another. What I hope this tale offers, though, is how it is possible to find a way around institutional abuse, to move forward as human beings who choose to teach from a place of inner sanity even if surrounded by insanity. My story helped me remember that it is we, ultimately, who hold all the keys that matter.

One place to find such keys is deep inside. At the height of my frustrations, I noticed a point of anxiety forming in my chest as I drove into the campus, as I walked among the gray buildings with the familiar office-complex-low-security-prison air that most of the schools I've experienced exhale. That day, feeling the need to uproot the heartache, I started repeating a kind of silent morning mantra: "I am here to be with people." Over and over I repeated it, smiling as I met students, administrators and security guards in the elevator; as I passed my former student at the end of the hall from my office who is now a part-time receptionist; as I walked into my first morning class. "I am here to be with people." I found comfort in my mantra almost every day for the remainder of the year. It helped to open my heart and let out the poison. I can refuse to reproduce that poison in my interactions with my colleagues and students. I know I have to cleanse as much of its bitterness as possible before I can truly get on with my work.

Finding creative, at times direct, at times more poetic and roundabout ways of speaking out about the insanity became necessary for my psychic survival. I and two of my closest friends and colleagues, caught up together in the web of the grant and performance review incidents, started sharing our experiences in a variety of forums. Together, we called union and faculty leadership meetings, directly expressing our concerns. We got ourselves onto the agenda of department meetings and offered a workshop on community engagement, showing the quality of our work to the same administrator who had questioned it without basis a few months before. On Facebook, we posted videos of police pepper-spraying protesting students at UC-Davis, noted the administration's failure to respond there—and tagged our colleagues.

Throughout this year-long campaign to speak out, we worked on a letter to bring attention to the hostile climate we were experiencing. We showed it to at least 100 colleagues for feedback, debated to whom we'd send it, how to frame it, and what the tone should be. After several months and five drafts, we sent it to the whole faculty union membership and distributed it at meetings. The tone was conciliatory, the message was a call for dialogue.

Addressed to both "faculty and administration colleagues," the letter attributed the college climate to a "corporate managerial model" one that is inappropriate for the organic process of teaching and learning. The letter indicated that we as a college were losing "the notion of what it means to be an academic community and family," and that "questions pertaining to teaching and learning are boxed and put aside in spite of (or worse, because of) their potential to open our deepest desire to belong, create, engage and change."

The three of us, as we authored the letter, weren't sure what we wanted, exactly, but we became driven to reach out:

"We call on all of us, but specifically, our academic deans to take their rightful mantle and become present to their faculty. Engage us in meaningful conversations. Help create the conditions to do our jobs well. We, faculty, call on you to become the voice that transforms this institution into a place where we can confidently come forward and present ideas and projects, and where differences of opinions and beliefs are not seen as threats to be put aside through managerial sleight-of-hand, but instead embraced with vigor, honesty, and transparency" (link).

At the end, we provided a sign-up sheet for those who wanted to stay involved in the conversation and perhaps generate a document of specific grievances representing a more collective voice. About twenty faculty to date have expressed their interest in opening a dialogue. My direct supervisor, after reading the letter, said she was interested in learning more about the issues we were raising, but the rest of the administration gave no direct response.

For us, the process of writing the letter was probably more useful than the product. It gave us a chance to relieve pressure, to stand up, to simply bear witness. In hearing our own stories as faculty, we reassured each other that our perception of the climate was real. We expressed compassion for each other's struggles. And we learned that at the base of those struggles is fear.

The fear is understandable, especially when people's livelihoods face real threats, and especially in cases when faculty don't benefit from tenure or unions. Also vulnerable are administrators themselves, who often have no recourse if they displease the powers that occupy one step up on the pyramid. Some administrators may acknowledge an injustice in a private moment but say the very opposite in an official setting, or more frequently, official document. Almost no one else besides the writers of the letter would agree to sign the letter, and even I needed time to make that serious public commitment.

Friends and colleagues mostly encouraged me to press on, but many warned that administrators may "gang up on me," "make my life miserable," and that besides, "this wouldn't change anything." One colleague said he preferred to stay out of it, not because he was afraid or skeptical that it could work, but because he felt so alienated from "the politics," that he had made a conscious choice to disengage: "I come here, I teach, and I leave." Others shared stories of their own vocal resistance. One mentor, an activist educator for more than 30 years, told me this over dinner one night: "If you stay silent, don't think that means you're safe. They'll come up with something and get you later." Another veteran, weighing the risk of speaking out, advised me with this simple question: "Do you really want to work at a place where you're treated like this?"

As our chorus of voices grew louder, I found what I have often found in many of my life's most fearful moments, whether I was thinking about making the leap to love someone, to reinvent myself, or to take on a new project. Looking at fear closely, considering gains and losses, I saw that the *fear* of the action was much worse than the *results* could ever be. The decision became not that difficult, after all.

Fear seems often to be the most potent diluter of what ultimately brings about change: community. That last and most powerful entry point into sanity, I've rediscovered. In resisting administrative tyranny, I participated in planting new seeds of community. The autocratic wreckage led me and my two partners in crime to create community from the pain—a process that has nourished me since virtually the beginning of my teaching and through my fortunate connections with civically engaged educators.

One of these is an education professor at another college. She has been facilitating spaces for community-building since I started working with her as a graduate student—workshops, conferences, parent-teacher-student gatherings in public schools, and graduate courses designed for practicing teachers. At the end of one of her courses in 2005, I along with my two professor/friends/soul-mates, as well as a number of other fellow faculty, brainstormed a project called the *Imagination Federation* (IF), inspired by the "Republic of the Imagination" that Azar Nafisi describes in her memoir *Reading Lolita in Tehran*. The memoir describes the author's life as a professor in Iran during the Islamic Revolution and her formation of a secret group to read banned books. Our goal through the Imagination Federation (IF) was to formalize on some level our shared commitment to libratory education by opening free and joyful spaces like Nafisi's reading group and my mentor's courses. These experiences we created before the administration targeted me as an institutional ogre.

To inaugurate our IF experiment and playfully invite others to join, we requested time (and were given it) at our college convocation ceremony to present some civic engagement initiatives. After a few minutes of a sober PowerPoint, we played Pink Floyd's "Another Brick in the Wall" ("We don't need no education!") and bounced five beach balls through the audience—much to the delight of some colleagues, and to the chagrin of others. But the message, which Nafisi expresses powerfully, was out:

"I'd like to propose that there is such a thing as the Republic of the Imagination. It is a country worth building, a state with a future, a place where we can truly know freedom. . . a world that runs parallel to the real one. The key is an open mind, the restless desire to know, the indefinable urge to leave the mundane behind. We write and read not because we already know, not in order to reassert habits and expectations, but because we are in search of what we don't know, of what is dangerously new, unpredictable" (2004).

By naming our intentions, we are still creating a new world through the Imagination Federation.

Another activist and scholar, Gustavo Esteva, suggests that we may feel stifled in the face of an unsatisfying world that seems too entrenched to dismantle. Yet, he insists, in the midst of that entrenchment, we can attempt to make a world-within-a-world. He describes the challenges of creating a free, open-access, non-credentialed university in Mexico called Unitierra (roughly translated, "One Earth"). He asks "How can we create our own new world, at our own, small, human scale, in our little corner in Oaxaca? How can we deschool our lives and those of our children in this real world, where the school still dominates minds, hearts and institutions?" (2007)

I think of the *Imagination Federation*, at its core, not as an organization or a project, but as a psychic space. It is a matrix of relationships. It is essentially invisible, a bubble that surrounds me at all times, totally porous to anyone who wants to enter, but also a shield against the weight of the gray, soul-drained, corporate world bearing down. Our irrepressible imaginations can encompass everything. Simultaneously, that bubble can be as small as the space I occupy with one student in one moment, able to squeeze into the smallest crevices and live in the most airless environments. It is a Freirean, all-loving space (1996).

Our hope is to bring into being, without buildings, curriculum or hierarchies, "the other college," as we like to call it, through our presence and intention. Living in the Imagination Federation, we have sustained long-term community partnerships in Miami with urban gardens and after-school programs; we have created literary magazines; we have marched in support of immigration reform and farm worker's rights; we have created websites brimming over with the curriculum of everyday life; we have organized music festivals and walk-a-thons; we have created summer programs for underserved youth; we have taken students and friends to the Everglades and other natural preserves; we have hosted student retreats at the beach; we have created learning communities across disciplines, campuses and international borders; and we have formed a non-profit organization dedicated to supporting education in rural Nicaragua while raising global consciousness in the United States.

We have read countless books, engaged in countless dialogues, gotten into and out of all kinds of trouble together, offered each other countless words of succor, loved each other with the deepest parts of our beings, celebrated weddings and births—all as a family of human beings who also happen to be interested in education. Some of these activities have had the approval of the institutions we work for. Some of them have been ignored. Some of them have been rejected and made us the object of disciplinary action. But the idea is that they create a free space unto its own, one that I know I can conjure at any time by saying the magic words: "I am here to be with people."

Here is the ultimate wisdom of IF for young teachers: Get together, and do it outside the school walls. Talk honestly about what turns you off. Talk about what turns you on. Then get creative. Pour some of your precious life and energy into action, and trust that doing so will merge your life and work in a beautiful way. It may make things more fun and relieve some of the pain. If you get stuck, speak up, and someone will come. Be smart about it, but don't hesitate to break a rule or two if you need to—and you probably will. And if you're wondering how you can join the *Imagination Federation*, know that in asking the question, you already have.

REFERENCES

Esteva, G. (2007, November 07). *Reclaiming the freedom to learn. Yes!*, (44), Retrieved from http://www.yesmagazine.org/issues/liberate-your-space/reclaiming-our-freedom-to-learn

Freire, Paulo. (1996) *Pedagogy of the oppressed*. New York, NY: Penguin Press.

Imagination Federation: link

Nafisi, A. (2004, December 5). The republic of the imagination. The Washington Post. Retrieved from http://www.washingtonpost.com/wp-dyn/articles/A30117-2004Dec2.html

Section 11: Liberating Schools from Hegemony Inspires Teachers and Students to Excel

Please take 10 minutes and write about the following:

1. How can teachers use in the classroom the lessons about connections and context that Lisa Delpit learned in Alaska?

_____

_____

_____

_____

2. What kind of imaginative ideas about teaching come to your mind after having read the Salinas article?

_____

_____

_____

3. As a class, please view the *YouTube* video of Ken Robinson's ideas about schools: http://bit.ly/o3Epsg

   ◆ After viewing the video, discuss with your partner, how Robinson's ideas about education compare with the lessons learned by Delpit in Alaska.

_____

_____

_____

_____

_____

_____

4. Now watch the TED.com video below on your laptop or other device: http://www.ted.com/talks/jr_one_year_of_turning_the_world_inside_out.html

5. Discuss with a partner how teachers might involve their students and themselves in JR's Project of "Turning the World Inside Out." Write a list of your major ideas in the space below:

SECTION 12

KNOWING 'WE ARE THE LEADERS WE HAVE BEEN WAITING FOR' FOSTERS CREATIVITY

Image copyright Lakomanrus, 2012. Used under license from Shutterstock. Inc.

My basic sense of it has always been to get people to understand that in the long run they themselves are the only protection they have against violence or injustice . . . . People have to be made to understand that they cannot look for salvation anywhere but to themselves.
—*Bob Moses, Radical Equations*

CHAPTER 12

TEACHERS AS LEADERS IN URBAN SCHOOLS: TESTIMONIES OF TRANSFORMATIONS

Joan T. Wynne

The stories people tell have a way of taking care of them. If stories come to you, care for them. And learn to give them away where they are needed. Sometimes a person needs a story more than food to stay alive.

—Barry Lopez, *Crow and Weasel*, p.60

I began writing this piece because I wanted to tell the story of the dramatic changes I had witnessed in thirteen teachers who were participating in an Urban Teacher Leadership (UTL) Program. Not only had those teachers' changes been dramatic, but they were also quick in coming. After just one semester in the program, they spoke about transformations so compelling that, like the ancient mariner, I talked about these remarkable teachers and their testimonies of change to all who would listen. So I thought the UTL story was about them. However, when I asked my late friend and mentor, Dr. Alonzo A. Crim, to read their story, he asked, "but what is it that these teachers and the program taught you? What did you learn?"

Reflecting on Dr. Crim's question, I began to see more clearly that the teachers' stories of transformation and mine were intricately intertwined. Throughout our journey together, lessons unfolded for all of us. The most important lesson, I think, emerged one day when the teachers and I were in my office practicing for a panel discussion to be given at a national conference, an opportunity to describe our experiences in a new UTL Master of Science Degree Program. While practicing, one of the panelists, a teacher of African descent, Yolanda,[1] said to us "I don't want to tell that part of my story because I hate to admit that I once felt that way about my students." She was referring to some unconscious racist notions that she had held prior to her participation in our program, notions about the incapacities of children of color who live in poverty, notions that I, too, as a young teacher had once absorbed. Remembering her words, in a moment, crystallized for me what this program was really about. I had thought, when helping to design the program (a program that was the brain child of Lisa Delpit), that its major focus was developing teachers as leaders. Even though advocacy of urban children and their families was the theme under-girding all the components of the program, during the initial creating process, what seemed paramount to me was facilitating the development of leadership skills for teachers. Over a year into the program, however, after listening to these teachers and reflecting upon their experiences, I now realize that reckoning with the ravages of racism has been the central focus in the lives of the participants as well as mine—and the most important impact of the program.

As the story of that impact unfolds, like Yolanda, I have an admission. Though I have spent much of my life confronting racist attitudes, I know that being white I am riddled with racism. I have breathed in the disease that seems endemic in the US culture. Thus, none of my comments on society's addiction to racism or the UTL participants' struggle to unravel it, in any way reflect an assumption on my part that I am free of such unconscious attitudes or acts—only that I am on a journey of unlearning racism. So when I challenge educational institutions and society at large on their racist policies and belief systems, and when I tell of the journey of these teachers to shift their way of thinking, I am, at the same time, attempting to uncover that thinking buried in my own psyche—to constantly undo my own mis-education about children of color forced to live in poverty by a culture who devalues them.

Part of Yolanda's story as well as the other thirteen UTL teachers' testimonies, only one of whom is white, may be more fully understood if they are put in the context of the consequences of the mis-education of and about urban children who live in poverty, especially children of African descent, a mis-education that impacted all thirteen of the program's first cohort. The other part of their stories involves the power of education that liberates.

RACISM AND MIS-EDUCATION

From my experiences in and out of the classroom these last thirty years, from others' research and mine, and from conversations with scholars of African descent, I have learned that the mis-education *of* urban children of color typically comes from the mis-education of adults and society at large *about* those children and their families, a mis-education rooted in racism. Rooted there because the culture of the United States has been built upon a history, traditions, epistemologies, politics, and economics steeped in oppression. Those aspects of mainstream culture were part of the investigations of UTL teachers in the first semester of the program. They began such explorations in an orientation retreat co-facilitated by Dr. Alonzo Crim as well as during their first two courses, one team-taught by Dr. Asa Hilliard and me, "The Psychology of the Inner-city Child," and the other team-taught by Dr. Lisa Delpit and me, "Creating Excellence in Urban Education." During this same semester, the cohort further explored those issues while attending two professional conferences held at the university that dealt specifically with teaching children of African descent. After these early experiences, the teachers reported, during evaluation sessions, significant shifts in their thinking about their students, the parents of those students, and the communities where their students lived.

Those shifts that the cohort continued to make throughout the program constantly reminded me of the gravity of the impact of our biased notions about the performance of urban children of the poor. Years ago Jean-Paul Sartre best captured that impact when he spoke of his European history and what he called 'that super-European monstrosity, North America': "It seems that we are the enemies of mankind; the elite shows itself in its true colours—it is nothing more than a gang. Our precious sets of values begin to moult; on closer scrutiny you won't see one that isn't stained with blood (1963, p.618)."

When hearing the UTL teachers talk about previous attitudes they had held about the children they taught, the children outside the circle of the "elite," and when remembering my own previous notions of obnoxious pity for poor children of color, I began to understand again the full weight of Sartre's assertion that "we [the larger society] are the enemy." Yes, our larger, hegemonic society, "super-European monstrosity" had effectively seduced itself, me as a young teacher, and these present teachers of color into thinking that students of their same ethnicity, who happened to be poor, were intellectually limited, unmotivated to learn, and academically crippled by uncaring parents. At the end of the first year of the program, when reading evaluation forms written by this first cohort, I continued to recognize the level of the seduction through their words of change:

"I learned that urban children can succeed just like any other child in any other setting."

"I learned that urban children have a lot of strengths. Their environment should not be used to hold them back. They are intelligent beings. Their environment does not indicate what they can do."

"I have a new conversation about what our urban children can achieve—a conversation I would not have had before."

"My philosophy has changed since the program. I now believe teaching is a service, and I'm on a mission to nurture my students academically and emotionally. I want to connect them to the world."

Before reading these admissions of change, I had witnessed with the cohort what I had seen previously during my own experiences as a new teacher and with other urban teachers—"internalized oppression"—believing the distorted messages about one's own group"(Tatum, p.6). Because of the dominant culture's "stained values," our history and continued practices of oppression, even teachers of African descent often absorb faulty notions about people of color. These distortions permeate the society. Consequently, teachers, both black and white, of the urban poor often act out of an unconscious assumption that those students, their parents, and their communities bring no real value to the educational experience. Like many in society (and myself when a first year teacher), most of the UTL teachers came to the program assuming that if their students of color failed to achieve academically, then the students, their parents, and their "dysfunctional" communities were responsible, not the schools and not the teachers. During the cohort's candidate interviews as well as during their Orientation Retreat for the program, the teachers consistently complained about lack of parental support for their students' education.

Until my experiences with the UTL program and my work with a co-reform effort, I didn't fully realize the complexities and the heavy weight of the impact of internalized oppression. Previously, while teaching at Morehouse College, the only all male Historically Black College in the nation, and Howard High School, an all black urban high school, I had worked alongside many professors and teachers of African descent who had refused to assume the societal stereotypes about their ethnic brothers and sisters. Thus, I had not fully understood the capacity of racist notions to infect the minds of so many of its victims. First in the co-reform effort and then in the UTL program, though, I began to see how pervasive and insidious are the distortions of power and privilege among oppressed people. Tatum's concept of "internalized oppression" seemed to unfurl.

In a recent conversation with Yolanda, more evidence of the depth of the grip of past internalized oppression unfolded. During the initial year, she along with the first cohort had gone through a process of developing a personal leadership profile. Her leadership skills, as well as the others, were individually assessed by their supervisors at their schools and by several of their peers, and, then, sent to a professional firm to be analyzed, where their strengths were identified and suggestions for growth were offered. During the year the cohort was asked to select a mentor at the school who would periodically assess the growth of a specific leadership skill chosen by the participant to develop. After the first 15 months of the program, during an individual evaluation session with two of the professors, each cohort member reported her profile progress. It was during that session that Yolanda revealed the distorted messages about her capacity to achieve—messages that she had absorbed during her growing-up years in a public school. She said,

While I attended school, an integrated school, I got the message that being black, I would never do as well as the white students. I mean I always thought 'You're black, so white students will always do better than you.' I took that with me into my classroom with my students. . . . And I almost dropped out my first semester of this program because I felt I didn't have what it takes to compete with the white students that were in one of my classes. Here I was in this majority white university wondering what I was doing at this place. If it hadn't been for you and Dr. Hilliard, I would have dropped out. But now I feel I can do anything. And, now, that I've been inducted into an honor society—well.

On that same day, another teacher confessed that before enrolling in the UTL program, she didn't set high enough standards for her students. "I just felt sorry for those children who were raggedy. I didn't think they could do very much. But now in my classroom, they are learning twice as much as they were—before I didn't understand how smart they really are."

These courageous confessions persuaded me that refusing to address the distortions of "internalized oppression" with teachers of urban children of color jeopardizes every player in the classroom. The teacher loses sight of her own power to teach all children, and she, unconsciously, sends messages to her students that they are unteachable. The cohort's admissions of their vulnerability due to racism's clasp may suggest that every white teacher, before she puts another foot in an urban classroom with children of color, needs to hear Yolanda's story as well as all the others' stories. They need to hear them because those stories indicate a new imperative in pre-service and in-service education: a long and honest dialogue that allows us as white teachers to confront the consequences of society's denial of the reality of oppression. The damage we do because of that denial is at times unthinkable! Through denial, we protect institutionalized racism, allowing it to continue to grow in our society like a cancer. And, thus, we become partners in creating and sustaining internalized oppression, damaging teachers of color like Yolanda, and, then, the children they teach by blaming all of them for the failures of the schools that so poorly serve them.

Because the UTL teachers were honest enough to confide their changes and because they were open enough to change, they taught me how unconscious I had been of one of the most significant root causes of the ills of urban education. I have spent decades in urban schools facilitating staff development about diversifying instructional strategies. For years I've taught urban faculties collaborative learning models. I have even facilitated diversity trainings. But until these teachers shared their testimonies of change, I had not understood how stupidly I had "followed the wrong god home" (Bly, 1981). I had spent much of my professional life asking teachers to change their teaching strategies, when this was only the tip of the iceberg. Paradigms of oppression, and all their disguises, not just bad pedagogy, lurk underneath the surface, blocking our hopes for building effective learning communities. It is those negative belief systems that disrupt the academic growth of our urban children of the poor, corroding every fiber of our school systems. It is those belief systems that I now realize I should have been confronting first within myself and within school circles all those years, not cooperative learning, not diversity training, not varying instructional strategies. All of those issues may, indeed, need to be raised, but examining attitudes about students and their parents needs to happen first. The experiences of the UTL program have persuaded me that dramatic shifts in thinking about how to teach more effectively by varying instruction seem to happen more quickly after first addressing erroneous belief systems about the intellectual capacity of children and parents living in poverty. Teachers need a safe space to take an honest look at the consequences of those attitudes on these communities, on themselves as professionals, and on the systems that are supposed to serve the students, parents, and teachers in communities besieged by poverty.

As a result of these cohort stories, I am clearer about what those systems lack because I now better understand the profundity of the lessons I thought I had learned years ago from some of the masters I've studied. I thought I had learned from Alonzo Crim about the importance of a "community of believers"(Crim, 1988). I thought I had learned from Lisa Delpit (1997, 1998) about the brilliance of all children, especially those "economically disenfranchised children of color." I thought I had learned from Asa Hilliard (1996, 1998, 1999) the imperative of teachers being in caring relationships with their students. And from all three I thought I had learned how important it was to acknowledge the gifts that children of the poor bring to the classroom. Yet, until, my experience with the UTL teachers, I had talked most often about other things—about more effective methods to teach reading, writing, even science.

This need for another kind of conversation, Ladson-Billings validates as well. While discussing a school restructuring effort, she said: ". . .even when there is wide support for change, without confronting the underlying beliefs of teachers about the educability of particular groups of students, that change is likely to be subverted" (Lipman, xiii).

In the UTL program, however, by continuously participating in a different dialogue, by exploring "underlying beliefs," I was witnessing the speedy changes this cohort made in their professional and intellectual lives as a result of examining erroneous societal assumptions about families of color who live in poverty. I heard these teachers speak about the powerful effect of learning that their own cultural history was rich in valuable lessons to be lived and taught. I listened as they talked in and out of the classroom about the profound significance of their discovery of an African worldview, of how that new knowledge had impacted their making sense of their own experiences and those of their students. I watched their faces as they revealed their surprise at how they had unconsciously "bought into" the dominant culture's false research, stereotyping their black male students as somehow antisocial and un-teachable. I understood when one of the cohort, Rachelle, confessed to me in my office one day: "Yes, the teachers at my school and I have often explained away a students' behavior by describing him as 'that bad-ass boy.'" We were all beginning to understand how easy it is to fall back on society's determination to negatively label these children and, thereby, to write them off, to do what Ladson-Billings insists that "far too often, teachers do." They "demonstrate a belief that it is more important to control and manage African American learners (particularly males) rather than teach them" (Lipman, p. x).

Developing an understanding of the consequences of those kinds of beliefs and learning the significance of integrating cultural histories and values into instruction seemed to impact the practices of all, including our only white cohort member. While visiting her classroom one day, I observed her using an African-centered affirmation with her mathematics class, a class composed only of African males. She began the class with every student reciting a libation which she had learned from one of her UTL colleagues of African descent. She was using the practice as a way of exploring the consequences of establishing a cooperative learning environment on academic achievement for students who were struggling with mathematics. Rather than trying to control the students' behavior as they loudly chanted the affirmation together, she pushed them to discuss the implications of the chant for their working together to achieve academic excellence. Her strategy stands in stark contrast to those teachers described by Ladson-Billings who want only to "manage African American learners." I am convinced that her life story was dramatically changed by her deep connection to her African American teacher cohort—and their willingness to support her growth while they grew.

Because of witnessing these teachers' unusual willingness to so quickly shatter their belief systems coupled with my previous experience researching a co-reform effort that was struggling with racism, I began to believe that all dialogue about school change should begin with a discussion about "the pain of racism, the necessity for constant surveillance lest it slip into our souls" (Delpit, 1999). The experiences of these courageous thirteen caused me to wonder if by my being in another conversation for so many years, I had forgotten the need for that "constant surveillance." Had I allowed it to "slip deeper into" my soul, the souls of the teachers I taught, and the children they taught? Because of my white privilege, had I too seldom addressed the "torment" that mothers of color face each time they are "confronted with racism's ugly face," (Delpit, 1999) especially those mothers of children in urban schools?

As I watched the UTL thirteen shed the trappings of their mis-education about these black mothers and their children, I was reminded again how seldom white educators address the accepted values of the culture that Sartre suggests are "stained with blood." Through the cohort's grappling with historical lies embedded in school curriculum that they and I had often unwittingly taught, I became more aware that the "how" to teach wasn't all that needed to change, it was, more importantly, the "what" we teach that had to change. I had not known enough or, maybe, been brave enough to talk to large faculties about changing the "what" we were teaching children. Over the years I had talked about infusing diverse cultural histories, art, literature, etc. into mainstream curriculum, but I had never challenged the lies we teach nor the values we teach. I most often stayed safe by teaching others "how" to teach. Yet, as Freire indicated, "There is no such thing as a neutral education." We either enculturate our youth by teaching within a context that sustains the present hierarchal epistemologies or we teach within a context of transformation (Freire & Macedo).

The limited and often dangerous perspective of teaching only the mainstream cultural values has created distortions about the integrity of other cultures. Thus, society at large ignores or worse condemns any philosophy that is inconsistent with Eurocentric values. Because such messages from the media bombard our every waking hour, many teachers cannot escape the misrepresentations about children and parents in poor neighborhoods of color. When teachers assume no value can come from these communities of color, they typically expect little from those students, teach less instead of more, and, therefore, get less (Delpit, 1997). Many teachers, both African-American and Anglo, have absorbed these false notions (I have met many African-American teachers, however, who have not). Regardless, though, the power of our culture's mis-education about the capacity of these students to achieve is so pervasive that it threatens the quality of their education and, ultimately, their lives.

That mis-education due to faulty belief systems threatens mainstream children as well. It threatens them on a number of levels. Intellectually, it distorts their world-view, keeping them from grappling with the fact that they are only a tiny percent of the earth's population. Its notions of superiority limit these children's ability to understand and learn from the wisdom of other cultures. And, as Rokeach found in his research in 1960, it hinders their problem solving skills. But the largest threat is to their sense of moral integrity. For, like James Weldon Johnson, I believe that dealing with racism "involves the saving of black America's body and white America's soul" (Carnegie, 2001, p. 4).

EDUCATION THAT LIBERATES

"Saving bodies and souls" is the other side of the thirteen teachers' story—the power of education when it liberates. From the dramatic testimonies of transformation that these thirteen offered while still participating in the UTL program, the possibility for education to unshackle the mind from mono-cultural intellectual traps and myopic visions of one-dimensional children becomes clear. As the program progressed, the teachers' unconscious negative attitudes and belief systems of hopelessness for their students unraveled. From their comments in class and the transcripts of their recorded program evaluations, we learned that these teachers were beginning:

- to see not only the problems but also the blessings of the child's home culture;
- to understand the value of connecting that culture to what the student was expected to learn in school;
- to see beauty in other dialects and languages—not just in standard English;
- to appreciate the need to value the language the child spoke at home in order to help the child develop a proficiency in the standard dialect;
- to understand the alienation of parents from the school;
- to look at the parents and their communities as possessing wisdom that could inform the schools;
- and, finally, to develop a "discipline of hope." (Kohl, 1998)

These new insights, spoken and written about by the teacher/leaders, may need consistent re-enforcement within a support network because as Pauline Lipman suggests: "In popular culture, African American inner-city neighborhoods are demonized as pathological, dysfunctional, and violent. . . .These images obscure the real strengths of supportive African American communities, families, and institutions" (1998). Being constantly bombarded by those images, within and outside the schools, our teacher/leaders may slip in and out of their new consciousness. If we are successful, however, in sustaining the support network we are developing with them, then their insights may be long lived and replicated throughout their schools and districts.

THE URBAN TEACHER LEADERSHIP MASTER OF SCIENCE DEGREE

In our country's culture, teachers are more often than not discouraged and disrespected by all levels of society. Politicians scorn them; legislators make laws to constrain them; the media scoffs them; parents and administrators blame them; and students often resist them. Many times I have heard undergraduate students ask pre-service teachers, "Why do you want to be *just* a teacher?" In designing the UTL program, we wanted to encourage teachers to see that they are much more than a "just," and that they don't have to leave the classroom and become administrators to be seen as worthy. Nor did we want them to assume they had to leave the classroom in order to assert their influence beyond the classroom. We wanted to foster the understanding that a career in the classroom is a profound privilege, a sacred trust, and, as Asa Hilliard says, "the most important profession" (Hilliard, 1999).

This understanding was affirmed by Karla, one of the members of our first cohort. After one year into the program, our department chair visited one of the UTL classes and asked the cohort to share any particular insights they might have gained as a result of their participation in the program. Karla responded, saying that one of her colleagues at her elementary school had asked her if pursuing this degree was going to get her out of the classroom. She told her colleague that "No, it makes me want to stay in the classroom; working with my kids is the most important thing I do."

The growth in their professional pride was a part of their journey toward development as leaders. For them, as for many teachers challenging negative notions about themselves and their students, teaching became both a personal and a public journey. Encouraging this cohort to take such a journey inside and outside their classroom became an important component in the UTL program. Many in the cohort were willing to address the issue for themselves, but because of their feelings of isolation within the school environment, they were, at first, reticent to share their ideas with their colleagues. The reasons for this seem evident. Teachers are typically left out of the loop of leadership in their schools; and, all too often, if given leadership roles, lack the skills that will lead to their success as leaders. Historically, education has excluded from its leadership the professional force whose experience and insights could inform and enrich its decision making process. And, an even bigger reality for this cohort were the results of investigations of scholars like Delpit (1998) which indicated that many schools have effectively shut out the voices of teachers, parents, and students of color.

As we designed the UTL program, besides being conscious of the necessity to initiate a dialogue with the cohort on such imposed silences, we also wanted to help develop the skills they would need to work within site-based management models and other school reform efforts that were increasing in the schools. In those systems, teachers are expected to collaborate with other teachers on issues of instruction and curriculum, to present innovative pedagogy to colleagues, to help define budgets, and to serve on school-wide and community councils, committees, and boards. They are asked to share instructional expertise across districts; collaborate with community and foundation leaders in finding resources for their classrooms and schools; become more intimately involved at local universities in the preparation of pre-service teachers; and organize diverse groups affiliated with schools in the larger community to encourage a bigger investment in the accomplishment of school goals set for student achievement.

We recognized that to adequately perform in those new roles, teachers need more opportunities for formal training in leadership skills and in principles of action research. They need encouragement to shift from their perception of isolation into recognition of themselves as active participants in a larger context. In developing this sense of the whole, they need support so that their contribution as professionals can grow beyond the walls of the classroom. They need encouragement to see themselves as professionals and as leaders, especially, if they are to deal with the debilitating impact of racist attitudes toward children and parents in urban schools.

Others, outside of educational reform, also have seen the necessity to change the way we think about who becomes leaders, who is included in the circles of power, an issue crucial to understanding the impact of racist epistemologies. Peter Block, a business consultant, warns:

Our task is to create organizations that work, especially in a world where everything constantly seems up in the air. We know that fundamental change is required. We keep talking about cultural change, but this will not be enough if we stay focused on changing attitudes and skills. No question that beliefs and attitudes need to change, but unless there is also a shift in governance, namely, how we distribute power, and privilege, and the control of money, the efforts will be more cosmetic than enduring.

One of the program's primary functions was to encourage the UTL teachers to see themselves as teachers and as leaders, not one or the other. We believed that as teachers they would empower their students to achieve academic excellence, and through each teacher's success in the classroom, she would, then, as a leader influence her colleagues by sharing her best practices to revolutionize individual schools so that every child at every school academically flies

Earlier, during their selection interviews, these teachers never mentioned the responsibility of faculties and schools to change to create more effective learning environments for their students. The teachers, in these sessions, seemed convinced that the children and their parents must change if the children were to achieve any modicum of academic success. There was an overwhelming collective conviction that if parents did not get involved in the children's education, the child would never succeed.

Surprisingly, though, after only one semester into the program, these teachers began to change their assumptions and to modify their instructional practices. After continuous exposure in the program to research that indicated a high level of achievement for all students was not only possible, but was occurring in schools in different parts of the country who served students from similar backgrounds as theirs,[5] the teachers began to expect and demand more from their students. In their program journals, the teachers began documenting their changes in beliefs about their students, the parents of their students, and the capacity of teachers to more effectively teach their students. All of these changes signified a tremendous leap in deconstructing the racist assumptions of the society in which they live.

Another characteristic of racism, the notion of elitism, at times, reared its ugly head. One of the teachers, Alice,[6] admitted in a conference after her first semester in the program that:

Frankly, I felt that I was better than these kids. I really hate to admit this, but before this program, I felt like I was above my students. Now, though, I don't believe in student failure. It goes back to me being a better educator. Now that I've been educated about urban children, I really do believe that all children can learn. And for the first time I really believe that my job is important. And now I want to become more intellectual, not in a stuffy sense, but in the sense of really knowing what I'm supposed to know to be a great teacher.

Her admission of believing that she "was better than these kids" spoke to the often unconscious negative attitudes held about children of color living in poverty.

Alice's sudden realization that her "job is important" suggested her need to combat the overall lack of status that the profession holds in the larger society. Her newfound professional pride insinuates the consequences of teachers' absorbing the dominant culture's attitudes toward economically disenfranchised people of color. Regardless of the teacher's ethnicity, for many of them, their sense of power seems to get distorted. No matter how vigorously they initially blame the students, the parents, or the communities for their students' academic failures, the teachers, on some level are aware, that they are not meeting the learning needs of those children. Because of that awareness, they tend to assume that teachers are powerless to produce results for urban children; thus, for many teachers, getting out of the classroom seems the only avenue to power and importance.

Another teacher/leader's comments spoke again to the proclivity to blame the students and their parents for academic failure. After just one semester into the program, she said, in a session where she was evaluating her participation in the program, that:

I used to constantly attack parents for not being involved in their children's education. But now I see them in a whole different light. I used to think it was the child's fault for not learning, but now I understand that they have different styles of learning. That even though I may be African American just like my students, still their home culture is different from mine and I need to understand that. Meanings are different, you know, according to cultural differences and socioeconomic status. I'm trying now to bring more of the students' culture into my lessons. I'm also surprised at how much I know now. . . .before I only had opinions, but now I have research based knowledge. . . .I can talk more intelligently to other teachers now about what we need to do to make it better for our kids, because I know more now. I can talk from a base of real knowledge. I understand the need for research to problem solve. I mean solutions need to come from research.

Her growing confidence as a spokesperson for her newly formed philosophies, as indicated in this assessment session, became apparent as well when she, in the beginning of the school year, gave a presentation to her faculty at her new school about more effective instructional strategies to teach writing. Quite an accomplishment for a teacher who had never addressed her faculty at her previous school.

In a later interview at the end of the first year of the program, the same teacher said that because of the program, she had expanded her instructional strategies to include cooperative learning and culturally responsive pedagogy. In addition, during this interview, she said she no longer blamed parents for the children's failure to achieve; she looked to herself to find the strategy to allow each child to succeed. The negative notions about parents and their inability to parent well if they are poor seemed ubiquitous in the beginning of the program with all thirteen teachers.

In her journal, another teacher/leader, Christine, spoke of changing her attitudes about students and parents:

I've gotten rid of my hopelessness about the children. I've changed my 29 year philosophy of teaching and children. I'm much more connected to my students. I feel more like the students are mine. If someone hurts my students, it's like they are my own. I've changed my attitude about parents. I don't blame them anymore.

These teachers were beginning to challenge their assumptions about the students, parents, and the communities where their schools were housed. Unconsciously these teachers, even though they were African, had bought into a Euro-centric worldview, "I think, therefore, I am." One ramification of that view in our educational systems is a belief that children can learn well without being connected to their teachers. It is a belief that doesn't work for most urban children of color living in poverty. The African centered worldview suggests that relationship is at the heart of everything, (Nobles, 1985; Hilliard, 1997, 2000) and that the African child learns best when she feels connected to her teacher (Delpit, 1997; Hilliard, 1999; Perry et.al, 2003; Siddle–Walker, 1996). Christine's realization that her children responded better to what she was trying to teach when they felt a kinship with her came after her study of African culture and the psychology of the inner city child. During these graduate experiences, she began to alter the way she related to her students in her classroom and began noting the difference in their academic performance.

SIGNIFICANT CHANGES FOR THE TEACHER LEADERS

I think it is important to recognize that these teachers were making dramatic changes in their classrooms and in their schools while at the same time teaching a full load during the day, five days a week, attending classes at the university, writing research papers, and giving professional presentations at local, state, and national conferences, and taking care of their families. In this cohort, only one participant lived without children and/or a spouse.

Repeatedly, the thirteen teachers seemed to unravel the severe impact that unconscious racism wreaked on the lives of their students and on the impotence of their schools to educate those students. All of the teachers taught in urban schools where the majority of their students of color suffered low academic achievement. I never dreamt that the transformations in belief systems and classroom practices could happen so quickly. But, indeed, they did.

I knew the magic that Crim, Delpit and Hilliard had worked on my thinking was formidable, but I had come to them after years of attempting to question my beliefs and after having been influenced by many other thinkers of African descent. These UTL teachers had come with previously unchallenged racist notions about children of color who lived in poverty and, as many said to me, either ignorant of the qualities of their own African culture or with unconscious notions of the inferiority of that culture. So how is it that in such a short time, so much could shift? For it was not just their words that told us they had changed, but also watching them in their classrooms with their children. We observed them modify their instructional strategies to include collaborative learning; writing circles for children–including kindergartners; literature honoring the child's culture; and more hands-on experiential learning tasks. We saw them begin to respect their children's gifts by giving them decision-making power in the classroom—one first grade teacher created an advisory board of two parents and two students each semester to help with curricular and disciplinary decisions. We began to see them demand high performance from their students instead of giving up on their students' ability to achieve at optimal levels.

We heard the cohort talk to each other about how they were being more creative about engaging the parents in the learning process of their children, and we heard one teacher say "Even if I don't get the parents involved like I want them to, I know it's my business to teach their children how to read and write and compute. I'll try to include the parents, but if I'm unsuccessful, I'll just move on because I'm responsible for my students' achievement." That was a mouthful for a teacher who had come into the program blaming parents for her students' inability to learn what she thought she was teaching.

In addition, while observing these teachers make presentations to their faculties, we heard them try to answer questions of resistant teachers. We heard them answer with confidence about the promise of their students, quoting research they had read and ideas they had learned from their teacher/leader mentors.

The evaluations submitted by the teachers, conversations in the college classroom, and the observations in their classrooms demonstrated that these teachers were becoming more effective instructors; more fluent in their writing and more aware of their need to continue to grow as writers; able researchers; bold leaders in their schools; and professionals who wanted to engage others in positive dialogue about important issues impacting the education of our urban children.

SIGNIFICANT CHANGES FOR ME

Though I learned many important lessons from this cohort of remarkable teachers, the most important one, I believe, is that until we confront the racist practices and philosophies that hinder many urban children's academic progress, those children will rarely "fly" in our institutions. Seeing these thirteen struggle to break away from negative notions about their students suggests to me that if we want to "reform" our schools, then we must collectively address negative belief systems. Since the profession in K-12 schools is comprised of at least 80% white females, then that confrontation should be initiated by them. As I have noted elsewhere (Wynne, 2003), we can't keep waiting for people of African descent to voice it, as though it's their issue, not ours. Too often I have seen them get nowhere when they raise the issue with white audiences. But when they raise it amongst themselves, it is powerful; and I have seen it in this program transform lives. If only white educators could hold such conversations with each other and get out of denial, we might make some serious headway in dismantling institutionalized racism. It seems, though, that our attachment to white power and privilege prevents us from "confronting racism's ugly face."

Confronting power and privilege is part of the challenge of any educator groomed for leadership. While the results of many research studies suggest that if we are to raise the level of academic achievement of our children, we need to empower their teachers as leaders (Pellicer, Anderson, 1995; Bolman & Deal, 1994; Lieberman & Miller, 2004; Moller & Katzenmeyer, 1996), few have tackled the issue of changing negative belief systems about urban communities as they try to empower teachers. In addition, too few school reform studies look at this issue. The Carnegie Forum on Education and the Economy (1986) reported that "without teacher support any reforms will be short lived" and that successful reform "lies in creating a new profession . . . of well-educated teachers prepared to assume new powers and responsibilities to redesign schools for the future" (p. 2). Nevertheless, since the initial implementation of the UTL program as well as my experiences with a K-8 co-reform effort, I am beginning to believe that until white educators confront racism head on, the Carnegie Commission's call to redesign schools will be as Kozol suggests "just moving around the same old furniture within the house of poverty"(p. 6), with nothing significantly happening to force schools to effectively educate children of color, especially those who live in urban settings.

Another significant lesson for me happened while watching masters like Crim, Delpit, and Hilliard facilitate the dialogue about these tough issues. Their ability to hold without rancor these discussions about the results of oppression kept me on a learning curve. Growing up in the south, in a segregated society, seeing the abuses that segregation wrought upon the entire culture kept me angry at my ancestors, white neighbors and colleagues most of my life. Seeing these three educators who have dedicated their lives to serving children and teachers, especially those of African descent, deliver without anger instruction that holds the promise to counteract the abuses of racism forced me to look again at my unwillingness to move beyond acrimony and blame. These three master teachers weaved a tapestry of truths so splendidly that often the cohort and I sat in awe. Some scholars might wince at the mention in a research study of expressions of naked admiration like these as well as at the telling of the soulful examinations brought forth by this program, but, for me, those experiences and outcomes are essential to the story of our research. Kozol suggests "that discipleship like this may be, in the last event, the only thing that can empower a person to live by his beliefs" (p. 195). Being surrounded by denial and psychic numbing about the devastation that my culture is wreaking through institutionalized racism, I occasionally need a certain reverence for those masters from another ethnicity to carry me forward so that I don't "slip imperceptibly backwards into deadness" (Kozol, p. 147) into that abyss of denial.

QUESTIONS AND CONCLUSIONS

After sifting through my research data, I still have several questions. What does it mean for these women of African descent, these teacher leaders, to be literate in this new way? Often their individual responses in journals, in classes, in evaluation interviews suggested that as a result of studying their rich and ancient cultural history, they had each grown personally as women of color. They talked about the influence of this history not only on their students in the classroom, but also on their children and families at home. They talked about their growth as writers, as leaders, as teachers using culturally responsive pedagogy. In reaching for a broader literacy, will they now be able to take on the mantle of powerful black women professionals in a racist society and transform those places in society where they interact? Will that literacy continue to advance them? Will that literacy encourage them to mentor other black women and/or teachers riddled with the same insecurities which these leaders initially possessed?

A question for all teacher educators is why, in such a short time, have these teachers, who came to us rife with confusions about urban children of the poor and their parents and unconscious of their negative beliefs about them, significantly changed not only their attitudes but also their behaviors? My hunch is that one of the most powerful factors is the opportunity to study with urban gurus like Crim, Delpit, and Hilliard. Yet because 12 of these 13 are teachers of African descent, did their ethnicity allow them to open sooner to the teachings of these masters. And, could it happen as quickly if 12 of the 13 had been white teachers? Without intimate contact in cohorts such as these with teachers of color, will white teachers be able to transform as quickly? Those questions were aroused again after a recent conversation with a colleague who is working with another urban education program at the university. In that conversation, she complained that she often still feels as though she is "banging her head against a brick wall" because several of her students after a year in that program are continuing to blame parents for the schools' failure to teach children. Most of her cohort are white. How much does their whiteness prevent them from shifting into new ways of thinking about urban children of color living in poverty?

In living these questions, I have a growing concern that no teacher leadership program can be successful raising the level of academic achievement of urban children of color until it opens up the discourse about racism in the classrooms, in the schools, and in society. I have learned from these exceptional UTL teachers how powerful that dialogue can be in shifting attitudes, behavior, and instructional strategies.

The impact of the program on exposing the distortions of the dominant culture seems significant. Hearing members of the 2nd cohort, who later entered the program and who are all teachers of African descent, slip into some of the same parroting of mainstream rhetoric about urban children of the poor and their families reminded me again of the need for and the power of the program's attempts to examine racist discourse. In addition, after having read Lipman's (1999) research on the restructuring of two schools in the south, I am more convinced of the imperative for serious conversation about belief systems if any positive change is going to happen in urban schools, especially where white people are in control. In Lipman's study, all the elements of school reform supported by white educators involved in engineering reform efforts were part of the change efforts of the two schools, elements such as teacher empowerment, shared governance, collaboration, professional development and more time for reflection. Yet, while involved in those strategies, many teachers at these two schools "unwittingly reproduced, perhaps even intensified, the marginalization of African American students" (p.296). Lipman suggests that a major cause for this result was the lack of any sustained conversations about belief systems steeped in race, class, and power inequities. Our program dealt, quite deliberately, with those attitudes and beliefs.

When left unchallenged, those negative belief systems subject the dominant culture not only to erroneous notions about its superiority to other humans, but also its assumptions of power over the natural world. Those notions many scientists suggest have caused irrevocable damage to the earth's resources and the species' life support system. We continue to dump toxic waste into our streams, rivers, oceans, soil, and air, and strip the land of oxygen producing trees and forests because we assume an entitlement to all the riches of the earth to meet our unquestioned demands for luxury, while one-half of the world's population goes hungry (Diversity Trainer's Manual, 1995). If the scientists are correct about the magnitude of the planetary damage, then failing to address the faulty assumptions of superiority, power, and privilege that racism begets becomes criminal negligence against the ability of future generations to recognize the perils of the planet, and, thus, their ability to steward the earth toward survival.

Choosing words like racism and planetary survival may seem too dramatic for some. Using words like diversity, multiculturalism, etc. over the last decade or two, however, has produced very little change, that I can observe, in epistemologies that continue to intellectually suffocate children and teachers across the country and that protect the power and privilege of the elite. Our euphemisms fail to lead toward real change in schools, in our society, and in the world. Moreover, they contribute to the telling of lies by reducing the lie to pabulum. John Mann said that "The term 'inequality' suggests a kind of passive accident . . . It is a gentler word than racism or exploitation . . . It is an easier word than oppression . . . Precisely for these reasons it is a useless word" (Kozol, 116). It seems to me that unless we can accurately name a problem, its solution will continue to escape us. Early in my life, my mother taught me that "Silence is consent." Whether her logic was right or wrong, it has always stuck with me. Thus, I believe that when we refuse to address racism, when we can't even say the word, we give consent to it.

A number of scholars have attempted to clarify the nature of the problem—to strip away the semantic barriers. Joao Coutinho, an African and Native American scholar said, "Education is either for domestication or for freedom" (1970, p. vi). No one seems to say it any clearer, however, than Jonathan Kozol (1975) when he admonishes those of us in the dominant culture that "It is not good enough . . . to feel compassion for the victims of the very system that sustains our privileged position. We must be able to disown and disavow that privileged position. If we cannot we are not ethical men and women, and do not lead lives worth living" (p. 6).

The program's attempt to address racism seems to have caused significant repercussions in the personal and professional lives of the teacher/leaders and in mine. Of course, the real test for our UTL program will be what happens to the children in these thirteen teachers' classrooms. If within three to five years of the end of their program, we are able to witness student transformations similar to their teachers', with raised levels of academic achievement and social consciousness for these students, then we will have much more to say about developing teachers as leaders.

To participate in this journey with these teachers was a gift of watching them "enter the fire of the world, and stand there shining" (Oliver, p. 2). As I continue to grapple with the "savage inequalities" in our public schools and in our society, I need the stories of these UTL teachers "more than food to stay alive."

REFERENCES

Bolman, L. & Deal, T. (1994). *Becoming a Teacher Leader: From Isolation to Collaboration,* Thousand Oaks, CA.: Corwin Press, Inc

Block, P. (1996*). Stewardship: Choosing Service over Self-Interest.* San Francisco: Barrett-Koehler, Inc.

Bly, R. (1981). *Selected Poems of Rainer Maria Rilke.* New York: Harper & Row.

Carnegie Forum on Education and the Economy (1986). New York: Carnegie Foundation

Carnegie Magazine (2001). Inhumanity. Pittsburgh: Carnegie Museums of Pittsburgh.

Crim A.A. (1991). Educating all god's children. *Reflections:Personal essays by 33 distinguished educators.* Bloomington: Phi Delta Kappa Educational Foundation.

Coutinho, J. (1970) Preface to Paulo Freire's article, "Cultural action for freedom," published in pamphlet form by the Harvard Educational Review and the Center for the Study of Development and Social Change.

Delpit, Lisa. (1997) "Ten Factors Essential to Success in Urban Classrooms," unpublished speech, UACC Town Meeting, Atlanta, GA.

_____ (1997) *Other people's children.* New York: The New Press,

_____ (1999) "A Letter to My Daughter on the Occasion of Considering Racism in the United States," *Racism explained to my daughter,* New York: The New Press.

Diversity Trainers' Handbook. (1995). Washington, D. C.: Multicultural Institute.

Educational Trust Report (1999). Washington. D.C.: Educational Trust Foundation.

Freire, P. & Macedo, D. (1987). *Literacy: Reading the word and the world.* South Hadley, MA: Bergin and Garvey.

Hilliard, III, A. G. (2000) Awaken the geniuses of children: The nurture of nature. Unpublished speech for Skylight 6th International Teaching for Intelligence Conference, (Cassette produced by: Chesapeake Audio/Video Communications, Inc. 6330 Howard Lane, Elkridge, MD, 21075 (00227–1160)

_____ (1999). The spirit of the African child. Unpublished speech at the Urban Atlanta Coalition Compact Town Meeting, Atlanta, GA.

_____ (1998) Characteristics of effective teachers. Conversation about his research.

_____ (1997). SBA: The reawakening of the African mind. Gainesville, FL: Makare Publishing Co., pp. 69–70.

_____ (1997) The structure of valid staff development. Journal of Staff Development. Spring, Vol.18, No.2

_____ (1997) Tapping the genius and touching the spirit: a human approach to the rescue of our children. The Ninth Annual Benjamin E. Mays Lecture, Atlanta, GA.

_____ (1991). Do we have the will to educate all children? *Educational Leadership*, 49(1), 31–36.

Kohl, H. (1998). A discipline of hope. Learning from a lifetime of teaching. New York: Simon and Schuster.

Kozol, J. (1975). *The night is dark and I am far from home*. Boston: Houghton Mifflin Co.

Lieberman, A & Miller, L. (2004). *Teacher Leadership*. San Francisco: Jossey-Bass, Inc.

Lipman, P. (1999) *Race, class and power in school restructuring*. Albany: State University of New York Press.

Moller, G. & Katzenmeyer, M. (eds.) (1996). *Every teacher as a leader: Realizing the potential of teacher leadership*, San Francisco, CA, Jossey-Bass Inc.

Nobles, W. (1985). *African Psychology: Toward it's Reclamation, Re-ascension and Revitalization*. San Francisco: Institute for Advanced Study of Black Family Life and Culture.

Oliver, M. (1992). *House of light*. Boston: Beacon Press.

Pellicer.,O. & Anderson, L.W. (1995). *Handbook for teacher leaders*. California: Corwin Press.

Perry, T., Hilliard, A., Steele, C. (2003). Young gifted and black: Promoting high achievement among African-American students. Boston: Beacon Press.

Sartre, J. (1963). Preface to *The Wretched of the Earth*. New York: Grove Press, Inc. Reprinted in Schwartz, B. & Disch, R. (1970). *White racism: Its history, pathology and practice*. N.Y: Dell Publishing Co.

Schwartz, B. & Disch, R. (1970). *White racism: Its history, pathology and practice*. N.Y: Dell Publishing Co.

Siddle–Walker, V. (1996). *Their highest potential: An African American school community in the segregated south*. The University of North Carolina Press.

Sizemore, B., et al (1982) An abashing anomaly: The high achieving predominately Black elementary schools. Pittsburgh, PA: University of Pittsburgh Press.

Wynne, J. (2003) "The elephant in the classroom: Racism in school reform," International Perspectives on Methods of Improving Education: Focusing on the Quality of Diversity, edited by R. Duhon-Sells, New York: The Edwin Mellon Press.

END NOTES

1. All teachers' names used in the chapter are pseudonyms

GRASSROOTS LEADERSHIP FOR THE 21ST CENTURY: LEADING BY NOT LEADING

Joan Wynne

Transformative leadership and educational excellence: Learning organizations in the information age.

INTRODUCTION

What kind of leadership does the 21st century demand? Many of us in education today realize that top-down hierarchal thinking and behaving is stultifying students' and teachers' imaginations, disenfranchising student voices, failing marginalized populations, and foiling national school reform. Asa G. Hilliard, III (1997), a decade ago, suggested that with a broken system, "revolution, not reform is needed." That revolutionary vision can be seen in a model of leadership, fully operationalized during the sixties in the Southern Freedom Movement (SFM) in the U.S.A., but honed in education during this new century by Bob Moses, founder and president of the Algebra Project, Inc. Grounded in a philosophy of empowering grassroots, bottom-up brilliance to find an equal voice alongside those in the power structure, the Movement's history did not start in the sixties. Rather, as Moses explains, it "came into existence when the first African walked off the first slave ship in chains" (Moses, 2001, p 174). And though the grassroots component of the SFM model may be as old as the leadership philosophy of Lao Tsu in 700 B.C.[1], its impact on educational circles is only now being examined.

Research, sponsored by the National Science Foundation, Florida International University (FIU), and some grassroots organizations is beginning to investigate SFM's educational offspring, the Algebra Project, as a possibility to revolutionize school reform, especially in the instruction of mathematics. Within the context of public schools, the Movement practice that seems unique in reform is its insistence on bringing together the disenfranchised into small circles to discuss, understand, and, then, demand what people say they don't want—a quality education (Moses, 2001, p.16).

In this chapter, I will discuss some of the components of this transformative leadership model as I witnessed them unfold during Moses' negotiation of the leviathan obstacles that stand in his path of delivering black, brown, and poor white children from the dismal dungeons of impoverished schools. His attributes as a leader reflect not only the grassroots experiences and wisdom learned through the Southern Freedom Movement (SFM) and from his mentor Ella Baker, but also from his disciplined intention of denying any attachment to charismatic leadership. Rather, he seems committed to fostering the leadership capacity of others. Moses suggests in *Radical Equations* this distinction between the two leadership styles, charismatic versus grassroots:

My basic sense of it has always been to get people to understand that in the long run they themselves are the only protection they have against violence or injustice. . . . People have to be made to understand that they cannot look for salvation anywhere but to themselves. (p. 33)

THE STORY

This chapter is more a narrative or portraiture than it is a research report explained through traditional reporting protocol. The story begins in 2004, when FIU invited Moses, Civil Rights legend and MacArthur Genius Fellow, to come to its campus as an Eminent Scholar in its Center for Urban Education & Innovation. He had been invited because of his 25 years of stewarding accelerated mathematics programs to disenfranchised communities across the country and because of his "focus on creative methods of teaching and learning as a strategy for empowerment and social change" (Ransby, p. 252). From the first time Moses came to Miami, I have followed him into a myriad of settings from classrooms and parent meetings and academic halls of various universities to foundation board meetings and superintendent offices in Miami and other cities. As a researcher, my observing and being in those arenas alongside Moses have been both humbling and transformative. So to write this chapter as an objective eye-witness is a challenge because I was observing not just a different mode of leadership, but also witnessing what I believe to be a different way of "being" in the world. My internal question has always been how do I wrap academic words around this multi-layered, innovative yet ancient, quasi "spiritual" leadership experience?

When Cornel West wrote in 2001 that Moses is the towering activist/intellectual of his generation, he captured two of the many facets of this leadership style manifested by SMF luminaries like Ella Baker, Fannie Lou Hamer, Vincent Harding and practiced by Moses in the field of education. One of those facets is his commitment to excavate the intellectual life of students scoring at the bottom quartile of academic measures. A second is the social activism, the intention to radically change an oppressive system (Moses, p.3). Moses suggests that "embedded in this work" of education and the concurrent building of a demand for positive change by people at the bottom "is the idea that if you can really bring about any kind of change at the bottom it is going to change everything" (Moses, 2001, p.188). Both of these commitments are integrated into the philosophy and practice of the Algebra Project and addressed whenever Moses is in a room with other people.

While exploring the intellectual life of students or their communities, what always seems to set Moses apart from others in a room is his stillness, a quality manifested also in many SFM leaders like Baker and Harding. That deep quiet lives in stark contrast to the monologues and directives that one often hears in classrooms, schools, or meetings with many leaders in the U.S.A. Indeed, that silence permeates Moses' teaching style and his persona in every group that he draws into a circle. It's a strategy that he often credits to the mentoring of Baker (Moses, 2001, chapter 3). Though, I find Moses' profound calm so integrated into his personality, that calling it a strategy seems a misnomer, like trying to separate the dancer from the dance. Yet, at the same time, I know that this "stillness" is a quality of leadership that is more powerful than any of the others I will write about, and one I believe necessary to emulate in the hyper-sensory-stimulated

21st century. Though other cultures may manifest this quality more widely, the fast-paced, efficiency driven American culture is not known for it.

YOU MUST ENTER INTO THE SMALL SILENCES (MOFFITT, 1961)

Several incidences of this disciplined quiet stand out in my research notes as strong demonstrations not only of its unique nature amidst hierarchal institutions in America, but also of the positive outcomes resulting from its practice. The first example is a meeting with Moses and a group of faculty who had been invited by the Executive Director of the Center, Lisa Delpit, to dialogue with the newly recruited Eminent Scholar. The dean's conference room was filled with about 26 faculty members. All seemed eager to meet and hear from this highly respected and reputed urban leader. After Delpit introduced Moses and asked the faculty to introduce themselves, Moses quietly asked "What is it that you would like to accomplish in these next two hours?" After the question, silence filled the room. Moses didn't speak. The professors didn't speak. People began to shift in their seats, either looking down or looking around for someone to speak. Approximately four or five minutes passed, which at the time seemed longer, and Moses remained still, looking straight at his audience, and seemed the only one in the room comfortable with the absence of words.

Professors are often wedded to fixed agendas, expectations of leader-dominated lectures, or pre-determined formats for discussions. Thus, being in the room with a leader, who believed that the wisdom needed for any effort lived within the people in the room and had to unfold with "leaderless" dialogue, seemed to bring this set of professors to palpable discomfort. They had come to hear his wisdom, not to be participants in the excavation of their own. Eventually, a professor broke the silence with a question which later gave way to a group decision of an open conversation about the challenges of being a college of education in the midst of the fourth largest school district in the nation. Later, after the meeting, one of my colleagues asked me, "Is that silence a strategy of Moses? I've never experienced that in an academic setting."

In the classroom with a cohort of 9th grade Algebra Project students and at a church basement where Moses led adult mathematics literacy workshops, I experienced that same quality as a means of allowing learners the space and time to answer their own questions about solving mathematical concepts, permitting them to dig deeper into their own reasoning for solving a problem. His pedagogy, a framework designed to develop conceptual knowledge, not rote formulaic answers, intends to build student confidence so that they and their small groups can probe within themselves for answers.

However, it was at our first parent-student meeting where Moses was beginning to organize the parents to support their students' new foray into the world of higher level mathematical thinking, that his stillness was again palpable and resourceful. Four professors, some from FIU and some from Miami Dade College, accompanied me to that meeting to become a part of this effort to sustain an AP site in Miami, where students performing in the bottom-quartile of academic measures were being offered an accelerated mathematics program. Moses and this team plan to shepherd these students from the 9th grade through the 12th grade, preparing them for access to and success in college.

At this parent meeting, where also some brothers and sisters, aunts and uncles came, Moses formed us into a circle, explained to the parents the scope of the project and then asked the question, "What steps do you want to take next to support your students on this four year journey?" Again, like the meeting with the college professors, an uncomfortable hush crept in. Moses sat quite still and never took his eyes away from the circle. Many, if not most, of these parents had never been asked what they thought or wanted to do about their children's education. The room remained quiet for what seemed again like a very long time. Even the professors wiggled a bit in their chairs, wondering if anything could be ushered in from this silence. Finally, one parent spoke, then another, then another and before the end of the night, the participants had planned the dates, the agenda, and a cross-cultural menu for subsequent meetings, as well as a commitment letter of support drafted by the parents to pledge their family's support for the work of the Algebra Project. After the meeting, in the parking lot, the professors and I confessed to each other our own discomfort with Moses' long silences while marveling at its brilliance, admitting that this had allowed the participants to find their way into shaping their own dialogue, strategies, and interventions to push their students toward college.

At another parent/student meeting, we watched as Moses sat quietly allowing students fifteen to twenty minutes to debate what time they wanted their classes to begin each morning at an upcoming summer institute. Later each of us professors, who had sat in the same circle, admitted that we would, heretofore, have impatiently intervened and made the decision for the students, unwittingly squashing their initiative and their ownership of the process. We, too, were learning from Moses' leadership.

Possibly, the most memorable example, though, of this quality unfolded the first day of a six-week residential summer academic institute that AP and FIU operated for this newly formed ninth grade cohort and for twenty-two students from another high school in the city. None of these students had ever been away from their parents for this length of time. Some had never been away from home. The students came from two rival schools where fear of one another surfaced at the parent/student information meetings held separately at both schools prior to this first day. Suddenly forty, fourteen-year old rivals arrived at the front door of a residence hall meeting space, disembarked from two separate buses, carrying their belongings and entered into a large meeting room in the hall. Some were driven there by their parents who also came into the meeting.

I welcomed the group who sat noisily in chairs and sofas, telling them how excited we were to have them at FIU, how long and with what enthusiasm the staff had planned for making their stay on campus a good experience, and, then, introduced their instructors, their college chaperones, and the other staff who would be working with them for the six weeks. The students listened yet chattered and sometimes giggled during introductions and comments from professors and staff. When everyone else had been presented, I, then, introduced Moses whom the 22 non-cohort students never before had met. After the introduction, Moses stood before them and said nothing. He stood looking at the students and their parents. Some of the students continued to chatter. Moses stood silent. Students began to hush other students. Moses stood silent. Some students then began to nervously giggle at the ensuing quiet. Professors shifted from foot to foot. The discomfort swelled.

For seven minutes, Moses stood silent, looking at everyone there. I had never before experienced this kind of patient waiting for a room full of anxious strangers and giggling teenagers, staring back, to settle into a respectful calm. The room became motionless and soundless, and, then, his quiet, calm voice began to tell the history and purpose behind the effort to bring them all together in this place at this time. He spoke of their obligation to bring the best they had to offer to the summer experience, not just for their own success, but to help build a movement to secure the rights of all students to a quality education. He, then, asked them to immediately decide if they were ready to make a serious commitment to the goals of the institute. If they were not ready, he indicated, there was no shame attached to leaving. He again insisted that if not eager then for rigorous academic pursuit, they might consider coming to a subsequent institute. He continued, saying that no one was forced to be there; that it was their choice, and they should not make that choice lightly. He paused and gave students the opportunity to leave. No one left. The rest of the day proceeded. I still remember standing there in awe of the courage and confidence to hold oneself silent and present to each moment and person for such a long time. The incident also reminded me of a description of Moses in *Parting the Waters* when Taylor Branch cites the first meeting between Martin Luther King, Jr. and Moses, who was then only twenty-five: "Moses carried about him the strong presence of an Eastern mystic. There was something odd about him, yet he also managed to communicate a soothing, spiritual depth" (Branch, 1988, p. 325).

SLOW THE BUS DOWN

Moses used similar acts of patience with me. Often before or after sessions at work-shops with adults or young people, I would proffer an idea about some content or pedagogy or activity that we might bring the next time we met with the group; and Moses, each time I asked, would suggest to me that we should wait for the group to decide what they needed or wanted. But on later occasions, because I was on such a steep learning curve about grassroots organizing and leadership, I would forget and ask the same question. Moses, as though it were the first time he had heard me ask the question, patiently gave the same answer. After one of these moments, I realized again the depth of the generosity that Moses, and people in the Movement trained by Baker, bring to any dialogue, and the huge philosophical shift this kind of leadership reveals. I had grown up in an Anglo-American world where a typical metaphor for describ-ing most processes, especially in education, was "Hurry up and get on the train; it is leaving the station, and you will be left behind." But Moses kept gently reminding me to, "Slow the bus down so the people can get on." His patient stillness in all of these instances made possible the gift of slowing the bus down so that everyone's talents and wisdom had time to emerge and to join the ride toward creative revolution.

In addition, this quality, the use of "small silences," demonstrates a profound faith in the wisdom of those living on the margins, "Black, Latino, and poor white students who are trapped at the bottom with prisons as their plantations" (Moses, p. 12). The silence, patience, and calm create a luxury of space and time for people to find their authentic voices in the midst of chaos, of confusion, of struggle, of discomfort; time to dig for their words, their ideas, their wisdom; space to piece them together so they can own and use them to invent their own solutions to the sometimes daunting realities they face and the educational monstrosities they suffer. Baker, too, believed that the people at the bottom of society's hierarchal ladder often offered the most ingenious ideas. (Ransby, 2007) In an unwelcoming culture, as academe typically is for disenfran-chised people, creating a safe container for them to let their ideas evolve is mutually beneficial for the institution and the people it serves. Indeed, such mutuality demands and shapes institutional change. As Moses explains it, "A network, a tradition like this, involving teachers, students, schools, and community, is not established in one fell swoop. You go around it and around it, and you keep going around it and deepening it. You keep returning to it until all the implications of what you are doing become clear and sink in." (Moses, p. 188)

HELPING TO CREATE THE DEMAND

Leading by not leading might be another way to describe the qualities that surfaced as I followed Moses into diverse arenas. That component, in fact, is what first drew me to Moses and his Algebra Project work. I had been immersed in urban school reform since the 70's and had become discouraged, always working for sweeping reform, but in three decades witnessing "so much reform, so little change" (Payne, 2007) in urban schools. Yet I know, as educators, most of us have desperately wanted to be co-creators of a democratic, quality educational experience for all of America's children, not just for the elite—as Moses puts it, "to recognize that all of the children *in* the nation are children *of* the nation." (Center, 2004). In hopes of accomplishing this, we educators have changed our curriculum, our pedagogy, our leadership styles, our textbooks, and our management systems. We have made large schools into groupings of small academies. We have promoted teacher leadership, shared governance, collaboration, rigorous professional development, reflective practice, and learning communities — yet still the majority of urban schools in every city continue to deliver inferior education to black, brown, and poor white children (Dropout factories, 2007).

After reading in 2001, *Radical Equations: Civil Rights to the Algebra Project*, however, I began to understand the missing piece of all of these reform efforts. That piece is the "demand side" of the work, or what Moses also calls "earned insurgency." Helping to develop that component within any group is the transformative leadership piece that too many of us don't' quite understand, or don't value, or don't feel we have the time or skill to cultivate. It's the knowledge that Moses learned in the sixties with the sharecroppers. While then the group was sacrificing for the constitutional right to vote, and in the present century, we struggle for the constitutional right of a quality education for *all* children, that same quality of leading without leading is vital. Moses often reminds us that now, as then, there is a place for advocates of all kinds—educators, lawyers, foundations, civic leaders, churches, businesses, community agencies—to push for democratic rights. But "the only ones who can really demand the kind of education they need and the kind of changes needed to get it are the students, their parents, and their community, which largely remains silent on issues like this." (Moses, p.151) For, in the absence of the community's demand, the country insists and teachers believe that black, Latino, poor white students and their parents do not value education and/or don't have the capacity to achieve academic excellence; thus, they become the scapegoats for low performance, a belief system that allows the nation to resist holding itself accountable for delivering "first class" instruction to all. The Algebra Project's insistence on building a base of student and parent demand for superior curriculum and pedagogy is a commitment and skill vital for all educational leaders, whether serving in colleges, universities, or public schools. But "leading without leading," an integral part of building a grassroots' demand is a painstakingly disciplined, back and forth process, that many leaders have little patience for.

Moses' shifting lately of the language from "demand" to "earned insurgency" (PBS) indicates his insight that students must make sacrifices for their education as did "sharecroppers" who made sacrifices (risking their jobs, homes, and sometimes their lives) to demand their right to vote. If today's students are to demand a quality education from the nation, they, Moses often explains, must be willing to take mathematics for 90 minutes every day for four years; sacrifice time at home to study; and devote time in their communities as math literacy workers. Moses' and the Algebra Project's demand on the students to pursue academic excellence, not mediocrity, is as deliberate as its demand on the nation to deliver quality education.

LEADERSHIP LESSONS LEARNED

When I think about my journey of being like an intern, shadowing a leader, gathering data, attempting to see the patterns of leadership, the nuances and the directions, I'm reminded of Harding's, *Hope and History*. In the book, Harding, while explaining "the transformative uses of biography," describes his encounter with a youngster caught up in a drug and gang world, a young man who speaks with "unconventional wisdom." Harding relates that after his lengthy exchange of dialogues with this young man, he began to recognize the need for young people to have "human signposts" who can help point them toward healthy visions and transformation (Harding, 1990). "They need to see and know the lives of women and men who provide intimations of our human grandeur, who open doors beyond darkness and invite us all toward the magnificent light of our own best possibilities, as mature, compassionate, evolving human beings" (p. 16).

In these dark times in urban education where the statistics of failure can overwhelm us, in a nation where all the old paradigms of social and economic polices have recently collapsed, I believe that knowing the success story of leadership demonstrated by Moses is especially valuable. Knowing that his qualities evolved through a crucible of darker times, fashioned by men and women like Amzie Moore, E. W. Steptoe and Fannie Lou Hamer, people pushed to the very bottom of society's rung deep in the Mississippi delta, yet who drew upon a vast, historic, and collective Movement wisdom to mount the struggle against racism, power, and privilege and won, we can unearth those qualities within ourselves to transform not only education, but also the nation.

So what are those qualities that I witnessed that seem the most relevant to a transformational leadership that might dig us out of the quagmire of inadequate public education, out of the vast inequities in urban and rural schools, and out of elite education that keeps the children of the wealthy lost in a sea of moral morass?

THE PRACTICE OF SILENCE

Harding suggests that Bob Moses calls it "the work of 'internal organizing' for anyone who seeks to work at serious reorganization of the world around us" (Harding, p. 24). It might unfold from a practice in yoga, or meditation, or simply developing a comfort with stillness. When witnessed, it is a potent force.

THE DISCIPLINE OF PATIENCE

A sense that the task is never complete so the need to rush becomes irrelevant and often counterproductive. If as Hamer suggested, "Freedom is a constant struggle; make a joyful noise," (Roberts, 2004) then there is always time to sink into the silences and wait for "the people" to lead their own struggle toward intellectual engagement and restorative justice. Moses, like Hamer, sees his work as a lifelong journey. Once when I was attempting to persuade him to accept a tenured position at the university, he asked what that would mean. I told him that for one thing, it would mean a retirement pension and benefits. He quickly informed me that neither would be necessary as he had every intention of "dying with his boots on." Moreover, with Moses the destination of the struggle seems integral to the careful attention to each moment in the journey, and the moment is met with complete integrity, like a doctor listening for the rhythms of a heartbeat.

THE BELIEF IN THE SMALL AND THE INTIMATE IN LIFE

Mother Theresa said, "We can do no great things, only small things with great love." Moses consistently manifests a belief that creating small groups with intimate connection to each other around a shared vision builds strong and bold movements. He did this kind of work in Mississippi; and, though, he has become what Dave Lawrence, a civic leader in Miami, calls a national treasure, Moses continues to spend time in the classroom working with one cohort at a time for four years at a time, teaching mathematics to keep the movement alive in the young while testing out theories of accelerated curriculum and pedagogy. His belief in the intimate of life seems counter to the typical national demand for grandiose schemes; its rush to "scale up" reform; its lust for big numbers to guide and shape us; its demand for answers without being willing to live the question; and its distaste for the prolonged struggle toward radical change. There is an organic nature to the leadership and work of Moses and the Algebra Project. He insists that AP "is a process, not an event" (p. 18). And he never seems to rush the process to grow it big—to force feed its success—his product is never a hot-house plant. Like a small farmer he knows the seasons of change. He knows that when rushed, when grown too fast or too big, ideas and practices like plants can become toxic or void of any nutrient or meaningful content. For twenty-five years, Moses has taken the Algebra Project step by step toward success. He's watched as young people grabbed hold of AP in Mississippi and spun it off into a different direction into a Young People's Project (YPP), managed by young people for young people, learning mathematics as they serve their communities as math literacy workers in after-school programs. Like Baker, he resists manipulating it to resemble his vision, but has stepped aside for it to organically grow its own leadership, directions, and intellectual base. After ten years of growth, YPP, too, now has a large National Science Foundation award and is developing new sites around the country.

THE PERSONAL CONNECTION

Moses consistently in Miami demonstrates a belief in personally connecting with whomever he works. When he was first forming the 9th grade cohort, he visited the homes of each student. Often the school had incorrect addresses for students; Moses kept at it until he found the home of every student. He visited those homes on multiple occasions as well as met parents and relatives at the school several times a year for brainstorming sessions. He visits sick students when they are stuck at home; he takes students to the doctor; he brings them groceries. This is the man who, in an interview with a journalist, President Barrack Obama called his "role model" (Lizza, 2007, p. 3).

In his book, Moses says that connecting is an essential part of the work of the Algebra Project: "The first thing you have to do is make a personal connection. You have to find out who it is you are working with. All across the South you could see that in grassroots rural people. That was their style. Miss Baker took this style to a sophisticated level of political work." (Moses, p. 32)

GIVING VOICE TO THE VOICELESS

Moses reminds us that "Young people finding their voice instead of being spoken for is a crucial part of the process" (Moses, p.19). Consequently, he creates opportunities at conferences, university classrooms, and diverse meeting halls where his high school students can tell their stories and share their mathematical knowledge across the country. Learning from Baker and his experiences in the SFM, he also insists that leadership "should emerge from the community and be helped in its growth by grassroots organizers" (Moses, p. 34).

With Moses, leadership itself seems a co-creative process, always moving, never culminating, a procession of people and ideas changing places in a circle, not a triangle. Resisting any attempts at making the national Algebra Project a center of power, Moses continuously pushes power into the hands of the local sites. He seeks, and sometimes helps to create, local grassroots cadres to develop a consciousness that nothing will be sustained without their owning personal leadership, without constantly re-evaluating successes and failures to keep their efforts fluid and responsive to the environment in which they live and the people with whom they work. Like a jazz musician who "modifies a musical rhythm by shifting the accent to a weak beat of the bar," Moses places his attention on the weakest voices in society and helps them find their song—and, like Hamer, they make a "joyful noise."

He orchestrated that "jazz" again in August of 2008 when a newly assigned principal at the local high school was considering closing the Algebra Project site. To counter her attempt, I suggested that Bob, I, and others might meet with the principal and extol the virtues of the project. Bob quietly said, "No." The students and parents, he suggested, should write a letter about their experiences in the project and then meet with the principal to share the letter. They did, and they alone persuaded the principal to maintain the project at their school. Moses' two years of work with these students, building them as a cohort and a community, produced a desire and a confidence in them to demand what they needed. They had earned their insurgency.

A PROFOUND CAPACITY TO LISTEN DEEPLY AND WELL

I have yet to find anyone who has not felt deeply heard after walking away from a meeting with Moses. Whether he agrees or not, he listens intently to whoever is speaking. He asks penetrating questions and waits patiently for others to digest the words and respond from their own experiences. Without taking the first note in most meetings, months later he can repeat who said what when. His capacity, though, to listen, really listen, to the young is remarkable to experience. His proclivity for prolonged silence with them and his honest curiosity to know their thinking allow them to push that thinking in new directions. Whether in the classroom or in sessions with students planning events, Moses consistently models this profound respect for what young people are saying. He explains that, "It is the voices of the young people I hear every day, more than anything, that gives me hope" (Moses, p. 191).

In most arenas, leaders who listen well are treasured. Historian, Charles Payne, suggests this quality of careful listening as one that Moses early in his life projected:

The broad outlines of the Mississippi movement of the sixties had been laid out, primarily between an older warrior [Amzie Moore] with little formal education but years of experience fighting Mississippi and a younger man [Bob Moses] with sense enough to listen, Harvard notwithstanding (Payne, p 106–107).

BUILDING THE NETWORK OF RELATIONSHIPS IN COMMUNITIES AND ACROSS THE NATION

Moses since the sixties, as a field secretary for the Student Non-violent Coordinating Committee (SNCC), has learned the necessity of always widening the web of the network both locally and nationally to support his work. In Mississippi, he, along with local insurgent leaders, organized sharecroppers, young people in the towns, thousands of white students from Northern universities, federal prosecutors, doctors, teachers, preachers, politicians and other social justice groups beyond SNCC around the issue of voting rights. This network proved invaluable, for as Moses puts it: "When Mississippi locked us up, the Feds could set us free" (Moses, 2009).

In the Algebra Project, he started in a classroom with his children, teaching them algebra, then other people's children in that same classroom, then organized other parents, former SFM activists, teachers across the country, elite mathematics researchers from Cornell, Kent State, the Mathematics and Science Research Institute (MSRI), foundations like MacArthur, Lilly, Open Society, the National Science Foundation, the Children's Trust, universities, professors and graduate students, lawyers, school board members, unions like the Industrial Areas Foundation (IAF), politicians, journalists and thousands of young people around the issue of delivering accelerated academic education to the nation's bottom quartile and creating a movement for Quality Education as a Constitutional Right. His circle spreads across the nation from Los Angeles to Miami: "The question of how we all learn to work across several arenas is unsolved. Those arenas are large and complicated . . . . Really working in all these arenas will require that many people adopt a more holistic outlook than they have ever done before" (Moses, 2001, p. 16). Moses nurtures this complex network while at the same time spending 3 days a week teaching mathematics to his local AP cohort. And always, living the words of Baker, to bring the family along, Moses' circle includes his family, his wife, his two sons and two daughters in the work.

REACHING FOR STRATEGIES TO MOVE FORWARD, INSTEAD OF GETTING STUCK IN A SEARCH FOR BLAME

Moses' rapid movement from problem to strategies for addressing thorny issues is often demonstrated with staff, circles of supporters, parents, and students. I have often observed and silently approved his response to students who might misbehave. At those times, like most "good" teachers, he moves immediately to discovering the reason behind the behavior instead of locking into ideas of punishment; he elicits student engagement in finding the root and the solution, not only in mathematics but also in their lives.

Recently, though, his propensity to move instantly from problem toward strategy stood in stark contrast to my own. He walked into my office immediately after a meeting where expected support was suddenly withdrawn. After he reported to me the outcome of the meeting, I instantly protested, "Why would they do that? How can they do that? How short-sighted." Without entertaining my outburst, Moses asked "What do you think are some strategies to now keep our work going in Miami?" My brain had shut down with the shock of the bad news, while Moses had already begun sharing ideas for garnering other support. Wallowing in blame is just not part of Moses' psyche. His intellect and imagination seem always in gear for moving creatively toward the next step. Yet, at the same time, he can surrender to the ideas of any group at hand, especially the young, if those ideas are congruent with the gestalt of the vision.

WORK WITHIN AND AGAINST VARIOUS STRUCTURES

Within most public school systems there are structures in place which might seem to enhance the system, yet often damage the humans within that system. Wise leaders recognize those structures and understand the need to work against them when they stifle the creativity and relationship building of the system's participants. While working in urban and rural systems, Moses, like many of us, has suffered arcane public school protocols and processes. The bigger the system, the more rigid and unimaginative the rules—-and the more unconscious the intimidation of the people it is supposed to serve. Against these monolithic systems, Moses' organic sense of life, learning, and leadership stands in stark and elegant relief. His refusal to replicate yet one more hierarchal, one-size-fits-all instructional and organizational model, though, is often misunderstood as unrealistic or somehow incomplete.

Nevertheless, during strategy sessions, Moses has often explained that we must continue to go up and down the hierarchy of the system, the chain of command, to keep the support alive for the students' intellectual development, and that we should maneuver around those structures we cannot change and create our own system for who contacts whom on each level of authority:

It is a little bit like guerrilla warfare. You're striking. You're pulling back. You're looking at where you are. You're striking again. You're looking for an opening. You're looking for a soft spot, trying to find out where you can penetrate. And you are working with and against various structures. You're in them, but you're working against them at various levels. (p. 17)

Yet always Moses reminds us that the students and parents must be the driving force behind the survival of the project's vision of "facing a system that does not lend itself to your needs and devising means by which you change that system." (p. 19) Though Moses continually attempts to build consensus and networks among diverse advocacy groups, the radical change needed, he insists, will result ultimately from disenfranchised communities pushing against the system, not from the well-meaning advocacy of outside agents.

When I get disheartened by the harsh realities and inequities in the public school system (Orfield, 2004) and the dearth of leaders with a vision, I think about Moses' almost fifty years of quiet revolution. I think of his front-line participation in the Southern Freedom Movement; of the times he was beaten and shot at; of the times he spent in jail when Civil Rights Attorney, John Doar had to come from D. C. and save Moses from southern sheriffs. I think also about Ella Baker and Fannie Lou Hamer and Amzie Moore and the thousands of Harding's "human signposts" who changed the south forever and who changed the nation's political system so that a Barrack Obama could become President of the United States of America. And, then, I go and sit with Moses' Algebra Project students and listen to them talk. That's when I sense that the system is not impenetrable, and that if I have the patience and the stillness, I will hear the strong shifting musical rhythm that comes from the "accent on a weak beat of the bar." Then I know we're closer to public schools making freedom's "joyful noise."

REFERENCES

Branch, T. (1988). *Parting the waters: America in the King years 1954–63*. New York: Simon and Schuster.

Center for Urban Education & Innovation (2004). "Interview with Bob Moses." Promotional DVD. Miami, FL: Florida International University.

Harding, V. (1990). *Hope and history: Why we must share the Movement*. Maryland: Orbis Books.

Henry A. & Curry, C. (2000). *Aaron Henry: The fire ever burning*. Jackson, Mississippi: University of Mississippi Press.

Hilliard, Asa G., III (1997), "The structure of valid staff development." *Journal of Staff Development*. Spring, Vol.18, No.2.

Lizza, R. (2007). Barack Obama's unlikely political education. *The Agitator*. (http://www. tnr.com/doc.mhtml?i=20070319&s=lizza031907)

Moffitt, J. (1961) "To look at anything." *The Living Seed*. New York: Harcourt Brace & Co.

Moses, R. & Cobb, C. (2001), *Radical equations: Civil rights from Mississippi to the Algebra Project*. Beacon Press: Boston, MA.

Moses, (2009) "Constitutional Property versus Constitutional People." In Perry, T., Delpit, L., Moses, R, & Wynne, J. eds. *Quality Education as a Constitutional Right*. Boston: Beacon Press. (due in fall '09)

Orfield, G., Losen, D., Wald, J. & Swanson, C. B. (2004). Losing our future: How minority yourth are being left behind by the graduation rate crisis. Urban Institute, available at http://www.urban.org/UplaodedPDF/410936_LosingOurFuture.pdf

Payne, C. (1995). *I've Got the Light of Freedom: The organizing tradition and the Mississippi freedom struggle*. Berkeley: University of California Press

Payne, C. (2008). So much reform, so little change: The persistence of failure in urban schools. Cambridge, MASS: Harvard Education Press.

Ransby, B. (2003). *Ella Baker & the Black Freedom Movement: A radical Democratic vision*. Chapel Hill, The University of North Carolina Press.

Roberts, Wally. (2004). E-mail sharing his experience living one summer in Fannie Lou Hamer's home.

Think Exist.Com. Quotations from Lao Tzu. http://thinkexist.com/quotation/go-to-the-people-live-with-them-learn-from-them/348565.html

END NOTES

1. Quotation by Lao Tsu from the *Tao Te Ching suggests* the general philosophy of Movement leadership style "Go to the people. Live with them. Learn from them. Love them. Start with what they know. Build with what they have. But with the best leaders, when the work is done, the task accomplished, the people will say 'We have done this ourselves.'" While at Harvard, Moses studied also the writings of Lao Tzu.

Section 12: Knowing "We Are the Leaders We Have Been Waiting For" Fosters Creativity

Please take 10 minutes and write about the following:

1. In the "Teachers as Leaders" article, what kinds of teacher transformations appealed to you the most?

_____

_____

_____

2. What seemed to be the main ingredients for fostering their change?

_____

_____

_____

3. Describe three of Moses' leadership qualities that you most admire and explain why you admire those qualities. What value could those qualities hold for teachers in the classroom?

_____

_____

_____

4. Discuss with your partner what you think Fannie Lou Hamer means when she says "Freedom is a constant struggle; make a joyful noise." Watch: http://typp.org/videos (go to second video on site "Building demand for math literacy")

After watching the 6-minute film, please address the following questions with a partner:

1. How does Moses explain the connection between Math Literacy & Voting Rights in Mississippi during the Civil Rights Movement?

_____

_____

_____

2. In the video how do the students explain the value of the FLAGWAY game for teaching mathematics to students who don't like mathematics?

_____

_____

_____

View the video: www.youtube.com/watch?v=PbEjwAdGNWQ

3. Describe qualities of a grassroots leader that seem different from a charismatic leader. _____

_____

_____

SECTION 13

'WE HAVE ALL WALKED IN DIFFERENT GARDENS AND KNELT AT DIFFERENT GRAVES'

Image copyright I. Quintanilla, 2012. Used under license from Shutterstock. Inc.

"First thing I'd say," said one student, "is too much kids is dying where I live. While I was here, there were four, no three people got shot and two died. . . . And those kids, those two that died were in my face telling me goodbye on the last day of school, hugged me. . . . killed at a school party. If I had not been here, that could have been me, that could have been me . . . I'm glad that I'm not there; I'm here learning something. All the kids here are learning."

—Student in Algebra Project
Summer Institute

CHAPTER 13

STORIES OF COLLABORATION AND RESEARCH WITHIN AN ALGEBRA PROJECT CONTEXT: OFFERING QUALITY EDUCATION TO STUDENTS PUSHED TO THE BOTTOM OF ACADEMIC ACHIEVEMENT[1]

Joan T. Wynne and Janice Giles

ABSTRACT

In an interview in 1981, former SNCC field secretary, Charlie Cobb, Jr. reminisced about the lessons young African Americans learned in the sixties:

"What we had learned essentially was that the things that affected blacks in Ruleville, Greenwood, or Sharkey County, Mississippi, didn't just stop at the county line or the state line. What we really had was a national structure. The sheriff and the Ku Klux Klan and White Citizens Council were all tied into the Congress and the president, and even if we got everybody registered to vote in Sunflower County it wasn't going to provide the complete answer for black people. We were beginning to see the relationship between economics and politics," (Minter, 2008)

As we have built partnerships across university and public school boundaries to create models of quality education for the disenfranchised, like Cobb, we have been reminded of the roots and the multiple layers of politics, power, and privilege that trap our youngsters into cycles of unequal and inferior education. Those structural forces at work in Mississippi and the nation in the sixties, and centuries before, still plague urban and rural schools in the 21st century. This chapter attempts to tell the story of the challenges and triumphs of working within such a context to create and demand quality education for the progeny of slaves and sharecroppers as well as for other children denied academic excellence.

INTRODUCTION

There have been great societies that did not use the wheel, but there have been no societies that did not tell stories. —Ursula K. LeGuin

My early educational background was literature. So I believe in the power of story. And for me, research is a story. Some researchers tell that story in numbers—some tell it in narrative. Some believe numbers are sacred; some believe narrative is; and still others believe nothing is. Regardless of the form, though, the research story comes from a human who goes into and out of her project with biases. For, all researchers come to those studies with specific cultural experiences, presuppositions and delusions.

My experience of growing up in a segregated south influenced my personal and professional life. It was a south of "white only" water fountains, restrooms, and public spaces; a place of white supremacy; of blacks in the back of the bus; a place of public lynchings and secret murders; a place of governmental double-speak; of public universities refusing to admit blacks into their institutions; a place where 6-year-olds had to be escorted by the National Guard to walk safely through the doors of public schools. All of these factors from my lived experience helped shape my sense of what needs to be researched—and what cultural assumptions undergird a research and educational agenda, and ultimately helped lead me to the present research project, which is firmly rooted in the south.

That particular shaping also has persuaded me that ethical research is more than just an abstract theory. Although, it too often gets cloaked in esoteric discourse, research is formed within a specific context of socio-political experiences and realities.

The poet, Rumi, said "We have all walked in different gardens and knelt at different graves" (Barks 2001). Those individual experiences of gardens and graves largely shape who we are—not only as humans but also as researchers—helping to determine what it is we choose to investigate; what it is we're hoping to find; and what the biases are that we bring to the table of research.

Researcher Linda Smith, who wrote the book, *Decolonizing Methodologies: Research & Indigenous People* (1999), indicates that as a Maori woman from New Zealand, her personal story of resisting and transforming methods of oppression has shaped her research. She suggests that sometimes when we frame research within a specific scientific or disciplinary approach, we forget that all of it, for urban and indigenous people across the globe, is deeply embedded in complex and multiple layers of imperial and colonial practices (Smith 1–18).

Unconscious colonial attitudes are often reflected in research journals that feature too many studies which seem stuck on discovering the deficits or dysfunctions of families of color, living in poverty. This propensity has created a sense in indigenous communities that research is a dirty word (Smith).

UNIVERSITY PARTNERSHIP WITH THE ALGEBRA PROJECT

In the spirit of countering that practice of "dirty research," the Center for Urban Education & Innovation at Florida International University (FIU), through a research grant awarded by the Urban Educators Corps, chose to investigate the work of Dr. Bob Moses and his Algebra Project (AP) in a 9th grade classroom in one of the nation's largest metropolitan school systems. The system operates in a state that holds the record for the second highest number of high school dropouts in the nation (Associated Press 2007). FIU is a large public university whose student population is a Latino/a majority. The extended collaboration is an attempt to create a school-based, university-affiliated school reform, where the accountability of the reform rests upon producing high academic achievement for students through four years of high school with "students standing on their own two feet" in college (PBS 2007). In this reform, the university comes to the school house. Professors, researchers, Center partners work in the classroom with the students alongside the high school teacher. Theories, curriculum, and pedagogy are worked out inside the classroom with students. In this model, the university leaves its "ivory tower" and becomes intimately involved with its real constituents, testing knowledge, shaping and re-shaping its visions of reality to consciously contribute to the public good.

THE CENTER AND THE ALGEBRA PROJECT

For decades, a multitude of educators, governments, foundations, and school systems have been concerned about creating more effective learning environments for disenfranchised students. But as Charles Payne discovered during his five-year study of the massive Chicago School Reform Effort, there has been "so much reform, so little change" (2001). Our experiences and research in urban schools suggest the same conclusion (Wynne 2003; Delpit 2005). That is, until investigating the work of Bob Moses and the Algebra Project. In fact, Payne cited AP as one of the few successful projects involved in Chicago's huge reform effort (2001).

AP is steeped in experiential learning pedagogy that, since Dewey, has proven effective in most disciplines. Within that context Moses and AP have developed imaginative approaches, responsive to youth culture, to teach mathematics to students who have been tracked out of higher level abstract thinking. Moses & AP are doing what very few others dare—demanding excellence from children at the bottom instead of settling for their meeting minimum standards. But what is radical about AP's approach is its philosophy that: The only ones who can really demand the kind of education they need and the kind of changes needed to get it are the students, their parents, and their community (Moses 2001, 18–21). Moses believes that the young people must create a culture in which they begin to make a demand on themselves and then on the larger society, a kind of "earned insurgency" (PBS 2007).

That philosophy puts the power in the hands of the people who are being abused by inadequate education, not in the hands of well meaning advocates, or worse, in the hands of people who are intent on maintaining a "sharecropper" education for the descendents of slaves, or other children of color (Moses 2001). The Center believes that few in reform efforts fully comprehend this crucial component. Student and parent voices typically are either uninvited or rarely taken seriously in the decision-making process in school reform. Though many districts are establishing parent academies, there often is distrust in the capacity of the disenfranchised to create powerful learning communities. And where there might be trust, there is little experience in organizing communities to address quality education for its children. The Algebra Project has been founded upon a long tradition of grass-roots organizing and has developed, as an integral part of its program, strategies for organizing parents and students to demand academic excellence.

Central to AP is the belief that "a real breakthrough would not make us happy if it did not deeply and seriously empower the target population to demand access to literacy for everyone. That is what is driving the project" (Moses 2001, 19). Many of us do not understand the profundity of that belief. Too often in school reform we are caught up in believing that improving instruction, empowering teachers, developing school leadership, teacher/administrative shared decision-making and other facets of educational change will transform low-performing schools. Certainly these components are significant in whole school change, but they are not sufficient. When community and student demand for excellence for "everyone" is not organized and sustained, the other strategies for change provide only fleeting results, if any, for disenfranchised children.

In her five-year study of two school reform efforts in South Carolina, Pauline Lipman observed numerous progressive reform components operating within the two schools. However, at the end of the five years, she found that the academic achievement of African American students' actually decreased during that time. She indicated that the failure to address the absence of community, power and privilege within the schools played a significant role in thwarting the other reform components (Lipman 1999). AP works within this essential dimension of school reform. Their work is a deliberate attempt to prove to the nation that all children, no matter how poor or how alienated from the society at large, can and will learn higher level mathematics, given the appropriate curriculum, pedagogy, and support. A present example of AP's success is found at Mississippi's Lanier High School where large numbers of students take trigonometry and introductory engineering (West 2004). Eighty-five percent of AP's 2006 cohort graduates from Lanier successfully completed their 1st year of college (West 2006). In essence, AP is changing the story about America's disenfranchised children and communities.

EARLIER RESEARCH STUDIES OF AP

In a 5 year study funded by the National Science Foundation (NSF), researchers found that AP students in several large cities around the country performed at a higher level when compared to the general population. The AP students enroll in 9th and 10th grade mathematics courses at a significantly higher rate. They enroll in college preparatory courses at twice the rate, and they pass state mathematics exams at significantly higher rates. The researchers also found that teachers who were taught the AP pedagogy and curriculum became more effective in the classrooms with higher levels of mathematical conceptual understanding by students (West, 2004).

THE LOCAL CHALLENGE

The size of the local school system and its history of failing schools within poor neighborhoods (39 chronically low-performing schools) make this system an excellent model for addressing the issues that face urban schools across the country. A majority of the system's students are ethnic minorities; a high percentage of them are poor; many are from immigrant backgrounds; and sixty-two percent speak English as their 2nd language (System, 2006–2007).

STRUGGLES IN FORMING THE COLLABORATION

Although the system's superintendent proclaimed at the first district level partners' meeting, "Bob Moses, you are a gift to this county," it took subsequent months of meetings with other district and school administrators, students and parents for Moses to finally begin his AP work at Eagle High School[2]. Eagle is located in a neighborhood where some of the students are African-American and some are Latino, but many more of its students are bi-lingual Haitians—their first language is Kreyol. Moses and his FIU teaching fellow, Mario Eraso, began the process of bringing AP to Eagle High School in September, 2006 in a classroom with 24 students who were achieving at the bottom quartile of academic measures (state tests and grade averages). The only criterion for selecting the members of the cohort was that they be in the bottom quartile.

PARENT VISITS

A significant piece of the partnership has been meeting with parents to explain the program and the kind of commitment that it takes from parents and students for success in mathematics. These meetings are crucial in building the "demand side" of the quest for academic excellence. In the beginning, however, meeting with cohort parents posed quite a challenge. Because student records and addresses are confidential, the school administration offered to contact parents to invite them to a dinner in August, 2006 where Dr. Moses could explain his program before the students started the school year. Over fifty parents were invited. One parent came. After that trial, a concerted effort was made to obtain phone numbers and addresses of students so that we could make home visits. It took months to go up and down the chain of command to obtain addresses and many visits to erroneous addresses, even to houses that did not exist, before finally getting correct addresses from the students themselves as Eraso and Moses tutored them in small groups. By the end of October, 2006, twenty of the original twenty-four students' homes had been visited. These visits continued throughout the school year.

But finding the students' parents was just the tip of the iceberg of troubles confronted when attempting to unfold the project in the new location. Eagle's administration decided that the students needed to use the first six and one-half months of their 9th grade mathematics class to prepare for the state "high-stakes" test, the Florida Comprehensive Assessment Test (FCAT). Therefore, Moses & Eraso were allowed to work only as aides in the teacher-of-record's classroom to help the students prepare for the FCAT. The full AP curriculum and pedagogy finally began on March 19, 2007.

Observations in the cohort classroom in January, February, and the first part of March, 2007, along with the observations of the class after March 19th, yielded the following results:

Before instituting the curricular process of the Algebra Project with the cohort in March, a traditional pedagogy was used by the teacher-on-record. Students sat passively as the teacher advanced to new topics without pausing to check for student understanding. Just a few students participated. Those who did, reproduced procedural mathematics, but could not explain the meaning of their work. The students were intimidated by a teacher who repeatedly yelled at them to control the class discipline. On the first week of the transition to AP in March, two different students asked Moses' assistant: "Why does Dr. Moses talk so softly?" (Eraso, 2006–07)

The Algebra Project's curricular process is based on a shared student experience, therefore, in March, these 9th graders used a bus fieldtrip to FIU as their first AP collective experience. It allowed students an opportunity to discuss among themselves the mathematics of the location of different landmarks found on the bus route taken the day of the fieldtrip. Students took careful notes that described the shared experience, simulating the detailed process a scientist or artist goes through to describe a phenomenon. Once back in the classroom, the students drew iconic representations of the shared experience before being exposed to the symbolic representation of mathematics. Most of the work done by the instructors is to get students to think abstractly and to apply what they learn. The mechanism for this strategy, "people talk," involves students using their own informal language, to describe what they observe. Following this stage, the teacher introduces "feature talk," technical mathematical language that allows students to communicate explicitly. Prior to the talk, however, the students produced a class trip line that graphically and pictorially illustrated the fieldtrip from their high school to the university. Colorful poster boards full of pictures serve as the context to learn the mathematics of integers. Mathematical objects, actions and relationships are introduced. For example, movement, an object, and moving, an action, are distinguished as students use displacement vectors, location integers, and addition. Mathematical relationships are developed, too, finally arriving at abstract formulations such as (Eraso):

- x1 + delta x = x2, where x1 and x2 are location integers assigned to landmarks on the trip line,
- delta x is the movement (left or right) needed to go from x1 to x2,
- and the symbols "+" and "=" mean "to move" and "to arrive," respectively

Moses created the trip line strategy while teaching in Boston in the 80's. Later with his team of mathematicians, he developed a consistent pedagogy that is explained in *Radical Equations* as the "Five Crucial Steps in the Algebra Project curriculum process" (Moses, pp. 120–124).

1. **Physical Events:** A trip taken by the students and teacher is the central experience of the transition curriculum designed to illustrate the concept to be learned.

2. **Pictorial Representation/Modeling:** Students move through a series of linked and progressively abstracted representation of the physical event, describing the event through pictures and everyday talk which the teacher builds on to introduce the language of the discipline and symbolic representation.

3. **Intuitive Language/"People Talk":** Students are asked to discuss and write about the physical event in their language.

4. **Structured Language/"Feature Talk":** This is "regimented" language aimed at explicitly selecting and encoding features of the event that are deemed important for further study.

5. **Symbolic Representation:** Once students have worked through steps 2–4, they construct symbols to represent these ideas. Through this activity, they begin to better understand the nature of symbol making, which moves them toward a fuller understanding and discussion of the symbols associated with mathematics. Many students have difficulty understanding the abstractions represented by a discipline's symbols until they experiment with creating symbols for their own ideas.

CHANGES OBSERVED DURING FIRST 3 MONTHS OF PROGRAM AT EAGLE H. S.

By the end of the 2006–2007, the differences in student participation in the cohort math class at Eagle were stark between the first six months and the last three months. The last 3 months, after FCAT preparation, the students were offered the full AP curriculum and pedagogy implemented from March to June, 2007. The observations suggested that (Eraso):

- During the 3 months of AP curriculum, students were more engaged during class time. More students participated in group discussions and more answered questions posed by the teacher. For the first 6 months of instruction with the teacher-on-record, the same 3 or 4 students answered questions aloud. All students, during AP instruction, were required to stand and present how they had solved a math problem, rather than repeating the method of the teacher.

- A class culture of respect and responsibility was developed during AP instruction. Group work continued even when the teacher or assistant was not in the group.

Prior to AP, when students were placed in groups, there was no discussion among group members, and in small groups usually 2 students would work individually to solve the problem, with the other 2 to 3 students sitting passively or talking to each other about irrelevant concerns.

- Part of AP's pedagogy is for teachers to give no answers; students must struggle through the problem-solving collaboratively; thus, students became dependent on collective small group discussion as well as individual critical thinking to solve problems.

- A general positive group attitude towards fieldtrips, college, and learning increased. Before their field trip to FIU, none had mentioned college as a goal. After the trip, students began to advise others: "If you want to go to college or have a nice living, study."

- Students started to view themselves as a group, capable of moving together and forward in their education. The cohort began reminding each other of why they were studying math and what their ultimate goals were, a departure from the previous sense of isolated individualism observed. The students also began calling to remind each other to bring their parents to monthly AP meetings at night.

- Students began to volunteer for role playing the mathematician when reading the textbook dialogues. Previously, no one volunteered.

- Attendance and homework completion improved. From January to March, the attendance was typically 20 students out of 24, with some days as low as 18 out of 24. After March 19, the average daily attendance was 23 out of 24, with many days of perfect attendance. Before March 19th and the inception of the full curriculum and pedagogy of the Algebra Project, average homework completion was 1 to 2 students out of 24; after March 19th, average homework completion was 8 to 10 of 24 students.

AP COHORT, 2007–2008 SCHOOL YEAR

Because of students' leaving the neighborhood, the Algebra Project cohort in the beginning of the new school year, 2007–2008, decreased to 20 Eagle students. Records for these 20 students and for a group of 20 students who are similar in academic performance at Eagle were checked, representing their last five years with the system from their middle and the high school records.

DEMOGRAPHIC BACKGROUND OF THE AP COHORT

- Three students speak Spanish with limited English proficiency; ten students speak Kreyol and English; three speak Kreyol, with limited English proficiency; four speak English and Ebonics.

- Eighteen of the 20 receive free or reduced lunch.

- All twenty students represent those who fall within the lowest FCAT math categories.

The Florida Comprehensive Achievement Test (FCAT) scores are based on a 1 to 5 scale, with 1 being the lowest score and 3 being considered a proficiency score. Seventeen of the cohort scored in a level-1 category and three of the cohort scored in a level-2 category for the 2005/2006 school year—the year before the intervention. Although, typically administered only in the 3rd, 8th and 10th grades, until a student reaches a score of 3, the student must continue to take the appropriate, grade specific FCAT every year.

Based upon the Math measures data as obtained through the Eagle Student Score Database, 18 of the 20 students have shown gains from the inception of their AP at Eagle. Of the 20 selected students, 25% achieved scores that afforded them the advance from the level-1 category to the level-2. One of the three level-2 students within the program shifted in Math Achievement, which allowed her to move into a level-3, placing her at the appropriate FCAT proficiency level for her grade. The 2 remaining level 2 students maintained their level 2 status, although one of the students was able to make gains within that level-2 categorization (System's data bank 2006–07).

When measured against a control group, a cohort of 20 students selected on the basis of their comparative likeness on variables such as race, gender, rates of those whose records reflect a former repeated grade, qualification for the receipt of free or reduced lunch, and limited English proficiency, the Algebra project cohort made higher achievements, Only 5% of the control group made gains which advanced their level in FCAT Math measurement.

THE SUMMER COMPONENT OF THE ALGEBRA PROJECT COHORT PROGRAM

The 2007 summer institute for the Eagle cohort was initiated as a result of lessons learned from the previous years in Mississippi with the AP Lanier High School cohort. Realizing that its Mississippi cohort needed more academic support if they were to be successful in being admitted into college, the Algebra Project in 2005 instituted its first summer program for that cohort at the end of their junior year. The Center co-sponsored the institute with Mississippi State University at their campus. The next year the Center hosted the same cohort for the summer on the FIU campus at the end of the Lanier students' senior year. In the summer of 2007, the Center, with funding from the Children's Trust, Inc., hosted its first six-week residential summer institute at the FIU campus for AP students from the 9th grade Eagle cohort, along with a similar group of students from another high school in the city, Brandon High School. The Brandon students had no previous training with Moses and the Algebra Project. Although twenty-five students from each school were invited, only 40 students attended.

The summer program provided the students with a series of courses designed to help them strengthen their mathematics and language skills and to prepare them for college. The academic component of the program included courses in mathematics, communications, reading, and "writing circles." Several electives, limited to 10–12 students per course, were offered: Spanish, computer graphics, yoga, drama & spoken word, film production, photography, visual arts, and basketball. The students were allowed to choose two electives.

This effort was labor intensive and expensive. We cobbled together funds from many sources, the bulk of which, however, came from The Children's Trust, and the Center. The cost to house, feed, and instruct forty students amounted to approximately $185,000 for six weeks. Beyond Moses, six other professors, one language arts consultant, and one psychologist were involved in the academic pieces of the institute, from FIU; a local community college; City College of New York; and Cornell University. Two reading specialists spent three weeks assessing reading levels and delivered daily instruction to two small groups: one male and one female. Seven other instructors delivered the "elective" afternoon courses. The intensity of the work and the constant attention to emotional as well as academic needs for forty 9th graders kept teachers and students fully engaged.

The students met for mathematics class every day, Monday through Friday, for ninety minutes a day. Part of the mathematics course offered to both sets of high school students at different times in the morning were modules in geometry offered by two professors who taught for two full weeks each. A Math researcher taught algebra for one full week. Moses was in the mathematics classes the majority of the summer. These classes were consistently highly rated by the students as superior learning opportunities (See focus group comments below).

While the Brandon students were receiving Action-Research instruction, the Eagle students received a language arts program which included "writing circles/peer editing" and linguistic instruction. Students wrote personal stories, learned the international phonetic alphabet, Grimm's Law, and role-played international "accents." At the ending summer ceremony with students, instructors, and parents, every student in that course chose to recite in unison linguistic rules and derivations to inform the parents of the lessons they had learned from the class. The enthusiastic class response to this course resounded through the banquet hall; the written evaluations on the final day of class were equally as enthusiastic as were the focus group responses about the language arts program.

In the Student Action-Research (SAR) course, students engaged in activities that taught them how to document their successes and challenges in high school. The students said they wished the class could be offered at their school in the fall. Their final products detailed their growth in grappling with self-reflective practices, critical thinking about their learning environment, and knowledge of data collection and analysis (Cook 2006).

In addition to these academic classes, students were offered experiences in building social and conflict resolution skills. Every afternoon, small groups divided into male and females, met with a psychologist for 45 minutes. Because the institute was the students' first experience of dormitory life, these sessions became invaluable in learning to work out conflicts during the 6-weeks.

During the first two days of the summer program, the students attended team-building workshops. These two days were designed as a result of discovering tensions between the two high school groups prior to students' arrival on campus. During several recruiting meetings in the spring, individual students from both schools raised concerns about sharing rooms with participants from the "other" high school. Eagle High's mostly Haitian population lived across town from Brandon High's students, who lived in the oldest African-American neighborhood in the city. Both sets of students lacked any sense of trust or safety about the other set. Eight students at each school, all of them female, told the graduate researcher that they were afraid to be in the room with girls from the other school, afraid that violence would occur. In fact, a couple of weeks before the program began, after meeting with students and parents to explain the institutes goals and activities, the fears and mistrust between the schools became so palpable that we began to wonder whether inviting two schools with such intense rivalries had been a good idea. And certainly the first week of the institute was a trial by fire! Student and classroom conflict abounded, but by the end of the 2nd week, life settled and students began taking on the responsibility of holding each other accountable for appropriate behavior.

Five chaperones, recruited from the AP Mississippi graduates, played a key role in reducing students' fears of dormitory life, negotiating interpersonal conflicts, and assisting with academic classes. Chaperone contributions resulted in a standing ovation for them at the ending banquet.

FOCUS GROUP INTERVIEWS

On the last day of the institute, Janice Giles, an FIU/Ph.D. student researcher, interviewed two separate focus groups consisting of seven students from each high school for two hours each. The students were asked what parts of the institute they would like to change; what parts they thought were valuable; why they had chosen to come to the institute; how their parents felt about the experience; and would they choose to come again if the institute were offered the following summer. The final question hypothesized that if they were to attend a meeting with local foundations, how might they persuade the foundation that its money would be well spent in funding another three years of summer institutes.

The students' overwhelming response to the institute was positive. Both focus groups unanimously said they wanted the next summer to be 12 weeks instead of six weeks. Several said that they wished the institute could become "a year long school." Some of the most telling responses came from several students who attended Brandon High School, especially when asked, "What would you say to possible funders for next year's summer institute to persuade them that this effort is worth their support?"

"First thing I'd say," said one student, "is too much kids is dying where I live. While I was here, there were four, no three people got shot and two died. . . . And those kids, those two that died were in my face telling me goodbye on the last day of school, hugged me. . . . killed at a school party. If I had not been here, that could have been me, that could have been me . . . I'm glad that I'm not there; I'm here learning something. All the kids here are learning." Another chimed in saying, "One of them killed—I knew since I was in third grade; the boy was smart, but he decided to drop out, and if we had more programs like this, people wouldn't drop out. We learned stuff. I swear to God."

All the students from both focus groups said consistently that they had "learned more math in these six weeks" than in their nine years in schools. The Brandon students, who prior to the summer had not known Moses, and who in the beginning weeks found his instruction too rigorous, in unison during the interviews, mentioned how much they had learned from him and the other mathematicians. They all commented on the surprise of learning about geometry through designing "pop-up" books with the mechanical engineer from CCNY and about learning math theories from the Cornell geometer, about creating one-dimensional geometric shapes, which they later connected together to make one huge hyperbolic "soccer ball" shape. Through these experiences, they learned about positive and zero curvatures, and the constant negative curvatures of heptagons.

Another component of the summer that students applauded was the small group "life skills" sessions led by Gaynor. One student described the sessions as a surprise: "I hated them at first. I thought, 'What is this woman doing, asking all of those questions, in my face, in my business?' I just clammed up and didn't say a word. But after two sessions, I started lovin' goin' there. She helped us talk to each other in a positive way, even when we were mad at each other." Commenting further, another student said, "I wish our school had ten Dr. Gaynor's. Counselors at our school don't help us solve problems; they don't even know us." All students rated the group sessions as one of their favorite experiences.

Students also made equally enthusiastic comments about all of the academic courses offered. All of the electives involving movement as well as the Spanish immersion class were mentioned as particularly enjoyable. The only two consistent student criticisms about the institute were that it was not long enough and that late night "room-checks" were annoying.

LESSONS LEARNED

Through the collaboration, we have learned a number of valuable lessons for working in tandem with public school systems to create access to and success in colleges for disenfranchised children.

1. DEMANDS OF LEADERSHIP

◆ This collaboration necessitated calling upon the leadership of the academic, department chairs and deans, as well as the civic community. The role of the university is crucial in sustaining the initiative because of the resources that it offers and its perceived credibility as an agent of academic expertise.

◆ The financial support through local community grants and donors is critical to creating enrichment opportunities like the summer institute.

◆ Receiving approval from the top echelon of a system is crucial in maintaining the partnership before gaining the program's access to a school. Going up and down the chain of command is often required to move from one piece of the program to the next. In large systems, a complex set of unwritten procedures seems to exist that are often difficult to ascertain.

◆ State tests seem to dominate the curriculum and pedagogy of "failing schools." In these schools, teaching for the test becomes not a cliché but a harsh reality in mathematics and language skills courses (While attempting to explain to our new teaching fellow the dilemma we consistently face in getting cooperation to fully implement the AP process, Moses said, "Reaching our kids in huge urban systems is like the days of Jim Crow in Mississippi, where we had to sneak onto the plantation to reach our people who wanted to vote.")

2. STUDENT ACHIEVEMENT MECHANISMS

◆ Through student evaluations during the summer institute, we now know that it is an imperative piece of the over-all program for access and success; that the achievement level of the students in the bottom quartile demands a year-long program of support. Others' research also suggests that it takes 3 months during the fall semester each year to recoup the academic losses due to summer vacations away from school (Cooper, 2003; Phi Delta Kappan, 2003; Planning, 2000).

◆ Through the success of the non-academic support systems offered during the summer, i.e. group and peer counseling, team building skills, action-research empowerment skills, etc., we've learned that academic press is not enough to shepherd our students toward success in academe. The cognitive and affective domains must be addressed.

◆ Attention to raising the level of achievement in mathematics is not enough. Through the summer institute, we learned that the students' reading skills fell below state levels.

3. ROLE OF RESEARCH MATHEMATICIANS

◆ Regular visits of research mathematicians from universities to the classroom created a consistent grounding of theory into practice and a practice grounded in sound mathematical content. The high school math teacher's working alongside research mathematicians raised the level of content knowledge available for students. One of the challenges of urban mathematics classrooms is the scarcity of teachers with adequate content knowledge (Schmidt 2007).

4. BUILDING RELATIONSHIP

◆ Building relationships with students and their parents, visiting their homes, hosting parent events are essential. Other research suggests the efficacy of positive relationships between disenfranchised students' and their teachers (Delpit 1997; Hilliard 2000; Perry 2003; Blanchard 2007).

- ◆ Because the summer institute produced an intense bonding experience for the cohort, those who did not attend sometimes manifest a sense of being "outsiders," a factor that seems to impact their academic performance.
- ◆ Bringing the cohort to the FIU campus to speak to two classes of undergraduate pre-service teachers was a powerful experience, not only for the cohort, but for the pre-service teachers.[3]

CONCLUSION

We have many more lessons to learn as we work with the local cohort and possibly other cohorts. The data gathered as we continue the work will reveal more about the program; yet we know that student voices are essential in grappling with what we know and what we need to know to imagine a way for total access to and success in college for our children at the bottom. A conversation in one of Alice Walker's novels, *By the Light of My Father's Smile*, suggests the power of these children's stories in conjuring their future:

> You are saying . . . that stories have more room in them than ideas? . . .
> That is correct, Senor. It is as if ideas are made of blocks. Rigid and hard.
> And stories are made of a gauze that is elastic. You can almost see through it, so what is beyond is tantalizing. You can't quite make it out; and because the imagination is always moving forward, you yourself are constantly stretching. Stories are the way spirit is exercised.
> But surely you people have ideas! I said.
> Of course we do. But we know that there is a limit to them. After that, story! (193–194).

We believe that along with shifting the politics of education and influencing the will of the nation to educate all of its children, we must also, as Walker suggests, "stretch our imaginations" to offer the content and instruction that will ensure all of the country's children can tell stories of academically soaring in schools.

EPILOGUE

Two years after the above story was written, a newly assigned principal at the local high school planned to eliminate the Algebra Project. To counter her attempt, Moses suggested that the students and parents write a letter about their experiences in the project and that they, only the students and parents, should meet with the principal to share the letter. They did, and they alone persuaded the principal to maintain the project at their school. Moses' two years of work with these students, building them as a cohort and a community, produced a desire and a confidence to demand what they needed. They had earned their insurgency (Wynne, 2009, pp. 96–97).

However, the next year another principal was hired who refused to allow the Algebra Project to remain at the school for the cohort's senior year. (No reason was given. The principal would not meet with anyone associated with the program; thus, we never could ascertain the reason it was eliminated.) In the three years that AP existed in the school, three different principals led the school, an unfortunate urban school practice prevalent in low-performing schools.

That same year Moses' five-year contract with FIU was not renewed. Consequently, he left the city to work with other AP sites in the nation. Two of the six FIU and local community college professors who had worked with the AP program during those 3 years continued to work with the students during after-school hours with the Young People's Project (YPP), a national spin-off of the Algebra Project founded and directed by young people to create math literacy workers who mentor younger children, using the AP pedagogy. The local site of the YPP was organized during the third year of the AP program at the school. Evidence is being gathered now to explore the implications of YPP's impact on these students as they navigate the rigor of the Algebra Project curriculum.

Though the official program ended prematurely, significant gains for these students occurred. The following graph explains the results of the AP students who remained with the program for 3 years and who continued to work with YPP after school. Another graph depicts the results of all of the other low-performing students at the high school who entered the 9th grade at the same time as the AP ninth-graders.

During the 2006–07 school year, 280 students entered the selected high school as 9th graders. 202 of those students entered with level 1 or 2 Math scores (1–5 scale with 5 being the high score). Of the 202 ninth-graders entering the high school in 2006 as low-performing students, the following statistics exist.

IN 2010:

25.7% (52 students) graduated with a Standard Diploma and also passed the FCAT; 21.8% were ESE students who graduated with a Standard Diploma, did not take FCAT—passed an
   Alternate Assessment
 2.5% graduated with FCAT waived
  .5% graduated with Special Diploma
   No statistics available for this school's graduates attending post-secondary education.
All statistics above made available from the System's Director of Evaluation, Research Office.

The Following Are the Results of Local Algebra Project Graduates:
Twenty-four students in original ninth-grade program—All students in the cohort were in the bottom quartile of academic performance; 18 remained in the program throughout the 3 years due to student transfers to other schools, with 4 leaving and going back home to Honduras. Of those 18 AP students, 17 graduated with a standard diploma, with all 17 passing the FCAT exams.

In addition, of those 18 AP students, 17 applied for and were admitted into post-secondary education in August, 2010.

Proportion of Student Passing FCAT
2010

☐ AP Students   ■ non-AP Students

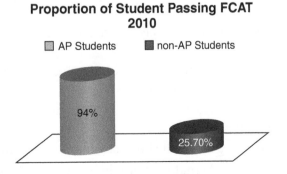

94%

25.70%

**Proportion of 202 Low Performing
2006 freshmen Graduated in 2010**

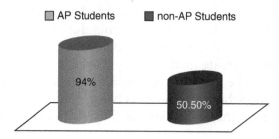

Six of these local Algebra Project students in the summer of 2011, during a Mathematics and Civics institute at FIU, taught math to twenty-four 3rd, 4th, and 5th graders from a local elementary school. The institute was a collaborative designned and operated by the College of Law, College of Education, and the Algebra Project. These six students continue to work with the Young People's Project and will be working again in the summer, 2012 for the 2nd Mathematics and Civics Summer Program held on the FIU campus.

At the time of this writing, conversations have begun with another low-performing school in the same district to develop an AP pilot program of 50 students while exploring the possibilities of creating multiple AP cohorts so that the entire 9th grade at the high school receives the accelerated and rigorous mathematics curriculum and pedagogy created by the Algebra Project. The pilot will include AP professional development for the mathematics teachers and summer institutes for the students, along with other major support systems that AP uses to scaffold academically struggling students. Moses, the district, and FIU are intending to partner again on this effort through a comprehensive program defined by FIU and the District as "The Education Effect."

Currently, Moses is working at Princeton University as a Distinguished Scholar to explore the structures needed to develop the Algebra Project cohort model as a mathematics "whole-school reform" strategy in districts across the nation to raise the level of performance for students currently scoring at the bottom of academic achievement measurements. At this time, FIU in partnership with a local historically African-American community, the School District, and multiple other partners, intend to be part of that national study. Moses is dedicated to proving to the nation that "all the children *in* the nation are children *of* the nation" and, thus, all are deserving of quality education (Wynne, 2009).

REFERENCES

Analysis: Florida drop-out rates high. The Associated Press. http://floridatoday.com/ (accessed October 30, 2007).

Barks, Coleman. trans. 2001. *The Soul of Rumi: A new collection of ecstatic poems.* San Francisco: Harper-Collins Publishers, Inc.

Blanchard, Wanda, and Joan Wynne. 2007. Reframing urban education discourse: A conversation with and for teacher educators. In *Theory into practice* 46: 187–194.

Cook-Sather, Alison. 2006. Sound, presence, and power: 'Student Voice' in educational research and reform. *Curriculum Inquiry* 36: 359–390.

Cooper, Harris. 2003. Summer Learning Loss: The Problem and Some Solutions. *ERIC Digest*: ED475391.

Davis, Frank. 2006. Transactions of mathematical knowledge in the Algebra Project. In N. S. Nasir & P. Cobb (Eds.), *Improving access to mathematics: Diversity and equity in the classroom* (pp. 69–88). New York: Teachers College Press.

Davis, Frank, and West, Mary. 2000. *The impact of the Algebra Project on mathematics achievement.* Cambridge, MA: Program Evaluation & Research Group, Lesley University.

Delpit, Lisa. 1997. *Other people's children.* New York: The New Press,

———— Interview with Lisa Delpit. 2005. In *Racism, research, & educational reform: Voices from the city.* Eds. Dowdy, Joanne, and Joan Wynne. New York: Peter Lang.

Dowdy, Joanne, and Joan Wynne. co-eds. 2005. *Racism, research, & educational reform: Voices from the city,* New York: Peter Lang.

Eraso, Mario. 2006–07. Fieldnotes.

Giles, Janice. 2007. Focus Group Video. Center for Urban Education & Innovation: Florida International University.

Hilliard, III, Asa. G. 2000. Awaken the geniuses of children: The nurture of nature. Unpublished speech for Skylight 6th International Teaching for Intelligence Conference, (Cassette produced by : Chesapeake Audio/Video Communications, Inc. 6330 Howard Lane, Elkridge, MD, 21075 (00227–1160)

Lipman, Pauline. 1999. *Race, class and power in school restructuring.* Albany: State University of New York Press.

Le Guin, Ursula. L. 1982. *Language of the Night: Essays on Fantasy and Science Fiction.* New York: Berkley Publishers.

Minter, William, Gail Hovey, and Charles Cobb, Jr. eds. 2008. *No easy victories: African liberation and American activists over a half century, 1950–2000.* Trenton, N.J.: Africa World Press, Inc.

Making use of summer time. In Phi Delta Kappan. www.ecs.org Denver, CO.: Education Commission of the States. (accessed March, 2003)

Moses, Robert, Frank Davis, and Mary West (in preparation). Why does A minus B equal A plus negative B? In *Culturally responsive mathematics education.* Mahwah, NJ: Lawrence Erlbaum

Moses, Robert, and Charles C. Cobb. 2001. *Radical Equations: Civil Rights from Mississippi to the Algebra Project.* Boston: Beacon Press.

Payne, Charles. 2001. So Much Reform, So Little Change: Building-Level Obstacles to School Change. In *Education policy for the 21st century: Challenges and opportunities in standards-based reform,* Joseph, L. (ed.). Chicago: Center for Urban Research and Policy Studies.

Perry, Theresa, Asa G. Hilliard, III, and Claude Steele. 2003. *Young gifted and black: Promoting high achievement among African-American students.* Boston: Beacon Press.

Planning for summer school: A tool to help students achieve high standards. 2000. *The Informed Educator Series.* Arlington, VA: Education Research Services.

Robert Moses & The Algebra Project. July 15, 2007. *NOW with David Brancaccio.* New York: PBS.

Schoenfeld, Alan. 2002. Making mathematics work for all children: Issues of standards, testing, and equity. *Educational Researcher* 3: 13–25.

Smith. Linda. 1999. *Decolonizing methodologies: Research and indigenous peoples.* London: Zed Books Ltd.

Schmidt, William. 2007. *The Preparation Gap: Teacher Education for Middle School Mathematics in Six Countries.* (MT21 Report) http://usteds.msu.edu/MT21.

School System's Statistical Abstract. 2006–2007, accessed September, 2007 (Confidential High School data bank made available only through high school administrators. Information also acquired through scores and data distributed to students on their " Student Score Card.")

Walker, Alice. 1998. *By the light of my father's smile.* New York: Random House.

West, Mary, et al. 1998. *The Algebra Project's middle school intervention in 1997–98.* Cambridge, MA: Program Evaluation & Research Group, Lesley University

————, and Frank Davis. 2004. *The Algebra Project at Lanier High School, Jackson, MS.* Cambridge, MA: Program Evaluation & Research Group, Lesley University.

_____, and Frank Davis, 2006. *The Algebra Project's high school initiative: An evaluation of the first steps.* Cambridge, MA: Program Evaluation & Research Group, Lesley University.

Wynne, Joan. 2003. The elephant in the classroom: Racism in school reform. In *International Perspectives on Methods of Improving Education: Focusing on the Quality of Diversity*, ed. Rose Marie Duhon-Sells, 114–156. New York: The Edwin Mellon Press.

Wynne, J. 2009. "Grassroots leadership for the 21st century: Leading by not leading." *Transformative leadership and educational excellence: Learning organizations in the information age.* Selah, I. M. & Khine, M. S. (eds.). The Netherlands: Sense Publications.

ENDNOTES

1. An earlier version of this chapter without the EPILOGUE was published in *Quality Education as a Constitutional Right: Creating a grassroots movement to transform public schools* (2010) Perry, et.al. (eds) Boston: Beacon Press.

2. Eagle H.S. is a pseudonym for the school as are all references to school or district names.

3. An anecdote about the cohort visits to the university: During three visits to FIU, the cohort "wowed" the adults with their discussion of newly acquired math skills. One pre-service teacher who was sitting next to me said, "They know more math than I do. If I had been taught that way, I might not be struggling now." Later the cohort shared with the FIU class, "What New Teachers Should Know" for students to excel. Many stereotypes inadvertently arose. For instance, one student was explaining that she hates hearing teachers say to her, "I got mine; you get yours." To emphasize her frustration about those kinds of comments, she said she felt like throwing a chair at teachers when they say that. An FIU student was over-heard mumbling, "That's why we don't want to teach at schools like yours." When the Eagle student challenged the FIU student about his comment, a good discussion ensued between the two groups about the fear and myths that pre-service teachers harbor about urban schools

SHOULD WE CONTINUE TO BRING UP GENDER ISSUES IN EDUCATION?

Mildred Boveda

As I looked around the inn, my eyes caught Tameka and Anthony engaged in a lively conversation. All three of us were in the same cohort at the Graduate School of Education, and they were the first familiar faces that I recognized at the mixer. We eventually started talking about our classes. I remember turning to Anthony and asking him if he ever felt weird about being one of the few males in our courses. The usually cool and collective young man from the west coast surprised me with his stunned reaction: "Why should I feel weird?" I do not remember how I replied, but the three of us kept the conversation moving and enjoyed the rest of the night.

A couple of weeks later, after a substantive discussion about race and poverty during the final class session of an urban education course, a group of us got on an elevator. I saw Daniel standing there, the only male student in this class and the only man in the elevator. So, out of curiosity, I asked him if he ever felt out of sorts when outnumbered by women. His answer echoed the reply I received from Anthony. Daniel scrunched up his face and then said:

"Why should I?"

"Wow… that's power!" I quickly retorted.

The ensuing conversation made everyone in the elevator uncomfortable. Daniel and I had an impassioned exchange where I explained how I feel whenever I walk into a room filled with men or when I realize that I am the only person of color. Daniel, clearly offended by my use of the word "power," kept insisting that he fought for and earned everything that he had accomplished and acquired in life. Perhaps, some may argue, that instead of power I should have used the words "entitlement" or "privilege" in my retort. But it was my initial questioning of these two men's status among a group of women that evoked the outraged responses in the first place. They questioned my question.

Had Daniel, or the more affable Anthony simply answered my inquiry with a "yes" or a "no," I probably would not have reacted so strongly to Daniel's, "Why should I?" In both instances, I mistakenly attributed minority status to the men due to their being "outnumbered" by women. As tempting as it may be to view minority status numerically, sociologists have long asserted that membership to a minority group refers to belonging to a category that is defined by those who hold the majority of positions of social power in a society. As such, minority status does not necessarily correlate to population. Powerful examples of this are apartheid in South Africa where blacks accounted for 33 million of the population yet held minority status while whites comprised only 3 million with majority status; or blacks in the south of the United States where a number of counties comprise a majority black population while whites hold majority power; or the 99% that "Occupy Wall Street" suggests is the majority of U.S. population who are resisting the 1% with economic power; and, as is the focus of this paper, the minority status of women in most societies where they represent 50% of the world population. So the very word "minority" in our society is loaded with conscious or unconscious distortions.

The exchanges described above forced me to reflect heavily about patriarchy and the status of women in education (Collins, 2000; hooks, 1981). I now realize that my questioning the young men had less to do with their status as members of the under-represented gender in the field of education and more about me understanding why I, an Afro-Latina woman living more than forty years after the height of the civil rights and feminist movements, continue to feel uneasy in certain social and academic situations. As can probably be assessed by the above stories, I have always been vocal about my thoughts and ideas. Being vocal, however, as is the stereotypical perception of black women and Jewish mothers (hooks, 2011), is not the same as having voice. Perhaps Anthony and Daniel interpreted my question as a statement that they SHOULD feel uncomfortable when outnumbered by women. But, as an active pursuant of social justice, I do not wish for anyone else the sense of smallness that I have felt in certain contexts.

When I have shared with women and some of my close male friends of color my exchanges with these two men, my friends understood the intention behind my question, and they understood my frustration with those two male responses. The stunned reaction to my question made it clear to me that these two men could not empathize with me as a woman of color. A second reflection that came out of these exchanges was the realization of the lack of substantive critiques on gender issues in most of my education courses. With the exception of a course on international education policy, where we examined blatant gender disparities in access to education in certain developing nations, for the most part discussions on the overrepresentation of black boys in special education or the feminization of the teacher profession remained at best, shallow. Why is it then easier to talk about racial and economic achievement gaps in education rhetoric and yet, as exemplified by Anthony and Daniel's reaction, so absurd to bring up gender?

GENDER INEQUALITY IN EDUCATION: A COMPLEX PICTURE

Through concerted efforts from advocacy groups and educators that have challenged education policies, the United States has closed many of the gaps in education attainment between male and female students (White House, 2012). Today, in the U.S. younger women are more likely to graduate from college than are men and are more likely to hold a graduate school degree. Higher percentages of women than men have at least a high school education, and higher percentages of women than men participate in adult education. "Educational gains among women relative to men can be seen across racial and ethnic groups and this trend is also present in other developed countries" (White House, 2012).

Although gender gaps have narrowed, many scholars continue to question the effects of gender on educational outcome. For example, by the end of high school there are differences in course taking patterns between boys and girls. Curriculum analyses continue to find that some differences in the portrayal of boys and girls continue in curricular materials (Correll, 2004). The federal government acknowledges that differences remain in the relative performance of female and male students at younger ages, with girls scoring higher than boys on reading assessments and lower on math assessments. These disparities can be seen in the fields that women pursue in college; female students are less well represented than men in science and technology-related fields, which typically lead to higher paying occupations (White House, 2012). In attempting to find why there are gender differences in subject area performance, researchers have found that there were no skill differences, but that girls in the U.S. tend to lack "interest," in the STEM (science, technology, engineering, and mathematics) areas, perhaps attributing to the impact of gender stereotypes on performances and assessments of ability (Correll, 2004). Furthermore, in the mid 1990's renowned social psychologist Claude Steel (2010) first described stereotype threat as the experience of anxiety or concern in a situation where a person has the potential to confirm a negative stereotype about their social group as the experience of anxiety or concern in a situation where a person has the potential to confirm a negative stereotype about their social group. In his book, "Whistling Vivaldi", Steele (2010) examined experiments and studies that repeatedly show how exposing participants to stereotypes—such as merely reminding a group of female math majors about to take a math test that women are considered inherently inferior to men at math—impairs their performance in the area affected by the stereotype.

A closer examination of the U.S. gender trends in education, reveals that gender inequality increases as you move up from primary, secondary and post-secondary education. At the post-secondary level, bachelor's degrees earned by gender and race reveal some interlocking inequalities. Women earn 56% of all bachelor's degrees earned by white students; they earn 59% of all bachelor's degrees earned by Hispanic students; and they earn 66% of all bachelor's degrees earned by African American students (Correll, 2004) demonstrating an under-representation of black and brown men in higher education. Gender segregation further complicates the discourse, because segregation continues to exist within college majors (such as the education majors in the introductory narrative of this paper). As the White House (2012) notes, "gender differences in college majors alone explains" 12% of the gender gap in wages segregation of college majors (U.S. Department of Education, National Center for Education Statistics, 2011; Correll, 2004).

To truly understand the nuances involved in relationships between colleagues, teachers and learners within educational spaces, we need to pursue a framework that goes beyond statistical measurements or the dualistic oppressed/oppressor paradigm often used to describe inequalities. Black feminist thought re-conceptualizes the social relations of domination and resistance, focusing on the multiple levels of oppression, and how each is linked to an interlocking system of privilege or domination. Black feminists thought arose from scholars that saw that privilege and oppression each ran on a continuum (Collins, 2000). Girls are not always oppressed and boys are not always the oppressor, but depending on context and other factors that confluence in systematic ways, members of either sex may play either of these roles. For example, consider the possible relationship between the overrepresentation of white, female teachers in the field of education and the overrepresentation of black, male students in special education. By embracing a paradigm that acknowledges the intersection of race, class, and gender as interlocking systems of oppression, black feminist theorists (who are not always black or female) argue that relationships of domination are structured through social institutions such as schools, businesses, hospitals, the work place. Race, gender, and class, religion, etc. place people in distinct institutional niches with varying degrees of penalty and privilege. Educators must be aware of themselves as practitioners and as human beings if they wish to teach students in a non-threatening, anti-discriminatory way. For example, hooks (1994) contends that teachers and students must speak on traditional roles and challenge the ways patriarchal females reinforce patriarchal gender roles in the classroom. Although her teaching has been typically at the college level, in recent years hooks has written several children's books, such as *Grump Groan Growl* and *Be Boy Buzz*, featuring boys and girls in non-traditional ways.

RETURNING TO THE NARRATIVE

The relative silence in my education courses regarding issues of gender dynamics speaks volumes about the complexities involved in closing the gender gaps in schools and society. The statistics presented above indicate that women have made great strides in achieving higher levels of education. The numbers, however, do not tell the entire story, and I am thankful for the great scholarship available that unpacks gender inequalities in our field. Just as is the case with racism and classism, the struggle for gender equality is a dynamic one, influenced by several social institutions. The media, especially, stereotypes women in destructive ways. Cartoons, TV and magazine ads, movies, story books depict sexist notions of women. As educators, we must invite our students, no matter how young, to critique the distorted images that pervade the representation of women in the media. We need only look at our female students in K-16 and observe the convoluted fashions they wear, many painful and injurious to their bodies, to understand the power of the media to contort females' visions of what they should look like.

Feminist thinkers push the gender conversation beyond graduation rates and woman-as-oppressed group rhetoric. My two male friends were not my oppressors and, as a college-educated, vocal woman, I was far from the "oppressed" in the situations that drove our two exchanges. Nevertheless, their inability to understand my questioning of their status as males within a female "dominated" profession demonstrated their lack of understanding and empathy towards my positions as a woman of color within a Western, patriarchal society. It is my hope that as I continue to ask questions and work to address social injustices within the education sector, that one day, when I ask someone to think about their position of privilege, regardless of their ethnicity, gender or any other social identity marker, that their response would have more depth and understanding than a naive "Why should I?"

REFERENCES

Collins, P. H. (2000). Black feminist thought: Knowledge, consciousness, and the politics of empowerment (2nd ed.). NY: Routledge.

Correll, S. (2004). Gender inequality in education. Center for the Study of Inequality: Forum theme "Equity and Excellence: Shared Challenges, Shared Opportunites." Retrieved from http://inequality.cornell.edu/events/correll_draft2.pdf

hooks, b. (1981). *Ain't I a woman: Black women and feminism*. Boston, MA.

hooks, b. (1994) *Teaching to transgress: education as the practice of freedom*. New York: Routledge.

Jbadalament. (2011). bell hooks on Voice. <Video file> Retrieved from [http://www.youtube.com/watch?v=j5ThEoA0ESA]

Steele, C. (2010). Whistling Vivaldi: And other clues to how stereotypes affect us. New York: W.W. Norton & Company

U.S. Department of Education, National Center for Education Statistics. (2011). *The Condition of Education 2011* (NCES 2011–033), Retrieved from [http://nces.ed.gov/fastfacts/display.asp?id=72]

White House, The. (2012). Women in America: Indicators of social and economic well-being. Retrieved from [http://www.whitehouse.gov/administration/eop/cwg/data-on-women#Education]

Section 13: "We Have All Walked in Different Gardens and Knelt at Different Graves"

Please take 10 minutes and write about the following:

1. Why do you think it is important to deliver "gifted" curriculum and pedagogy, instead of remedial learning, to students at the bottom of the educational ladder (as AP/YPP do)?

_____

_____

_____

2. In a conversation with faculty in the College of Education at FIU, Charles Payne said that current research indicates that "academic push" is not enough to create long-term educational reform for struggling learners. He said that along with the delivery of rich academic curriculum, struggling learners need social support systems. What are some support systems offered by the Algebra Project that you think all schools should include?

_____

_____

_____

3. What kinds of gender discrimination have you observed or experienced in your professional or personal life that are different from those noted in Boveda's article?

_____

_____

_____

With your classmates, view the YouTube short video "The People Speak" www.youtube.com/watch?v=GAxH28s29dA

- After viewing it, discuss with a partner why you think students in a K-12 classroom should know about "The People Speak."

_____

_____

_____

_____

_____

The complete version of the *The People Speak* (DVD) by Howard Zinn can be found in the university library: Watch that together with a small group and discuss your reactions to the film.

SECTION 14

'NOT ONLY IS ANOTHER WORLD POSSIBLE . . . SHE IS ON HER WAY'

We seek to raise the voices of Katrina's survivors and connect them with the voices of America's survivors, the brothers and sisters in all corners of the country who remain on the margins of citizenship. We seek to use the tools of education, documentation, healing, and organizing to explore and discuss the conditions that led to the devastating impact of Katrina; to join the voices of resistance, the veterans of past and continuing movements, with the voices of Hip-Hop, Blues and Jazz; to celebrate African and indigenous cultures as they have been expressed in New Orleans and throughout the world; to find our folk, to reconnect the individuals, families and communities that are scattered across the country, living in exile. In finding our folk, we hope to find ourselves.

—Finding Our Folk, The Young People's Project

CHAPTER 14

SCHOOL

Alex Salinas

This poem emerged from a period in which the community of educators I belong to made a local spoken-word venue a class text. A couple of us started going to the Inner Look in Miami, FL and fell in love with the mission captured in the name of the place, the commitment of the resident poets to provide a community space for public self-reflection. The Inner Look became another opportunity to learn outside the school building, another in a long line of experiments designed to make our work free, authentic, joyous.

Over a period of about a year, hundreds of our students came to fulfil their assignments on Thursday and Friday nights, reflecting on poems covering the whole range of the human experience—everything from the pain of broken hearts; rage against the system; the survival of diseases, sexism and racism; and the sustaining power of love, beauty, and just having a good time. Some of our students even wrote their own poems and got on stage to try out the elusive art of voice in front of a live audience. I wanted to add something to the conversation about that other part of our lives that transforms us every day, for better or worse. Our educations. I wanted to say it in my own emerging voice as a young teacher trying to figure out who I was and what I was trying to do. And I mostly wanted my students out in the audience to smile. The piece works best out loud.

> I learned everything I need to know back in kindergarten.
>
> I remember tiny roots and buds in the garden of children
>
> The first thing I learned was my teacher's smile
>
> My other mother with that crayola air about her
>
> Who first made the ABC's mean
>
> Communications
>
> And pictures of apples equal
>
> Mathematics
>
> Remember kindergarten?
>
> Now remember third grade
>
> According to researchers
>
> That's when children start losing interest in going to school
>
> Start saying they can't go in the morning because they're sick
>
> They're fighting us but not really lying to us
>
> They got a deadly virus called school-sucks-itis

Put five paragraphs in your essay
Not one word more not one line less
Don't say a word standing in line
Never use "you" never ever use "I"
Shape up your grammar
by banging it flat with a hammer
Be objective in your expression
Make everything a thing
Remove yourself from
That thing

I don't care if long division's no fun
Don't ask why you have to carry the one
I don't care if the page is a graveyard
Scratched up with dead symbols
Referring to nothing you know
Don't ask why you have to memorize
The periodic and multiplication tables
Or why all the black brown and white kids
Sit at different lunch tables
Yes, F does stand for fear
Yes, you will take the FCAT, every grade
And that's that, and do it now and don't be late
Or say bye bye to a proper career
As a customer service rep at the corporate headquarters
Yes, I'm your teacher, and no I don't care what you do
Because I already got mine

School is a machine with razor sharp edges
That teachers and students
Pass through on a conveyor belt
Squeezing through a jaw of prison bars
Number two pencils
overcrowded homerooms
Until they have been drained
Bloodless
Expertly trained
But terribly educated
Emerging on the other side
Packed in boxes
With little breathing holes punched out

But we can resist
We are artists

with monkey wrenches
We make paper mache volcanoes
That erupt spaghetti sauce
Just for the kicks
We make magic
That turns toxics
Into tonics

Get unhooked from phonics
We are black and brown kids
who speak in ebonics
brown and white kids
who speak in cubonics
who speak to each other
in the universal language of story
about living and loving our lives
We challenge the teacher
Because we can teach each other
How to read write and figure out puzzles
Take our nose out the book
To take an inner look
At the neighborhood poetry spot
With discussion out in the parking lot
Before and after the show
The poets are the ones who know it
Not just the textbooks from the Phd's
I will write I
I will write me

Every mind has an idea
A genius-one-of-a-kind-light-bulbs-going-off-everywhere idea
Every idea has a story
A sitting-on-the-edge-of-your-desk-I-can-really-relate-wow-factor story
Every story has a student
A thirsty-for-the-first-time-in-my life-drinking-up-every-last-drop-of-it
student
Every student has a teacher
A trip-you-out-eyes-wide-open-and-a-third-eye-too-whispering-wisdom
teacher
Every teacher has a river rushing between the peaceful temples of the mind
And the heart
Every teacher is a student is a teacher is a student
Unteaching the walls
Destandardizing the ceilings

Of the principal's office
Expeling the beauracrats with their report cards
Learning backwards to the basics
So that the kindergarten
Is a fun place to learn

KATRINA STILL CALLS OUR NAMES[1]

Joan T. Wynne

When I was invited here to talk to you about the theme of this conference, "Where We Stand: Issues in Educational Leadership," I was intrigued because I grew up in a segregated south when the answer to "Where I stand" could be a life-defining moment. Some schools were closed in answer to that question. Some teachers went to jail answering that question. And some people died answering that question.

Yet often in the field of education, I believe, too many slink away from addressing, "Where we stand." That this body here today gathered to make its stand clear is a significant democratic act; it is a counter to the country's recent inclinations for cowardice. And I feel fortunate to be amongst you.

To help explain where I stand, I would like to call forth the spirits of those who one year ago lost their lives in a nation who refused to stand up for them, victims of a storm the government calls Katrina. After watching the horrid images of that national disaster unfold in New Orleans, I promised myself and the staff of our Center at FIU, that no matter in what circle I found myself, I would raise the issues that caused this human tragedy—in hopes that together we who educate the children of our country will take a united stand to stop the madness that allows debacles like the aftermath of Katrina to wreak havoc in the lives of children. A way to look at stopping that madness is suggested in a poem by one of my favorite poets, Wm. Stafford, who said:

> *For it is important that awake people be awake,*
>
> *or a breaking line may discourage them back to sleep;*
>
> *the signals we give—yes or no, or maybe—*
>
> *should be clear; the darkness around us is deep*

William Stafford, "A Ritual to Read to Each Other" from The Way It Is: New and Selected Poems. Copyright © 1960, 1998 by William Stafford and the Estate of William Stafford. Reprinted with the permission of The Permissions Company, Inc. on behalf of Graywolf Press, www.graywolfpress.org

Yes, "The darkness around us in education is deep."—Yet, all of us in this room, I believe, as well as parents, students, teachers can be some of the voices that bring light into that deep darkness. As Ella Baker said, "We are the people we have been waiting for." And the Winds of Katrina are still calling our names. What will we say, yes, no, or maybe?—for the outrage spurned by the memory of watching live news footage of thousands of people abandoned by their government in a major U. S. city, for days on end, becomes almost unbearable. Televised images of bodies, faces down, floating in toxic waters, babies and elders, people in wheelchairs dying before our eyes, as we sat in the comfort of our living-rooms, will continue to shake the inner stuffings of our souls—those images become the newest nightmares in our tormented sleep, a sleep already crowded by pictures of Iraqi women and children blown to bits through military strategies of "shock and awe," dead 18, 19, 20 year old U. S. soldiers, and tortured prisoners in secret cells.

Those images, that outrage—How do we as educational leaders address it? How do we stop the nightmares? For ourselves? For teachers? For students? How do we counter the national propensity to return to denial, to "business as usual?" How do we discourage the nation from "falling back asleep?"—"Where do we stand?" How do we use this horrific travesty of justice as a catalyst for teaching us to become active participants in the formidable task that the poet Langston Hughes long ago charged us to do—to remake America; to renew its dream; and to redeem the land that the ancestors of all its disenfranchised helped steward and shape (Rampersad).

How do we bring that message into the public school discourse? Katrina brutally exposed the "two America's" that have always existed, but this dichotomy has rarely before been so dramatically unmasked in so many living rooms of so many homes in America at the same moment, creating a giant opportunity for us to raise this conversation about race, class, and redemption. When I was in New Orleans after Katrina and witnessed the gripping difference in the damages in one part of the city, the 9th Ward, versus that of the powered-up garden district, I was struck once again by the stark disparities in the distribution of our country's resources. When I saw whose schools were open, and whose were shut, I cringed at the echoed sounds of ole "Dixie" playing in my head. Indeed, has the confederate south, I wondered, risen again, only this time in D.C. or did it never really go away?

I asked myself then as I ask you now—how do we as educators use this nationally shared, excruciatingly painful, historical experience, this blight on the soul of America, to catapult us into a new direction for our colleges, our schools, and the country? Vincent Harding, in 1999, asked us in *Hope and History*, "Who are the teachers and what is the curriculum that will prepare us to redeem the land, to remake a nation?" His question seems the one most worthy of attention in reckoning with our responsibility as teachers and as teachers of teachers to rectify the wrongs of racist policies and practices that use schools to help sustain a divided nation.

There are teachers and students in New Orleans who are right now participating in answering Harding's question, teachers like Chris Mayfield; Adriane Frazier; and the co-directors of Students at the Center, Kalamu Ya Salaam and Jim Randels. We as educators can shine our spotlights on those teachers and students, and others like them in the nation, on their pedagogy, their grassroots driven, culturally responsive, student-centered curriculum. We might invite them into these circles, have them do our keynotes, invite them into our college classrooms and our leadership meetings to learn lessons from them. We need to stop talking and listening only to each other. What might we learn if we invited the grassroots energy and wisdom into this room, into this circle, in this time, and in all our circles.

What might we learn from those in the Young People's Project (YPP), those youngsters who in the immediate aftermath of Katrina designed the "Finding Our Folks Tour" (FOF), Omo Moses, Chris Adagbonyin, Anasa Phoenix, and many other young people. They traveled the southeast, reaching out through educational workshops, to the displaced students and parents who had been tossed to the four winds, landing in unfamiliar cities and states, living in stadiums and armed camps in Boston, insulted in Texas by the mother of the president of the United States of America. One year later, over 300,000 African American students and parents are still dispersed, still unable to go back home.

I'd like to share with you the vision of the Finding our Folks tour:

"We seek to raise the voices of Katrina's survivors and connect them with the voices of America's survivors, the brothers and sisters in all corners of the country who remain on the margins of citizenship. We seek to use the tools of education, documentation, healing, and organizing to explore and discuss the conditions that led to the devastating impact of Katrina; to join the voices of resistance, the veterans of past and continuing movements, with the voices of Hip-Hop, Blues and Jazz; to celebrate African and indigenous cultures as they have been expressed in New Orleans and through out the world; to find our folk, to reconnect the individuals, families and communities that are scattered across the country, living in exile. In finding our folk, we hope to find ourselves" (typp website)

And I would like to suggest that if we as educators find and privilege the voices of those folks, then, maybe, we too can hope to find ourselves---to reconnect with the visions, the ideals that brought us to this work in the beginning of our professional lives. Without these kinds of continuing conversations, reality-based curricula, and constant challenges to the country at large, how will we as educators find ourselves? After all, each of us in this room works for institutions that for over 400 years have been steeped in racist and classist epistemology, policies, and practices.

If we are serious about being literacy advocates, then, we also need to be serious about including the history, the art, the science, the music, the voices of those who are on the margins of citizenship. And not just for their sakes, but also for ours. For until our children, mainstream children, learn the truth of the histories of indigenous and marginalized people, they will have learned not only an incomplete American story, but a 400 year old lie that will continue to bamboozle them as they try to navigate a global society that does not match the story they were told in their schools. They will cherish not what is great about America, but what is false about America. And the repercussions from that lie will haunt their days, for the lie follows them, corrupting their judgment in world affairs, stifling their acquisition of knowledge of that which is different, keeping them separate from the very diversity that the planet demands for survival.

Stafford says,

> *If you don't know the kind of person I am*
> *and I don't know the kind of person you are*
> *a pattern that others made may prevail in the world*
> *and following the wrong god home we may miss our star.*

We do not want our children "missing their star" because they do not know each other's stories, each other's music, art, culture, values.

From these diverse stories, from the descendents of the African, the Appalachian, the Lakota, the Mexican, the Korean, the Muslim, the youngsters like the creators of FOF, we can all learn. With these stories schools might become lively places of engagement with elders and parents—places where we design together a curriculum grounded in healing, in human and earth justice. In these kinds of learning circles, might we as teacher leaders, instead of researching the deficits, dysfunctions, disadvantages of communities, study the ways these unconventional movements tap into the creativity and genius of their people—to co-create Langston's dream of a new America?

All children, but especially the survivors of Katrina, have much to teach us. We need to sit and listen to the past and present stories of the people who for over four centuries we have tried to silence in this country. If we are to keep the promise of democracy alive, to rebuild Langston's dream of America, we need our classrooms to be brimming over with story, with everyone's story, and especially those stories of creative resistance.

Let us together shake up the rigid hierarchal structures that privilege only the stories of the elite in our midst—Let us practice radical philosophies like that of Ella Baker, who always listened for the wisdom of the folks at the bottom. She sought after their insights, their inspiration (2003). In light of those traditions, might we, then, break down the walls of our schools and be with and learn from the people at the bottom—let those transactions together change all of us. Through such a process might we begin in schools to build a new democracy that includes and responds to everyone?—that leaves no one, face down, abandoned in toxic waters? Is that where we stand?

When will we as teacher leaders become the driving force in dismantling, what Bob Moses calls, "sharecropper" schools, that forever doom some students to 2nd class citizenship or worse to a life of poverty or prison? Can we, unlike our political leaders, in the aftermath of Katrina, find the moral ground to stand, speak and act, as a collective power, against the tyranny of unequal education, against schooling that keeps our black and brown children doomed to standing on rooftops watching the waters of an undemocratic system rise to sink them? When will we, as a united community of teacher leaders, take that stand?

Can we use Katrina—an event that continues to graphically expose the grotesque and savage inequalities of the status quo—as the crucible to transform the mission of our colleges and schools? Can we join with other educators across the country to demand that public schools in New Orleans, in Miami, in Atlanta, in America be protected from the profiteers who plan to deny the community its legitimate participation in the decision-making process about its own schools?

Colleges, schools, and professional organizations have historically been stuck in sustaining the status quo. We rarely, if ever, as a body politic, have challenged our institutions to eliminate the racist policies and practices that keep schools separate and unequal. In fact, most often, faculties run as fast as we can away from any conversation about such policies. Certainly, individuals in many colleges and public schools, and many of you sitting in this room, address the impact of race, class, and power on schools, yet the institutions as a whole continue, even a year after Katrina, to ignore the imperative to explicitly and consistently deal with these issues. Human Justice must become an institutional mantra, not just the conversation of a few. The outrage produced by the continuing neglect and abuse of the citizens of New Orleans, America's citizens, must be addressed. And if colleges of education and public schools are not up to the task, then we need to close our doors. If we cannot redeem ourselves, then we are not the ones to lead Langston's dialogue on redeeming America.

The darkness around us is deep. What will we say, yes? No? or maybe? When and Where will we take our stand?

When I think about teachers across this country taking that collective stand, I

hear the words of Arundhati Roy when she said, "Another world is not only possible, she's on her way. . . on a quiet day . . . . I can hear her breathing."

REFERENCES

Brown, C. ed. (1986) *Ready from within: Septima Clark and the civil rights movement.* Navarro, Calif: Wild Trees Press.

Center for Community Change, (2006) *Dismantling a Community*, Washington D.C. http://www.communitychange.org/issues/education/publications/

Finding Our Folks Tour, (2006) http://www.findingourfolk.org/

Freire, P. (1998/1970). *Pedagogy of the Oppressed* (trans. by Myra Bergman Ramos). New York: Continuum.

Harding, V. (1999). *Hope and history: Why we must share the story of the movement.* New York: Orbis Books.

Hilliard III, A.G. (1997). SBA: *The reawakening of the African mind.* Gainesville, FL: Makare Publishing Co.

Moses, R. & Cobb, Jr., C. (2001) *Radical Equations: Civil rights from Mississippi to the Algebra Project.* Boston: Beacon Press.

Payne, C. (1996). *I've got the light of freedom: the organizing tradition and the Mississippi freedom struggle.* Berkeley & Los Angeles: University of California Press.

Polier, N. & Mayfield, C. (2006). "After Katrina: Tales from a Chartered School Classroom," *Radical Teacher,* 76, pp. 20–23.

Rampersad, A. (1986) *The life of Langston Hughes: Volume 1: 1902–1941. I, too, sing America.* New York, NY: Oxford University Press.

Ransby, B. (2003). *Ella Baker and the Black freedom movement: A radical democratic vision* Chapel Hill: University of North Carolina Press.

Roy, A. *Come September* (9–29–2002). ZNET: A community of people committed to social change. Retrieved http://www.zcommunications.org/come-september-by-arundhati-roy

William Stafford, "A Ritual to Read to Each Other" from *The Way It Is: New and Selected Poems.* Copyright ©1960, 1998 by William Stafford and the Estate of William Stafford. Reprinted with the permission of The Permissions Company, Inc. on behalf of Graywolf Press, www.graywolfpress.org

END NOTES

1. Keynote for Conference on English Leadership, National Council of Teachers of English (NCTE) November 19, 2006; later an abbreviated version was published in Multicultural Education Magazine, Special Issue, Katrina: Schools, Culture, and Trauma, Caddo Gap Press: Progressive Education Publications, Spring, 2007

GLOBAL LEARNING FOR THE 21ST CENTURY: ARE YOU READY?

Stephanie P. Doscher and Hilary Landorf

In July 2011, the United States reached a tipping point, one that arrived sooner than anticipated but had been long predicted. For the first time, minority groups—including Hispanics, blacks, Asians and those of mixed race—composed the majority of births (50.4%) in a preceding 12-month period, while non-Hispanic whites accounted for a minority (49.6%) of children born. This statistic sent a shock wave through the media, with commentators citing implications for politics, economics, immigration reform, and social dynamics. William Frey, senior demographer at the Brookings Institution, observed that the nation was now unquestionably transitioning from a culture dominated by white baby boomers to one formed by a more multiethnic, globalized populace. This shift would have particularly strong implications for educators. "This is a polite knock on the door to tell us to get ready," warned Ruy Teixeira, a senior fellow at the Center for American Progress. "We do a pretty lousy job of educating the younger generation of minorities. Basically, we are not ready for this" (Tavernise, 2012, A1).

Born in the 20th century yet charged with preparing students for life in the increasingly diverse and interconnected 21st century, today's pre-service teachers cannot depend on their own formal educational experiences to ready them fully to meet this challenge. Educational leaders are only just beginning to recognize the urgent need for educational reform that goes beyond raising standards for the three R's. Some scholars are trying to shift the national conversation from accountability towards the state to the needs of individual students, particularly those in diverse underserved populations. According to Marcelo Suarez-Orozco, New York University Professor of Globalization and Education, "The little teaching that goes on is neither culturally relevant to the immigrant students' backgrounds nor pertinent to the realities of the global culture and global economy these youth will eventually have to face." Consequently, unacceptable numbers of immigrant youth, especially those coming from poor backgrounds, are leaving school before acquiring the tools needed to navigate today's bitterly competitive global economy" (Tavernise, 2012, A1).

But is it enough merely to prepare students to make their way through the complexities of life in the public sphere? We contend that a culturally and socially relevant education must prepare individuals to *shape* the circumstances of their lives. Educators must engage all students in the act of problem solving through collaboration, in order that they may live and work with diverse others to create the conditions within which interconnected communities thrive. Today's learning must be global learning, marked by intentional outcomes, active pedagogies, and authentic assessments that enable and empower students as global citizens.

The concept of global citizenship was born in classical Greece, but it has taken on new significance in the 21st century. Global citizenship is a distinctly different notion than that of national citizenship. Whereas national citizenship is defined as a set of rights and responsibilities granted by the nation-state, global citizenship is a disposition that guides individuals to take on responsibilities within interconnected local, global, intercultural, and international contexts. National citizenship is granted by virtue of birth, heritage, or naturalization, but according to Martha Nussbaum (2004), Ernst Freund Distinguished Service Professor of Law and Ethics at the University of Chicago, global citizenship is an outlook developed through education. This involves an approach to knowledge that was rarely provided for American students in the past. Global citizens do need to be knowledgeable about world conditions—history, geography, current events—but in addition, they need to understand how these conditions are deeply interrelated.

In their book *Coming of Age in a Globalized World: The Next Generation* (2006), Adams and Carfagna likened knowledge of interrelatedness to a connect-the-dot puzzle, warning of the danger of focusing on the isolated dots rather than the connections between/among them: "As a society, we are flooded with information. It can be overwhelming, but it is critically important to find meaning. . . . Without understanding relationships and connections, we are forced only to react to isolated events. We can never make decisions or act in a way that anticipates or takes advantage of trends or events. We must each therefore develop the ability to connect the dots" (2).

Global citizens also need to be able to discern the distinctive and common qualities between their own perspectives on the world and the perspectives of others. One's perspective consists of ordinarily unexamined assumptions, evaluations, explanations, and conceptions of time, space, and causality (Hanvey, 1982). Once a person has developed a sense that she has a perspective that is shaped by subtle influences, she can then learn that others have different perspectives, and that people use multiple methods to create meaning from their varying experiences. Nussbaum (2004) has asserted that education for global citizenship involves a comparative, rather than an evaluative approach to diversity, by helping students to discern "the ways in which common needs and aims are differently realized in different circumstances" (43). The ability to understand issues from multiple perspectives will only become more critically necessary for American global citizens living and working in a nation transitioning towards the New Majority.

Alongside the development of their global knowledge and perspective, global citizens must be encouraged to participate in and influence change. National citizenship carries with it rights and responsibilities, but global citizens are motivated to define rights and take on responsibilities as a result of their positive attitude towards engagement. Understanding that they live in an interconnected world and that the well-being of others impacts their own well-being, global citizens accept shared responsibility for solving problems (Hanvey, 1982). What's more, global citizens are willing to take action to solve these problems (Falk, 1994). In short, global citizens view themselves as change agents. They base their actions on an in-depth understanding of interrelated world conditions and a multi-perspective analysis of problems and their potential solutions.

For teachers to be able to prepare students for global citizenship, it is essential that they themselves possess global knowledge, analytical skills, and attitudes. Beginning in pre-service and continuing throughout their careers, teachers must actively pursue their own global learning opportunities. As professional educators and models of global citizenship, teachers must take responsibility for the development of their own global consciousness. Awareness of the world's interconnectedness can be cultivated through regular consumption of multiple media sources, from multiple points of view, a diversity of disciplines, on the issues and trends affecting education, and the socio-cultural context of their students' lives. The teacher as global citizen also intentionally seeks experiences of cultural and cognitive contrast, in order to learn to respect difference and guide students through similarly challenging yet fruitful opportunities for growth. Moreover, teachers must ready themselves, and by extension the diverse children and families they serve, by actively engaging in the decision-making processes that determine the course of their school, their profession, and their local and global communities. They must model ways their hard won knowledge and skills can be used to enhance their own well-being and the well-being of others, both within and outside the classroom. In so many ways, the global and the local are one, and now is the time for all of us to prepare to thrive within our increasingly interconnected world.

REFERENCES

Adams, M. J. & Carfagna, A. (2006). *Coming of age in a globalized world*. Bloomfield: Kumarian Press.

Falk, R. (1994). The making of global citizenship. In B. V. Steenbergen (Ed.), *The condition of citizenship* (pp. 127–140). London: Sage Publications.

Hanvey, R. G. (1982). An attainable global perspective. *Theory into Practice, 21*, 162–67.

Nussbaum, M.C. (2004). Liberal education and global community. *Liberal Education, 90* (1), 42–48.

Tavernise, S. (2012, May 17). Whites account for under half of births in U.S. *The New York Times*. A1.

Section 14: "Not Only Is another World Possible . . . She Is on Her Way"

Please take 10 minutes and write about the following:

1. What are some of the rigid institutional practices that Salinas seems to argue against in his poem?

_____

_____

_____

2. What seems different to you about the "Finding Our Folks" vision of education and the practices seen most often in schools? (FOF vision mentioned in Wynne's article)

_____

_____

_____

3. What changes in education does Wynne argue for in her article "Katrina is calling our names"?

_____

_____

_____

_____

_____

4. Share your writing with a group of four to five other students.

After sharing, please do the following:

♦ Divide yourselves into ten separate groups.

♦ Choose a number from one to ten as your group number.

♦ Choose the corresponding number in Delpit's list below and create a K-12 classroom activity that illustrates that particular "essential factor to success in urban classrooms."

♦ Share that activity with the class.

> *Lisa Delpit -"Ten Factors Essential to Success in Urban Classrooms"**:
>
> 1. Do not teach less content to poor, urban children, but understand their brilliance and teach more!
>
> 2. Whatever methodology or instructional program is used, demand critical thinking.

3. Assure that all children gain access to "basic skills," the conventions and strategies that are essential to success in American education.

4. Provide the emotional ego strength to challenge racist societal views of the competence and worthiness of the children and their families.

5. Recognize and build on strengths.

6. Use familiar metaphors and experiences from the children's world to connect what they already know to school knowledge.

7. Create a sense of family and caring.

8. Monitor and assess needs and then address them with a wealth of diverse strategies.

9. Honor and respect the children's home culture(s).

10. Foster a sense of children's connection to community–to something greater than themselves.

*Found in the article: "The Elephant in the Classroom" printed in Section 1.

- Visit the website http://typp.org/findingourfolk and read the page; then view the short 2-minute video "The Hot 8 and FOF slide show." Discuss with a partner or group the value of the FOF project for empowering young people to contribute to their communities.

Watch the short video from the Color of Fear on *YouTube*:
www.youtube.com/watch?v=-vAbpJW_xEc&feature=related

After watching it, with your partner or a small group discuss the following:
How do the responses from the white man in the video reflect the issues of denial of power and privilege that are discussed in the introduction, and other articles and videos in this book?

- Write some of your responses in the space below:

_____

_____

_____

_____

_____

_____

_____

_____

With your partner or small group, create an activity in which you use culturally responsive theory and practice to help develop students as global citizens.

CONTRIBUTORS

Michael Baugh is deeply concerned with the social injustices within this society. He is passionate about sociocultural issues and looks forward to increasing his involvement in the community to better address the great lies that have been told in our culture. He has recently completed his Master's in Urban Education and will seek his doctorate in the next few years.

Barbre Berris received her B.B.A in Marketing and Management from North Georgia College and State University; her M.S. in Higher Education and Student Affairs from Florida State University; and is currently pursuing her Ph.D. in Counseling and Student Personnel Services at the University of Georgia. As a higher education professional, her background includes experience in Housing and Residence Life, Orientation and New Student Programs, and Greek Life. Research interests include diversity and social justice initiatives including LGBT outreach and the role of race in Greek-lettered organizations.

Wanda J. Blanchett is Dean of UMKC's School of Education and the Ewing Marion Kauffman Endowed Chair in Teacher Education. Previously she served as Associate Dean for Academic Programs and Curriculum and Associate Professor of Urban Special Education for the School of Education and Human Development (SEHD) at the University of Colorado [CU] Denver. Earlier she served as the Associate Dean for Academic Affairs in the School of Education at the University of Wisconsin-Milwaukee [UWM]. She has a national reputation in urban education and issues of social justice, and her research has focused on urban teacher preparation, issues of race, class, culture, and gender, and the overrepresentation of African American students in special education, and issues of sexuality and disability.

Mildred Boveda is a doctoral student at Florida International University. Before beginning her doctoral studies, she taught for five years as a special education teacher in Miami Dade Country Public Schools. Mildred holds a master's in Special Education from Florida International University and a master's in Education Policy and Management from Harvard Graduate School of Education.

Princess Briggs works in the Miami-Dade County Public School system and has over seventeen years of experience working with children with special needs and their families as a teacher, as a curriculum support specialist, and as an instructional supervisor. These experiences throughout the district and beyond Miami-Dade County have offered her the opportunities to hone her skills and provide support, mentoring, and professional development to parents, teachers, and administrators. She is currently working toward her doctorate degree in special education and hopes to one day join a university faculty and conduct research to improve the education of children with special needs who live in urban communities.

Lisa Delpit is an award-winning writer, scholar, and researcher of education in urban schools and diverse cultural settings, including Alaska and New Guinea. Her latest book, *Multiplication Is for White People: Raising the Expectations for Other People's Children*, has created another national stir in the dialogue about schools and children just as did one of her previous books, *Other People's Children: Cultural Conflict in the Classroom*. Currently, she is the Felton G. Clark Distinguished Professor at Southern University, College of Education in Baton Rouge.

Stephanie Doscher is Associate Director of the Office of Global Learning Initiatives at Florida International University. She has published and presented internationally on topics ranging from global education leadership and assessment strategies to ethics in educational leadership. Recent publications include, "Promoting Engagement in Curriculum Internationalization" in *IIE Networker* and "The Moral Agency of the Educational Leader in Times of National Crisis and Conflict" in *Journal of School Leadership*.

Jeremy Glazer received his undergraduate degree in Anthropology from Amherst College and his M.S. Ed. from the University of Pennsylvania. He went on to teach high school in both Philadelphia and Miami in a wide range of schools. He currently works in local government.

Paul Gorski is an assistant professor of Integrative Studies in George Mason University's New Century College, where he teaches classes on class and poverty, educational equity, and environmental justice. He created and continues to maintain the Multicultural Pavilion, a website focused on critical multicultural education. He has published three books and more than thirty-five articles in *Educational Leadership, Equity and Excellence in Education, Rethinking Schools, Teaching and Teacher Education, Teachers College Record, Teaching Tolerance*, and others.

Catharine Graham is a Native Atlantan, a former public high school special education teacher and a department chair. She received her B.S. degree from Florida State University and her Master's in Special Education and an Administration Certificate at Georgia State University. She has also worked as a consultant in Team Building for school faculties and business executives and is presently a business analyst/computer application specialist for the telecommunications industry.

Ceexta Hall is a college student, studying to earn a bachelor's degree in Early Childhood Education. She is currently a teacher's aide, aspiring to become a preschool teacher. Her ambition is to acquire as much knowledge as possible from the children with whom she interacts daily at a Learning Center.

Renatto Hernandez for the last ten years has taught Language Arts and Reading in an urban high school setting in Miami, while coaching football, track and field, and sponsoring the Key Club, a community service organization. He is a second-year special education doctoral student at Florida International University and a National Board Certified teacher with a Master's degree in Special Education and Reading from the University of Miami.

Alexandre Lopes is a National Board Certified teacher who, for the last eight years, has been teaching Pre-K SPED at Carol City Elementary School. Alexandre, who is currently pursuing his doctoral degree in Special Education at Florida International University's School of Education, and was awarded the 2013 Francisco R. Walker

Miami-Dade County Teacher of the Year and 2013 Florida Department of Education Teacher of the Year.

Hilary Landorf is an Associate Professor in the College of Education at Florida International University and Director of the Office of Global Learning Initiatives. She has published widely in national and international journals and is regularly consulted for her expertise in globalizing K-20 curricula across the curriculum. Recent publications include, "Toward a Philosophy of Global Education" in *Visions in Global Education*, and "Education for Sustainable Human Development: Towards a Definition" in *Theory and Research in Education*.

Maria Lovett is an assistant professor in the College of Education at Florida International University and the Partnership Director for the Education Effects, a university-assisted community school partnership with Miami Northwestern Senior High School and the feeder schools in the Liberty City community of Miami. With an extensive background in documentary production and teaching youth media, she uses video as a tool to fight for social justice both in the classroom and the community.

Cindy Lutenbacher is Associate Professor of English at Morehouse College, where she has taught composition and creative writing since 1990. She is the single mother of two daughters and is a lifelong activist for a progressive and just public education and for an end to racism.

Carlos González Morales lives and works in South Florida. He teaches English along with monkey-wrenching skills at Miami Dade College. He is a member of the Imagination Federation, a community of presence engaged in creating soulsustaining teaching/learning bubbles with the aim of encouraging all to live life well and fully. He was an endowed chair at MDC for seven years and also taught at FIU in the English Department as well as in the College of Education/Algebra Project Summer Institutes for high school youth.

Ronald E. Miles, upon completing a BA in Spanish Literature and Language from Columbia University, began teaching in Oakland, CA. Ron's career includes teaching primary, secondary and university students; providing PD to public school teachers; and working as a publishing firm executive. He is earning a Ph.D. in Curriculum and Instruction at FIU after completing a graduate certificate in African New World Studies and an MS degree in International and Intercultural Education. His research focuses on Teaching Diverse Populations and Teaching English as a Second Language.

Ruba Monem was born and raised in New Jersey and currently lives in Southwest Florida with her son. Ruba is a doctoral student and adjunct instructor in technology and Special Education at Florida International University. She also teaches Social Studies in one of Southwest Florida's largest middle schools.

Fernanda Pineda is a doctoral student in International & Intercultural Studies at Florida International University and a graduate assistant in the Office of Global Learning Initiatives. She has published and conducted research in Mexico and the Philippines. Her home is in Mexico where she first began investigating issues of social justice, her primary interest for study in all arenas and especially in education.

Alex Salinas has been a Communications Professor at the Miami Dade College InterAmerican Campus in Little Havana since 2003. He also was the public relations coordinator and writer for the FIU Center for Urban Education & Innovation until 2009. Since 2010, he has been the Vice-Chair of Imagination Federation Inc., a nonprofit organization committed to bringing greater educational opportunities to students of the rural Nicaraguan community of Chacraseca while raising awareness about issues of global poverty in the United States. As an educator, he consciously tries to create spaces in which students feel in community with him, with each other, and with the village outside the classroom.

Michael Skolnik is the Editor-In-Chief of GlobalGrind.com and the political director to Russell Simmons. Prior to this, Michael was an award-winning filmmaker. Follow him on twitter @MichaelSkolnik

Joan Wynne is an Associate Professor and directs the Urban Education Master's Degree Program at FIU in Miami, where she also serves as Director of Community Relations/ COE. The influence of her students and educators like Lisa Delpit, Catharine Graham, Carlos Gonzalez, Asa G. Hilliard III, Robert P. Moses, Theresa Perry and many others has driven her research and writing about transformation, school change, and the impact of racism on youth, schools and communities. Earlier she taught in the Atlanta Public School System; at Morehouse College, directing The Mays Teacher Scholars Program; and at Georgia State University where she served as a faculty member and administrator, directing the Urban Teacher Leadership Master's Degree Program.